CHANGE AND CONTINUITY
IN THE 2000 AND 2002 ELECTIONS

Paul R. Abramson
MICHIGAN STATE UNIVERSITY

John H. Aldrich
DUKE UNIVERSITY

David W. Rohde
MICHIGAN STATE UNIVERSITY

CQ PRESS

A Division of Congressional Quarterly Inc.
Washington, D.C.

CQ Press
1255 22nd St., N.W., Suite 400
Washington, D.C. 20037

Phone, 202-729-1900
Toll-free, 1-866-4CQ-PRESS (1-866-427-7737)

www.cqpress.com

∞ The paper used in this publication meets the minimum requirements of the American National Standard for Information Sciences—Permanence of Paper for Printed Library Materials, ANSI Z39.48-1992.

Printed and bound in the United States of America

07 06 05 04 03   5 4 3 2 1

Typeset by Picas Rule, Baltimore, Maryland

Cover design: Rich Pottern

Library of Congress Cataloging-in-Publication Data

In process

ISBN: 1-56802-742-7

To Richard F. Fenno Jr.

Contents

Tables and Figures

Tables

Figures

Preface

◆◆◆

Beginning in 1994 a remarkable series of events occurred in American politics. A political earthquake in November gave the Republicans control of the House of Representatives for the first time in forty years. They also won control of the Senate for the first time in eight years. Although President Bill Clinton was thrown on the political defensive, two years later he easily won reelection. But with his victory came another unusual occurrence. In nineteen of the forty-two presidential elections between 1828 and 1992, the Democrats had won the White House; and in all nineteen they had also won control of the House of Representatives. But although the Democrats gained nine House seats in 1996, they failed to win control, and they lost two seats in the Senate.

The 2000 elections were remarkable for a different reason: their closeness. Republican candidate George W. Bush won half a million fewer popular votes than did his Democratic opponent, Al Gore, and just 271 electoral votes, only one more than the majority of 270 needed for election. The Democrats gained two House seats, but the Republicans held control, the first time in seventy-two years that they had won four or more elections in a row. The Democrats also gained four Senate seats, giving each party fifty seats, with the Republican control contingent upon Vice President Dick Cheney's tie-breaking vote. In June 2001, after Republican senator James M. Jeffords of Vermont became an independent, the Democrats regained control of the Senate. In 2002 the Republicans retained control of the House, gaining six seats and coming close to their streak of winning six consecutive House elections between 1918 and 1928. They also regained control of the Senate by a fifty-one to forty-eight seat margin. Both the 1998 and the 2002 midterm elections broke a long-established pattern. Between 1842 and 1994 there were thirty-nine midterm elections, and the party holding the White House lost strength in the House in thirty-eight of them. But in the last two midterms the party holding the presidency has made narrow gains in the House.

George Bush's election to the presidency in 1988 was the third straight presidential victory for the Republicans. Many scholars argued that the GOP had become the dominant party in presidential elections. But with Democratic presidential victories in 1992 and 1996, and with a virtual tie in 2000, Republican dominance appears to have ended. What happened to it? And what happened to Democratic congressional dominance? What are the prospects for ending the prevailing postwar pattern of divided government, and which party is likely to end it? Have the major parties weakened their hold on the U.S. electorate, and if so, what are the prospects for a new political party?

To answer these questions we must study the 2000 and 2002 elections in their historical context. To do this we have examined a broad range of evidence, from election results to surveys of the electorate conducted since 1944. We utilize many sources, but rely mostly on the 2000 survey of the U.S. electorate conducted by the Survey Research Center and the Center for Political Studies (SRC-CPS) of the University of Michigan as part of an ongoing project funded by the National Science Foundation. We also use each of the twenty-six election studies conducted between 1948 and 2000, studies often referred to as the National Election Studies (NES). (The NES study conducted in 2002 will not be available for scholars to analyze until after our book is published.)

These surveys, disseminated by the Inter-university Consortium for Political and Social Research (ICPSR), can be analyzed worldwide. The data we use were provided in April 2001. Unless otherwise indicated, all tables and figures in Chapters 2, 4–8, and 10 are based on surveys provided by the CPS and the ICPSR. The standard disclaimer holds: the consortium is not responsible for our analyses or interpretations.

Several institutions aided us financially. John H. Aldrich received financial support from Duke University. Paul R. Abramson and David W. Rohde received support from the Department of Political Science at Michigan State University and from the Political Institutions and Public Choice Program at Michigan State University.

We would also like to thank several individuals. John D. Griffin and Amy McKay at Duke University helped with the data analyses for chapters 1, 6, 7, and 8, and Dana Ellington assisted in turning those analyses into text. Jamie Carson at Michigan State University helped with data analyses in chapters 2, 4, 5, 9, 10, and 11, and Suzanne Gold at Michigan State University assisted with the analysis in chapter 11. In addition, we are grateful to Walter Dean Burnham at the University of Texas at Austin for supplying us with estimates of voter turnout among the politically eligible population and to Tom Smith of the National Opinion Research Center for providing us with the distribution of party identification in the 2002 General Social Survey. We are also grateful to Dennis P. Patterson of Texas Technological University and to Kaare Strøm of the University of California at San Diego for their comments on chapter 12.

Once again we are thankful to the staff at CQ Press. Many thanks to Charisse Kiino, Elizabeth Jones, and Niall O'Donnell for their guidance and support in helping to prepare the manuscript; to Jarelle Stein, Molly Lohman, and Christopher Karlsten for a superb job of copyediting the manuscript; and to Belinda Josey and Lorna Notsch for managing the book's production.

Like our earlier books, this was a collective enterprise, but we did divide the labor. Paul R. Abramson had primary responsibility for chapters 3, 4, and 5; John H. Aldrich for chapters 1, 6, 7, and 8; and David W. Rohde for chapters 2, 9, 10, and 11. Abramson and Aldrich are primarily responsible for chapter 12.

Paul R. Abramson
John H. Aldrich
David W. Rohde

PART 1

The 2000 Presidential Election

Presidential elections in the United States are ritual reaffirmations of our democratic values, but they are far more than that. Upon its occupant the office of president confers great power, which has expanded over the course of American history. Presidential elections have at times played a major role in determining public policy.

The 1860 election, which brought Abraham Lincoln and the Republicans to power and ousted a divided Democratic Party, focused on whether slavery should be extended to the western territories. After Lincoln's election, eleven southern states attempted to secede from the Union, the Civil War erupted, and the U.S. government abolished slavery completely. Thus an antislavery plurality (Lincoln received only 40 percent of the popular vote) set in motion a chain of events that freed some four million black Americans.

The 1896 election, in which Republican William McKinley defeated the Democrat and Populist William Jennings Bryan, beat back the challenge of western and agrarian interests to the prevailing financial and industrial power of the East. Although Bryan mounted a strong campaign, winning 47 percent of the popular vote to McKinley's 51 percent, the election set a clear course for a policy of high tariffs and the continuation of the gold standard for American money.

Lyndon B. Johnson's 1964 landslide over Republican Barry M. Goldwater provided the clearest set of policy alternatives of any election in the twentieth century. In his campaign, Goldwater had offered "a choice, not an echo," advocating far more conservative social and economic policies than Johnson. When Johnson received 61 percent of the popular vote to Goldwater's 38 percent, he saw his victory as a mandate for his Great Society programs, the most far-reaching social legislation since World War II. The election also appeared to offer a choice between escalating American involvement in Vietnam and restraint. But American involvement expanded after Johnson's election, and four years later the Democrats lost the presidency.

WHAT DID THE 2000 ELECTION MEAN?

Some scholars have argued that elections have become less important, and there is a certain amount of truth to their arguments. [1] Still presidential elections often do offer important policy choices, though those offered during the 2000 elections were not dramatic ones. After the Republican victories in the 1994 midterm elections, Bill Clinton had moved to the political center, proclaiming that "the era of big government is over." In his campaign, Al Gore, partly in response to Ralph Nader's Green Party candidacy, made some populist appeals, especially with tax proposals aimed at helping poor- and middle-income Americans. But since he could not disavow Clinton's policies, Gore was constrained from moving too far from mainstream policies. Bush, in turn, was not as opposed to government involvement as the conservative wing of his party. As E. J. Dionne Jr. argues, "Perhaps the most significant Clinton contribution was to end old battles on the role of government. Ronald Reagan's cry was 'The government is not the solution. The government is the problem.' George W. Bush put the case much more modestly. 'Government if necessary,' he said, 'but not necessarily government.' "[2]

Though no dramatic choices existed, Bush and Gore did differ on several policy issues. Bush's major emphasis was on large tax cuts, which Gore argued would mainly benefit wealthy Americans. After Bush's victory, Congress enacted his proposed plans, with some modifications, in May 2001, providing a tax cut of $1.35 trillion over the next decade, down from the $1.6 trillion he had originally proposed. Many of the bill's provisions will not take effect for several years, and economists disagree about its consequences. But a large tax cut will make it more difficult to begin new federal funding or to increase funding for existing programs, especially because weak economic performance eliminated future budget surpluses. This reform was a clear victory for conservatives who want to reduce the role of the federal government.

Gore and Bush differed on many other issues.[3] For example, Gore was much more in favor of abortion rights, although he said he would sign a bill banning late-term abortions (often called "partial-birth" abortions) if they included exemptions to protect the life of the mother. Bush was against abortion except in the case of rape or incest, or to save the mother's life. He favored a constitutional amendment banning abortion but acknowledged that such an amendment could not be passed.

Gore was also more supportive of civil rights, favoring affirmative action, and allowing homosexuals to serve openly in the military. Bush did not want to use the term affirmative action, saying he opposed quotas and racial preferences. He favored the current "don't ask, don't tell" policy, which allows homosexuals to serve in the military as long as they do not reveal their sexual orientation.

Both candidates argued that the military should be stronger. The main difference was that Bush wanted to create a missile defense system to protect the United States from "rogue states," even if this led to canceling the Anti-Ballistic

Missile Treaty with the former Soviet Union. Bush has argued in favor of such a missile defense since being elected, although he has encountered opposition not only from Russia and China, but from our NATO allies as well.

Bush also offered a major reform for education, calling for a program of school vouchers to help parents send their children to private schools; Gore strongly opposed vouchers. Despite Bush's election, this proposed reform was defeated early in the 107th Congress.

Finally, the candidates differed on environmental policies. Gore had long been seen as a major proponent of protecting the environment, although Ralph Nader argued that Gore had abandoned this commitment. Gore favored ratifying the Kyoto accords to reduce global warming by reducing carbon dioxide emissions, as well as banning drilling off the Florida and California coasts. Bush opposed the Kyoto accords, instead favoring increased research on global warming. He did promise to reduce carbon dioxide emissions, however. After his election, Bush announced that he would not ask the Senate to ratify the Kyoto accords but withdrew his promise to reduce emissions. The candidates also strongly disagreed about whether oil exploration should be permitted on Alaska's Arctic National Wildlife Refuge, with Bush favoring exploration and Gore strongly opposed. Thus on balance the electorate did have a set of policy differences to choose between in 2000.

When Bush took office on January 20, 2001, the Republicans held both chambers of Congress and the presidency for the first time since January 1955. Despite receiving half a million fewer votes than Gore, Bush was elected with 271 electoral votes, only 1 more than the required majority. Moreover, the Republicans narrowly held control of the U.S. House of Representatives, and by virtue of Dick Cheney's role as a tiebreaker, they held control of an evenly divided Senate (although they lost that control in June 2001 after erstwhile Republican James M. Jeffords of Vermont became an independent).

The extremely narrow Republican victories of 2000 underscore the close competitive balance between the Democratic and Republican Parties. James W. Ceaser and Andrew E. Busch argue that if one looks at the House, Senate, and presidential elections as a whole, one can demonstrate that the 2000 contest was the closest in American history.[4] They argue that the 2000 election "delivered an unambiguous and unmistakable message. George W. Bush received nothing more than a key to his office. Neither party could make a plausible claim to be unambiguously in power."[5] But presidents can change the direction of public policy, and it would be unwise to write off Bush's capacity to introduce change,[6] especially after the dramatic surge in his approval ratings following the September 11, 2001, terrorist attack on the World Trade Center and the Pentagon.[7]

Although the 2000 election provided only the narrowest of wins, the Republicans did regain the presidency, an office they have won in four of the six elections since 1980. During the Republican presidential victories of the 1980s, many political scientists raised the possibility that a realignment had occurred or was about to occur. In 1985 President Reagan himself proclaimed that a Republican realignment was at hand. "The other side would like to believe that our victory last November was due to something other than our philosophy," he asserted. "I just hope that they keep on believing that. There's a change happening in America. Realignment is real."[8]

In November 1984 Reagan won 59 percent of the popular vote. George Bush's victory in 1988 (with 53 percent of the vote) raised the possibility of continued Republican dominance. But in 1992 Bush won only 37 percent of the popular vote, a 22-point decline from Reagan's high-water mark. Not only had the Republican winning streak been broken, but the Republicans had suffered one of the greatest popular vote defeats since the Civil War as well. And in 1996 Bob Dole won only 41 percent of the popular vote.

Obviously, the 1992 and 1996 presidential elections call into question any claims about a pro-Republican realignment. But Clinton won only 43 percent of the popular vote in 1992 and only 49 percent in 1996. In 1992 nearly one out of five voters voted for H. Ross Perot, and in 1996 one out of ten voters voted for Perot and other minor-party candidates. Moreover, the divided partisan outcome between the presidency and the Congress in 1996 suggests that a substantial number of Clinton voters voted for Republican House and Senate candidates. In 2000 Bush won the election with only 47.9 percent of the popular vote, while Gore lost with 48.4 percent. Although the minor-party vote was small, only 3.7 percent, 2000 was the third consecutive election in which the presidential winner failed to gain a majority of the popular vote. Some scholars argue that voters have reservations about both of the major parties. This raises the possibility that past voting patterns are breaking down, something that political scientists have called a "dealignment."

What do the terms *realignment* and *dealignment* mean?[9] Political scientists define *realignment* in different ways, but they are all influenced by V. O. Key Jr., who began by developing a theory of "critical elections" in which "new and durable electoral groupings are formed."[10] Elections such as 1860, in which Lincoln's victory brought the Republicans to power; 1896, in which McKinley's victory solidified Republican dominance; and 1932, which brought the Democrats under Franklin D. Roosevelt to power, are obvious choices for this label.

But later Key argued that realignments take place over a series of elections—a pattern he called secular realignment. During these periods, "shifts in the partisan balance of power" occur.[11] In this view, the first Republican realignment might have begun in 1856, when the Republicans displaced the Whigs as the major competitor to the Democrats, and might have been consolidated by Lincoln's reelection of 1864 and Ulysses S. Grant's election in 1868. The realignment of the late nineteenth century may well have had its beginnings in 1892, when Democrat Grover Cleveland won election, but the Populist Party, headed by James B. Weaver, won 8.5 percent of the popular vote, won four states, and won electoral votes in two others. In 1896 the Populists supported Bryan and were co-opted by the Democrats, but the electorate shifted to the Republicans. The realignment might have been consolidated by McKinley's win over Bryan in 1900 and by Theodore Roosevelt's victory in 1904.

Though the term *New Deal* was not coined until 1932, the New Deal realignment, forged by Franklin D. Roosevelt, may be seen as beginning in Herbert C. Hoover's 1928 triumph over Alfred E. Smith (the first Roman Catholic to be nominated by the Democratic Party). Although badly defeated, Smith carried two New England states, Massachusetts and Rhode Island, which later became the most Democratic states in the nation.[12] As Key points out, the beginnings of the shift toward the Democrats can be seen in Smith's defeat.[13] The New Deal coalition was not created by the 1932 election, but after that, and it was consolidated in Roosevelt's 1936 landslide over Alfred M. Landon and his 1940 defeat of Wendell Willkie.

Although scholars disagree about how long it takes to create a new partisan alignment, they all agree that durability is an essential element of realignment. As James L. Sundquist writes, "Those who analyze alignment and realignment are probing beneath the immediate and transitory ups and downs of daily politics and periodic elections to discover fundamental shifts in the structure of the party system."[14] According to Lawrence G. McMichael and Richard J. Trilling, a realignment is "a significant and durable change in the distribution of party support over relevant groups within the electorate."[15]

Partisan realignments in the United States have had five basic characteristics. First, party realignments have always involved changes in the regional bases of party support. Between 1852 and 1860 the Republicans replaced the Whigs. In all of the elections between 1836 (when the Whigs first opposed Democrat Martin van Buren) and 1852, the Whigs drew at least some of their support from the slave states. The last Whig candidate to be elected, Zachary Taylor in 1848, won 66 of his 163 electoral votes from the fifteen slave states.[16] In his 1860 victory Lincoln did not win a single electoral vote from any of the slave states, in twelve of which he did not even compete. But Lincoln won all of the electors in seventeen of the eighteen free states, as well as the majority of the electoral votes in New Jersey. Subsequent realignments have not involved this degree of regional polarization, but they all display regional shifts in party support.

Second, past party realignments appear to have involved changes in the social bases of party support. Even during a period when one party is becoming dominant, some social groups may be moving to the losing party. During the 1930s, for example, Roosevelt gained the support of industrial workers, but at the same time he lost support among business owners and professionals.

Third, past realignments have been characterized by the mobilization of new groups into the electorate. Between Calvin Coolidge's Republican landslide in 1924 and Roosevelt's third-term victory in 1940, turnout rose from 44 percent to 59 percent. Although some long-term forces were pushing turnout upward, the sharp increase between 1924 and 1928, and again between 1932 and 1936, resulted at least partly from the mobilization of new groups into the electorate.

Ethnic groups that were predominantly Catholic mobilized to support Smith in 1928, and industrial workers were mobilized to support Roosevelt in 1936.

Fourth, past realignments have occurred when new issues have divided the electorate. The most obvious example is the emergence of the Republican Party, which reformulated the controversy over slavery to form a winning coalition. By opposing the extension of slavery into the territories, Republicans divided the Democratic Party. No issue since slavery has divided America as deeply, but subsequent realignments have always been based on the division of the electorate over issues.

Last, most political scientists argue that partisan realignments occur when voters change not just their voting patterns, but the way they think about the political parties. For example, during the Great Depression in 1932 many voters who thought of themselves as Republicans voted against Hoover. Many of these voters returned to the Republican side in subsequent elections, but others began to think of themselves as Democrats. Likewise, in 1936 some voters who thought of themselves as Democrats may have voted against Roosevelt and his policies. Some of these Democrats returned to the Democratic fold during subsequent elections, but others began to think of themselves as Republicans.

During the three Republican victories of the 1980s, some of these changes occurred. As we will see, there were shifts in the regional bases of party support and in the distribution of party loyalties among the electorate. There were further shifts among some social groups (especially southern whites) away from the Democratic Party, and some political observers argued that the Republicans had established a winning position on issues that gained votes in presidential elections. Despite these changes, however, the Republicans never emerged as the majority party among the electorate, although they came close to parity with the Democrats in the mid-1980s. Moreover, even though the Republicans gained control of the U.S. Senate between 1981 and 1987, they never came close to winning control of the U.S. House of Representatives. Clearly, if a realignment had occurred, it was incomplete, leading some scholars, such as Michael Nelson, to speculate about the possibilities of a "split-level realignment," a pattern in which the Republicans became the dominant party in presidential elections while Democratic dominance in the House of Representatives remained intact.[17] And Byron E. Shafer argued that a "new electoral order" had been achieved. The 1988 election, Shafer argued, had institutionalized a new division in American politics, a new system begun twenty years before with the controversy over the Vietnam War. "What was to emerge, instead of realignment," he wrote, "was a different *type* of electoral order: one in which there was a new Republican majority to lay claim to the presidency, an old Democratic majority to keep the House, and a wavering Democratic majority to strive to hold on to the Senate."[18] But this electoral order was disrupted by Clinton's election in 1992 and appears to have ended with the Republican capture of the House in 1994.

Clinton's victories in 1992 and 1996 and the narrowness of Bush's electoral vote majority in 2000 call into question the thesis that there has been a pro-

Republican realignment. Moreover, Bush trailed Gore by half a million popular votes. On the other hand, the Republicans have won four consecutive House elections for the first time since the 1920s, and they briefly held control of the Senate after the 2000 elections. In addition, the large vote for Perot in 1992, and the sizable vote for Perot and other minor-party candidates in 1996, raises the prospect of the breakdown of the traditional party system. Therefore the term *dealignment*, introduced by Ronald Inglehart and Avram Hochstein in 1972, may provide a better description of current political realities than realignment.[19]

A dealignment is a condition in which old voting patterns break down without being replaced by newer ones. Most scholars who use this term stress the weakening of party loyalties as a key component. As Russell J. Dalton, Paul Allen Beck, and Scott C. Flanagan point out, dealignment was originally viewed as a preliminary stage leading to a new partisan alignment. But, they argue, dealignment "may be a regular feature of electoral politics."[20] As Dalton and Martin P. Wattenberg have written, "Whereas realignment involves people changing from one party to another, dealignment concerns people gradually moving away from all parties." The large Perot vote in 1992, they argue, may have come mainly from voters who have few feelings—either positive or negative—toward the political parties. The move worries a number of observers. "Many scholars," Dalton and Wattenberg write, "express concern about potential dealignment trends because they fear the loss of the stabilizing, conserving equilibrium that party attachments provide to electoral systems."[21]

The concept of dealignment is by no means restricted to U.S. politics. Bo Särlvik and Ivor Crewe have characterized British politics in the 1970s as "the decade of dealignment."[22] And Harold Clarke and his colleagues argue that Canadian politics may have reached the stage of "permanent dealignment." "A dealigned party system," they write, "is one in which volatility is paramount, where there are frequent changes in electoral outcomes as well as lots of individual flexibility."[23]

Raising questions about prospects for realignment and dealignment leads to three basic questions that we will ask throughout our book. First, what happened to the Republican presidential dominance that appeared to have been established in the 1980s? Did George Bush's loss in 1992 occur mainly because the electorate judged him a failure, or did the Republican coalition have conflicting components that contributed to his defeat? Did Bob Dole's failure to recapture the presidency for the GOP result mainly from a poor campaign, or did it demonstrate that the Republicans may face difficult problems in rebuilding a winning coalition? Now that the Republicans have recaptured the presidency, do they have good prospects for building a winning presidential coalition?

Second, what are the Democrats' prospects for building a new presidential majority? Were Clinton's victories genuinely something new, or did his winning coalitions resemble those of past Democratic winners? Did he win reelection in 1996 based on his policy positions on newly emerging issues, or did he win mainly because the voters were relatively satisfied with the economy and the job he was doing as president? And, given the robust economy in the fall of 2000, as well as high levels of approval for Clinton's performance as president, why did Gore lose the election? Did Clinton build a basis for Democratic support that future candidates will be able to exploit more successfully than his vice president?

Last, what ended Democratic congressional dominance? With the 1992 election, the Democrats had won the U.S. House of Representatives in twenty consecutive elections, by far the longest period of one-party dominance in U.S. history.[24] The capture of the House by the Republicans in 1994 was largely unexpected, but they held the House in 1996, 1998, and 2000, although by ever narrower margins. When the House convened in January 2001 the Republicans held only 221 seats, just three more than the 218 necessary to command a majority.[25] Moreover, the Republicans added to their margin in 2002, despite the tendency for the party holding the presidency to lose seats in midterm elections. Can the Republicans become the dominant party in House elections, as the Democrats were for four decades?

SURVEY RESEARCH SAMPLING

Our book relies heavily upon surveys of the American electorate. It draws upon telephone polls conducted during the election year, an exit poll conducted by the Voter News Service, and interviews conducted inside the respondents' households by the National Opinion Research Center and the U.S. Bureau of the Census. But for the most part we rely upon surveys conducted during the two months before and two months after the 2000 election, 56 percent of which were conducted in the respondents' households, and 44 percent by telephone by the Survey Research Center (SRC) and the Center for Political Studies (CPS) of the University of Michigan.[26] The SRC has been conducting surveys of the American electorate in every presidential election since 1948, and of every midterm election since 1954; these surveys are generally known as the National Election Studies (NES). Since 1952 the NES surveys have measured party identification and feelings of political efficacy. The CPS, founded in 1970, has developed valuable questions for measuring issue preferences. The NES data are the best and most comprehensive source of information about the political attitudes and partisan loyalties of the American electorate.

Readers may question our reliance on the NES survey of 1,807 adults when there are some 195 million Americans of voting age.[27] Would we obtain similar results if all adults had been surveyed?[28] The NES surveys use a procedure called multistage probability sampling to select the particular person to be interviewed. These procedures ensure that the final sample is likely to represent the entire U.S. citizen population of voting age (except for Americans living in institutions, on military bases, or abroad).[29]

Given the probability procedures used to conduct the NES surveys, we are able to assess the likelihood that the results represent the entire U.S. citizen resident population. The 2000 survey sampled only about one American in 100,000, but, provided the sample is drawn properly, its representativeness depends far more on the size of the sample than on the size of the population being studied. For most purposes, samples of 1,500 are adequate to study the electorate. With samples of this size, we can be fairly confident (confident to a level of .95) that the results we obtain fall within 3 percentage points of the results we would get if the entire population had been surveyed.[30] For example, when we find that 39 percent of the sample in the 2000 NES survey thought the nation's economy had gotten better in the past year, we can be reasonably confident that between 36 percent (39 − 3) and 42 percent (39 + 3) of the electorate thought the nation's economy was improving. The actual result could be less than 36 percent or more than 42 percent. But a confidence level of .95 means that the odds are 19 to 1 that the proportion in the entire electorate falls within this range. The range of confidence becomes somewhat larger when we look at subsamples of the electorate. When we study groups of 500 respondents, the range of confidence grows to ±6 percentage points. Because the likelihood of error grows as our subsamples become smaller, we often supplement our analysis with the reports of other surveys.

Somewhat more complicated procedures are necessary to determine whether the difference between two groups is likely to reflect the relationship that would be found if the entire population were sampled. The probability that such differences reflect real differences in the total population is largely a function of the size of the groups being compared.[31] Generally speaking, when we compare the results of the 2000 sample with an earlier NES survey, a difference of 4 percentage points is sufficient to be reasonably confident that the difference is real. For example, back in 1988, when George Bush was elected, only 19 percent thought the nation's economy had improved in the last year. In 2000, as we saw, 39 percent thought the economy had improved. Because this difference is greater than 4 points, we can be reasonably confident that the electorate was more likely to think that the economy was improving in 2000 than they were to think it was improving back in 1988.

When we compare subgroups of the electorate sampled in 2000 (or subgroups sampled in 2000 with subgroups sampled in earlier surveys), a larger percentage point difference is necessary for us to be reasonably confident that differences do not result from chance. For example, when we compare men with women, a difference of about 6 points is necessary. When we compare whites with blacks, a difference of 9 points is necessary because only about 200 blacks are sampled in most NES surveys.

These numbers provide only a quick ballpark estimate of the chances that the reported results are likely to represent the entire population. Better estimates can be obtained using formulas presented in many statistics textbooks. To make such calculations, or even a ballpark estimate of the chances of error, the reader must know the size of the groups being compared. For this reason, we always report in our tables and figures either the number of cases upon which our percentages are based or the information necessary to approximate the number of cases.[32]

THE 2000 CONTEST

Part 1 of our book follows the chronology of the campaign itself. In chapter 1, we begin with the struggle to gain the Republican and Democratic Party nominations. As Clinton was prevented from seeking reelection by the Twenty-second Amendment, twelve major Republican candidates sought the GOP nomination, although by the time first delegates were actually chosen in the Iowa caucuses only six candidates remained. On the Democratic side, Al Gore was the clear front-runner from the outset, with former Senator Bill Bradley of New Jersey his only major opponent. We begin by examining the decision of candidates to run—or not to run—for their party's nomination, explaining why the Republican field in 2000 was so large and the Democratic field so small. We show that most candidates hold, or have held, high political office, although there has been a growing tendency for nonpoliticians to seek the presidency.

We then examine the regularities of the "nomination system of 1972," as well as the unique features of the 2000 contests. We study the rules structuring the nomination of candidates, showing how the electorate has a far larger role in choosing presidential candidates than it did before the reforms introduced after the 1968 election. These new rules, we argue, make it very likely that a party's nominee will be chosen before its presidential nomination convention is held. We examine the process by which the Republican field was winnowed down to two viable candidates and see how George W. Bush captured the nomination by early March 2000. We also show how Gore had an easy run against Bradley, winning every primary and caucus contest. We discuss Bush's choice of Dick Cheney, a former member of the U.S. House of Representatives and a former secretary of Defense, as his running mate, and Gore's more surprising choice of Joseph I. Lieberman of Connecticut, an Orthodox Jew who had been a critic of Bill Clinton's conduct in the Monica Lewinsky scandal.

Having gained their parties' nominations, Gore and Bush faced the task of winning the 270 electoral votes necessary to win the general election. We discuss the strategic context that confronted the candidates as the general election campaign began, showing how the Republicans appeared to have an advantage based upon the past pattern of state-by-state results. We see how the Democrats tried to take advantage of the "bounce" that they had received from their successful convention and see how the Republicans sought to stop the Democratic momentum. The three presidential debates, and the one vice-presidential debate, seemed to provide the Democrats with the opportunity to take the lead, since Gore was an experienced debater who had participated in vice-presidential debates in 1992 and 1996. We examine how the low expectations for Bush's debate performance actually worked to his advantage when he surpassed them. We then look at the final efforts in the "battleground" states, which both sides believed held the key to winning the election. And we analyze the way in which Gore reacted to the threat posed by Ralph Nader, the Green Party candidate, who could drain away enough support from Gore to cost him the electoral votes in close states. More than in past elections, both political parties and their allies made a major effort to identify their supporters and to get them to vote, and we examine the techniques that they used. Finally, we turn to the question of whether the campaign mattered.

Chapter 3 presents and interprets the election results. We briefly examine the postelection contest for Florida's twenty-five electoral votes, concluding that by most standards Bush would have won a hand recount. We next examine the rules for electing the president, showing how Bush was able to win a majority of the electoral votes even though he trailed Gore in popular votes. We then look at the pattern of results since World War II, showing that there has been a great deal of volatility, although with a slight advantage for the Republicans. We next turn to the state-by-state results, examining the margin of victory for the winning candidates over the past six elections. We examine partisan change in the post–World War II South and explain why the South was transformed politically into one of the most Republican regions in the nation. We see that though differences among the states rose somewhat in 2000, regional differences are substantially smaller than they were before World War II. Finally, we turn to the electoral vote balance between the Democrats and the Republicans. We argue that neither party is in a dominant position and that each has a mixture of problems and opportunities.

Chapter 1

The Nomination Struggle

❖❖❖

On March 9, 2000, both former senator Bill Bradley, D-N.J., and current senator John McCain, R-Ariz., held press conferences announcing their withdrawals from their respective party's presidential nomination campaign. By doing so, they conceded the Democratic nomination to Vice President Al Gore and effectively conceded the Republican Party's nomination to Texas governor George W. Bush, respectively. Bradley was Gore's only formally declared opponent. While Alan Keyes remained in the Republican contest, only McCain presented Bush with any serious competition, and now that challenge, like Bradley's, had ended little more than a week into March.

In 1988 Bush's father, George H. W. Bush, like Gore in 2000, had run for the presidential nomination as the sitting vice president, seeking to succeed an incumbent president who was completing the constitutional maximum of two four-year terms, and who was bequeathing unusually high approval ratings from the public to his successor.[1] At the comparable point to March 9, 2000, Bush in 1988 still faced a crowded field of challengers. Although he was in the process of vanquishing his strongest foe, Sen. Bob Dole, Kan., neither Bush nor anyone else could be certain at the time that he was poised for effective victory. In fact, he would not reach a point comparable to that of his son until after a majority of delegates had been selected, with Dole withdrawing on March 29th, some three weeks after "Super Tuesday" and its southern regional primary.

On the other side, Massachusetts governor Michael S. Dukakis was in a position even more analogous to George W. Bush's in 2000. Each was governor of a state integral to his party's current identity and at the center of his party's electoral coalition. Neither was a particularly well-known national figure at the outset of his bid, and both would prove successful in large measure because they had amassed much larger campaign war chests and built substantially more effective national campaign organizations than any of their numerous challengers. Dukakis, however, was barely the front-runner, if front-runner at all, at the point comparable to March 9, 2000, and Al Gore's and George W. Bush's effective victories. Dukakis, moreover, had just faced one of his most important tests, the so-called southern primary. He did surprisingly well in that test but still had a long way to go, including tackling then senator Al Gore's challenge, before victory was assured.[2]

In many respects, however, the presidential nomination contests of 2000 looked similar not only to those of 1988 but to all those that have been fought since 1972. Reforms in the late 1960s and early 1970s had induced a new form of nomination campaign, one that required public campaigns for resources and for votes. The system was sufficiently different from that which preceded it and sufficiently in place by the 1972 campaign that we refer to it as the "new nomination system of 1972." It has shaped many aspects of all contests since then, and we will examine similarities that have endured over its thirty-year existence. Each contest, of course, differs from all others due to the differing electoral contexts (for example, state of the economy, of war and peace) and differing sets of contenders. And in the new nomination system, the rules change to some degree every four years as well. The changes in rules and the strategies candidates adopt in light of these rules combine with the context and contenders to make each campaign unique in certain aspects.

In 2000 the rules changes that had the most impact on candidate strategy and the ultimate outcome of the nomination were the dates on which each state held its presidential primaries or caucuses. Many states, including some of the largest (for example, California and New York), moved their primaries to as early in the year as possible. "Front loading," as it had come to be called, has been the trend for most of the past thirty years, becoming even more pronounced since 1988. It became one of the most important forces shaping the campaigns of 1996 and 2000. Learning from the experiences of their predecessors in 1996, the candidates in 2000, especially the eventual victors, carefully designed their strategies around the front loading of the campaigns. This confluence of circumstances accounts for the most evident aspects of the 2000 campaigns—their early beginnings and their remarkably early endings. This confluence also helps us understand why it was Bush and Gore who won rather than McCain and Bradley, some other candidates, or even some prominent politicians who did not run at all.

In this chapter, we will examine some of the regularities of campaigns since 1972 and seek to understand some of the newer features revealed in the 2000 nomination contests. Next we turn to the first step of the nomination process, the decision of politicians to become—or not to become—presidential candidates. Then we will examine some of the rules of the nomination system they face. Finally, we will consider how the candidates ran and why Bush and Gore succeeded in their quests.

WHO RAN

It is a regularity of the nomination campaign that when incumbents seek renomination, only a very few candidates will contest them, and perhaps no one will at all. In 1972, while President Richard M. Nixon did face two potentially credible challengers to his renomination, they were sufficiently ineffective that he was essentially uncontested; Ronald Reagan was actually uncontested for renomination in 1984; and Bill Clinton was also actually unopposed in 1996. The other incumbents—Gerald R. Ford in 1976, Jimmy Carter (the only Democratic incumbent besides Clinton in this era) in 1980, and George Bush in 1992—each faced one or at most two credible challengers. Bush was expected to have little difficulty in defeating his challenger, Pat Buchanan, but had some difficulties at the outset, in part because he did not anticipate any struggle. Still, he defeated Buchanan rather easily.[3] Ford and Carter, however, had great difficulty in defeating their opponents (Reagan and Sen. Edward M. "Ted" Kennedy, D-Mass., respectively). These two presidents, while demonstrating that incumbents are not assured victory, nonetheless demonstrate the power of presidential incumbency, because both were victorious despite facing the strongest imaginable challengers and despite being relatively weak incumbents.

A second regularity in the nomination system is that a relatively large number of candidates will run for the nomination when no presidential incumbent is seeking it. Twelve major Republicans sought their party's nomination, though only six were still actively campaigning by January 1, 2000. A six-candidate field is quite typical for parties that do not have an incumbent president seeking the nomination. There have been eight such campaigns since 1980, and the number of major candidates that were in the race as the year began varied remarkably little: seven in 1980 (R); eight in 1984 (D); eight (D) and six (R) in 1988; eight in 1992 (D); and eight in 1996 (R). Yet on the Democratic side in 2000, only Gore and Bradley sought their party's nomination. Thus the field of only two Democrats in 2000, to go along with the more typical six on the Republican side in 2000, is all the more surprising and seems to be the first exception to this second regularity in the system.

Perhaps, however, having two Democrats in 2000 is not really an exception, but rather a reflection of both similarities with prior campaigns and adaptations to this extremely front-loaded primary season. Six major Democratic figures were often considered to be, and often gave signs that they were considering being, contenders to Gore. Besides Bradley, these included three current senators: Robert J. Kerrey, Neb., John Kerry, Mass., and Paul Wellstone, Minn. Also included on that list were the minority leader of the U.S. House of Representatives, Richard A. Gephardt, Mo., and the Rev. Jesse Jackson Jr. Like Gore, Kerrey, Gephardt, and Jackson had already run for presidential nomination at least once (and Jackson twice). While some indicated their interest in the race and Wellstone went so far as to establish an exploratory committee, only Bradley actually chose to run. Each, of course, cited unique personal reasons. Each recognized as well that Gore was the clear front-runner, with a strong base, a proven record as a fund-raiser, and the enthusiastic backing of the president (who was, of course, an outstanding fund-raiser). While in these ways Gore was in a stronger position than even George W. Bush in 2000, he was not in a stronger position than Bush's father in 1988. The differences between the two campaigns of sitting vice presidents are that front loading had increased substantially since 1988 and that experience had since demonstrated the increasing difficulty in defeating front-runners in the new nomination system, especially one so front loaded. Note, finally, that the number of Democrats (six) in this position in 2000 compares favorably with the number of Republicans (six) in the category of those strongly considering but ultimately choosing not to run in 1996.[4]

The twelve Republican candidates who declared their candidacy for the 2000 contest were: Lamar Alexander, Tenn., who most recently had been secretary of Education in the Bush administration and had been governor directly before then; Gary Bauer, a policy activist; Pat Buchanan, former speech writer in the Nixon administration and media commentator more recently; George W. Bush; former cabinet secretary and more recently head of the American Red Cross Elizabeth Dole; publisher Steven Forbes; current senator Orrin G. Hatch, Utah; Rep. John Kasich, Ohio; Alan Keyes, a former ambassador who is a black conservative; John McCain; former vice president Dan Quayle; and current senator Robert C. Smith, N.H. Alexander, Buchanan, Forbes, and Keyes had all run for the Republican nomination in 1996 (and Buchanan had done so in 1992 as well). Half of this list announced the end of their campaigns before the close of 1999: Alexander, Buchanan, Dole, Kasich, Quayle, and Smith. This list included some of those thought to have been Bush's strongest competitors for the nomination.

These lists of potential and actual candidates reveal further regularities over the past three decades. A third regularity is that, while one might expect current officeholders to dominate the list of candidates, in actuality a significant fraction of them do not hold office during the campaign. In 2000 only Bush, Gore, Hatch, and McCain were currently in office, while Kasich and Smith, holding office at the time, had dropped out of the campaign in 1999. The substantial proportion of out-of-office candidates illustrates the extreme amount of time, energy, and effort required to run for a presidential nomination. In addition, it exemplifies the (apparently increasing) attraction voters have to the "nonpolitician," the candidate who can claim to have played little or no role in politics, especially in Washington politics. The modest, if surprising, 1992 showing of Buchanan, who took great pains to be seen as an outsider, was trumped by the nearly 20 percent of the vote that businessman H. Ross Perot won in that general election. Businessman Forbes made an impressive showing in the 1996 nomination campaign, as well. While Bush prepared for strong efforts from Buchanan, Forbes, or perhaps some other nonpolitician (the strongest of which, had he run, was surely Gen. Colin Powell), none happened to have a strong impact in 2000.

A fourth regularity is that, of those candidates who were politicians, most held or had recently held high political office. This list (counting all twelve Republicans) included two vice presidents, four senators, two cabinet officers (one of whom had just retired from a governorship when he first ran), and another governor. This regularity follows from "ambition theory," developed

TABLE 1-1   Current or Most Recent Office Held by Declared Candidates
for President: Two Major Parties, 1972–2000

Office held[a]	Percentage of all candidates who held that office	Number 1972–2000	Number 2000
President	7%	6	0
Vice president	4	4	2
U.S. senator	37	34	3
U.S. representative	11	10	1
Governor	21	19	2
U.S. cabinet	4	4	1
Other	8	7	3
None	9	8	1
Total	101%	92	13

Sources: The list of candidates between 1976 and 1992 is found in *Congressional Quarterly's Guide to U.S. Elections,* 4th ed. (Washington, D.C.: CQ Press, 2001), 562. Those in 1972 may be found in ibid., 522–525. Candidates for 1996 are listed and discussed in Paul R. Abramson, John H. Aldrich, and David W. Rohde, *Change and Continuity in the 1996 and 1998 Elections* (Washington, D.C.: CQ Press, 1999), 13. Year 2000 candidates are discussed in *CQ Weekly,* Jan. 1, 2000, 22. *CQ Weekly* does not classify Robert C. Smith as a candidate.

[a] Office held at time of candidacy or office held most recently prior to candidacy.

originally by Joseph A. Schlesinger to explain how personal ambition and the pattern and prestige of office will tend to emerge from political offices that provide the strongest electoral bases.[5] This base for the presidency includes the offices of vice president, senator, governor, and of course, the presidency itself. Note that Kasich was the only member of the U.S. House actually to run for nomination (although he withdrew before 2000 began). House candidates do not have a strong electoral base for the presidency and ordinarily must forgo a safe House seat. As a result, few run and fewer still are strong contenders.

Most candidates in 2000, as in all earlier campaigns under the new nominating system, emerged from such a strong electoral base. Table 1-1 reports such data for 2000 and for all campaigns from 1972 through 2000 combined. Sixty-nine percent of all candidates emerged from the four offices that provide a strong electoral base, 54 percent in 2000, a year in which so many ran from outside electoral politics. Of the candidates running in 2000, only Hatch was up for reelection. None of the rest was up for reelection to a currently held office and therefore did not have to consider how to resolve a dilemma of having to choose between offices without knowing the outcome of the presidential nomination contest.

These two slates of contenders now prepared for the difficult and complicated task of actually conducting the campaign. How they ran depended, as we noted above, on the other candidates and on the rules (both formal and informal) of the nomination campaign. Knowing the list of candidates, we now turn to consider the remarkably complex game of nomination politics that characterizes campaigning in the new nomination system of 1972. As we shall see, front loading is but one of the many features of this game.

The method used by the two major parties for nominating presidential candidates is unique and amazingly complicated. To add to the complication, the various formal rules, laws, and procedures for the nomination are changed, sometimes in large ways and invariably in numerous small ways, every four years. Beyond the formal rules lie informal standards and expectations, often set by the media or the candidates themselves, that help shape each campaign. As variable as the rules are, however, the nomination system of 1972 has one pair of overriding characteristics that define it as its own system. Beginning in 1972, for the first time, the major-party presidential nominees were selected in public and by the public; as a result, all serious candidates have sought the nomination by seeking the support of the public through the various media of communication.

The complexity of the nomination contests is a consequence of four major factors. The first of these, federalism, or the state as unit of selection for national nominees, is as old as the Republic. The second, rules concerning the selection (and perhaps instruction) of delegates to the convention, and the third, rules concerning financing the campaign, are the (often revised) products of the reform period. The final factor is the way candidates react to these rules and to their opponents. This factor is the invariable consequence of keen competition for a highly valued goal.

Federalism, or State-Based, Delegate Selection

National conventions to select presidential nominees were first held for the 1832 election, and it has been true for every nomination from then to today that the votes of delegates attending the conventions determine the nominees.[6] Delegates have always been allocated at the state level; whatever particulars may apply, each state selects its parties' delegates through procedures adopted by its state party organizations or by state law (which determines primary elections, as well as their dates, rules, and procedures) or by both. Votes at the convention are cast by state delegation, and in general, the state (including the District of Columbia, various territories, and, for the Democrats, even Americans living abroad) is the basic unit of the nomination. Thus there are really fifty-one separate delegate selection contests in each party (plus procedures the remaining units use). There is no national primary, nor is there serious contemplation of one.

That there are more than fifty separate contests in each campaign creates numerous layers of complexity, two of which are especially consequential. First, each state is free to select any method of choosing delegates consistent with the general rules of the national party. Many states choose to select delegates via a primary election, which is a state-run election like any other, except each primary selects delegates for only one party's convention (as well as, often, serving as a primary election for selecting candidates for the party's nominees for the various other electoral offices). The Democratic Party requires that its party's primaries be open only to those who register as Democrats.[7] States not holding primaries use a combination of caucuses and conventions. Caucuses are simply local level meetings of party members. Those attending the caucuses typically report their preferences for the presidential nomination (and must do so on the Democratic side), and attendees choose delegates from their midst to attend higher level conventions, perhaps at the county level, then the congressional district, state, and eventually national-level conventions. In addition to selecting delegates, caucuses and subsequent conventions may endorse possible platform proposals and conduct other party business.

The second major consequence of this federalism is that the states are free (within bounds) to choose when to hold their primaries or caucuses.[8] As a result, they are spread out over time. New Hampshire's has been the first primary in the nation since the state began to hold primaries in 1920, and state law requires that New Hampshire's primary be held (invariably in February or March) before any other state's. A more recent tradition that began in 1976 is that Iowa holds the first caucuses, in advance of the New Hampshire primary (a "tradition" challenged by other states that have scheduled even earlier caucuses). The primary season in 2000 ended, as usual, in early June. In prior years, the seasons had ended with something of a flourish because June primaries included the largest single prize, California. Even when California moved the date of its primary to earlier in the year, delegate selection was still spread over essentially the same time as in earlier years. The result has been a months-long process that features dramatic ebbs and flows of candidates' fortunes, albeit a more truncated one in 2000 than earlier. The lengthy and dynamic nature of these fifty-plus events preceded the reforms that created the nomination system of 1972, but those reforms have greatly accentuated the importance of length and enhanced its dynamism.[9]

The Nomination System of 1972: Delegate Selection

Through 1968 presidential nominations were won by appeals to the party leadership. To be sure, public support and even primary election victories could be important in a candidate's campaign, but their importance would lie in the credibility they would give his or her candidacy to party leaders. But the 1968 Democratic nomination, as so many other events that year, was an especially tumultuous one, with the result that the Democratic Party began a series of reforms, initiated by proposals from the McGovern-Fraser Commission as adopted by the party convention in 1972, that created one of the two major components of the new nomination system, that concerning delegate selection. While much less aggressive in reforming its delegate selection procedures, the

Republican Party did so to a certain degree. Moreover, the most consequential results of these reforms for our purposes—the proliferation of presidential primaries and media treatment of some (notably the Iowa) caucuses as essentially primary-like—spilled over to the Republican side in full measure.

In 1968 Sens. Eugene J. McCarthy, D-Minn., and Robert F. Kennedy, D-N.Y., ran highly visible, public, primary-oriented campaigns in opposition to the policies of President Lyndon B. Johnson, especially the conduct of the war in Vietnam. Before the second primary, in Wisconsin, Johnson surprisingly announced that he would not seek renomination. Vice President Hubert H. Humphrey took Johnson's place in representing the establishment and the policies of the Democratic Party. Humphrey, however, waged no public campaign, winning nomination without entering a single primary.[10] The nomination split an already deeply divided party. Whether Humphrey would have won had Robert F. Kennedy not been assassinated the night he defeated McCarthy in the California primary, effectively eliminating McCarthy as a serious contender, is unknowable. The chaos and even violence that accompanied Humphrey's nomination made it clear to Democrats, however, that the nomination process should be opened to more diverse candidacies and that public participation should be more open and more efficacious, perhaps even determinative.

The two most significant consequences of these reforms were the increasing decisiveness of the public in each state's delegate selection proceedings (even binding delegates to vote in support of the candidate for whom they were chosen)[11] and the proliferation of presidential primaries. Caucus-convention procedures were made more timely, better publicized, and, in short, more primary-like. Until recently, the media treated Iowa's caucuses as critical events, and the coverage of them was similar to the coverage of primaries—how many "votes" were "cast" for each candidate, for example. At the state level, many party officials concluded that the easiest way to conform to the new Democratic rules in 1972 was to use a primary election. Thus the number of states holding Democratic primaries increased from seventeen in 1968 to twenty-three in 1972 to thirty in 1976, with the number of Republican primaries increasing comparably. By 1988 thirty-five states held Republican primaries (thirty-three did on the Democratic side), which selected three of every four delegates to the Republican convention that year. In 2000 forty Democratic and forty-three Republican primaries were held. Thus it is fair to say that the parties' new nomination systems have come to be based largely on primaries. Even the one set of caucuses that might attract considerable media (and therefore candidate) attention, Iowa, has become less newsworthy and salient to the candidates since its heydays of 1976 and 1980.

The only major exception to this conclusion is that about one in five delegates to the Democrats' national convention is chosen because he or she is an elected official or a Democratic Party official. Supporters of this reform to party rules (first used in 1984) wanted to ensure that the Democratic leadership would have a formal role to play at the conventions of the party. However, though these "superdelegates" may have played a decisive role in the 1984 nomination of

Walter F. Mondale, they have not played a pivotal role in the past four nomination contests.

While national Democratic Party rules were unchanged for 2000, the Republican Party modified their rules between 1996 and 2000.[12] They adopted two changes of note, partly in response to the increased front loading of primaries in 1996 and the attempts by several state GOP parties to move their caucuses ahead of Iowa's.[13] To forestall such moves and to keep the formal campaign from starting even earlier, the Republicans required that delegates be chosen during the "window" of the first Monday in February to the third Tuesday in June. Secondly, they provided incentives for state parties to select their delegates later in the season. In particular, they offered to add a bonus of a 5 percent increase to the number of delegates a state would otherwise have if they selected their delegates between March 15 and April 14, a 7.5 percent bonus for selections between April 15 and May 14, and a 10 percent bonus to those states selecting delegates from May 15 to the end of the window.

The Republican reforms went along with some sentiment that the effects of front loading were deleterious to the nomination process. These reforms, however, proved ineffective in slowing the rush to the front of the calendar. After discussions among various party leaders about holding one regional primary or another, often later in the year, the incentives for the individual states to move to the beginning of the season outweighed Republican delegate bonuses. Most important, the two largest states, California and New York, became two of eleven states to hold their primaries at the earliest time after New Hampshire, as permitted by the Democratic window, March 7. As a result, candidates had to run coast-to-coast campaigns on the seventh, if not earlier. In Figure 1-1, we graph the cumulative percentage of Democratic delegates (not including super-delegates) selected to date, in weeks elapsed since the New Hampshire primary, for 1976 and 2000. (New Hampshire ended up moving its primary in 2000 to an early, rather than the more usual late, February time slot, well before the Democratic window opened for other states.) It is clear that many more delegates were selected early in 2000 than were selected early in 1976.

The rationale for front loading is clear enough. California's (actual or near) end-of-season primary was last consequential in the 1964 Republican and the 1972 Democratic nomination contests. Once candidates, media, and other actors realized, and reacted to, the implications of the reformed nomination system, the action shifted to the earliest events of the season, and nomination contests, especially those involving multiple candidates, were effectively completed well before the end of the primary season. More and more state parties and legislatures realized the advantages of front loading, bringing more attention in the media, more expenditures of time and money by the candidates, and more influence to their states if they held primaries earlier rather than later.

If the rationale for front loading was clear by 1996, when it first became controversial, the consequences were not. Some argued that long-shot candidates could be propelled to the front of the pack by gathering momentum in Iowa and

FIGURE 1-1   Cumulative Percentage of Democratic Delegates Selected since
New Hampshire Primary, 1976 and 2000

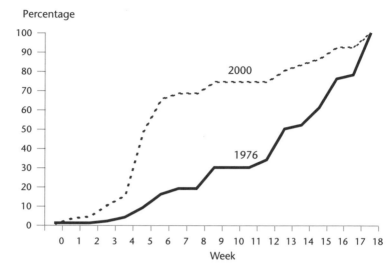

New Hampshire and, before the well-known candidates could react, lock up the nomination early. The alternative argument was that increasing front loading helps those who begin the campaign with several advantages associated with being a front-runner, such as name recognition, support from state and local party or related organizations, and most of all money.

Indeed, as the primary season has become more front loaded, the well-known, well-established, and well-financed candidates have increasingly come to dominate the primaries. Sen. George S. McGovern, S.D., and Carter won the Democratic nominations in 1972 and 1976 even though they began as little-known and ill-financed contenders. George Bush, successful in the 1980 Iowa Republican caucuses, climbed from, in his words, "an asterisk in the polls" (where the asterisk is commonly used to indicate less than 1 percent support) to become Reagan's major contender and eventual vice presidential choice, and Gary Hart nearly defeated former vice president Mondale in 1984. In 1988 the two strongest candidates at the start of the Republican race, Bush and Dole, contested most vigorously, with Bush winning, while Gov. Michael S. Dukakis, Mass., was the best-financed and best-organized Democrat and won nomination surprisingly easily. Clinton's victory in 1992, then, appeared the culmination of the trend toward the strongest and best-financed candidates' seemingly insuperable advantages. For his part, he was able to withstand scandal and defeat in the early going and eventually cruise to victory. One important reason for Clinton's victory was illustrated by the campaign of former Sen. Paul Tsongas, Mass. He defeated the field in New Hampshire, and as usual, the victory and its consequent media attention opened doors to fund-raising possibilities unavailable to him even days earlier. Yet he faced the dilemma that taking the time to raise the funds and use them to increase the chances of winning votes would let too many primaries pass without his competition. Conversely, if he campaigned in those primaries, he would not have the opportunity to raise and direct the funds he needed to be an effective competitor. Front loading had, simply, squeezed too much into too short a post-New Hampshire time frame to be able to capitalize on early victories as, say, Carter had in 1976 in winning nomination and election. The events of 1996 supported the second argument also, even though it took nearly all of Dole's resources to effect his early victory. This lesson was not lost on the candidates for 2000. George W. Bush, especially, was able to learn from Dole's experience and to act on the lesson, as we shall see below.

The Nomination System of 1972: Campaign Finance

The second part of the reforms of the presidential nomination process began with the Federal Election Campaign Act of 1971, but it was the amendments of 1974 and 1976 that fully altered the nature of campaign financing. The Watergate scandal included revelations of substantial misuse in the raising and spending of money in the 1972 presidential election (facts discovered in part because of the implementation of the 1971 act). The resulting reforms limited contributions by individuals and groups, virtually ending the impact of individual "fat cats" and requiring presidential candidates to raise money in a broad-based campaign. Small donations for the nomination could be matched by the federal government, and candidates who accepted matching funds would be bound by limits on what they could spend (a provision that effectively limited Dole's campaign efforts in the spring of 1996, after he had won the primaries but before the nominating conventions).

These provisions, created by the Federal Election Commission to monitor campaign financing and regulate campaign practices, altered the way nomination campaigns were funded. Still, just as candidates learned over time how to contest most effectively in the new delegate selection process, so too did they learn how to campaign in light of the financial regulations. Perhaps most important, presidential candidates learned that, while it is not as true for them as for congressional candidates that "early money is like yeast" (the acronym for EMILY's List, the group that supports female candidates), it is true, or so they believed in both 1996 and 2000, that lots and lots of early money is necessary to compete effectively.[14]

The costs of running presidential nomination campaigns have escalated dramatically since 1972. This fact does not, of course, make the new presidential nomination system unique. The costs of campaigning for all major offices have escalated dramatically. But a special chain of strategic reactions have added to escalating campaign costs in the presidential nomination system.

The McGovern-Fraser Commission reforms did not specify that delegates should be chosen via primary elections. Indeed, they indicated a preference for the use of (more open and accessible) caucuses and conventions instead of primaries. The commission, however, sought to achieve a variety of goals, and state parties and legislatures found that compliance to the full set of reform measures made the caucus-convention method complicated, while compliance via primary elections was less cumbersome for the state. Thus, as noted above, increasing numbers of states chose to comply by using primaries. This led to more media coverage of particular events, to the greater possibility of a campaign's developing momentum, and to the enhancement in value of early victories (and harsher costs of early defeats). As we saw earlier, these reactions, in turn, led states to create the front-loaded season candidates faced in 2000. All of these factors, therefore, created not only a demand for more money to be raised but also a demand for that money to be raised early, in advance of the primary season. The result, using 2000 for illustration, was that only by raising large sums of money in 1999 could candidates hope to compete effectively in the eleven coast-to-coast primaries held on March 7. Finally, Bob Dole in 1996 demonstrated that even the primary victor could not rest on his or her laurels and spend the interim between the primary and general election seasons preparing for the fall. Instead, the victor had to plan on being able to fill the interregnum with expensive, public campaigning.

Not only was fund-raising one of the most important events of 2000, but also its story, like that of the campaigns themselves, was nearing an end and not a beginning when the primary season of 2000 opened.[15] Therefore, we turn now to the two party nominations themselves, starting with the Republican campaign, which most fully illustrates the impact of the chain of strategic reactions described above.

WHY BUSH WON

George W. Bush's easy reelection as governor of Texas in November 1998 catapulted him to the status of front-runner for the Republican presidential nomination. Still, his hold on the lead was uncertain and more tenuous than that of many other apparent front-runners before him. When 2000 opened, however, his front-running status had become so strong that his nomination appeared all but certain. As noted earlier, he had already driven out more than half of his competition, including many of those who had seemed likely to become his strongest competitors.

How had he done so? The answer is that Bush was in a position to take advantage of the various elements in the chain of strategic reactions described above, and he used that potential with remarkable effect. Central to this ability to defeat so many strong opponents before the first vote was cast was his ability to build by far the most effective campaign organization among the Republican candidates. Three factors helped Bush to achieve success: his popular standing, his campaign financing, and his support among party leaders. His popular standing in the polls started off well. He led his closest rival (Elizabeth Dole) by sixteen points among Republicans as their first choice for nomination (30 percent to 14 percent) in a May 1998 Gallup poll, and by twenty points (42–22) in January 1999. By September that lead had ballooned to forty-nine points, mostly by a dramatic increase in his support (62 percent) and to a lesser extent by a decline in hers (to 13 percent, down from a May peak of 24 percent), with no one else gaining ground. This lead did not materialize out of nowhere, of course. While his gubernatorial reelection attracted positive media attention, so too did his efforts to create an effective presidential campaign organization.

Most remarkable of the three factors that aided Bush in his success is the second, his ability to raise funds. The Bush campaign attracted considerable attention by announcing that he had raised the remarkable figure of $36.3 million by July 1999, more than six months before the start of the primary season. He proved so successful that he decided to forgo federal matching funds. Doing so would free him from the limitations on expenditures that come with accepting matching funds and that had hamstrung Dole in 1996. Third, Bush was able not only to raise money, but also to attract considerable support among party leaders. On August 8, 1999, he received the endorsement of twenty-one Republican governors. Adding himself and his brother Jeb, governor of Florida, to the list, he could count on the backing of twenty-three of the thirty-one GOP governors.[16] By the end of 1999 Bush had secured numerous other endorsements, as well. Elizabeth Dole, the second most popular candidate in 1999 and contender for some of the same, more moderate Republican support, found many of her potential sources of funds and other kinds of support already committed to Bush. There was a form of momentum in 1999 similar in some respects to that previously found building from primary victories.

The Bush juggernaut had effectively defeated most of his strongest rivals as 2000 opened—but not all. Bauer, Forbes, Hatch, Keyes, and McCain remained. While the Bauer, Forbes, and Hatch campaigns fizzled and Keyes's did not have much impact, McCain showed surprising strength. He bypassed the Iowa caucuses, helping render them relatively unimportant (results of Republican caucuses and primaries are reported in Tables 1-2 and 1-3 respectively). McCain focused instead on New Hampshire. While his voting record in the Senate was quite conservative (seeming to match up well against Bush's reputation of moderate conservatism and bipartisan cooperation), he developed a more moderate, reformist reputation due to his unflagging efforts on behalf of campaign finance reform, especially in the guise of the bill he cosponsored with Democratic senator Russell D. Feingold, Wis. McCain defeated Bush soundly in New Hampshire. Having, however, placed great emphasis on South Carolina's primary (in part due to his expected appeal to veterans as an especially heroic POW in Vietnam), McCain's loss there seemed likely to derail his campaign and clear the road for Bush. Conversely, McCain's appeal for campaign finance reform proved strong among Democrats and independents. While neither could vote in South Carolina's GOP primary, they could in several others, including Michigan's.

TABLE 1-2   Republican Caucus Results, 2000

State	Date	Total votes	Bush	McCain	Keyes	Others
Alaska	Jan. 24	4,330	36.3%	9.5%	9.5%	44.8%
Iowa	Jan. 24	87,233	41.0	4.7	14.2	40.0
Hawaii	Feb. 7					
North Dakota	Feb. 29	9,066	75.7	18.9	5.3	0.0
Minnesota	March 7	18,390	62.7	17.4	19.9	0.0
Washington	March 7	—	80.0	15.3	3.3	1.3
Wyoming	March 10	944	77.5	10.3	11.7	0.5
Nevada	Feb.–Mar.					
Montana	April					
Kansas	May 25					

Source: http://www.thegreenpapers.com

Notes: The total votes cast in Washington are not available. For that state the percentages shown are based on the county convention delegates won by the candidate. Caucus results are not available for Kansas, Montana, and Nevada. No vote was taken in Hawaii.

There was no Democratic primary campaign in Michigan in 2000, and therefore many did "cross over" to vote on the GOP side. Combined with a home-state victory that day to go along with his surprise victory in Michigan, momentum appeared to swing back to McCain once again, and he seemed poised to become a serious challenger.

It was at this point that the advantages of a large, well-funded campaign organization became clear. Bush's advantages in this area were significant, and so too was his support among Republicans, a support base largely unaffected by McCain's emergence. These factors combined with the vast and complex set of primaries on March 7 to render Bush's advantages decisive. With too few delegates remaining to be chosen after the seventh for McCain to imagine overcoming Bush's lead in delegate commitments, he conceded two days later. Although Keyes continued to campaign, McCain's concession effectively gave Bush the nomination.

WHY GORE WON

That a dozen candidates declared on the Republican side but only two did so on the Democratic side might lead one to conclude that the two parties' contests differed dramatically. In fact, there were more striking similarities than differences between them. Gore, for example, might well have anticipated a large set of challengers, and as we saw earlier, a considerable number of potentially competitive Democrats did consider running. That they did not reflected Gore's solid front-runner status. In that respect, the biggest difference between the Republicans and the Democrats may have been the clarity of Gore's position from the outset. In

TABLE 1-3   Republican Presidential Primary Results, 2000

State	Date	Total votes	Bush	McCain	Keyes	Others
New Hampshire	Feb. 1	238,206	30.4%	48.5%	6.4%	14.7%
Delaware	Feb. 8	30,060	50.7	25.4	3.8	20.0
South Carolina	Feb. 19	573,101	53.4	41.9	4.5	0.2
Arizona	Feb. 22	322,669	35.7	60.0	3.6	0.7
Michigan	Feb. 22	1,276,770	43.1	51.0	4.6	1.4
Virginia	Feb. 29	664,093	52.8	43.9	3.1	0.3
Washington	Feb. 29	491,148	57.8	38.9	2.4	0.9
California	March 7	2,847,921	60.6	34.7	4.0	0.7
Connecticut	March 7	178,985	46.3	48.7	3.3	1.7
Georgia	March 7	643,188	66.9	27.8	4.6	0.6
Maine	March 7	96,624	51.0	44.0	3.1	1.9
Maryland	March 7	376,034	56.2	36.2	6.7	1.0
Massachusetts	March 7	501,951	31.8	64.7	2.5	1.0
Missouri	March 7	475,363	57.9	35.3	5.7	1.0
New York	March 7		51.0	43.4	3.3	2.3
Ohio	March 7	1,397,528	58.0	37.0	4.0	1.1
Rhode Island	March 7	36,120	36.4	60.2	2.6	0.8
Vermont	March 7	81,355	35.3	60.3	2.7	1.7
Colorado	March 10	180,655	64.7	27.1	6.6	1.6
Utah	March 10	91,053	63.3	14.0	21.3	1.4
Florida	March 14	699,503	73.8	19.9	4.6	1.6
Louisiana	March 14	102,912	83.6	8.9	5.7	1.8
Mississippi	March 14	114,979	87.9	5.4	5.6	1.0
Oklahoma	March 14	124,809	79.1	10.4	9.3	1.2
Tennessee	March 14	250,791	77.0	14.5	6.7	1.7
Texas	March 14	1,126,757	87.5	7.1	3.9	1.5
Illinois	March 21	736,857	67.4	21.5	9.0	2.1
Pennsylvania	April 4	651,809	72.5	22.4	1.1	4.1
Wisconsin	April 4	495,769	69.2	18.1	9.9	2.8
Dist. of Columbia	May 2	2,433	72.8	24.4	—	2.8
Indiana	May 2	406,664	81.2	18.8	—	—
North Carolina	May 2	322,517	78.6	10.9	7.9	2.7
Nebraska	May 9	185,758	78.2	15.1	6.5	—
West Virginia	May 9	109,404	79.6	12.9	4.8	2.8
Oregon	May 16	349,831	83.6	—	13.4	3.0
Arkansas	May 23	44,573	80.2	—	19.8	—
Idaho	May 23	158,446	73.5	—	19.1	7.4
Kentucky	May 23	91,323	83.0	6.3	4.7	5.9
Alabama	June 6	203,079	84.2	—	11.5	4.2

TABLE 1-3   (continued)

State	Date	Total votes	Bush	McCain	Keyes	Others
Montana	June 6	113,671	77.6	—	18.3	4.1
New Jersey	June 6	240,810	83.6	—	16.4	—
New Mexico	June 6	75,230	82.6	10.1	6.4	0.8
South Dakota	June 6	45,279	78.2	13.8	7.7	0.3

Source: Richard M. Scammon, Alice V. McGillivray, and Rhodes Cook, *America Votes 24: A Handbook of Contemporary American Election Statistics* (Washington, D.C.: CQ Press, 2001), 42–43, 326.

Notes: "—" indicates that the candidate was not listed on the ballot or that votes for the candidate or others were not tabulated separately. Total votes figures were not available for New York Republicans. Results are based on official returns except for Arkansas, Indiana, Massachusetts, and North Carolina.

any event, 2000 opened with two strong candidates on the Democratic side, roughly comparable to the two who would prove to be competitive on the Republican side. It was therefore perhaps fitting that Gore's rival withdrew on the same day and for the same reason as Bush's only serious rival did.

Bradley had the difficult task of facing the best-known politician besides the president himself. He needed something to help him catch up to Gore. Unfortunately for Bradley, while Gore was not an especially stirring speaker, neither was he. Bradley also did not seem to react in a strategically adept way to Gore's campaign. He did prove to be a surprisingly effective fund-raiser, virtually matching the success of the vice president. However, though money is necessary to run a vigorous campaign, it must be combined with an effective message for the campaign to be successful. Bradley's general stance as a moderately liberal Democrat did not sharply distinguish him from the better-known Gore, and thus he could not convincingly represent himself as a genuinely different alternative, such as a clear liberal, to the moderately liberal Gore. Bradley also had difficulty in convincingly representing himself as an outsider, having been in the Senate for eighteen years. While Bradley ran strongly in New Hampshire, he came up four points short of Gore, losing 50 to 46 percent (see Tables 1-4 and 1-5 for results of Democratic caucuses and primaries). He had the resources but apparently not (quite) the message, so from that peak his success declined. To be sure, he ran strongly against Gore in several more states (albeit mostly in New England), but he won none of them and fared worse in the larger states, losing New York by two to one and California by four to one, for example. Thus, like McCain, Bradley realized that the March 7 primaries were in fact decisive, and he too withdrew on March 9, completing Gore's nomination victory.

THE CONVENTIONS

With both nominations effectively resolved on March 9, an unusually long hiatus quieted most political considerations until the national nominating conventions neared, more than four months later. It is, of course, only the convention

TABLE 1-4   Democratic Caucus Results, 2000

	Date	Total votes	Gore	Bradley	Other
Iowa	Jan. 24	61,000	63.4%	34.9%	1.7%
Hawaii	March 7	1,364	79.8	17.4	2.8
Idaho	March 7	1,500	62.8	33.0	4.2
North Dakota	March 7	2,291	77.7	21.7	0.6
Washington	March 7		68.4	28.2	3.4
South Carolina	March 9	7,519	92.2	1.9	5.8
Michigan	March 11	19,160	82.7	16.3	1.0
Minnesota	March 11	10,764	74.2	14.2	11.7
Nevada	March 12	1,089	90.2	2.2	7.6
Texas	March 14				
Wyoming	March 25	581	85.4	4.8	9.8
Delaware	March 27	800	100.0	—	—
Virginia	April 15	10,000	96.0	—	4.0
Alaska	April 22				
Kansas	May 6	566	95.6	—	4.4

Source: http://www.thegreenpapers.com

Notes: "—" indicates that the candidate was not listed on the ballot or that votes for the candidate or others were not tabulated separately. Total votes were not available for Washington; caucus results were not available for Texas or Alaska. Total votes were estimated in Iowa, Idaho, Delaware, and Virginia. Percentages reflect the candidate preferences of caucus attenders except in certain states, in which the percentages reflect shares of the following won by the candidate: Delaware and Idaho (state convention delegates), Virginia (congressional district and state convention delegates), and Washington (legislative and county convention delegates).

delegates who choose the nominees and only they who adopt the party's platform. But with opposition gone, all of the drama was also gone from the presidential nominations. And in these two cases, as in most, the soon-to-be victorious nominees kept a tight hold over the deliberations and the content of their respective party's platform.

Convention delegates make two other decisions, either of which can become controversial. One is the adoption of party rules (ordinarily considering what rules should govern for the coming four years, but also considering any challenges to current delegations—for example, for alleged violations of party rules in their selection). The other is the selection of vice-presidential running mates. In these cases, as in all else in both successful nomination campaigns, Bush and Gore were adept at eliminating any potential concerns. This was especially apparent in the selection of running mates to offer to the conventions for formal nomination, as both selections received high marks from party leaders and the media. Bush ended up choosing the head of the team advising him on this choice. Dick Cheney is an experienced political veteran, a former member of Congress, and secretary of Defense in Bush's father's administration. Most saw Cheney as balancing Bush's relative youth and inexperience in Washington, if

TABLE 1-5   Democratic Presidential Primary Results, 2000

State	Date	Total votes	Gore	Bradley	Others
New Hampshire	Feb. 1	154,639	49.7%	45.6%	4.7%
Delaware	Feb. 5	11,141	57.2	40.2	2.6
California	March 7	2,654,114	81.2	18.2	0.6
Connecticut	March 7	177,301	55.4	41.5	3.0
Georgia	March 7	284,431	83.8	16.2	—
Maine	March 7	64,279	54.0	41.3	4.7
Maryland	March 7	507,462	67.3	28.5	4.2
Massachusetts	March 7	570,074	59.9	37.3	2.8
Missouri	March 7	265,489	64.6	33.6	1.8
New York	March 7	974,463	65.6	33.5	0.9
Ohio	March 7	978,512	73.6	24.7	1.7
Rhode Island	March 7	47,079	56.9	40.4	2.7
Vermont	March 7	49,283	54.3	43.9	1.8
Washington	Feb. 29	297,001	68.2	31.4	0.4
Colorado	March 10	88,735	71.4	23.3	5.3
Utah	March 10	15,687	79.9	20.1	—
Arizona	March 11	86,762	77.9	18.9	3.2
Florida	March 14	551,995	81.8	18.2	—
Louisiana	March 14	157,551	73.0	19.9	7.1
Mississippi	March 14	88,602	89.6	8.6	1.8
Oklahoma	March 14	134,850	68.7	25.4	5.8
Tennessee	March 14	215,203	92.1	5.3	2.6
Texas	March 14	786,890	80.2	16.3	3.4
Illinois	March 21	809,667	84.3	14.2	1.4
Pennsylvania	April 4	704,150	74.6	20.8	4.6
Wisconsin	April 4	371,196	88.5	8.8	2.7
Dist. of Columbia	May 2	19,417	95.9	—	4.1
Indiana	May 2	293,172	74.9	21.9	3.1
North Carolina	May 2	544,922	70.4	18.3	11.3
Nebraska	May 9	105,271	70.0	26.5	3.6
West Virginia	May 9	253,310	72.0	18.4	9.6
Oregon	May 16	354,594	84.9	—	15.1
Arkansas	May 23	246,900	78.5	—	21.5
Idaho	May 23	35,688	75.7	—	24.3
Kentucky	May 23	220,279	71.3	14.7	14.1
Alabama	June 6	278,527	77.0	—	23.0
Montana	June 6	87,867	77.9	—	22.1
New Jersey	June 6	378,272	94.9	—	5.1
New Mexico	June 6	132,280	74.6	20.6	4.8
South Dakota	June 6				

Source: Richard M. Scammon, Alice V. McGillivray, and Rhodes Cook, *America Votes 24: A Handbook of Contemporary American Election Statistics* (Washington, D.C.: CQ Press, 2001), 44–45.

Notes: "—" indicates that the candidate was not listed on the ballot or that votes for the candidate or others were not tabulated separately. Total votes were not available for New York. Write-in vote figures were not available for Pennsylvania. No vote was taken in South Dakota.

not positively adding *gravitas* to the ticket. Gore selected Sen. Joseph I. Lieberman, Conn., a moderate liberal like Gore himself. An immediate advantage of this choice was the strong stance Lieberman had taken in criticizing Clinton's personal behavior in the various scandals, demonstrating both ethical priorities and political independence from the Clinton-Gore administration. This stance was reinforced because he is a devout Orthodox Jew.

The nominating convention serves not only as the culmination of the nominating campaign and as the locus through which the party conducts its business, but also as the transition to the general election campaign. The last event of the convention, the presidential nominee's acceptance speech, is the first major event of the general election campaign. Once again, Bush's and Gore's speeches were similar in being received by the media and apparently by the public as solid if not resounding successes. With so many similarities between the two nominees' roads to the conventions, it should not be a surprise that the general election campaign would prove to be a close contest as well. The account of how and why this proved true with a vengeance in 2000 is the subject of the next chapter.

Chapter 2

The General Election Campaign

♦♦♦

Once they have been nominated, candidates choose their general election campaign strategies based on their perceptions of what the electorate wants, the relative strengths and weaknesses of their opponents and themselves, and their chances of winning. Candidates who are convinced that they have a dependable lead may choose strategies very different from those used by candidates who believe they are seriously behind. A candidate who believes that an opponent has significant weaknesses is more likely to run an aggressive, attacking campaign than one who does not perceive such weaknesses.

After the 2000 conventions, the race was close. Most observers, and both candidates' organizations, believed that either George W. Bush or Al Gore could win and that the campaign could really make a difference. Part 2 of this book will consider in detail the impact of particular factors (including issues and evaluations of Clinton's job performance) on the voters' decisions. This chapter will provide an overview of the campaign—an account of its course and a description of the context within which strategic decisions were made.

THE STRATEGIC CONTEXT AND CANDIDATES' CHOICES

One aspect of the strategic context that candidates must consider is the track record of the parties in recent presidential elections. In presidential races the past is certainly not entirely prologue, but it is relevant. From this perspective, the picture was slightly more encouraging for the Republicans than for the Democrats. From 1952 through 1996 there had been twelve presidential elections, and the Republicans had won seven of them. Similarly, the GOP had won three of the five races since 1980, and two of their three victories were electoral college landslides while neither of the Democrats' wins was that large.

The nature of the American system for electing presidents requires that we examine the state-by-state pattern of results. U.S. voters do not directly vote for president or vice president. Rather, they vote for a slate of electors pledged to support a presidential and a vice-presidential candidate. Moreover, in every state except Maine and Nebraska, the entire slate of electors that receives the most popular votes is selected. In no state is a majority of the vote required. Since the 1972 election, Maine has used a system in which the plurality-vote winner for the whole state wins two electoral votes. In addition, the plurality-vote winner in each of Maine's two House districts receives that district's single electoral vote. Beginning in 1992, Nebraska allocated its five electoral votes in a similar manner: the statewide plurality-vote winner gained two votes, and each of the state's three congressional districts awarded one vote on a plurality basis.

If larger states used the district plan employed by Maine and Nebraska, the dynamics of the campaign would be different. For example, candidates might target specific congressional districts and would probably campaign in all large states, regardless of how well they were doing in the statewide polls. But given the winner-take-all rules employed in forty-eight states and the District of Columbia, candidates cannot safely ignore the pattern of past state results. A state-by-state analysis of the five presidential elections from 1980 through 1996 suggests that the Democrats did not face an easy task in the effort to win the 270 electoral votes required for victory.

As Figure 2-1 reveals, sixteen states voted Republican in all five of these elections. Only one state (Minnesota) and the District of Columbia were equally loyal to the Democrats. (See chapter 3 on long-term voting patterns.) These perfectly loyal states and the District of Columbia provided a prospective balance of 135 electoral votes for the Republicans to only 13 for the Democrats. Also problematic for the Democratic candidates were the next groups of states. Four states had voted Republican in every election but one, with a total of 44 electoral votes. Balancing these were only three small states (Hawaii, Rhode Island, and West Virginia), with a total of 13 electoral votes, that had supported the Democrats in four of the five contests. Thus, if each state's (and the District's) political leanings were categorized solely on the basis of the past five elections, one might expect that 179 electoral votes would go to the GOP, while only 26 would go to the Democrats.

If this past pattern had completely controlled the 2000 election, the prospects would have been bleak for the Democratic ticket. But, of course, things were not that simple, and many factors made Democratic chances considerably better than they had been in the Reagan era. Most obviously, the Democrats had *won* the two previous elections. They had carried many large states that were not sure things for the GOP, winning comfortable (albeit not overwhelming) majorities in the electoral college. In particular, they had pried the largest state, California—which had once leaned Republican—away from the GOP. The state now appeared to have a definite Democratic tilt, although victory there was far from certain. That, plus very good prospects in a number of the other big states, formed the basis for a plausible Democratic victory.

Thus either party could win, and both campaign organizations saw virtually the same set of states determining the outcome. These would be the battle-

FIGURE 2-1   States That Voted Republican at Least Four out of Five Times, 1980–1996

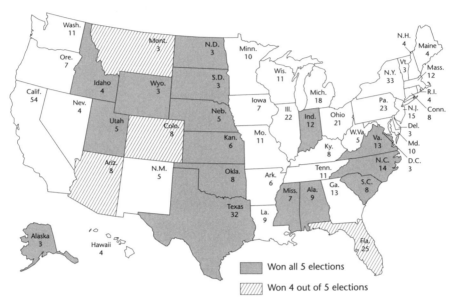

Source: Election results based on Richard M. Scammon, Alice V. McGillivray, and Rhodes Cook, *America Votes 24: A Handbook of Contemporary American Election Statistics* (Washington, D.C.: CQ Press, 2001), 13, 17, 21, 23, 25.

Note: Each state's electoral vote equals the total number of its representatives and senators in Congress. The electoral votes are the number allocated to each state for the 1992, 1996, and 2000 elections.

ground states, where both campaign organizations would concentrate the lion's share of their time, money, and effort. The larger states in this group—particularly Florida, Illinois, Michigan, New Jersey, Ohio, and Pennsylvania—would be the main focus of campaign efforts. On the other hand, many of the remaining states, such as New York, North Carolina, and Texas, would see little evidence that a presidential campaign was in progress. A state perspective through the lens of the electoral college would dominate the strategy of the 2000 campaign.[1]

FROM LABOR DAY TO THE DEBATES

The Democrats: Trying to Exploit the "Convention Bounce"

From the Democratic convention to the traditional kickoff of the general election campaign on Labor Day, Gore was uncharacteristically upbeat and relaxed. The year-long Bush lead that had expanded to double digits after the Republican convention had been wiped out, and many polls showed the Democrat with a slight advantage.[2] Gore flatly denied Republican claims that his populist speech at the Democratic convention was divisive or inconsistent with his past. He said: "It's who I am and what I've done for 24 years. . . . When I first went to Congress in January 1977, I took on the big oil companies, big polluters, and I have always fought for working families."[3] And he felt comfortable enough to joke about his unsuccessful race for the 1988 Democratic presidential nomination and about his reputation for "stiffness."

Gore and Joseph Lieberman led off the campaign with a five-city, four-state nonstop tour lasting 28 hours. The trip began in Pennsylvania and continued through Michigan, Kentucky, and Florida. (Democratic strategists promised that every week until the election at least one of the Democratic candidates would visit the last of these states, a reflection of its strategic importance.) During the marathon trip Gore tried to stay connected with the voters' desires and to establish a link with the country's long economic expansion. In Philadelphia he spoke to workers, claiming, "I'm not asking you to vote for me on the basis of the economy we had; I'm asking for your support on the basis of the better, fairer, stronger economy we're going to create together over the next four years."[4] Polls showed that the vice president had improved his personal popularity and that voters agreed with him on the issues they considered most important. The polls also indicated that Gore had made gains among the public on personal characteristics such as leadership and trustworthiness.

Another point of the tour had been to draw a symbolic contrast with the laid-back style of the Republican candidate, who had taken the weekend before Labor Day off.[5] In succeeding weeks the Gore campaign helped focus media attention on Bush's campaign tactics that cast the Texas governor in an unflattering light. While none of these stories was seriously damaging, the Democrats achieved their desired effect of impeding Bush from getting the media to focus on his own message.[6] One news story involved an ad that the Republicans created but then withdrew without running it. The ad used six-year-old footage of Gore to create the misleading impression that he was defending Clinton in the affair involving Monica Lewinsky. Another instance involved a Bush ad that flashed the word *rats* on the screen for a thirtieth of a second. The Republicans contended it was just a fragment of the word *bureaucrats,* but the Democrats said it was subliminal advertising.

As the first month of the campaign ended and the first debate approached, however, the tide began to turn. The Bush camp launched a series of effective attacks putting Gore on the defensive. The polls began to move in the Republican's favor, showing first a reduced Gore advantage, and then a small but consistent Bush lead. The Democrats, seeking to regain momentum, began running ads that attacked Bush's record in Texas on public health and the environment. Gore also continued the campaign's emphasis on Florida. By the first week of October, the vice president had visited the state eleven times (Bush had been there fifteen times).[7] The Democrats were convinced that they had a real chance in Florida and that if they won the state it would be difficult for Bush to win the presidency. Moreover, even if they were unsuccessful in Florida, keeping the pressure on there would prevent Bush from allocating desired campaign time elsewhere.

The Republicans: Stopping the Democrats' Momentum

The lead in the polls that Bush had held all year had given his campaign a false sense of security. To be sure, the Bush team expected Gore to get a bounce from the Democratic convention, but team members also expected the bounce to fade by Labor Day, leaving the GOP candidate with a dependable lead. They were confident that the American people would be eager to replace the Clinton administration with a Republican one as long as they were convinced it would not be too extreme ideologically. Toward that end, Bush began the postconvention period with a major campaign tour, focused on education, through seventeen states (most of which had been carried by Clinton in 1996). The Texas governor also attacked Gore's acceptance speech with its long list of policy proposals. He said that it sounded like "nothing got done" during the Clinton-Gore administration.[8]

But Gore's lead did not disappear, and problems became apparent in the Bush operation. At a Labor Day rally, Bush offered a vulgar characterization of a *New York Times* reporter to Dick Cheney as they stood before a microphone that the candidate didn't know was turned on. Then the Republicans launched a sarcastic ad referring to the vice president's fund-raising visit to a Buddhist temple during 1996 (juxtaposed with his claimed commitment to campaign finance reform) and his statement that he had invented the Internet. Reporters asked the Texas governor how he could square this ad with his often-stated pledge to alter the hostile tone of politics in Washington. Bush's response noted that the ad was "tongue-in-cheek" and that it had been created only after many attacks on his own record. He also drew a distinction between campaigning and what he would do as president, which caused reporters to portray him as equivocating.[9] Perhaps most problematic, polls showed that the effort to undermine Gore's credibility was not working; Bush's campaign claims were seen as no more credible than Gore's.[10] Shortly thereafter came the episode with the word *rats* flashing in the Republican ad. Bush tried to ridicule the idea that he and his team were secretly trying to influence the electorate, but he unfortunately had another bout with tangled language by pronouncing the word *subliminal* a number of times as "subliminable."[11]

In the wake of Bush's difficulties, tensions developed among various factions of his campaign and the national Republican Party over the best strategy to pursue. But the impetus for a change in approach came from within Bush's own family, from his wife, Laura. She had been away from the campaign until early September, preparing their twin daughters to leave for college. When she rejoined her husband, Mrs. Bush urged him and his managers to seek more "free media." "She believed that chatting with Oprah and Larry King and their ilk would show off the candidate to his best advantage."[12] At first Bush resisted, indicating that he did not want to do those shows, but then he relented. He appeared on Oprah Winfrey's show, beginning with a kiss on the talk-show host's cheek. He followed up with guest shots with Regis Philbin and Jay Leno. Bush discovered that he was comfortable and successful in this new role, and his mood about the campaign became more upbeat. On September 23 the candidate said, "I felt like we turned a corner about 10 days ago."[13]

With nearly a month gone and little more than a month to go, the Bush campaign began making some serious strategic choices. It was clear that Florida was likely to remain closely competitive, perhaps going down to the wire. That meant the GOP would have to spend more time and money there than originally planned and cut back elsewhere. For example, in late September the Bush campaign decided to sharply reduce spending in Illinois. They had hoped to contest the state, but polls indicated that Gore had a double-digit lead.[14] In early October, as the debates approached, Bush kept putting pressure on. Attempting to make headway on a traditional Democratic issue, he charged that the United States was in an education "recession." The GOP followed this up with one television ad making the same claim and another contending that Gore's education plan did not require any real testing of students. In his response ad, Gore could not come up with anything stronger than the statement that "George Bush and I actually agree on accountability."[15]

THE DEBATES: THE REPUBLICANS SURPASS LOW EXPECTATIONS

The first round of the presidential debates was actually a debate about the debates. Bush disliked the prospect of debates, telling reporters that they "suck the air out of the campaign."[16] The nonpartisan Commission on Presidential Debates, which had run every debate since 1988, had scheduled three presidential debates and one vice-presidential debate for October. The Republicans sought to improve their strategic position by proposing five debates (three presidential and two vice-presidential) starting in September, with a more informal format than usual, including presidential candidate appearances with NBC's Tim Russert and with CNN's Larry King. Gore had said that he would debate Bush any time, anywhere, and because of that GOP strategists thought Gore would either have to accede to their proposal or look like he was ducking debates.

The Republican expectations proved to be mistaken. When Gore turned down the Republicans' proposal, Bush began charging him with going back on a promise, saying, "it's time to elect people who say what they mean."[17] The media, however, chose to focus on Bush's refusal to accept the traditional debate format, and they emphasized the fact that only one of his proposed presidential debates was likely to be carried in prime time by all networks. Thus it appeared that Bush was trying to limit the size of the audience because he feared Gore's prowess as a debater. Eventually, the Republicans concluded that they were losing on this issue and that it was distracting from their ability to control their own message.

Consequently, Bush made a turnabout and accepted the commission's plan regarding the number of debates as well as locations and dates. In subsequent negotiations, a single moderator was agreed to for all four debates (Jim Lehrer of PBS), but the GOP campaign was successful in obtaining agreement for varying formats for the encounters. (Both sides readily accepted the commission's decision to exclude both Ralph Nader of the Green Party and Pat Buchanan of the Reform Party.)

Stakes were seen as high for the first debate. Democratic polls showed that the race was narrowing, with Gore's margin down to two points.[18] Their side felt the need to go for a knockout in the initial contest, and strategists urged Gore (as his handlers had for decades) to loosen up. The Bush people sought to lower expectations, frequently emphasizing Gore's substantial experience in national debates and arguing that Gore had "spent the better part of his career debating," while Bush had "been leading."[19] In the first debate, both candidates emphasized their contrasting approaches to governing, with Gore offering a number of proposals for government to help people of varying economic circumstances, while Bush emphasized his view that the federal government was too powerful. Gore repeatedly attacked Bush's tax proposal, claiming that he "would spend more money on tax cuts for the wealthiest 1 percent than all of the new spending that he proposes for education, health care, prescription drugs and national defense all combined." Bush responded that Gore was using "fuzzy math" and that he was trying to "scare" the people.[20] Bush in turn sought to emphasize his experience as chief executive of the second largest state and his history of working with both Democrats and Republicans in Texas. Observers thought that Bush looked more relaxed and less "scripted" than in previous debates. On the other hand, Gore was frequently heard sighing and seen shaking his head during Bush's statements.

The postdebate coverage and the ways it shapes popular perceptions is often more important than the initial reactions of the actual debate audience, and this seemed to be the case again in this instance. Two of the three overnight polls done by the news media showed that Gore had performed better in the debate, while the third indicated the candidates were even. However, the television audience for the debate was small, more than 20 million fewer viewers than the average of all presidential debates from 1976 through 1992.[21] Many commentators rated the event as a draw, but subsequent coverage focused increasingly on a number of Gore's exaggerations in the debate and on his attacking style. For example, Gore had claimed to have accompanied the director of the Federal Emergency Management Agency on a trip to survey the aftermath of fires in Texas, but it turned out he had been elsewhere. (Gore claimed that he must have been thinking about another trip.) The subjects of the slips were relatively trivial, but the coverage played into the Bush campaign's efforts to portray Gore as someone who stretched the truth for his own advantage. Luckily for the Bush people, they had a commercial titled "Trust" ready to go. It emphasized that the Republican candidate would earn the people's trust in the White House by his personal responsibility and that he would in turn trust the people to make their own decisions. In the wake of the ad, Bush gained in the main battleground states.

Next came the vice-presidential debate, which was actually a discussion with the candidates and the moderator sitting together at a table. Reporters had found Dick Cheney lackluster on the campaign trail, while Lieberman was seen to be effective and witty. Thus expectations were that the Democrat would be the winner. However, Cheney was relaxed and effective while Lieberman seemed to many observers to be overcoached (he was urged to begin most sentences with "Al Gore and I") and forced.[22] Then came the second presidential debate, with national polls showing Bush moving into a narrow lead. The format was the same as the vice-presidential debate, and the early questions focused on foreign policy, supposedly a Bush weakness. The GOP candidate, however, seemed relaxed and comfortable with the issues, and subsequent analysis emphasized how well he had done compared with what had been anticipated. (Ironically, Bush had made a number of misstatements, but the press did not focus on them, partly because of attention paid to new violence in the Middle East.) Gore, on the other hand, seemed subdued. He had apologized for his misstatements in the first debate and was apparently resolved not to appear too aggressive.

That left the finale in St. Louis, Missouri, on October 17. In this case, the rules called for the candidates to be seated on stools on a stage and to answer questions from ordinary voters chosen by the Gallup polling organization. The stakes were high, especially for Gore. A new *Washington Post* poll gave Bush a four-point lead nationally. It also showed that the proportion of people who thought Gore was honest and trustworthy had been cut in half since before the first debate.[23] The early questions dealt with health care and education, and Gore sought to be aggressive. He tried to pressure Bush by walking up close to him while responding, claiming Bush opposed a patients' "bill of rights" and attacking him on support for school vouchers. Bush in turn emphasized that he would be able to get things done and that Gore was for too much government. Gore believed he had clearly won the day, but much to his chagrin tracking polls showed him losing a couple of points in the aftermath.[24]

FINAL EFFORTS

Focusing on the Battleground States

As the campaign moved into its two last weeks, both candidates recognized that the race was close. Each had a chance to win, and the focus—as in the initial planning—was on the battleground states. Unlike in previous races, however, the number of such states was increasing as time ran out, with eighteen states still up for grabs (where the number would normally be a dozen or fewer).[25] Polls showed that voters retained doubts about both candidates. Fewer people saw

Bush as prepared for the job of president, and Gore was viewed as better able to deal with an international crisis and more caring about the needs and problems of people. On the other hand, Bush was seen as trying to show what kind of person he was rather than touting his experience and as more likely to say what he believed.[26] The weaknesses of the two candidates matched the themes that each campaign had tried to press in undermining its opponent.

Of the two, Gore's problem was the more serious. He was behind in most polls, and while the deficit was small, it was significant because he needed to change more minds, a task that became progressively more difficult as time ran down. Moreover, Gore had to contend with the serious threat from Ralph Nader (which we will discuss shortly). Dealing with the dual threat left the Democrats frantically trying to pin down states that had been safe by this point in 1992 and 1996. For example, the vice president spent precious time trying to rally support in his home state of Tennessee, and at the national level he was unable to gain an edge on the economic issues. A *New York Times* poll showed that voters saw Bush as better on both holding taxes down and keeping the stock market rising.[27] To compensate, Gore intensified his attacks on Bush's alleged inexperience and charged that his proposed tax cut would threaten Social Security.

Another Democratic strategic problem involved Clinton. He was eager to campaign, and many Democratic activists wondered why he was not being used more. But there was a problem. The Gore people claimed that poll data showed that while the president could rally core Democratic constituencies such as minorities when he appeared, he also turned off swing voters and energized core Republicans. This made his campaigning a net negative in most places, and the Democrats limited him to places such as Louisiana and New York, and told him to stay away from the big swing states of Pennsylvania and Michigan.[28] Of course, everything about the Democrats' situation was not negative. In particular, Florida remained one of the toss-up states, and Democratic polls showed Gore with a three-point lead on the Friday before the election, as well as with slim leads in some other big states.[29]

Bush faced the reverse situation to Gore's in the last weeks of the campaign: he was ahead only narrowly, but he *was* ahead. Having come from behind, he had a new confidence in the prospects of victory. The GOP candidate continued to emphasize his promise to change the style of politics in Washington by working with both Democrats and Republicans as he had in Texas. He recognized the narrowness of his lead, however, and began to escalate his rhetoric in the closing days rather than leaving the harsher attacks to party ads as earlier in the fall. For example, in a speech in late October, Bush offered a lengthy rebuke to the administration for its scandals and governing style. He said he was convinced that the government could show "more integrity in the exercise of power" and that another Democratic administration would continue "the bitter, negative tone that had nearly destroyed bipartisanship in Washington."[30] Despite the heat and closeness of the race, Bush felt good about his prospects, good enough to take a day off on the second Sunday before Election Day.[31]

Yet even with this positive picture, the Republicans were far from out of the woods. For one thing there was the continuing problem of Florida. The campaign's early expectations that Governor Jeb Bush would easily be able to deliver the state for his older brother obviously had been misplaced. The GOP would have to work hard there. The Republicans far outspent the Democrats in the state, and George W. Bush, Cheney, and others appeared there frequently. In late October, George and Jeb Bush toured the state with Sen. John McCain to try to attract enough moderates and independents to carry the day.[32] But George W. Bush continued to have problems expressing his ideas. For example, in early November he sought to respond to the Gore campaign's claims that his proposal to invest part of Social Security funds in the stock market would leave the program short of money to pay benefits. Bush wanted to continue to paint Gore as a big-spending liberal and said: "They want the federal government controlling Social Security like it's some kind of federal program."[33] Of course, the Democrats then tried to use this as more evidence that Bush was not ready for the job he sought.

Then on the Thursday before the election, a new problem came from nowhere. A report emerged that Bush had been arrested in 1976 in Maine for drunken driving. The candidate had never revealed this (to spare his daughters, he later said), and the news touched off a brief firestorm in the media. However, the story lost saliency rather quickly, and a lot of the remaining attention focused on whether the revelation was some kind of Democratic "dirty trick." There was no evidence from the polls that Bush had been damaged.

Gore Copes with the Nader Threat

Ralph Nader's campaign was a special and serious problem for Gore. Given the closeness of the race, even a few percentage points drained off to the Green Party candidate could be the difference between winning and losing. Nader limited Gore's flexibility in trying to appeal to moderate centrist voters because such moves might give credence to charges that there was no real difference between the major-party candidates. Early in the campaign, the Democrats largely ignored Nader, hoping that his prospects would fade, as had those of so many other third-party contenders, or that Gore would do so well that Nader's small share of the vote would not matter. As it became clear that events would not be that kind, Gore sought to avoid alienating Nader voters while leaving to surrogates the job of persuading his supporters to desert. For example, in late October Gore's deputy campaign manager said, "Mr. Nader is a good man, he's raised important issues. . . . But he himself admits that he can't win." Meanwhile, people with impeccable liberal credentials, such as Gloria Steinem and the heads of the Human Rights Campaign (the largest gay rights group), the Sierra Club, and the A.F.L.-C.I.O., urged voters to support Gore.[34]

Of course, Nader was not the only minor-party candidate. Pat Buchanan, a candidate for the Republican presidential nomination in 1992 and 1996, had bolted the GOP and become the candidate of the Reform Party in a disputed nomination fight. This gave Buchanan a recognizable party label and access to the $12.6 million in federal presidential campaign funds that the party had qualified for because of its showing in 1996. However, his right-wing views turned out not to be attractive to the independent and relatively moderate Reform voters of the past, and the cultural conservatives who had been Buchanan's previous constituency were sufficiently satisfied with Bush to stick with him in order to win. During the campaign, Buchanan tried to gain traction with issues such as immigration and English as the official language, but without success.[35] As Election Day approached, Buchanan was irrelevant, mired at 1 percent or less in the polls.

Nader, however, was far from irrelevant. He posed a threat to the Democrats in every state where the margin between Gore and Bush was close. As time grew short, the Democratic candidates and their supporters became more pointed. Both Gore and Lieberman contended that their views were much more in tune with Nader's issues than were Bush's. And Sen. Paul Wellstone of Minnesota, probably the most liberal Democrat in the Senate, said: "If you're really committed to environmental protection or economic justice or what the Supreme Court is going to look like, you don't want George W. Bush and his supporters to take over the national government. . . . It is too dear a price to pay."[36] In the face of these arguments, Nader grew more defiant. Responding to the claim that support for him would elect Bush, he said, "here is my answer. I'll be very sorry if either of them is elected."[37] And in his last rally he urged supporters to cast a "vote for your hopes, a vote for your dreams. . . . Those are the votes that you need to register, not a lesser of two evils where, at the end of the day, you're stuck with evil."[38] The Republicans were, of course, happy with the Nader effort and sought to reinforce it. A group of Bush supporters funded an ad that aired in a number of competitive states. It showed a Nader speech denouncing Gore's environmental record and speaking about "eight years of principles betrayed and promises broken."[39] Not surprisingly, the ad omitted the part of the same speech where Nader attacked Bush's record.

The Focus on Turnout

The expectations of a competitive race, and the realization of those expectations, led both parties to engage in unprecedented efforts to turn out supporters.[40] They began building on and expanding previous elections' efforts immediately after the conventions. The Republicans created Victory 2000, a program of the national committee and state party committees with a projected budget of $100 million to pay for ads and organization, as well as to identify and contact potential Bush voters.[41] Democrats did not have as big a budget allocation as the GOP, but they did have more experience to build on. The Democratic National Committee had been using and improving an organized turnout effort since

1988, and the new chairman of the committee had begun organizing the state turnout efforts for 2000 in March of 1999.[42]

Part of the reason for the intense efforts on getting out the vote was the concern in both camps that, compared to previous years, potential voters were not very enthusiastic about the candidates. Bush had had an "enthusiasm advantage" in the polls most of the year, which had ebbed after the Democratic convention and then resurfaced after the debates.[43] But no one could be sure how the people would react on Election Day, and it looked like every vote would be important, so get-out-the-vote (GOTV) efforts intensified as the campaign neared its end.

The Republicans had identified 15 percent of the potential voters in each of the battleground states as swing voters. To each of these people the party sent five to seven pieces of mail, a total of about 140 million items. In Florida alone the total was 17 million pieces.[44] The GOP even spent $1 million on radio ads targeted on black voters in urban areas, who might be responsive to the party's positions on school vouchers and Social Security investments.[45] The Democrats' effort was 50 percent larger than the Clinton-Gore turnout operation in 1992. They targeted 40 million pieces of mail in the last ten days of the campaign.[46] In addition to the party effort, the Democrats had substantial help from their allies. Particularly important were the efforts of organized labor, which had switched its tactics to emphasize targeting and GOTV among union members and their families in 1998, with substantial success. The unions escalated their activities in 2000, including a final push in which they sought to distribute a piece of Gore campaign literature to every union member three times in the last week.[47] The Democrats were also reinforced by an unprecedented effort by the NAACP to register and turn out black voters.[48] And the Republicans too had help from allies, especially the National Rifle Association.

The presidential campaign of 2000 ended with most polls showing a small Bush lead as they had for weeks. Gore closed with an even more frenetic effort than had followed the Democratic convention—a seven-city, thirty-hour swing that included stops in Iowa, Missouri, Tennessee, and Florida, and ended in Flint, Michigan. There Gore continued the turnout effort, telling two hundred people in a union hall: "I need each one of you to get me one more vote in each of your precincts."[49] Bush, as usual, pursued a lighter schedule than his opponent. He stopped in a number of the smaller toss-up states, including Clinton's and Gore's home turfs in Arkansas and Tennessee, where he returned to his theme of promising to unite the country and end partisan bickering. He also emphasized the efforts to turn out the faithful, saying: "Not only do I want your vote, . . . I want your help. I hope you continue to man those phones, and for those of you who are calling on my behalf, thanks from the bottom of my heart."[50] Many members of Bush's campaign staff were confident of victory, and the candidate shared that confidence. "Privately, aides said, the candidate predicted a big win, and even talked of calling potential cabinet appointees in the morning."[51] As Bush and the rest of the nation were to discover shortly, things would not be that easy or that simple.

DID THE CAMPAIGN MATTER?

It is appropriate to ask whether the general election campaign made any difference. The answer depends on the yardstick used to measure the campaign's effects. Did it determine the winner? Did it affect the choices of a substantial number of voters? Did it put issues and candidates' positions clearly before the voters? Would a better campaign by one of the candidates have yielded a different result? Did the campaign produce events that will have a lasting impact on American politics? We cannot provide firm answers to all of these questions, but we can shed light on some of them.

The event with the longest lasting effect is the set of occurrences on Election Day that left the country with such an unusual and indeterminate result. The state of Florida has already adopted election reforms with regard to voting procedures and recounts, and other states are likely to follow suit. It is thus probable that the next very close presidential election may come to a resolution more smoothly. It is, on the other hand, extremely unlikely that the nation will adopt constitutional changes to remove the possibility that the plurality winner will again lose the election. The kind of popular sentiment that would be required to pressure the politicians to alter our basic election structure is simply not present.

Regarding the outcome and voters' decisions, it seems quite clear that the campaign did indeed have an effect.[52] As noted above, Gore trailed Bush from January 2000 until late August, then he moved ahead. This was more than simply a bounce from the convention, for the lead lasted until the first debate, when Bush overtook his opponent again. Finally, Gore secured a plurality of more than half a million popular votes. While we may not be certain of the import of various events from August to November, or the magnitude of their impact, we can conclude that either of the major candidates could have won if the voting had taken place at a different date during the period.

Another perspective on these questions is offered by data from the 2000 National Election Studies (NES) survey. Table 2-1 shows the percentage of respondents that reported voting for each of the three top candidates, controlling for their party identification and when they claimed to have made their vote choice.[53] Overall, about 12 percent of the sample indicated that they knew all along how they were going to vote, less than half of the proportion (29 percent) that said the same after 1996 when Clinton was running as the incumbent. It was also slightly less than the 15 percent after 1988, a more similar race. Gore narrowly carried this group, while Bush led narrowly among those who decided up through the convention period. Then Gore won by somewhat larger margins in the two remaining groups that decided later. Nader's vote was largest among respondents who decided in the last two weeks. It was almost entirely confined to independents. In addition, among respondents who decided in the last period, Nader took a larger percentage from independents who leaned Republican than from those who leaned Democratic.

TABLE 2-1   Vote for President, by Time of Vote Decision and Party Identification, 2000 (in percentages)

Party identification	Vote	When voter decided			
		Knew all along	Through conventions	After conventions through debates	Last two weeks or later
Strong Democrat	Bush	0	2	3	10
	Gore	100	98	97	90
	Nader	0	0	0	0
	(N)	(45)	(111)	(37)	(39)
Weak Democrat	Bush	19	11	0	36
	Gore	81	89	100	62
	Nader	0	0	0	2
	(N)	(16)	(65)	(42)	(42)
Independent, leans Democrat	Bush	0	15	23	29
	Gore	89	74	73	61
	Nader	11	11	5	10
	(N)	(9)	(54)	(44)	(41)
Independent, no partisan leanings	Bush	40	62	52	43
	Gore	60	31	32	54
	Nader	0	8	8	3
	(N)	(5)	(13)	(25)	(37)
Independent, leans Republican	Bush	100	88	81	53
	Gore	0	7	16	26
	Nader	0	5	2	21
	(N)	(9)	(60)	(43)	(34)
Weak Republican	Bush	92	94	75	66
	Gore	8	6	19	31
	Nader	0	0	6	0
	(N)	(12)	(50)	(36)	(35)
Strong Republican	Bush	100	100	97	71
	Gore	0	0	3	21
	Nader	0	0	0	7
	(N)	(36)	(100)	(30)	(14)
Total	Bush	46	50	45	40
	Gore	53	48	51	52
	Nader	1	2	3	6
	(N)	(132)	(453)	(257)	(242)

Note: The numbers are weighted. The sixteen respondents for whom the direction of vote was not ascertained and the ten voters who voted for other candidates have been excluded from the analysis.

Finally, there is the question of whether a better campaign by a candidate, specifically by Gore, would have led to a different result. Many observers (mostly Democrats) believe that because the United States was in a period of peace and had eight years of economic growth, Gore should have been an easy winner. Indeed, academic forecasting models—which predict the prospective vote based primarily on the country's economic performance and the president's approval ratings—universally anticipated a comfortable Gore margin of victory.[54] Thus many of these commentators conclude that Gore ran a bad campaign and that a reasonably good one should have led to certain success. We dissent from that view. We do not say that Gore could not have won, but simply that the view that his victory should have been easy and sure is off the mark.

First, campaigns without an incumbent are usually close, and close elections can go either way. One should not expect the positives from Clinton's perform-ance to easily transfer to his vice president. Indeed, from this perspective, Gore did fairly well. This was the fifth presidential race with no incumbent since the Second World War. (The others were 1952, 1960, 1968, and 1988.) Both 1960 and 1968 were closer races in terms of the popular vote, and even though Bush's father won fairly easily in 1988, he had trailed in the polls that year as well.

Second, Gore came from behind twice, in August and again on Election Day. That is remarkably good for a candidate. Third, Gore had disadvantages that countered the positives of peace and prosperity. Most poll results throughout the campaign show that issues of personal likeability and trust were not positives for him. We saw that Gore's campaign staff was worried about having Clinton cam-paign for him, and Voter News Service (VNS) exit poll data justify that concern.[55] Twenty-four percent of respondents said the Clinton scandals were very impor-tant, and another 20 percent said they were somewhat important. Bush won 80 percent of the first group and 70 percent of the second, and Gore's own prob-lems reinforced this disadvantage. Among the 24 percent of the electorate that said honesty and trustworthiness were the qualities that mattered most in their vote, 80 percent voted for Bush. Moreover, when respondents were asked which candidate would say anything to get elected, 74 percent said Gore and only 50 percent said Bush.

Finally, and perhaps most important, Gore was at a significant strategic dis-advantage because of Nader. Many centrist Democrats argue that Gore ran too much to the left with populist themes and that a more centrist strategy (such as those of Clinton-Gore in 1992 and 1996) would have easily prevailed. It is not at all certain, however, that a shift toward the center—which would have been strongly decried by the Green Party candidate—would not have lost more votes (either through defection to Nader or through abstention) than it would have gained, especially in a number of larger, very closely contested states. Gore might well have won if he had done better in the first debate or if he had emphasized the good economy more, but that is far from a sure thing.

Chapter 3

The Election Results

◆◆◆

The 2000 campaign ended with pundits believing that the election was likely to be extremely close. Within the candidates' camps, George W. Bush's advisers were more confident of victory than Al Gore's. Because all of the networks were using the Voter News Service (VNS) exit polls to guide their projections, they projected victories at nearly the same time. Between 7:59 P.M. and 8 P.M. (EST) on Election Night, November 7, the networks projected that Gore would carry Florida and win its twenty-five electoral votes. As much of the Florida Panhandle is in the central time zone, and as the polls were still open there, this call infuriated the Republicans because these counties were heavily Republican and they feared that an early projection would reduce turnout. But at 10:13 P.M. VNS withdrew its call. At 2:16 A.M. the Fox News Network announced that Bush had carried Florida, and at that hour carrying Florida meant winning the election. Other networks followed suit, and at 2:30 A.M. Gore telephoned Bush to concede. But it shortly became clear that this second call by the news networks was questionable, and an hour later Gore withdrew his concession. Indeed, as Bush's margin of victory was only 1,784 votes out of six million votes cast, a recount became automatic under Florida law.[1]

A machine recount of the ballots showed Bush ahead: with sixty of the state's sixty-seven counties reporting, Florida officials stated that Bush held a 960-vote lead. But the Gore team demanded a hand recount in four counties—Broward, Miami-Dade, Palm Beach, and Volusia. In Palm Beach, the use of a "butterfly" ballot, with the names of the candidates on facing pages, had further complicated results. The Gore-Lieberman ticket appeared as the second set of candidates on the left-hand side of the ballot, but the punch hole for the Democratic ticket was the third one down. The second punch hole was for the Buchanan-Foster Reform Party ticket. Pat Buchanan received 3,400 votes in Palm Beach County, more than in any other county in the state. In addition, 19,000 voters punched more than two holes, and these "overvotes" were invalid.

Protracted court battles followed. A circuit court ruled that the courts had no authority to order a new election in Palm Beach County; higher courts upheld this decision. Gore's best hope for overturning the Bush margin came on December 8, when the Florida Supreme Court, in a four–three vote, ordered a statewide manual recount. But as the recount was underway, the U.S. Supreme Court, by a five–four vote, granted a stay that put the recount on hold. Then, on December 12, by another five–four vote, the U.S. Supreme Court overturned the Florida Supreme Court decision, ruling that there was not enough time to establish statewide standards for a recount. On the following day, Gore conceded.

Subsequent analyses of the ballots by *USA Today* and *The Miami Herald* reveal that errors by Florida voters probably resulted in the loss of 15,000 to 25,000 votes for Gore and cost him the election. However, under most standards for manually counting ballots Bush would have retained his lead.[2] It also seems likely that voting irregularities were much more likely to lead to black voters' ballots being rejected than to white voters' being rejected.[3] In addition, an analysis by the *New York Times* shows that overseas absentee ballots with irregularities under Florida law were more likely to be counted in Republican counties than in Democratic counties, although these different counting procedures probably did not affect the outcome.[4] A year after the election, a comprehensive analysis of the Florida election results by eight media organizations concluded that Bush would have won if the recount ordered by the Florida Supreme Court had continued.[5]

Of course, it is understandable that Bush wanted to avoid a recount, since he could not be sure of the outcome. Throughout the postelection contest in Florida, Bush was aided by the state's Republican Party machinery and by the Republican secretary of State, Katherine Harris, who had served as the Bush campaign's Florida cochair. Throughout the contest, the main goal of the Republicans was to prevent Gore from taking the lead at any stage of the recount. As Adam Nagourney and David Barstow report, "The overriding concern, one senior Bush aide said, was that any tally putting Gore even fleetingly in the lead, especially since the vice president was carrying the popular vote nationwide, would be politically devastating for Bush."[6]

In the final tally, Bush won thirty states, while Gore won twenty states and the District of Columbia. Ralph Nader, the candidate of the Green Party came in third in all forty-eight states (including the District) for which results for Nader were reported. Buchanan, the Reform Party candidate, was on the ballot in every state except Michigan but finished behind Nader everywhere that votes for Nader were reported. Bush won 50.5 million popular votes, Gore won 51.0 million, and Nader won 2.9 million, while Buchanan won only about 450,000 votes.

George W. Bush was the first presidential candidate since 1888 to be elected without winning a plurality of the popular vote. Indeed, as noted above, he trailed Gore by half a million votes and half a percentage point. Bush had won 49.7 percent of the major-party vote. The other Republican winners since 1980 had all won a majority of the vote. In 1980 Ronald Reagan won by 9.7 points over Jimmy Carter, in 1984 he defeated Walter F. Mondale by 18.2 points, and in

TABLE 3-1 Official Presidential Election Results, by States, 2000

(Based on reports from the secretaries of state for the 50 states and the District of Columbia)

State	Total vote	(George W. Bush) Republican Votes	%	(Al Gore) Democratic Votes	%	(Ralph Nader) Green Votes	%	Other	Rep.-Dem. Plurality	
Alabama	1,666,272	941,173	56.5	692,611	41.6	18,323	1.1	14,165	248,562	R
Alaska	285,560	167,398	58.6	79,004	27.7	28,747	10.1	10,411	88,394	R
Arizona	1,532,016	781,652	51.0	685,341	44.7	45,645	3.0	19,378	96,311	R
Arkansas	921,781	472,940	51.3	422,768	45.9	13,421	1.5	12,652	50,172	R
California	10,965,856	4,567,429	41.7	5,861,203	53.4	418,707	3.8	118,517	1,293,774	D
Colorado	1,741,368	883,748	50.8	738,227	42.4	91,434	5.3	27,959	145,521	R
Connecticut	1,459,525	561,094	38.4	816,015	55.9	64,452	4.4	17,964	254,921	D
Delaware	327,622	137,288	41.9	180,068	55.0	8,307	2.5	1,959	42,780	D
Florida	5,963,110	2,912,790	48.8	2,912,253	48.8	97,488	1.6	40,579	537	R
Georgia	2,596,645	1,419,720	54.7	1,116,230	43.0	13,273	0.5	47,422	303,490	R
Hawaii	367,951	137,845	37.5	205,286	55.8	21,623	5.9	3,197	67,441	D
Idaho	501,621	336,937	67.2	138,637	27.6	12,292	2.5	13,755	198,300	R
Illinois	4,742,123	2,019,421	42.6	2,589,026	54.6	103,759	2.2	29,917	569,605	D
Indiana	2,199,302	1,245,836	56.6	901,980	41.0	18,531	0.8	32,955	343,856	R
Iowa	1,315,563	634,373	48.2	638,517	48.5	29,374	2.2	13,299	4,144	D
Kansas	1,072,218	622,332	58.0	399,276	37.2	36,086	3.4	14,524	223,056	R
Kentucky	1,544,187	872,492	56.5	638,898	41.4	23,192	1.5	9,605	233,594	R
Louisiana	1,765,656	927,871	52.6	792,344	44.9	20,473	1.2	24,968	135,527	R
Maine	651,817	286,616	44.0	319,951	49.1	37,127	5.7	8,123	33,335	D
Maryland	2,020,480	813,797	40.3	1,140,782	56.5	53,768	2.7	12,133	326,985	D
Massachusetts	2,702,984	878,502	32.5	1,616,487	59.8	173,564	6.4	34,431	737,985	D
Michigan	4,232,711	1,953,139	46.1	2,170,418	51.3	84,165	2.0	24,989	217,279	D
Minnesota	2,438,685	1,109,659	45.5	1,168,266	47.9	126,696	5.2	34,064	58,607	D
Mississippi	994,184	572,844	57.6	404,614	40.7	8,122	0.8	8,604	168,230	R
Missouri	2,359,892	1,189,924	50.4	1,111,138	47.1	38,515	1.6	20,315	78,786	R

Montana	410,997	240,178	58.4	137,126	33.4	24,437	5.9	9,256	103,052	R
Nebraska	697,019	433,862	62.2	231,780	33.3	24,540	3.5	6,837	202,082	R
Nevada	608,970	301,575	49.5	279,978	46.0	15,008	2.5	12,409	21,597	R
New Hampshire	569,081	273,559	48.1	266,348	46.8	22,198	3.9	6,976	7,211	R
New Jersey	3,187,226	1,284,173	40.3	1,788,850	56.1	94,554	3.0	19,649	504,677	D
New Mexico	598,605	286,417	47.8	286,783	47.9	21,251	3.6	4,154	366	D
New York	6,821,999	2,403,374	35.2	4,107,697	60.2	244,030	3.6	66,898	1,704,323	D
North Carolina	2,911,262	1,631,163	56.0	1,257,692	43.2	—	—	22,407	373,471	R
North Dakota	288,256	174,852	60.7	95,284	33.1	9,486	3.3	8,634	79,568	R
Ohio	4,701,998	2,350,363	50.0	2,183,628	46.4	117,799	2.5	50,208	166,735	R
Oklahoma	1,234,229	744,337	60.3	474,276	38.4	—	—	15,616	270,061	R
Oregon	1,533,968	713,577	46.5	720,342	47.0	77,357	5.0	22,692	6,765	D
Pennsylvania	4,913,119	2,281,127	46.4	2,485,967	50.6	103,392	2.1	42,633	204,840	D
Rhode Island	409,047	130,555	31.9	249,508	61.0	25,052	6.1	3,932	118,953	D
South Carolina	1,382,717	785,937	56.8	565,561	40.9	20,200	1.5	11,019	220,376	R
South Dakota	316,269	190,700	60.3	118,804	37.6	—	—	6,765	71,896	R
Tennessee	2,076,181	1,061,949	51.1	981,720	47.3	19,781	1.0	12,731	80,229	R
Texas	6,407,637	3,799,639	59.3	2,433,746	38.0	137,994	2.2	36,258	1,365,893	R
Utah	770,754	515,096	66.8	203,053	26.3	35,850	4.7	16,755	312,043	R
Vermont	294,308	119,775	40.7	149,022	50.6	20,374	6.9	5,137	29,247	D
Virginia	2,739,447	1,437,490	52.5	1,217,290	44.4	59,398	2.2	25,269	220,200	R
Washington	2,487,433	1,108,864	44.6	1,247,652	50.2	103,002	4.1	27,915	138,788	D
West Virginia	648,124	336,475	51.9	295,497	45.6	10,680	1.6	5,472	40,978	R
Wisconsin	2,598,607	1,237,279	47.6	1,242,987	47.8	94,070	3.6	24,271	5,708	D
Wyoming	218,351	147,947	67.8	60,481	27.7	4,625	2.1	5,298	87,466	R
District of Columbia	201,894	18,073	9.0	171,923	85.2	10,576	5.2	1,322	153,850	D
United States	105,396,627	50,455,156	47.9	50,992,335	48.4	2,882,738	2.7	1,066,398	537,179	D

Source: Richard M. Scammon, Alice V. McGillivray, and Rhodes Cook, *America Votes 24: A Handbook of Contemporary American Election Statistics* (Washington, D.C.: CQ Press, 2001), 9.

Note: "—" indicates that no votes for Nader were recorded.

FIGURE 3-1   Electoral Votes by States, 2000

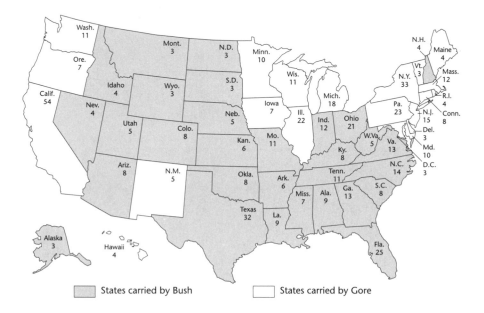

Source: Richard M. Scammon, Alice V. McGillivray, and Rhodes Cook, *America Votes 24: A Handbook of Contemporary American Election Statistics* (Washington, D.C.: CQ Press, 2001), 9.

Note: Bush won 271 electoral votes; Gore won 266 electoral votes. One elector from the District of Columbia abstained.

1988 George Bush defeated Michael S. Dukakis by 7.7 points. Although Bill Clinton failed to win a majority of the popular vote in either election, he defeated Bush by 5.6 points in 1992 and Bob Dole by an 8.5 percent margin in 1996. Table 3-1 presents the official election results, by state, for the 2000 presidential election.[7]

Bush's electoral-vote victory was the second closest contest since states began choosing electors by popular vote. As Figure 3-1 reveals, Bush won 271 electoral votes to Gore's 266,[8] while Nader and Buchanan won no electoral votes. George W. Bush won every state that his father had carried in 1992, as well as every state that Dole had carried in 1996. Gore, on the other hand, carried nine of the ten states that Dukakis carried in 1988 (all but West Virginia), as well as the District of Columbia. The 2000 contest was much closer than the 1988 Bush victory (in which Bush won 426 electoral votes to Dukakis's 111)[9] because George W. Bush failed to win eleven of the forty states his father had carried twelve years earlier (California, Connecticut, Delaware, Illinois, Maine, Maryland, Michigan, New Jersey, New Mexico, Pennsylvania, and Vermont), while winning only one state that his father had lost (West Virginia).

THE ELECTION RULES

The past three elections illustrate the importance of the election rules in affecting election outcomes. Perhaps most important in all three elections, no candidate won a majority of the popular vote, but in every election a single candidate won a majority of the electoral vote. Moreover, in all three elections independent or minor-party candidates received no electoral votes, even though in 1992 H. Ross Perot won nearly a fifth of the popular vote. In 1996 Perot won only 8 percent of the popular vote and again failed to gain a single electoral vote. Ironically, though Nader and Buchanan in 2000 received a far smaller share of the vote than Perot had, those votes may have had more impact on the results. Although Nader won only 3 percent of the popular vote, his presence on the ballot may have led to Gore's defeat. And even with only half a percent of the popular vote, Buchanan may have cost Bush New Mexico and Wisconsin.

As we saw in chapter 2, U.S. voters do not vote directly for president. Rather, they vote for a slate of electors pledged to support certain presidential and vice-presidential candidates. Moreover, in every state except Maine and Nebraska, the slate that receives the most popular votes wins all the electoral votes. In no state is a majority required to win. In fact Bush (or to be more precise the slate of electors pledged to Bush) won a majority of the vote in twenty-six states, yielding 217 electoral votes, while Gore won a majority in fourteen states (plus the District of Columbia), yielding 223 electoral votes.

The plurality-vote winner-take-all system usually transforms a plurality of the popular vote into a majority of the electoral vote. And it takes an absolute majority of the electoral votes to produce a winner. If there is no clear majority winner in the electoral college, the U.S. House of Representatives, voting by state delegations, chooses among the three candidates with the largest number of electoral votes. But the House has not chosen a president since 1825, mainly because the plurality-vote system is very likely to produce a winner in the electoral college. In forty-one of the forty-four elections from 1828 through 2000, the candidate with the most popular votes has won a majority of the electoral vote. The two exceptions before 2000, 1876 and 1888, were also very close elections, and the 1876 election was even more bitterly contested after the balloting than the 2000 election.[10] During this period, there have been fourteen elections in which a candidate won a plurality of the vote, but not a majority, and won a majority of the electoral vote.[11]

The system takes a heavy toll on third-party or independent candidates. A successful third-party candidate usually receives a far smaller share of the electoral vote than of the popular vote.[12] We can review the fate of the four most successful third-party or independent candidacies (in popular-vote terms) since World War II: those of George C. Wallace (who won 13.5 percent of the popular vote in 1968), John B. Anderson (who won 6.6 percent in 1980), and Ross Perot (who won 18.9 percent in 1992 and 8.4 percent in 1996). In 1980 and 1992 Anderson and Perot, respectively, had some modest regional support. Both fared better in New England than elsewhere, and both fared worse in the South.[13] In addition, Perot did well in the mountain states. He even finished second in two states, Maine, where he came in ahead of Bush, and Utah, where he came in ahead of Clinton. In 1996 Perot fared somewhat better in New England, but regional differences were very small. Wallace, by contrast, had a clear base of regional support in the South. Even though he won a smaller share of the popular vote than Perot in 1992, Wallace came in first in five states (winning a majority of the vote in Alabama and Mississippi) and gained forty-six electoral votes (including that of one faithless elector from North Carolina). But even Wallace won only 8.5 percent of the electoral vote, less than his popular vote share.[14]

The U.S. plurality-vote system can be seen as a confirmation of Duverger's law, a proposition advanced by Maurice Duverger in the 1950s. According to Duverger, "the simple-majority single-ballot system favors the two-party system."[15] In other words, a plurality-vote win system with no runoffs tends to favor the dominance of two political parties. Indeed, Duverger argued that "the American procedure corresponds to the usual machinery of the simple-majority single-ballot system. The absence of a second ballot and of further polls, particularly in the presidential election, constitutes in fact one of the historical reasons for the emergence and the maintenance of the two-party system."[16]

According to Duverger, this principle applies for two reasons. First, the plurality-vote system has a "mechanical" vote effect. Third-place parties may earn a large number of votes but fail to gain a plurality of the vote in many electoral units. Second, the plurality-vote system has a "psychological" effect. Some voters who prefer a candidate or party they think cannot win will cast a vote for their first choice among the major-party candidates. This behavior is called "sophisticated" or "strategic" voting. William H. Riker defines strategic voting as "voting contrary to one's immediate tastes in order to obtain an advantage in the long run."[17] As we will see in chapter 6, it seems highly likely that a substantial number of voters who preferred Nader voted for Gore.

Of course we do not know what the results would have been if the electoral rules had been different because the candidates might have had different strategies and some voters might have voted differently. The main virtue of the electoral college system is that it does produce a clear winner, recognized as legitimate by most opposition leaders even when, as in the 2000 election, he has lost a majority of the popular vote. Gerald M. Pomper goes even further in praising the merits of the electoral college and its role in the election of 2000. "The election," he argues, "vindicated the genius of the seemingly plodding institutions of the American republic, the Constitution and particularly the electoral college. . . . By providing a long interval between the popular vote and the meeting of the electors, the system provided time to count and recount votes, to argue and settle lawsuits, to begin cooling passions, and to allow a degree of routine transition to a new administration."[18]

Most Americans favor the direct popular-vote election of the president. But as Pomper points out, under such a system a close election might lead to calls for a national recount, whereas in 2000 the recount was restricted to Florida. In addition, such a change would require a definition of what share of the vote was necessary to win. For example, in the French Fifth Republic the president is directly elected by the popular vote, and an absolute majority is required to win. All seven presidential elections held under these rules (1965, 1969, 1974, 1981, 1988, 1995, and 2002) have required a runoff.[19] However, it seems likely that the 2000 election did not meet a criterion of fairness, for Gore was probably the Condorcet winner, that is, the candidate who would have won in head-to-head contests against all his opponents.[20]

THE PATTERN OF RESULTS

Two basic facts emerge from the 2000 presidential election results. First, consistent with the closeness of the 2000 election itself, the postwar pattern of results reveals a close balance between the two parties, with a small Republican edge. The Republicans have won eight of the fourteen elections held since World War II. The Republicans have also won four of the past six elections, and most of the Republican wins were by substantially bigger margins than the Democratic victories. In fact, the Republicans have won a majority of the popular vote six times since World War II (1952, 1956, 1972, 1980, 1984, and 1988), whereas the Democrats have won a popular-vote majority only twice (1964 and 1976). Moreover, the average (mean) level of Republican presidential support has been 49.0 percent, whereas the average level of Democratic support has been 46.1 percent.

This Republican advantage goes hand in hand with a pattern of considerable electoral volatility since World War II. Table 3-2 shows the presidential election results since 1832, the first election in which parties used national nomination conventions to select their candidates. From 1832 through 1948 we find four periods in which the same party won a series of three or more elections. The Republicans won six elections in a row from 1860 through 1880, although in 1876 Rutherford B. Hayes beat Samuel J. Tilden by a single electoral vote and Tilden won a majority of the popular vote. The Republicans also won four elections from 1896 through 1908, as well as three elections from 1920 through 1928. The Democrats won five straight elections from 1932 through 1948.

After 1948 the period of volatility began. From 1952 through 1984, neither party was able to win more than two elections in a row. The Republicans won in 1952 and 1956, the Democrats in 1960 and 1964, and the Republicans in 1968 and 1972. In all three cases the second win was bigger than the first (substantially bigger in 1964). Volatility increased in 1980, when the Democrats, who had won the White House in 1976, failed to hold it in 1980. The 1980 and 1984 elections, however, reverted to the pattern of a win followed by a bigger win. (Reagan's second win was by a substantially bigger margin than his first one.)

TABLE 3-2　Presidental Election Results, 1832–2000

Election	Winning candidate	Party of winning candidate	Success of incumbent political party
1832	Andrew Jackson	Democrat	Won
1836	Martin Van Buren	Democrat	Won
1840	William H. Harrison	Whig	Lost
1844	James K. Polk	Democrat	Lost
1848	Zachary Taylor	Whig	Lost
1852	Franklin Pierce	Democrat	Lost
1856	James Buchanan	Democrat	Won
1860	Abraham Lincoln	Republican	Lost
1864	Abraham Lincoln	Republican	Won
1868	Ulysses S. Grant	Republican	Won
1872	Ulysses S. Grant	Republican	Won
1876	Rutherford B. Hayes	Republican	Won
1880	James A. Garfield	Republican	Won
1884	Grover Cleveland	Democrat	Lost
1888	Benjamin Harrison	Republican	Lost
1892	Grover Cleveland	Democrat	Lost
1896	William McKinley	Republican	Lost
1900	William McKinley	Republican	Won
1904	Theodore Roosevelt	Republican	Won
1908	William H. Taft	Republican	Won
1912	Woodrow Wilson	Democrat	Lost
1916	Woodrow Wilson	Democrat	Won
1920	Warren G. Harding	Republican	Lost
1924	Calvin Coolidge	Republican	Won
1928	Herbert C. Hoover	Republican	Won
1932	Franklin D. Roosevelt	Democrat	Lost
1936	Franklin D. Roosevelt	Democrat	Won
1940	Franklin D. Roosevelt	Democrat	Won
1944	Franklin D. Roosevelt	Democrat	Won
1948	Harry S. Truman	Democrat	Won
1952	Dwight D. Eisenhower	Republican	Lost
1956	Dwight D. Eisenhower	Republican	Won
1960	John F. Kennedy	Democrat	Lost
1964	Lyndon B. Johnson	Democrat	Won
1968	Richard M. Nixon	Republican	Lost
1972	Richard M. Nixon	Republican	Won
1976	Jimmy Carter	Democrat	Lost
1980	Ronald Reagan	Republican	Lost
1984	Ronald Reagan	Republican	Won
1988	George Bush	Republican	Won
1992	Bill Clinton	Democrat	Lost
1996	Bill Clinton	Democrat	Won
2000	George W. Bush	Republican	Lost

Sources: Presidential Elections, 1789–1996 (Washington, D.C.: CQ Press, 1997), 23–75; Richard M. Scammon, Alice V. McGillivray, and Rhodes Cook, *America Votes 24: A Handbook of Contemporary American Election Statistics* (Washington, D.C.: CQ Press, 2001), 9.

Then in 1988 George Bush's election gave the Republicans three presidential wins in a row, breaking the postwar pattern of volatility. With Clinton's victory in 1992 volatility returned. (As with the other postwar elections, Clinton won his election in 1996 by a larger—though only slightly—margin.) George W. Bush's defeat of Al Gore in 2000 has continued the postwar pattern.

The 1976 and 1980 elections are the only successive elections in the twentieth century in which incumbent presidents lost.[21] But two periods in the nineteenth century were actually more volatile than postwar America. Four elections were lost by the incumbent party from 1840 through 1852, a period of alternation between the Democrats and the Whigs, and again from 1884 through 1896, a period of alternation between the Republicans and the Democrats. Both of these periods preceded major realignments of the parties. After the Whig Party loss in 1852, the Republican Party replaced it. Although many Whigs, including Abraham Lincoln, became Republicans, the Republican Party was not just the Whig Party renamed. The Republicans had transformed the political agenda by capitalizing on opposition to slavery in the territories.[22]

The 1896 contest, the last in a series of four incumbent losses, is usually viewed as a critical election because it solidified Republican dominance. Although the Republicans had won all but two of the elections since the Civil War, many of their victories were by narrow margins. In 1896 the Republicans emerged as the clearly dominant party, gaining a solid hold in Connecticut, Indiana, New York, and New Jersey, states they had frequently lost between 1876 and 1892. After William McKinley's defeat of William Jennings Bryan in 1896, the Republicans established a firmer base in the Midwest, New England, and the mid-Atlantic states. They lost the presidency only in 1912, when the GOP was split, and in 1916, when Woodrow Wilson ran for reelection.

The Great Depression ended Republican dominance. The emergence of the Democrats as the majority party was not preceded by a series of incumbent losses. The Democratic coalition, forged in the mid-1930s, relied heavily on the emerging working class and the mobilization of new groups into the electorate.

As the emergence of the New Deal coalition demonstrates, a period of electoral volatility is not a necessary condition for a partisan realignment. Nor, perhaps, is it a sufficient condition. In 1985 Reagan himself proclaimed that a Republican realignment had occurred. Political scientists were skeptical about this claim, mainly because the Democrats continued to dominate in the U.S. House of Representatives. With George Bush's victory in 1988, however, some argued that a "split-level" realignment had occurred.[23] But although Bush's election suggested that a period of Republican dominance may have arrived, Clinton's 1992 victory called this thesis into question, and his 1996 reelection cast further doubt on the idea that a realignment has occurred. On the other hand, the Republicans' capture of the House and the Senate in 1994, and their ability to hold control of these chambers in 1996, 1998, and 2000, call into question any claim that Democratic dominance has been reestablished. After the 2000 elections, the Republicans held control of the U.S. House, the Senate, and the presidency for the first time since 1953. But their narrow margin in the House, the fifty-fifty distribution in the Senate after the election, and the narrow margin of George W. Bush's election cast serious doubts on any claim of Republican dominance.

STATE-BY-STATE RESULTS

Because states deliver the electoral votes necessary to win the presidency, the presidential election can be viewed as fifty-one separate contests, one for each state and one for the District of Columbia. As we saw in chapter 2, the candidate with the most votes in each state, with the exception of Maine and Nebraska, wins all of the state's electoral votes. Regardless of how a state decides to allocate its electors, the number of electors for each state is the sum of its senators (two) plus the number of representatives in the House.[24] There are 538 electors, and an absolute majority of 270 is required to be elected by the electoral college. In 2000 the number of electors ranged from a low of 3 in Alaska, Delaware, Montana, North Dakota, South Dakota, Vermont, Wyoming, and the District of Columbia to a high of 54 in California.

Because each state regardless of its size gains two electors for its senators, the larger states are underrepresented in the electoral college and the smaller states are overrepresented. In 2000 the ten largest states, which had 54 percent of the population in the 1990 census, had only 48 percent of the electors. The twenty-two smallest states and the District of Columbia, each of which had between three and seven electors, made up 13 percent of the population, but they chose 19 percent of the electors. Some have argued that the overrepresentation of the smaller states played an important role in Bush's victory, but the evidence is unclear because both candidates had successes in large and small states.[25] Gore won six of the ten largest states and Bush four, which gave Gore 165 electoral votes and Bush 92. In these larger states, Gore won 27.8 million votes to Bush's 25.2 million, a 2.6 million vote margin. But Bush won fourteen of the smallest states and Gore eight plus the District, earning Bush 61 votes to Gore's 40. In these states Bush won 7.2 million votes to 6.1 million for Gore, a 1.1 million vote margin for Bush. The main problem for Gore was that he built up his popular-vote majority in a small number of states. As Michael Nelson points out, among the six states that provided a margin of 400,000 or more votes for a candidate, only Texas voted for Bush.[26]

Even though small states are overrepresented, presidential candidates tend to focus on the larger states, unless polls indicate that they are unwinnable. Despite being underrepresented on an electoral-vote basis, California still provides one-fifth of the electoral votes necessary to win the presidency. Even so, in 1992 George Bush quit campaigning in California in early September because the polls showed that Bill Clinton had a commanding lead. In contrast, in 1996 Bob Dole focused on California during the final weeks of the campaign, although this strategy may have been aimed more at helping Republicans retain control of the U.S. House of Representatives. In 2000 George W. Bush spent last-minute resources in California, even though he trailed Gore badly in statewide polls.

States are the building blocks of winning presidential coalitions, but state-by-state results can be overemphasized and can sometimes be misleading. First, as we saw, in forty-one of the forty-four elections from 1828 through 2000, the candidate with the largest popular vote has also gained a majority of the electoral vote. Thus, candidates can win by building a broad-based coalition throughout the nation, although they must also consider the likelihood of winning specific states. Moreover, given the nature of national television coverage, candidates must run national campaigns. They can make targeted appeals to specific states and regions, but these appeals may be broadcast by the national media.

Second, state-by-state results can be misleading, and these comparisons may actually conceal change. To illustrate this point we can compare the results of two close Democratic victories—John F. Kennedy's defeat of Richard M. Nixon in 1960 and Jimmy Carter's defeat of Gerald R. Ford in 1976. There are many parallels between these two Democratic victories. In both 1960 and 1976 the Republicans did very well in the West, and both Kennedy and Carter needed southern support to win.[27] Kennedy carried six of the eleven states of the old Confederacy (Arkansas, Georgia, Louisiana, North Carolina, South Carolina, and Texas) and gained five of Alabama's eleven electoral votes. Carter carried ten of these states (all but Virginia) for a total of 118 electoral votes.

The demographic basis of Carter's support was quite different from Kennedy's, however. In 1960 only 29 percent of the African American adults in the South were registered to vote, compared with 61 percent of the white adults. According to our analysis of the National Election Studies (NES), only one voter out of fifteen who supported Kennedy in the South was black. In 1976, 63 percent of the African Americans in the South were registered to vote, compared with 68 percent of the whites.[28] We estimate that about one out of three southerners who voted for Carter was black. A simple comparison of state-by-state results would conceal the massive change in the social composition of the Democratic presidential coalition.

Third, state-by-state comparisons do not tell us why a presidential candidate received support. Of course, such comparisons can lead to interesting speculation, especially when the dominant issues are related to regional differences. But it is also necessary to turn to surveys, as we do in part 2, to understand the dynamics of electoral change.

With these qualifications in mind we can turn to the state-by-state results. In our earlier books we presented maps displaying Reagan's margin of victory over Carter in 1980, Reagan's margin over Mondale in 1984, Bush's margin over Dukakis in 1988, Clinton's margin over Bush in 1992, and Clinton's margin over Dole in 1996.[29] In Figure 3-2 we present George W. Bush's margin over Al Gore in 2000. These maps clearly reveal differences among the four Republican victories and also show continuities in Clinton's two victories.

FIGURE 3-2   Bush's Margin of Victory over Gore, 2000

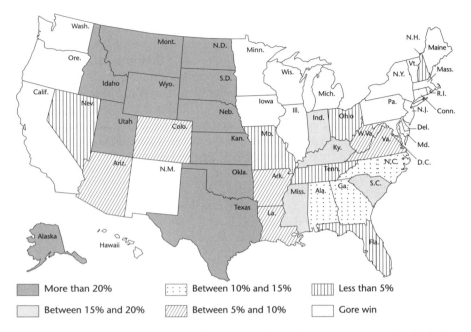

▨ More than 20%	⸭ Between 10% and 15%	▥ Less than 5%
▦ Between 15% and 20%	▨ Between 5% and 10%	☐ Gore win

Source: Richard M. Scammon, Alice V. McGillivray, and Rhodes Cook, *America Votes 24: A Handbook of Contemporary American Election Statistics* (Washington, D.C.: CQ Press, 2001), 9.

In 1980 Reagan did far better in the West than in other regions. We consider eighteen states to be western from the standpoint of presidential elections (see note 27), and Reagan won all of them except Hawaii. He carried thirteen of them by a margin of 20 percentage points or more. Outside the West, Reagan carried only a single state (New Hampshire) by a 20-point margin. Although he carried ten southern states (all except Carter's home state of Georgia), he carried many of them by relatively narrow margins.

In 1984 Reagan won by a far larger margin than in 1980, carrying every state except Minnesota. Although he still had a massive margin of victory in the West, Reagan now had an impressive margin in many more states and carried seventeen states outside the West by at least 20 points. He made his biggest gains in the South. In 1980 he carried none of the southern states by a 20-point margin. In 1984 he carried ten of them by 20 points and Tennessee by 16. Although southern blacks voted overwhelmingly for Mondale, his losses in the South were massive. Whereas in 1980 Carter had won more than one-third of the southern white vote, only about one white southerner in four voted for Mondale.

The 1988 results show a clear improvement for the Democrats. Dukakis won two New England states (including his home state of Massachusetts), gaining nearly half (49.9 percent) of the vote in this region. He carried three Midwestern states (Iowa, Minnesota, and Wisconsin). Dukakis fared somewhat worse than Carter in the border states, where he won only West Virginia. Like Mondale, Dukakis lost all eleven southern states.

George Bush's overall margin of victory over Dukakis was much smaller than Reagan's margin over Mondale in 1984, and it was somewhat smaller than Reagan's 1980 margin over Carter. Moreover, Bush's regional strength differed from Reagan's. Bush's best region was the South, and he was far less dominant in the West than Reagan. Bush won five southern states with a margin of 20 points and three others by 15 to 20 points. He won the three remaining states by a margin of 10 to 15 points. Bush won every southern state by more than his national margin (7.7 points) and carried the South as a whole by 17.5 points.

Of the eighteen western states, Bush actually lost three and won by less than 10 percentage points in five others, including California, which he carried by less than 5 points. If we restrict our attention to the eight mountain states, we find that Bush carried five by a margin greater than 20 points, but he carried the remaining three by less than 10 points. The combined results for these states show Bush with a 16.8 margin over Dukakis, slightly smaller than his margin in the South.[30] Bush's margin in all eighteen western states was only 7.5 points, slightly less than his national average.

In 1992, as in 1988, the South was the best region for the Republicans. Clinton lost seven of the eleven southern states, and he carried three others by less than 5 points, winning by a wider margin only in his native Arkansas. For all eleven states, Bush won 42.6 percent of the popular vote, compared with 41.2 percent for Clinton, and the South was the only region where Bush won a majority of the electoral vote, carrying 108 of the South's 147 electors. Among the eighteen western states, Bush and Clinton each won nine. Clinton even won four of the eight mountain states, although three of his victories were by less than 5 percentage points. But the mountain states were Perot's best region, and he won 25.2 percent of the vote there. Bush won 38.1 percent of the vote in these states, Clinton 36.3 percent. By winning by nearly 1.5 million votes over Bush in California, Clinton fared better in the eighteen western states than Bush. He carried 41.2 percent of the vote in all the western states, compared with 36.5 percent for Bush. Clinton's margin there was the same as his national average.

In 1996 Dole slipped slightly in the South compared with Bush, but he still won seven states, carrying 96 of the region's 147 electoral votes. Bill Clinton actually won slightly more of the popular vote in these states than Dole, carrying 46.2 percent to Dole's 46.1 percent. Dole did better than Clinton in the mountain states. Although Perot won 12 percent or more of the vote in Idaho, Montana, and Wyoming, his overall share of the vote in the mountain states fell to 8.7 percent, and Dole appears to have been the beneficiary. Dole carried five of these eight states, winning 23 of their 40 electoral votes. He also won a plurality of their popular vote, winning 46.4 percent to Clinton's 42.6 percent. But Clinton won California by 1.3 million votes. In the eighteen western states, Clinton received 46.7 percent of the popular vote, Dole 42.1 percent.

Clinton's greatest margin of victory was in New England and the mid-Atlantic states. He carried every Midwestern state except Indiana, winning Illinois and Minnesota by 15 percentage points. He won California and Washington by more than 10 percentage points and carried traditionally Democratic Hawaii by more than 20 points. Clinton won by a narrow margin in Arizona, but that ended an eleven-election winning streak for the Republicans. Arizona had been the only state to have consistently voted the same way in every presidential election since Dwight D. Eisenhower's 1952 victory.

In 2000 there were once again clear regional differences, with Democratic strength concentrated in the Northeast, the Midwest, and the Pacific coast states. Bush, too, had regional areas of strength as illustrated in Figure 3-2, which shows Bush's margin of victory over Gore. First of all Bush carried every southern state, although he won only his home state of Texas by more than a 20-point margin. Overall, he won 54.4 percent of the popular vote in the South, while Gore won only 43.4 percent. Bush's largest margins of victory occurred in the prairie states, as well as in the mountain states. He won four of the eight mountain states by 20 points or more, although he narrowly lost New Mexico. In these eight states Bush won 54.8 percent to Gore's 39.7 percent, a somewhat larger margin than in the South. But Gore won five of the eighteen states we classify as western. For all eighteen states, Bush held only a small overall margin of victory, capturing 48.2 percent of the popular vote to 46.7 percent for Gore.

As we shall see, state-by-state variation did increase in 2000, reaching its highest level since 1968. The South is now a Republican region, but the Republicans do not have dominance in that region. In both 1992 and 1996 the Republicans lost four southern states (Arkansas, Georgia, Louisiana, and Tennessee in 1992 and Arkansas, Florida, Louisiana, and Tennessee in 1996).

However, the Democrats would have won in both 1992 and 1996 without carrying a single southern state. Lyndon B. Johnson was the only other Democratic winner since World War II who would have won without southern electoral votes, but Johnson, unlike Clinton, won an electoral-vote landslide. Harry S. Truman in 1948, Kennedy in 1960, and Carter in 1976 all needed southern support to win.

Indeed, it is instructive to compare Clinton's victories in 1992 and 1996 with Jimmy Carter's victory. Although Carter won many southern states by narrow margins, his electoral-vote victory depended very heavily upon southern electoral votes. Of the 297 votes he won, 118 came from southern states. Of the 370 electoral votes that Clinton won in 1992, only 39 came from the South; of the 379 votes he won in 1996, only 51 did.

Likewise, it is instructive to compare George W. Bush's 2000 win with Richard M. Nixon's 1968 victory. Nixon won five southern states, losing five to Wallace and one to Hubert H. Humphrey. All the same, 57 of Nixon's 301 electoral votes came from the South, and without southern support, he would have failed to win an electoral-vote majority. Bush won 147 of his 271 electoral votes from the South, making the South crucial to his victory.

Clearly, the South has been transformed from one of the most Democratic regions of the country to one of the most Republican. Perhaps the most striking feature of postwar presidential elections has been the decline of regional differences, which can be demonstrated by statistical analyses. Joseph A. Schlesinger has analyzed state-by-state variation in presidential elections from 1832 through 1988, and we have updated his analyses through 2000. His measure is the standard deviation among the states in the percentage voting Democratic. State-by-state variation in 2000 was 8.51. This was the highest state-by-state variation since 1968 (9.50), although well below the 11.96 level in the 1964 Johnson-Goldwater contest. But Schlesinger's analysis also clearly reveals the relatively low level of state-by-state variation in all fourteen postwar elections. According to his analysis (as updated), all fifteen of the presidential elections from 1888 through 1944 displayed more state-by-state variation than any of the fourteen postwar elections. To a large extent, the decline in state-by-state variation has been a result of the transformation of the South.[31]

ELECTORAL CHANGE IN THE POSTWAR SOUTH

The transformation of the South was a complex process, but the major reason for the change was simple. As V. O. Key Jr. brilliantly demonstrated in *Southern Politics in State and Nation* (1949), the major factor in southern politics is race. "In its grand outlines the politics of the South revolves around the position of the Negro. . . . Whatever phase of the southern political process one seeks to understand, sooner or later the trail of inquiry leads to the Negro."[32] And it is the changed position of the Democratic Party toward African Americans that has smashed Democratic dominance in the South.[33]

Between the end of Reconstruction (1877) and the end of World War II (1945), the South was a Democratic stronghold. In fifteen of the seventeen elections from 1880 through 1944, all eleven southern states voted Democratic. In his 1920 victory over James M. Cox, the Republican Warren G. Harding narrowly carried Tennessee, but the ten remaining southern states voted Democratic. The only major southern defections occurred in 1928, when the Democrats ran Alfred E. Smith, a Roman Catholic. The Republican candidate, Herbert C. Hoover, won five southern states. Still, six of the most solid southern states—Alabama, Arkansas, Georgia, Louisiana, Mississippi, and South Carolina—voted for Smith, even though all but Louisiana were overwhelmingly Protestant.[34] After Reconstruction ended in 1877, many southern blacks were prevented from voting through illegal intimidation, and in the late nineteenth and early twentieth centuries several southern states changed their voting laws to further disenfranchise blacks. The Republicans ceded the southern states to the Democrats. Although the Republicans had black support in the North, they did not attempt to enforce the Fifteenth Amendment, which bans restrictions on voting on grounds of "race, color, or previous condition of servitude."

In 1932 a majority of African Americans in the North remained loyal to Hoover, although by 1936 Franklin D. Roosevelt had won the support of northern blacks. Roosevelt made no effort to win the support of southern blacks, most of whom remained effectively disenfranchised. Even as late as 1940 about 70 percent of the nation's blacks lived in the states of the old Confederacy. Roosevelt carried all eleven of these states in each of his four victories. His 1944 victory, however, was the last contest in which the Democrats carried all eleven southern states.

World War II led to a massive migration of African Americans from the South, and by 1948 Truman, through his support for the Fair Employment Practices Commission, made explicit appeals to blacks. In July 1948 he issued an executive order ending segregation in the armed services.[35] These policies led to defections by the "Dixiecrats" and cost Truman four southern states (Alabama, Louisiana, Mississippi, and South Carolina). But he still won all seven of the remaining southern states. In 1952 and 1956 Democratic candidate Adlai E. Stevenson de-emphasized appeals to blacks, although Eisenhower made inroads in the South.

In 1952 Eisenhower picked up Florida, Tennessee, Texas, and Virginia, and in 1956 he picked up Louisiana as well. In 1960 Kennedy played down appeals to African Americans, and southern support was crucial to his win over Nixon.[36] Kennedy also may have aided himself in the South by choosing a Texan, Lyndon B. Johnson, as his running mate. Clearly, Johnson helped Kennedy win Texas, which he carried by only 2 percentage points.

But if Johnson as running mate aided the Democrats in the South, Johnson as president played a different role. His support for the Civil Rights Act of 1964, as well as his explicit appeals to African Americans, helped end Democratic dominance in the South. Barry M. Goldwater, the Republican candidate, had voted against the Civil Rights Act, creating a sharp difference between the presidential candidates. In 1968 Hubert H. Humphrey, who had long championed black causes, carried only one southern state, Texas, which he won with only 41 percent of the vote. (He was probably aided by Wallace's candidacy, since Wallace carried 19 percent of the Texas vote.) Wallace's third-party candidacy carried Alabama, Arkansas, Georgia, Louisiana, and Mississippi, while Nixon carried the remaining five southern states. Nixon carried every southern state in 1972, and his margin of victory was greater in the South than outside it. Although Carter won ten of the eleven southern states (all but Virginia), he carried a minority of the vote among white southerners.

In 1980, as noted earlier, Reagan carried every southern state except Georgia, Carter's home state. In his 1984 reelection Reagan carried all the southern states, and his margin of victory in the South was greater than outside it. In 1988 George Bush carried all eleven southern states, and the South was his strongest region. As we saw, Clinton made some inroads in the South in 1992 and somewhat greater inroads in 1996. All the same, the South was the only predominantly Republican region in 1992, and in 1996 Dole won a majority of the electoral vote only in the South and the mountain states. In 2000 the South was the only region where George W. Bush carried every state, and over half of his electoral votes came from this region. The transformation of the South is clearly the most dramatic change in postwar American politics.

THE ELECTORAL-VOTE BALANCE

The Republicans dominated presidential elections from 1972 through 1988. After his relatively narrow win over Humphrey in 1968, Nixon swept forty-nine states in his defeat of George S. McGovern four years later. Although Carter won a narrow victory in 1976, the Republicans swept most states during the Reagan and Bush elections, winning forty-nine states in Reagan's triumph over Mondale.

As a result of these victories, the Republicans carried many states over the course of these five elections,[37] leading some scholars to argue that the Republicans had an electoral vote "lock." According to Marjorie Randon Hershey, the Republicans had won so many states during this period that they had a "clear and continuing advantage in recent presidential elections."[38] This advantage, Hershey argued, came mainly from Republican strength in a large number of small states, which are overrepresented in the electoral college. But Michael Nelson argued that the Republicans did not have an electoral-vote advantage, and James C. Garand and T. Wayne Parent argued that the electoral college was biased toward the Democrats.[39]

We tested for the possibility of a pro-Republican bias in the electoral college in 1992 and 1996 by assuming that Clinton and George Bush won the same percentage of the popular vote in 1992 and that Clinton and Dole won the same percentage of the popular vote in 1996. For example, in 1992 Clinton defeated Bush by 5.6 points. To assume that each candidate received the same percentage of the popular vote, we added 2.8 percentage points to Bush's total in each state and subtracted 2.8 percent from Clinton's. With such a shift Bush would have won the election with 275 electoral votes.[40] This suggests a slight pro-Republican bias existed in 1992. But following the same logic with the 1996 results, Dole did not emerge as the winner. As Clinton won by 8.5 percentage points, we added 4.25 percentage points to Dole's margin in every state, and subtracted 4.25 points from Clinton's. This hypothetical shift boosted Dole's electoral-vote count to 259 votes, but still left Clinton with a majority.[41]

The 2000 result clearly demonstrated a pro-Republican bias, since George W. Bush won even while trailing Al Gore by .45 percentage points. Adding .225 percentage points to Bush's total and subtracting .225 points from Gore's would have led to Bush's winning Florida by a safer margin, although Bush's margin would still have been less than half a percent. But this slight shift would have

FIGURE 3-3   Results of the 1988, 1992, 1996, and 2000 Elections[a]

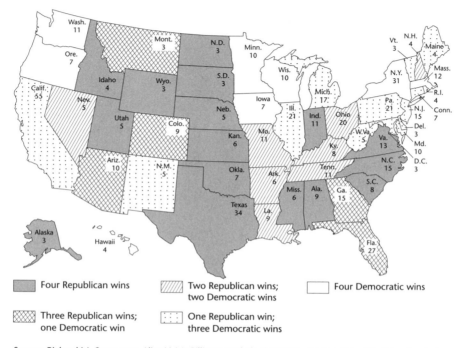

▓ Four Republican wins	▨ Two Republican wins; two Democratic wins	☐ Four Democratic wins	
▩ Three Republican wins; one Democratic win	⬚ One Republican win; three Democratic wins		

Source: Richard M. Scammon, Alice V. McGillivray, and Rhodes Cook, *America Votes 24: A Handbook of Contemporary American Election Statistics* (Washington, D.C.: CQ Press, 2001), 9, 13, 17, 21.

[a]Electoral votes for the 2004 and 2008 elections.

moved Iowa, New Mexico, Oregon, and Wisconsin from Gore's column to Bush's, adding thirty votes to Bush's total.

But if partisan biases exist in the electoral college they are very small. Even small biases, however, can lead to a "wrong winner," as they appear to have done in 2000, and as they did in 1876 and 1888.[42] Despite the election of a "wrong winner" in 2000, the likelihood of such an election is lower than it was before World War II, when the Democrats often won southern states by large popular-vote majorities.

Today's elections are more national in scope, and the electoral college provides no significant barrier to either political party. Figure 3-3 illustrates the results of the past four elections, showing the electoral votes that each state will have as a result of the reapportionment following the 2000 census. It shows the states that the Republicans have won in all four elections from 1988 through 2000, those that they won in three of the four contests, the states that the Republicans and Democrats have split, those that the Democrats have won in three of the four contests, and those that the Democrats have won in all four elections.

First, there are sixteen states, which yield 135 electoral votes that the Republicans have won in all four of these elections. Six of these states are in the South, and they include all four prairie states, three of the eight mountain states, as well as Alaska, Indiana, and Oklahoma. There are five additional states that the Republicans have won in three of these four contests, and they are worth 64 electoral votes. Two of these states are in the South, and three are mountain states. On the Democratic side there are nine states, as well as the District of Columbia, which the party has won in all four elections, together yielding 99 electoral votes. They include two New England states, New York, three Midwestern states, and the two Northwestern states, as well as Hawaii. And there are twelve states, yielding 166 electoral votes that the Democrats have won in three of these four contests. Most important, several large states are in this group, including California, Illinois, Michigan, New Jersey, and Pennsylvania. Together, these twelve states yield 166 electoral votes. On balance, there are twenty-one states that vote predominantly Republican, yielding 199 electoral votes, and twenty-one states, plus the District of Columbia, that vote predominantly Democratic and yield 265 electoral votes. And there are eight states, yielding 74 electoral votes, which have split their vote between the two parties in all cases by voting for Clinton in 1992 and 1996 and for George Bush in 1988 and George W. Bush in 2000.

This mixture shows problems and opportunities for both parties. The Republicans have strong prospects in the South, but they may have overinvested in that region. For example, the conservative appeals that helped George Bush and George W. Bush in the South may have cost them votes in California. The Democrats have demonstrated that they can win without the South, but many of Clinton's victories in the Midwest were in states that he won by relatively narrow margins. The potential for the Republicans to gain a "lock" on the presidency has disappeared, but the Democrats have no solid hold on the presidency either.

To assess the future prospects of the major parties we must go beyond analyzing official election statistics. We must attempt to understand the reasons that electoral politics are being fought among a shrinking percentage of the adult population and to try to understand why voting participation has declined. To do this we must turn to surveys that examine why some Americans vote and others do not. To determine how social coalitions have changed over time, as well as the issue preferences of the electorate, we must also turn to surveys. We must use surveys to try to understand why Gore failed to capitalize upon the widespread perception that Clinton was doing a good job as president. And we must study surveys to examine the way partisan loyalties have changed during the postwar years. Part 2 of our study uses survey data to examine the prospects for change and continuity in American electoral politics.

PART 2

Voting Behavior in the 2000
Presidential Election

The collective decision reached on November 7, 2000, was the product of 195,000,000 individual decisions. Two questions faced American citizens eighteen years and older: whether to vote, and, if they did so, how to cast their ballots. How voters make up their minds is one of the most thoroughly studied subjects in political science—and one of the most controversial.[1]

Voting decisions can be studied from at least three theoretical perspectives.[2] First, voters may be viewed primarily as members of social groups. Voters belong to primary groups of family members and peers; secondary groups such as private clubs, trade unions, and voluntary associations; and broader reference groups such as social classes and ethnic groups. Understanding the political behavior of these groups is the key to understanding voters, according to the pioneers of this approach, Paul F. Lazarsfeld, Bernard R. Berelson, and their colleagues. Using a simple "index of political predisposition," they classified voters according to religion (Catholic or Protestant), socioeconomic level, and residence (rural or urban) to predict how they would vote in the 1940 presidential election. Lazarsfeld and his colleagues maintained, "a person thinks, politically, as he is, socially. Social characteristics determine political preference."[3] This perspective is still popular, although more so among sociologists than among political scientists.[4]

A second approach analyzes psychological variables. To explain voting behavior in the 1952 and 1956 presidential elections, Angus Campbell, Philip E. Converse, Warren E. Miller, and Donald E. Stokes, scholars at the University of Michigan Survey Research Center (SRC), developed a model of political behavior based on social-psychological variables, which was presented in their classic book, *The American Voter*.[5] They focused on attitudes most likely to have the greatest effect just before the moment of decision, particularly attitudes toward the candidates, the parties, and the issues. Party identification emerged as the major social-psychological variable that influences voting decisions. The Michigan approach is the most prevalent among political scientists, although many de-emphasize its psychological underpinnings. The work of Philip E. Converse provides outstanding examples of this research tradition.[6] Warren E. Miller and J. Merrill Shanks's *The New American Voter* provides an excellent example of this approach and is especially useful for understanding the long-term forces that have transformed the American electorate.[7]

A third approach draws heavily upon the work of economists. According to this perspective, citizens weigh the cost of voting against the expected benefits of voting when deciding whether to go to the polls. And when deciding for whom to vote, voters calculate which candidate favors policies closest to their policy preferences. Citizens are thus viewed as rational actors who attempt to maximize their expected utility. Anthony Downs and William H. Riker helped to found the rational choice approach.[8] The writings of Riker, Peter C. Ordeshook, John A. Ferejohn, and Morris P. Fiorina provide excellent examples of this point of view.[9]

In our view, however, none of these perspectives provides a complete answer to the questions of how voters decide whether to vote and for whom. Although individuals belong to groups, they are not always influenced by their group memberships. Moreover, classifying voters by social groups does not explain why they are influenced by social forces. Placing too much emphasis on social-psychological factors, however, can lead us away from studying the political forces that shape political behavior. And while the assumptions of economic rationality may lead to clearly testable propositions, the data used to test them are often weak, and the propositions that can be tested are often of limited importance.[10]

Therefore, we have chosen an eclectic approach that draws on insights from each viewpoint. Where appropriate, we employ sociological variables, but we also use social-psychological variables, such as party identification and feelings of political efficacy. The rational choice approach guides our study of the way issues influence voting behavior.

Part 2 begins with an examination of the most important decision of all: whether to vote. One of the most profound changes in postwar American politics has been the decline of electoral participation. Although turnout grew fairly consistently between 1920 and 1960, it fell in 1964 and in each of the next four elections. Turnout rose slightly in 1984, but in 1988 it dropped to a postwar low. Turnout rose 5 points in 1992, but in 1996 it fell 6 points, once again reaching a postwar low. And despite concerted get-out-the-vote efforts in 2000, turnout rose only 2 percentage points. In the 1960 contest between John F. Kennedy and Richard M. Nixon, 63 percent of the adult population voted; in 2000, only 51 percent voted. Turnout is somewhat higher in the United States than in Switzerland, but it is about 20 points lower than turnout in Canada. Turnout is usually much higher in all the remaining industrialized democracies. But although turnout was very low in 2000, it was not equally low among all social groups, and we examine group differences in detail. Drawing mainly upon a social-psychological perspective, chapter 4 studies changes in attitudes that have contributed to the decline of electoral participation. We attempt to determine whether the low turnout in 2000 affected electoral outcomes. Finally, we discuss the implications of low electoral participation for a partisan realignment.

In chapter 5, we examine how social forces influence the vote. The National Election Studies (NES) surveys enable us to analyze the vote for George W. Bush, Al Gore, and Ralph Nader by race, gender, region, age, occupation, union membership, and religion. The impact of these forces has changed considerably during the postwar years. Support for the Democratic Party among traditional members of the New Deal coalition of white southerners, union members, the working class, and Catholics has eroded. With the exception of differences between whites and African Americans, which were pronounced in 2000, all of our basic measures of social cleavage registered little difference between social groups in the Bush-Gore contest.

Chapter 6 examines attitudes toward the candidates and the issues. Because Bush narrowly lost the popular vote, and because Nader won 2.7 percent of the vote, we can ask how Bush would have fared in a two-candidate contest against Gore. Our evidence suggests that Gore might very well have won such a contest, possibly overcoming Bush's electoral-vote majority. As we will see, a relatively small share of the electorate was most concerned about economic issues, which might have been expected to favor the incumbent party. The electorate did appear to be somewhat closer to Bush on a series of issue scales used to measure where voters placed themselves and the candidates, but most voters favored relatively prochoice positions on abortion and more restrictions on the sale of handguns. As we will show, issue preferences were strongly related to the vote, especially among voters who understood the relative positions of Bush and Gore on the issues. However, overall, the issue preferences of the electorate did not clearly favor either candidate.

We then turn to how presidential performance influences voting decisions. Recent research suggests that many voters decide how to vote on the basis of "retrospective" evaluations of the incumbents. In other words, what candidates have done in office—not what candidates promise to do if elected—affects how voters decide. In chapter 7 we assess the role of retrospective evaluations in the past eight presidential elections. Voters' negative evaluations of Gerald R. Ford's performance in 1976 played a major role in the election of Jimmy Carter, just as four years later the voters' negative evaluations of Carter played a major role in electing Ronald Reagan. To a very large extent, George Bush's defeat in 1992 resulted from negative evaluations of his performance as president. And positive evaluations of Clinton's presidency played a major role in his reelection in 1996. The 2000 contest presents an anomaly, since positive evaluations of Clinton and the Democratic Party were nearly as high as they were four years earlier, but the Democratic share of the major-party vote fell from 54.7 percent to 50.3 percent. But Gore fared worse than Clinton among voters with slightly pro-incumbent evaluations and those with neutral evaluations. Perhaps by not emphasizing the accomplishments of the Clinton administration, Gore was unable to capitalize fully upon the good economic conditions in the fall of 2000.

How closely do voters identify with a political party? And how does this identification shape issue preferences and the evaluations of the incumbent and the incumbent party? Chapter 8 explores the impact of party loyalties on voting choices during the postwar era. Beginning in 1984 there was a shift in party loyalties toward the Republican Party, but that shift ended and was possibly reversed in 1990. Moreover, the balance between the parties changed little between 1990 and 2000. Among Americans who identified with a political party in 2000, there were nearly three Democrats for every two Republicans, although this Democratic advantage is partly offset by higher turnout among Republicans. In 2000 party loyalties appear to have played a major role in shaping issue preferences, retrospective evaluations, and voter choices. Still, the partisan loyalties of the electorate are clearly weaker than they were during the 1950s and early 1960s, a change that has led political scientists to argue that we are in a period of dealignment.

Chapter 4

Who Voted?

♦♦♦

Before discovering how people voted in the 2000 presidential election, we must answer an even more basic question: Who voted? Turnout is lower in the United States than in any other industrialized democracy except Switzerland. Only 51 percent of the voting-age population cast ballots in 2000, just a 2-point increase from 1996. Although George W. Bush and Al Gore both won just over 50 million votes, the 90 million Americans who did not vote could easily have elected any presidential candidate.[1] As the Democrats did a reasonably good job of turning out their supporters, it is not clear that increased turnout would have affected the outcome of the presidential election. Before turning to the study of the 2000 presidential elections, however, we must place that contest in a broader historical context.[2]

TURNOUT FROM 1828 THROUGH 1920

Historical records can be used to determine how many people voted in presidential elections, and we can derive meaningful estimates of turnout for elections as early as 1828. Turnout is calculated by dividing the total number of votes cast for president by the voting-age population.[3] But should the turnout denominator be all people who are old enough to vote, or should it include only people who are eligible to vote? The answer to this question will greatly affect our estimates of turnout in all presidential elections through 1916 because few women were eligible to vote before 1920.

Although women gained the right to vote in the Wyoming Territory as early as 1869, even by 1916 only eleven of the forty-eight states had fully enfranchised women, and these were mainly western states with small populations.[4] Because women were already voting in some states, it is difficult to estimate turnout before 1920. Clearly, women should be included in the turnout denominator in those states where they had the right to vote. Including them in those states where they could not vote leads to very low estimates of turnout.

TABLE 4-1   Turnout in Presidential Elections, 1828–1916

Election year	Winning candidate	Party of winning candidate	Percentage of voting-age population who voted	Percentage eligible to vote who voted
1828	Andrew Jackson	Democrat	22.2	57.3
1832	Andrew Jackson	Democrat	20.6	56.7
1836	Martin Van Buren	Democrat	22.4	56.5
1840	William H. Harrison	Whig	31.9	80.3
1844	James K. Polk	Democrat	30.6	79.0
1848	Zachary Taylor	Whig	28.6	72.8
1852	Franklin Pierce	Democrat	27.3	69.5
1856	James Buchanan	Democrat	30.6	79.4
1860	Abraham Lincoln	Republican	31.5	81.8
1864[a]	Abraham Lincoln	Republican	24.4	76.3
1868	Ulysses S. Grant	Republican	31.7	80.9
1872	Ulysses S. Grant	Republican	32.0	72.1
1876	Rutherford B. Hayes	Republican	37.1	82.6
1880	James A. Garfield	Republican	36.2	80.6
1884	Grover Cleveland	Democrat	35.6	78.3
1888	Benjamin Harrison	Republican	36.3	80.5
1892	Grover Cleveland	Democrat	34.9	78.3
1896	William McKinley	Republican	36.8	79.7
1900	William McKinley	Republican	34.0	73.7
1904	Theodore Roosevelt	Republican	29.7	65.5
1908	William H. Taft	Republican	29.8	65.7
1912	Woodrow Wilson	Democrat	27.9	59.0
1916	Woodrow Wilson	Democrat	32.1	61.8

Sources: The estimates of turnout among the voting-age population are based on Charles E. Johnson Jr., *Nonvoting Americans,* ser. P-23, no. 102 (U.S. Department of Commerce, Bureau of the Census, Washington, D.C.: U.S. Government Printing Office, 1980), 2. The estimates of turnout among the population eligible to vote are based on calculations by Walter Dean Burnham. Burnham's earlier estimates were published in U.S. Department of Commerce, Bureau of the Census, *Historical Statistics of the United States: Colonial Times to 1970,* ser. Y-27-28 (Washington, D.C.: U.S. Government Printing Office, 1975), 1071–1072. The results in the table, however, are based on Burnham, "The Turnout Problem," in *Elections American Style,* ed. A. James Reichley (Washington, D.C.: Brookings Institution, 1987), 113–114.

[a] The estimate for the voting-age population is based on the entire U.S. adult population. The estimate for the eligible population excludes the eleven Confederate states that did not take part in the election.

Table 4-1 presents two sets of turnout estimates. The first column, which presents results compiled by Charles E. Johnson Jr., calculates turnout by dividing the number of votes cast for president by the voting-age population. The second, based upon Walter Dean Burnham's calculations, measures turnout by dividing the total presidential vote by the total number of Americans eligible to vote.

Burnham excludes blacks before the Civil War, and from 1870 on he excludes aliens where they could not vote. But the main difference between Burnham's calculations and Johnson's is that Burnham excludes women from the turnout denominator in those states where they could not vote.

Most political scientists would consider Burnham's calculations to be more meaningful than Johnson's. For example, most political scientists argue that turnout was higher in the nineteenth century than it is today. But whichever set of estimates one supports, the pattern of change revealed is the same. There was clearly a large jump in turnout after 1836, when both the Democrats and the Whigs began to employ popular appeals to mobilize the electorate. Turnout jumped markedly in the 1840 election, the "Log Cabin and Hard Cider" campaign in which William Henry Harrison, the hero of the Battle of Tippecanoe (1811), defeated the incumbent Democrat, Martin Van Buren. Turnout waned after 1840, but it rose markedly after the Republican Party, founded in 1854, polarized the nation by taking a clear stand against extending slavery into the territories. In Abraham Lincoln's election in 1860, four out of five white men went to the polls.

Turnout waxed and waned after the Civil War, peaking in the 1876 contest between Rutherford B. Hayes, the Republican winner, and Samuel J. Tilden, the Democratic candidate. As the price of Hayes's contested victory, the Republicans agreed to end Reconstruction in the South. Having lost the protection of federal troops, many African Americans were prevented from voting. Although some southern blacks could still vote in 1880, overall turnout among them dropped sharply, which in turn reduced southern turnout. Turnout began to fall nationwide by 1892, but it rose in the 1896 contest between William Jennings Bryan (Democrat and Populist) and William McKinley, the Republican winner. It dropped again in the 1900 rerun between the two men.

By the late nineteenth century, African Americans were denied the franchise throughout the South, and poor whites often found it difficult to vote as well.[5] Throughout the country, registration requirements, which were in part designed to reduce fraud, were introduced. Because individuals were responsible for getting their names on the registration rolls before the election, the procedure created an obstacle that reduced electoral participation.[6]

Introducing the secret ballot also reduced turnout. Before this innovation, most voting in U.S. elections was public. The parties printed their own ballots, which differed from each other in size and color; hence any observer could see how each person voted. In 1856 Australia adopted a law calling for a secret ballot to be printed and administered by the government. The "Australian ballot" was first used statewide in Massachusetts in 1888. By the 1896 election, nine out of ten states had followed Massachusetts's lead.[7] Although the secret ballot was introduced to reduce coercion and fraud, it also reduced turnout. When voting was public, men could sell their votes, but candidates were less willing to pay for a vote if they could not see it delivered. Ballot stuffing was also more difficult when the state printed and distributed the ballots.

As Table 4-1 shows, turnout trailed off rapidly in the early twentieth century. By the time of the three-way contest between Woodrow Wilson (Democrat), William Howard Taft (Republican), and Theodore Roosevelt (Progressive) in 1912, fewer than three out of five politically eligible Americans went to the polls (column 2). In 1916 turnout rose slightly, but just over three-fifths of the eligible Americans voted (column 2), and only one-third of the total adult population went to the polls (column 1).

TURNOUT FROM 1920 THROUGH 2000

It is easier to calculate turnout after 1920, and we have provided estimates based upon U.S. Bureau of the Census statistics. Although there are alternative ways to measure the turnout denominator, they lead to relatively small differences in the overall estimate of turnout.[8] In Table 4-2 we show the percentage of the voting-age population that voted for the Democratic, Republican, and minor-party and independent candidates in the twenty-one elections from 1920 through 2000. The table also shows the percentage that did not vote, as well as the overall size of the voting-age population. In Figure 4-1 we show the percentage of the voting-age population that voted in each of these twenty-one elections.

As Table 4-2 reveals, George W. Bush received the vote of only about one-fourth of the voting-age population. His low share resulted from two factors. First, he received less than half the total votes cast, and second, overall turnout was low. The only winning candidates to receive a smaller share were Calvin Coolidge in 1924 and Bill Clinton in his two elections. In fact, before 2000 seven losing presidential candidacies received a larger share: Wendell Willkie in 1940, Thomas E. Dewey in 1944, Adlai E. Stevenson in 1952 and 1956, Richard M. Nixon in 1960, Hubert H. Humphrey in 1968, and Gerald R. Ford in 1976.

As Figure 4-1 reveals, turnout increased in seven of the ten elections after 1920 through 1960. Two of the exceptions—1944 and 1948—resulted from the dislocations during and after World War II. Specific political conditions accounted for increases in turnout in certain elections. The jump in turnout between 1924 and 1928 resulted from the candidacy of Alfred E. Smith, the first Catholic candidate to receive a major-party nomination, and the increase between 1932 and 1936 resulted from Franklin D. Roosevelt's efforts to mobilize the lower social classes, especially the industrialized working class. The extremely close contest between Nixon and the second Catholic candidate, John F. Kennedy, partly accounts for the high turnout in 1960. Turnout rose to 62.8 percent of the voting-age population and to 65.4 percent of the politically eligible population.[9] This was far below the percentage of eligible Americans that voted from 1840 through 1900, although it was the highest percentage of the voting-age population that had ever voted in a presidential election. Nonetheless, U.S. turnout in 1960 was still far below the average level of turnout attained in most Western democracies.

TABLE 4-2   Percentage of Adults Who Voted for Each Major Presidential Candidate, 1920–2000

Election year	Democratic candidate		Republican candidate		Other candidates	Did not vote	Total	Voting-age population
1920	14.8	James M. Cox	26.2	*Warren G. Harding*	2.4	56.6	100	61,639,000
1924	12.7	John W. Davis	23.7	*Calvin Coolidge*	7.5	56.1	100	66,229,000
1928	21.1	Alfred E. Smith	30.1	*Herbert C. Hoover*	.6	48.2	100	71,100,000
1932	30.1	*Franklin D. Roosevelt*	20.8	Herbert C. Hoover	1.5	47.5	100	75,768,000
1936	34.6	*Franklin D. Roosevelt*	20.8	Alfred M. Landon	1.5	43.1	100	80,174,000
1940	32.2	*Franklin D. Roosevelt*	26.4	Wendell Willkie	.3	41.1	100	84,728,000
1944	29.9	*Franklin D. Roosevelt*	25.7	Thomas E. Dewey	.4	44.0	100	85,654,000
1948	25.3	*Harry S. Truman*	23.0	Thomas E. Dewey	2.7	48.9	100	95,573,000
1952	27.3	Adlai E. Stevenson	34.0	*Dwight D. Eisenhower*	.3	38.4	100	99,929,000
1956	24.9	Adlai E. Stevenson	34.1	*Dwight D. Eisenhower*	.4	40.7	100	104,515,000
1960	31.2	*John F. Kennedy*	31.1	Richard M. Nixon	.5	37.2	100	109,672,000
1964	37.8	*Lyndon B. Johnson*	23.8	Barry M. Goldwater	.3	38.1	100	114,090,000
1968	26.0	Hubert H. Humphrey	26.4	*Richard M. Nixon*	8.4	39.1	100	120,285,000
1972	20.7	George S. McGovern	33.5	*Richard M. Nixon*	1.0	44.8	100	140,777,000
1976	26.8	*Jimmy Carter*	25.7	Gerald R. Ford	1.0	46.5	100	152,308,000
1980	21.6	Jimmy Carter	26.8	*Ronald Reagan*	4.3	47.2	100	163,945,000
1984	21.6	Walter F. Mondale	31.3	*Ronald Reagan*	.4	46.7	100	173,995,000
1988	23.0	Michael S. Dukakis	26.9	*George Bush*	.5	49.7	100	181,956,000
1992	23.7	*Bill Clinton*	20.6	George Bush	10.8	44.9	100	189,524,000
1996	24.1	*Bill Clinton*	19.9	Bob Dole	4.9	51.0	100	196,509,000
2000	24.7	Al Gore	24.5	*George W. Bush*	2.0	48.8	100	205,813,000

Sources: Results for 1920 through 1932 are based upon U.S. Department of Commerce, U.S. Bureau of the Census, *Statistical Abstract of the United States, 1972,* 92nd ed. (Washington, D.C.: U.S. Government Printing Office, 1972), 358, 373; results for 1936 through 1996 are based upon U.S. Bureau of the Census, *Statistical Abstract of the United States, 2000,* 120th ed, the (2000) 273, 291, from the U.S. Bureau of the Census Web site: www.census.gov/prod/www.statistical-abstract-us.html). For 2000 the total voting-age population is based upon U.S. Department of Commerce, U.S. Bureau of the Census, *Projections of the Population of Voting Age, for States, by Race, Hispanic Origin, Sex and Selected Ages, November 7, 2000,* Table 1 (downloaded July 5, 2001, from the U.S. Census Bureau website: landview.census.gov/population/www.socdemo/voting/tabs00). For 2000 the number of votes cast for each candidate and the total number of votes cast for president are based on Richard M. Scammon, Alice V. McGillivray, and Rhodes Cook, eds. *America Votes 24: A Handbook of Contemporary American Election Statistics* (Washington, D.C.: CQ Press, 2001), 9.

Note: The names of the winning candidates are italicized.

FIGURE 4-1   Percentage of Voting-Age Population That Voted for President, 1920–2000

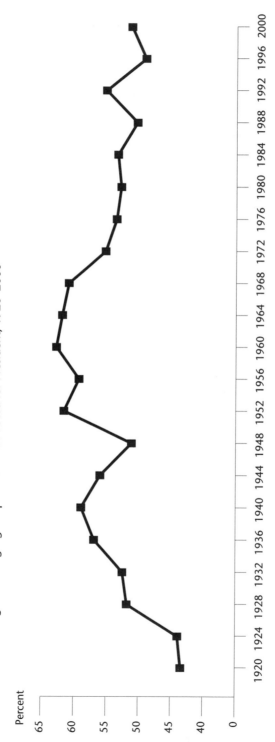

Percent

As short-term changes were driving turnout upward in specific elections, so long-term changes were driving overall turnout upward from 1920 through 1960. The changing social characteristics of the electorate contributed to the increase. For example, women who came of age before the Nineteenth Amendment often failed to exercise their right to vote, but women who came of age after 1920 had higher turnout and gradually replaced older women.[10] Because all states restricted voting to citizens, immigrants enlarged the voting-age population but could not increase the number of voters at the polls. But after 1921, as a result of restrictive immigration laws, the percentage of the population that was foreign born declined. Moreover, levels of education rose throughout the twentieth century, a change that boosted turnout. Americans who have attained higher levels of education are much more likely to vote than those with lower educational levels.

Between 1960 and the century's end, changes that might have been expected to increase turnout, such as the still rising educational levels, continued to occur. After the passage of the Voting Rights Act of 1965, turnout rose dramatically among African Americans in the South, and their return to the voting booth spurred voting among southern whites. Less restrictive registration laws during the past three decades have made it easier to vote. The National Voter Registration Act, better known as the "motor-voter" law, which went into effect in January 1995, may have added nine million additional registrants to the voter rolls.[11]

Yet despite these changes turnout declined after 1960, as can be seen in Figure 4-1. By 1960 generational replacement among the female electorate had largely run its course. In the 1960s and 1970s immigration laws were reformed, again increasing the noncitizen population. Except for a small increase in 1984, turnout declined continuously from 1960 through 1988, and in 1988 only 50.3 percent of the voting-age population voted. Turnout rose almost 5 percentage points in 1992, which may have resulted partly from H. Ross Perot's candidacy.[12] But in 1996, turnout fell some 6 percentage points, reaching only 49.0 percent, the lowest level since 1924. As we saw in chapter 2, the expectation that the 2000 election would be close led parties to unprecedented efforts to get their supporters to vote. But despite these efforts, turnout rose only 2.2 percentage points.

TURNOUT AMONG SOCIAL GROUPS

Although turnout was low in 2000, it was not equally low among all social groups. To compare turnout among social groups, we will rely on the National Election Study (NES) survey conducted by the Survey Research Center and the Center for Political Studies of the University of Michigan.[13] The 2000 NES survey is based exclusively upon whether or not respondents said that they voted; reported turnout is substantially higher than actual turnout. In 2000 actual turnout among the politically eligible population was about 53 percent, whereas in the 2000 NES, 72 percent said that they voted.[14]

There are three basic reasons that the NES studies overestimate turnout. First, even though they are asked a question that provides reasons for not voting, some people falsely claim to have voted.[15] Vote validation studies, in which the NES has directly checked voting and registration records, suggest that about 15 percent of the respondents who claim to have voted have not done so, whereas only a handful of actual voters say they did not vote.[16] Second, the NES surveys do not perfectly represent the voting-age population. Lower socioeconomic groups, which have very low turnout, are underrepresented. Third, during presidential years the same respondents are interviewed before and after the election. Being interviewed before an election provides a stimulus to vote and thus increases turnout among the NES sample.[17]

Race, Gender, Region, and Age

Table 4-3 compares reported turnout among social groups using the NES surveys. Our analysis begins by comparing African Americans with whites.[18] Our table shows that whites were only 1 percentage point more likely to report voting than blacks. As we pointed out in note 16, all eight vote validation studies showed that blacks were more likely to falsely report voting than whites, so it seems likely that these differences are greater than the NES survey suggests.[19] Of course, racial differences in turnout are far smaller than they were before the Voting Rights Act of 1965. The first Current Population Survey of U.S. turnout, conducted in 1964, found that whites were 12.5 percentage points more likely to vote than nonwhites. Racial differences in turnout may have been lowest in 1984, when Jesse Jackson's first presidential candidacy mobilized African Americans to vote.[20] Given the relatively small number of blacks in the NES surveys, we cannot make many comparisons among blacks. Southern blacks were less likely to vote than blacks outside the South.[21] The youngest group of blacks had very low turnout, as did blacks who had not graduated from high school. However, the NES survey found that black men were more likely to report voting than black women, whereas most studies find black women more likely to vote than black men.

As our table shows, Hispanics were a good deal less likely to vote than non-Hispanics.[22] The NES studies survey only citizens. The Current Population Study surveys include respondents who are not citizens, and Hispanics register very low turnout. For example, in the 1996 Current Population Survey, only 27 percent of the Hispanics voted.

Table 4-3 shows that white men were slightly more likely to vote than white women. In all presidential elections through 1976, surveys consistently showed that men were more likely to vote than women. The 1980 presidential election seems to mark a historical turning point, when the participation advantage among men was eliminated. In recent Current Population Surveys women have been slightly more likely to vote than men.

Of course, we do not need surveys to study turnout among various regions of the country. Because the Census Bureau estimates the voting-age population of

TABLE 4-3 Percentage of Electorate Who Reported Voting for President, by Social Group, 2000

Social group	Voted	Did not vote	Total	(N)[a]
Total electorate	72	28	100	(1,550)
Electorate, by race				
African American	72	28	100	(183)
White	73	27	100	(1,229)
Hispanic (of any race)	55	45	100	(87)
Whites, by gender				
Female	71	29	100	(691)
Male	74	26	100	(539)
Whites, by region				
New England and Mid-Atlantic	75	25	100	(258)
North Central	79	21	100	(334)
South	67	33	100	(317)
Border	80	20	100	(76)
Mountain and Pacific	67	33	100	(242)
Whites, by birth cohort				
Before 1924	78	22	100	(76)
1924–1939	81	19	100	(205)
1940–1954	84	16	100	(307)
1955–1962	73	27	100	(213)
1963–1970	69	31	100	(188)
1971–1978	51	49	100	(149)
1979–1982	50	50	100	(76)
Whites, by social class				
Working class	64	36	100	(358)
Middle class	79	21	100	(730)
Farmers	62	38	100	(21)
Whites, by occupation				
Unskilled manual	63	37	100	(150)
Skilled manual	65	35	100	(209)
Clerical, sales, other white collar	72	28	100	(312)
Managerial	81	19	100	(193)
Professional and semiprofessional	86	14	100	(226)

Table continues

TABLE 4-3   (continued)

Social group	Voted	Did not vote	Total	(N)[a]
Whites, by level of education				
Eight grades or less	41	59	100	(44)
Some high school	49	51	100	(110)
High school graduate	65	35	100	(411)
Some college	76	24	100	(348)
College graduate	92	8	100	(205)
Advanced degree	93	7	100	(108)
Whites, by annual family income				
Less than $15,000	39	61	100	(57)
$15,000 to $24,999	65	35	100	(83)
$25,000 to $34,999	71	29	100	(111)
$35,000 to $49,999	60	40	100	(146)
$50,000 to $64,999	77	23	100	(143)
$65,000 to $84,999	89	11	100	(157)
$85,000 to $104,999	84	16	100	(76)
$105,000 to $144,999	82	18	100	(65)
$145,000 and over	88	12	100	(43)
Whites, by union membership[b]				
Member	77	23	100	(195)
Nonmember	72	28	100	(1,027)
Whites, by religion				
Jewish	89	11	100	(28)
Catholic	80	20	100	(342)
Protestant	72	28	100	(649)
No preference	59	41	100	(190)
White Protestants, by whether born again				
Not born again	72	28	100	(327)
Born again	73	27	100	(313)
White Protestants, by religious commitment				
Medium or low	69	31	100	(316)
High	77	23	100	(210)
Very high	79	21	100	(101)

TABLE 4-3   (continued)

Social group	Voted	Did not vote	Total	(N)[a]
White Protestants, by religious tradition				
Mainline	80	20	100	(245)
Evangelical	69	31	100	(278)
Whites, by social class and religion				
Working-class Catholics	86	14	100	(92)
Middle-class Catholics	79	21	100	(208)
Working-class Protestants	62	38	100	(190)
Middle-class Protestants	79	21	100	(380)

[a] The numbers are weighted.
[b] Whether respondent or family member in union.

each state, we can measure turnout merely by dividing the total number of votes cast for president in each state by its voting-age population. In 2000 turnout varied a great deal from state to state, from a low of 40.5 percent in Hawaii to a high of 68.8 percent in Minnesota. Regionally, turnout was lowest in the South. According to our estimates, it was 47.7 percent in the South and 52.8 percent elsewhere.

Official election statistics do not present results according to race, so we do need surveys to compare turnout among blacks and whites in each region. As we have already noted, southern blacks were less likely to vote than blacks elsewhere. As Table 4-3 shows, white turnout, too, was lower in the South. Sixty-seven percent of southern whites reported voting; among whites elsewhere 75 percent did. The relatively low level of turnout in the South results partly from lower levels of education in that region.[23] Though such regional turnout differences still exist, they have declined dramatically during the past three decades. According to the 1964 Census Bureau Survey, southern whites were 15 percentage points less likely to vote than whites outside the South, and nonwhite southerners were 28 percentage points less likely to vote than nonwhites outside the South.

As in previous surveys, the 2000 NES survey found that turnout was very low among the young. Among the two cohorts born after 1970 (those too young to have voted in 1988), only half claim to have voted. Among older Americans, the cohort born before 1924 (which entered the electorate before or during World War II) had only a slightly lower level of turnout than those cohorts born between 1924 and 1954. Older Americans do not tend to disengage from politics as once thought. Even in surveys that find older Americans less likely to vote, this lower turnout results from their lower levels of formal education.[24]

Young Americans are more likely to have higher levels of formal education than their elders, and one might therefore expect them to have higher turnout.

They do not. However, as they age young Americans tend to participate more, although the reasons that their participation increases are not well understood.[25]

Social Class, Income, Education, and Union Membership

As Table 4-3 shows, there were clear differences in turnout between the working class (manually employed workers) and the middle class (nonmanually employed workers). Middle-class whites were 15 percentage points more likely to report voting than working-class whites.[26] Farmers registered lower than average turnout, but the number of farmers sampled is too small to lead to reliable conclusions. Although this distinction between the middle class and the working class is crude, it appears to capture a politically meaningful division, because when we further divide respondents according to occupation, we find that clerical, sales, and other white-collar workers (the lowest level of the middle class) are more likely to vote than skilled and semiskilled manual workers.

Annual family income was also related to turnout, with turnout very low among whites with family incomes below $15,000 a year.[27] Reported turnout was very high among whites with annual family incomes of $65,000 and above. Americans with high family incomes also are more likely to have higher levels of formal education, and both education and income contribute to turnout; however, education has a greater effect on turnout than income does.[28]

Surveys over the years have found a weak and inconsistent relationship between union membership and turnout. Although being in a household with a union member may create organizational ties that stimulate turnout, members of union households tend to have somewhat lower levels of formal education than nonmembers. In 2000 union leaders made a concerted effort to mobilize their members to support Democratic candidates. As Table 4-3 reveals, in 2000 whites in union households were somewhat more likely to report voting than whites who lived in households with no union members.

Religion

In postwar years Catholics have been more likely to vote than Protestants, although this difference has declined. As Table 4-3 reveals, in 2000 white Catholics were more likely to vote than white Protestants. Jews have higher levels of education than gentiles, and postwar surveys show that they have higher levels of turnout. The 2000 NES survey shows Jews to have the highest levels of turnout among these three basic religious groups, although the number of Jews sampled is too small to reach reliable conclusions. Whites with no religious preferences have the lowest level of turnout.

In recent elections, fundamentalist Protestant leaders have launched get-out-the-vote efforts to mobilize their followers, and we examined turnout among white Protestants in some detail. We found only limited evidence that these mobilization efforts were successful. As we show in Table 4-3, turnout was similar among white Protestants who had been "born again" and those who did not claim to have this religious experience.[29] However, we should remember that born-again Christians are more likely to live in the South, a low turnout region. Among white Protestants in the South, 62 percent said they had been born again; elsewhere, only 43 percent said they had had this religious experience. Outside the South, white Protestants who were born again and those who were not were equally likely to vote. Among white southern Protestants, those who were born again were 9 percentage points more likely to say that they voted than those who had not been born again.

David C. Leege and Lyman A. Kellstedt argue that religious commitment is an important dimension of voting behavior. We classified white Protestants according to their level of commitment. To receive a score of "very high" on this measure respondents had to report praying several times a day and attending church at least once a week, to say that religion provided "a great deal" of guidance in their lives, to believe that the Bible was literally true or "the word of God."[30] White Protestants with very high or high levels of religious commitment were more likely to vote than those with medium or low levels. Among white Protestants in the South, 55 percent had high or very high levels of commitment, while outside the South 47 percent did. Religious commitment was related to turnout both in and outside the South. Among southern white Protestants, those with high or very high levels of religious commitment were 12 percent more likely to report voting than those with medium or low levels; outside the South those with high or very high levels of commitment were 8 points more likely to vote.

Beginning in 1990 the NES has asked detailed questions that allow us to distinguish among Protestant denominations and thus to conduct analyses of religious differences that could not be conducted earlier. We can now divide Protestants into four basic groups: evangelical, mainline, ambiguous affiliation, and nontraditional. Most white Protestants can be classified into the first two categories, which, according to Kenneth D. Wald, make up almost half the total U.S. adult population.[31] According to R. Stephen Warner, "The root of the [mainline] liberal position is the interpretation of Christ as a moral teacher who told his disciples that they could best honor him by helping those in need." In contrast, Warner writes, "the evangelical position sees Jesus (as they prefer to call him) as one who offers salvation to anyone who confesses in his name." Liberal, or mainline, Protestants, stress the importance of sharing their abundance with the needy, while evangelicals stress the importance of sharing their creed. Evangelicals, Warner argues, see the Bible as a source of revelation about Jesus, "treasure it and credit even its implausible stories. Liberals argue that these stories are timebound, and they seek the deeper truths that are obscured by myths and use the Bible along with other texts as a source of wisdom."[32]

As Table 4-3 reveals, white mainline Protestants were 11 percentage points more likely to vote than white evangelicals.[33] White southerners are more likely to be evangelicals than whites outside the South. Among white southerners who can be classified into one of these two traditions, 69 percent were evangelicals;

elsewhere, only 43 percent were. Evangelicals also tend to have lower levels of formal education. Only 15 percent of the evangelicals were college graduates, while among mainline Protestants, 38 percent were. In the South we found no differences between the turnout among evangelicals and that among mainline Protestants. Outside the South, white mainline Protestants were 12 percentage points more likely to vote. We also found no differences in turnout among college graduates, but white mainline Protestants who had not graduated from college were 8 percentage points more likely to vote than evangelicals who had not.

In Table 4-3 we can note differences between white Protestants and white Catholics by looking at the combined effect of social class and religion. We find no differences between middle-class Catholics and middle-class Protestants, but find that working-class Catholics are 24 percentage points more likely to vote than working-class Protestants.

Education

We found a strong relationship between formal education and turnout. As Raymond E. Wolfinger and Steven J. Rosenstone demonstrate, formal education is the most important variable in explaining differences in turnout in the United States.[34] Better-educated Americans have skills that reduce the information costs of voting and can acquire information about how to vote more easily than less-educated Americans; the former are also more likely to develop the attitudes that contribute to political participation, especially the view that citizens have a duty to vote and that they can influence the political process.

As Table 4-3 shows, among whites who did not graduate from high school, fewer than half claimed to have voted; among whites who had graduated from college, more than nine out of ten claimed to have voted. Even though surveys may somewhat exaggerate the relationship between formal education and electoral participation, the tendency of better-educated Americans to be more likely to vote is one of the most consistently documented relationships in voting research.[35]

WHY HAS TURNOUT DECLINED?

Clearly, turnout within educational groups must have been declining so fast that the effect of rising educational levels was canceled out. This suggests that the decline of turnout since 1960 resulted from the offsetting of some forces that stimulated turnout by others that depressed it. Analysts have studied the decline extensively. A number of them have focused on social factors, such as the changing educational levels of the electorate, while others have studied political attitudes, such as changes in partisan loyalties, as a major source of turnout change. Some scholars have examined institutional changes, such as the easing of registration requirements. Others have pointed to the behavior of political leaders, arguing that they are making less of an effort to mobilize the electorate. Certain changes, such as the rise in educational levels and the easing of registration requirements, should have increased turnout in national elections. Because turnout declined in spite of these forces, Richard A. Brody views the decline as a major puzzle for students of political participation.[36]

We begin to explore this puzzle by examining the relationship between educational levels and reported turnout among whites in all presidential elections from 1960 through 2000. (African Americans have substantially lower levels of formal education than whites, and southern blacks have only been truly enfranchised since 1965. Therefore, including blacks in our analysis would substantially obscure the relationships we are studying.) We divide whites into five educational levels: college graduates, some college, high school graduates, some high school, and eight grades or less.

The NES surveys show no decline in turnout among college graduates, but they do show a decline among all other educational categories,[37] dropping 20 percentage points among whites who were high school graduates and even more among those who had not graduated from high school. Several studies of earlier Census Bureau surveys also suggest that turnout declined most among Americans who were relatively disadvantaged.[38] Ruy A. Teixeira's analysis of census surveys shows a 10-point drop in turnout among college graduates from 1964 to 1988, although the decline was greater among the lower educational categories; as with our analysis of NES data, he found that the decline of turnout was greatest among those who had not graduated from college.[39] And Jan E. Leighley and Jonathan Nagler's analysis of census surveys shows a similar pattern. In addition, studies by Teixeira and Leighley and Nagler show that turnout declines were greater among manually employed workers. But Leighley and Nagler argue that studies of turnout inequality should focus on income, since government policies affect Americans differentially according to their income levels. Leighley and Nagler's analyses suggest that the decline of turnout was consistent across all income levels.[40]

But it is the rise in educational levels that creates the greatest problem in accounting for the decline of turnout. Although the increase in educational levels did not prevent turnout from declining, it did play a role in slowing the decline. Between 1960 and 2000 the educational level among the white electorate increased substantially, an increase due almost entirely to generational replacement.[41] According to the NES surveys, the percentage of whites who had not graduated from high school fell from 47 percent in 1960 to 13 percent in 2000. During this same period, the percentage who had graduated from college rose from 11 percent to 26 percent. Between 1960 and 2000 reported turnout among the white electorate fell 9 percentage points. An estimate based upon an algebraic standardization procedure suggests that if educational levels had not increased, turnout would have declined 23 percentage points.[42] Although this procedure provides only a preliminary estimate of the impact of rising educational levels upon the decline of turnout, it suggests that the decline would have been two and a half times greater if educational levels had not risen.

Other social factors also tended to slow the rate of decline. In a comprehensive attempt to explain the decline of turnout between 1960 and 1988, Teixeira studied changes in turnout using the NES surveys. He found that increases in income and the growth of white-collar employment tended to retard the decline. But the increase in educational levels, according to Teixeira's estimates, was far more important than those two changes, its influence being three times as great as the impact of occupational and income levels combined.[43]

Steven J. Rosenstone and John Mark Hansen, too, have used NES surveys to provide a comprehensive explanation for the decline of turnout during these years. Their analysis also demonstrates that the increase in formal education was the most important factor preventing an even greater decline in voter participation. They also estimate the effect of easing registration requirements. They find that reported turnout declined 11 percentage points from the 1960s through the 1980s, but that turnout would have declined 16 points if it had not been for the combined effects of rising educational levels and liberalized election laws.[44]

Although some forces slowed down the decline in electoral participation, other forces contributed to it. After 1960 the electorate became younger, as the baby boom generation (generally defined as Americans born between 1946 and 1964) came of age. As we have seen, young Americans have lower levels of turnout, although as the baby boomers have aged (by 2000 they were between the ages of thirty-six and fifty-four), one might have expected turnout to rise. The proportion of Americans who were married declined, and because married people are more likely to vote than unmarried people, this change reduced turnout. And church attendance declined, reducing the ties of Americans to their communities. Teixeira identifies these three changes as major shifts that contributed to the decline of turnout and argues that the decline of church attendance was the most important of these changes.[45] Rosenstone and Hansen also examine changes that tended to reduce turnout, and their analysis suggests that a younger electorate was the most important factor reducing electoral participation.[46] Warren E. Miller argues that the decline of turnout resulted mainly from the entry of a post–New Deal generation into the electorate.[47] This change, Miller argues, resulted not only from the youth of these Americans, but also from generational differences that contributed to lower levels of electoral participation. During the late 1960s and early 1970s, Miller argues, a series of events—the Vietnam War, Watergate, and the failed presidencies of Ford and Carter—created a generation that withdrew from political participation. Robert D. Putnam also argues that civic disengagement was largely a product of the baby boom generation, although generational succession has played a different role in reducing differing forms of civic activity. Putnam writes, "The declines in church attendance, voting, political interest, campaign activities, associational membership, and social trust are attributable almost entirely to generational succession."[48]

Most analysts of turnout agree that attitudinal change has contributed to the decline of electoral participation. Our own analysis has focused on the effect of attitudinal change, and we have examined the erosion of party loyalties and the

decline of what George I. Balch and others have called feelings of external political efficacy, that is, the belief that the political authorities will respond to
attempts to influence them.[49] These are the same two basic attitudes studied by
Teixeira in his first major analysis of the decline of turnout, and they are among
the attitudes studied by Rosenstone and Hansen.[50] We found these attitudinal
changes to be an important factor in the decline of electoral participation, as did
Teixeira.[51] We have also estimated the impact of these changes upon turnout in
the 1984, 1988, 1992, and 1996 elections.[52] Although the effect of the decline in
party loyalties and the erosion of political efficacy has varied from election to
election, these variables have always played a major role in the decline of electoral participation. And they play a major role in accounting for the decline of
electoral participation between 1960 and 2000.

The measure of party identification we use is based upon a series of questions
designed to measure attachment to a partisan reference group.[53] In chapter 8 we
discuss how party identification contributes to the way people vote. But party
loyalties also contribute to *whether* people vote. Strong party loyalties contribute
to psychological involvement in politics, as Angus Campbell and his colleagues
argue.[54] Party loyalties also reduce the time and effort needed to decide how to
vote, and thus reduce the costs of voting.[55] In every presidential election from
1952 through 2000, strong party identifiers were more likely to vote than any
other partisan strength category. In every election since 1960, independents with
no party leanings have been the least likely to vote.

Between 1952 and 1964, the percentage of whites who were strong party
identifiers never fell below 35 percent. The percentage of strong identifiers fell
to 27 percent in 1966, and it continued to fall through 1978, when only 21 percent of the whites identified strongly with either party. Since then, partisan
strength has rebounded somewhat, but in 2000 only 29 percent of the whites
were strong party identifiers. The percentage of whites who were independents
with no party leanings averaged about 8 percent between 1952 and 1964. This
percentage increased to about 14 percent of the white electorate between 1974
and 1980. Since then, the percentage of independents with no party leanings has
declined in most surveys, but in 2000, 13 percent of the whites were independents who felt closer to neither major party. For a detailed discussion of party
identification from 1952 through 2000, along with tables showing the distribution of party identification among whites and among blacks during these years,
see chapter 8.

Feelings of political effectiveness also contribute to electoral participation.
Citizens may expect to gain benefits if they believe that the government is
responsive to their demands. Conversely, those who believe that political leaders
will not or cannot respond to their demands may see little reason for voting. In
eleven of the twelve presidential elections from 1952 through 1996, Americans
with high feelings of political effectiveness were most likely to vote, and in all
twelve of these elections, those with low feelings of political effectiveness were
the least likely to vote.

From 1960 to 1980 feelings of political effectiveness declined markedly. Scores on our measure are based on responses to the following two statements: "Public officials don't care much what people like me think," and "People like me don't have any say about what the government does."[56] In 1956 and 1960, 64 percent of the whites were classified as feeling highly efficacious. The decline in feelings of political effectiveness began in 1964, and by 1980 only 39 percent scored high. The percentage scoring high on our measure was 52 percent in 1984, 38 percent in 1988, and 40 percent in 1992, reaching an all time low of 28 percent in 1996. In 2000 the percentage scoring high rose somewhat, but only 35 percent scored high, far lower than levels of political effectiveness in 1956 and 1960. The percentage scoring low on our measure was only 15 percent in 1956 and 1960, but by 1980 had reached 30 percent. The percentage scoring low was 23 percent in 1984, 37 percent in 1988, and 34 percent in 1992, reaching 47 percent in 1996. Although the percentage with low feelings of political effectiveness declined somewhat in 2000, 40 percent scored low on our measure.

Although strength of partisan loyalties and feelings of political effectiveness are both related to political participation, they are usually weakly related to each other. In 2000 strong partisans did have somewhat higher feelings of political effectiveness than weak partisans; independents who leaned to a party and independents with no partisan leanings had lower levels of political effectiveness than any other group. Table 4-4 shows the combined impact of these attitudes on turnout in 2000.

Reading down each column we see that in all four partisan-strength categories, respondents with high feelings of political effectiveness were more likely to vote than those with medium feelings, and those with medium feelings were more likely to vote than those with low feelings of political effectiveness. Reading across each row we see that in all three efficacy categories, strong party identifiers were more likely to vote than any other partisan-strength group. In two out of three cases, respondents with no party leanings were the least likely to vote. As in most previous surveys, there are no consistent differences in turnout between weak partisans and independents who feel closer to a political party.[57] These attitudes have a strong cumulative impact. Among whites with strong partisan loyalties and high feelings of political effectiveness, nine out of ten say that they voted; among independents with no partisan leanings who have low feelings of political effectiveness, just over a third claim to have voted.

The decline in partisan loyalty and feelings of political efficacy clearly contribute to the decline of turnout. A preliminary assessment of the effects of these factors can be derived through a simple algebraic standardization procedure.[58] According to our calculations, the combined impact of this attitudinal change accounts for 65 percent of the decline of turnout, with the decline in political efficacy being twice as important as the decline of partisan loyalties.

Our estimates clearly demonstrate that these attitudinal changes are important, but they are not final estimates of the impact of these changes. We do not claim to have solved the puzzle of declining electoral participation; we believe

TABLE 4-4   Percentage of Whites Who Reported Voting for President, by Strength of Party Identification and Sense of External Political Efficacy, 2000

Scores on external political efficacy index	Strength of party identification							
	Strong partisan		Weak partisan		Independent who leans toward a party		Independent with no partisan leaning	
	%	(N)	%	(N)	%	(N)	%	(N)
High	92	(157)	82	(122)	78	(111)	79	(33)
Medium	88	(91)	75	(81)	68	(96)	61	(41)
Low	84	(116)	63	(134)	63	(147)	35	(74)

Note: The numbers in parentheses are the totals on which the percentages are based. The numbers are weighted.

that comprehensive tests, such as those conducted by Teixeira and by Rosenstone and Hansen, are needed to study the 1992, 1996, and 2000 NES results. As Teixeira demonstrates, a comprehensive estimate of the impact of attitudinal changes must calculate the contributions to changes in attitudes that would have occurred if there had been no social forces retarding the decline of turnout. In Teixeira's analysis, for example, the decline in party loyalties and the erosion of feelings of political efficacy contributed to 62 percent of the decline of turnout between 1960 and 1980. But these attitudinal changes contributed to only 38 percent of the decline that would have occurred if changes in educational levels, income, and occupational patterns had not slowed down the decline of turnout.

We analyzed the combined effect of rising educational levels, the erosion of feelings of party identification, and the decline of reported turnout among whites between 1960 and 2000. Our estimates show that attitude change would have accounted for 40 percent of the decline of turnout that would have occurred if rising educational levels had not slowed the decline.[59]

A comprehensive analysis of the impact of attitudinal factors would take into account other attitudes that might have eroded turnout. As has been well documented, there has been a substantial decline in political trust during the past three decades.[60] In 1964, when political trust among whites was highest, 77 percent of the whites said the government in Washington could be trusted to do what is right just about always or most of the time, and 74 percent of the blacks endorsed this view.[61] Political trust reached a very low level in 1980, when only 25 percent of the whites and 26 percent of the blacks trusted the government. Trust rebounded somewhat during the Reagan years, but it fell to very low levels in 1992, when only 29 percent of the whites and 26 percent of the blacks trusted the government. Trust rose in 1996 and again in 2000. In 2000, 45 percent of the whites trusted the government to do what is right just about always or most of the time, while 32 percent of the blacks did.

Back in 1964, 63 percent of the whites and 69 percent of the blacks said the government was run for the benefit of all.[62] By 1980 only 19 percent of the whites and 34 percent of the blacks held this view. Once again, trust rose somewhat during the Reagan years, but it was very low in 1992: only 20 percent of the whites and 19 percent of the blacks trusted the government on this question. Trust rose in 1996 and again in 2000, when 35 percent of the whites and 34 percent of the blacks said the government was run for the benefit of all. But in 2000, as in most previous elections, there was little difference in turnout between whites who trusted the government and those who were cynical. Whites who trusted the government to do what is right were no more likely to vote than those who thought it could be trusted only some of the time or never. However, among whites who said the government was run for the benefit of all ($N = 429$), 77 percent said that they voted; among those who said the government was run for a few big interests ($N = 738$), 70 percent said they voted.

Scholars will also need to examine short-term forces that may have contributed to low turnout in 2000. They will face problems, however, because there were short-term forces that should have boosted turnout. For example, Rosenstone and Hansen's analysis points to the importance of political parties in mobilizing voters. Rosenstone and Hansen present a fascinating analysis that focuses on the effect of elite behavior on the participation of the electorate. But there are problems with their interpretation. The percentage of Americans who said they had been contacted by a political party actually increased after the 1960 election. In 1960, 22 percent of the electorate said they had been contacted by a political party; in 1980, 32 percent said they had been contacted.[63] Yet turnout declined substantially. In 1992 only 20 percent said they had been contacted by a party, but turnout was higher in 1992 than in 1980. In 1996, 29 percent of the electorate was contacted, but turnout reached a postwar low. In 2000, 36 percent of the respondents said they had been contacted by a political party, and as in previous elections, people who had been contacted were more likely to vote than those who had not been contacted. For example, among whites who said they had been contacted by a political party ($N = 465$), 91 percent said that they voted; among those who said they had not been contacted ($N = 762$), only 61 percent voted. But even though there was a strong relationship between being contacted and voting, and even though the percentage contacted by a party was substantially higher than in 1960, turnout had declined markedly over the course of these decades.[64]

Moreover, one might have expected the closeness of the election to stimulate turnout. In most elections, Americans who think that the election will be close are more likely to vote than those who think that the winner will win by quite a bit.[65] Though these differences are usually not large, the percentage who think the election will be close varies greatly from contest to contest.[66] Orley Ashenfelter and Stanley Kelley Jr. report that the single most important factor accounting for the decline of turnout between 1960 and 1972 was "the dramatic shift in voter expectations about the closeness of the race in these two elections."[67] The percentage who thought that the election would be close rose dramatically between 1996 and 2000. In 1996 only 52 percent of the whites thought the election would be close; in 2000, 88 percent did. Moreover, among whites who thought the election would be close ($N = 1,063$), 76 percent voted; among those who thought it would not be close ($N = 148$), only 52 percent voted. Given the sharp increase in the percentage who believed the election would be close, as well as the strong relationship between expectations about the closeness of the election and voter participation, one might have expected a much greater increase in turnout than the 2-point rise between 1996 and 2000.

DOES LOW TURNOUT MATTER?

For the past two decades, Democratic political leaders have debated the importance of increasing turnout. Some argue that low turnout was a major reason for Democratic presidential losses. The Democrats could win, they argued, if they could mobilize disadvantaged Americans. In 1984 the Democrats and their supporters launched major get-out-the-vote efforts, but turnout increased less than 1 percentage point, and in 1988 it reached a postwar low. Other Democrats argued that the main problem the party faced was defections by its traditional supporters. Of course attempting to increase turnout and attempting to win back defectors are not mutually exclusive strategies, but they can lead to contradictory tactics. For example, mobilizing African Americans may not be cost free if doing so leads to defections among white Democrats.

In fact, as James DeNardo has pointed out, from 1932 through 1976 there was only a very weak relationship between turnout and the percentage of the vote won by Democratic presidential candidates.[68] In our analyses of the 1980, 1984, and 1988 presidential elections, we argued that in most reasonable scenarios increased turnout would not have led to Democratic victories.[69] In 1992 increased turnout went along with a Democratic victory, although not an increased Democratic share of the vote. Our analyses suggest that Clinton did benefit from increased turnout but that he gained more by converting voters who had supported Bush four years earlier.[70] Despite a 6-percentage-point decline in turnout between 1992 and 1996, Clinton was easily reelected. Even so, there is some evidence the decline in turnout cost Clinton votes. Moreover, the decline probably cost the Democrats votes for the U.S. House of Representatives as well. Low turnout, we concluded, may have thwarted the Democratic efforts to regain the House, although the evidence was by no means conclusive.

We begin this discussion by examining turnout among party identifiers. In 1980, 1984, and 1988 strong Republicans were more likely to vote than strong Democrats, and weak Republicans were more likely to vote than weak Democrats.[71] In 1992 partisan differences were small because turnout increased

TABLE 4-5   Percentage of Electorate Who Reported Voting for President,
by Party Identification, Issue Preferences, and Retrospective
Evaluations, 2000

Attitude	Voted	Did not vote	Total	(N)[a]
Electorate, by party identification				
Strong Democrat	82	18	100	(292)
Weak Democrat	71	29	100	(234)
Independent, leans Democratic	64	36	100	(230)
Independent, no partisan leaning	51	49	100	(178)
Independent, leans Republican	72	28	100	(205)
Weak Republican	72	28	100	(185)
Strong Republican	92	8	100	(197)
Electorate, by scores on the balance of issues measure[b]				
Strongly Democratic	78	22	100	(50)
Moderately Democratic	64	36	100	(84)
Slightly Democratic	58	42	100	(173)
Neutral	67	33	100	(82)
Slightly Republican	71	29	100	(182)
Moderately Republican	68	32	100	(148)
Strongly Republican	78	22	100	(120)
Electorate, by summary measure of retrospective evaluations[c]				
Strongly Democratic	74	26	100	(34)
Moderately Democratic	91	9	100	(107)
Leans Democratic	73	27	100	(177)
Neutral	72	28	100	(119)
Leans Republican	74	26	100	(90)
Moderately Republican	65	35	100	(106)
Strongly Republican	89	11	100	(70)

[a] Numbers are weighted.

[b] Chapter 6 describes how the "balance of issues" measure was constructed.

[c] Chapter 7 describes how the "summary measure of retrospective evaluations" was constructed.

more among Democrats than Republicans. In 1996 we once again found that strong Republicans were more likely to vote than strong Democrats and that weak Republicans were more likely to vote than weak Democrats.[72]

In Table 4-5 we show the percentage of the electorate who reported voting, according to party identification, issue preferences, and evaluations of Clinton and the Democratic Party performance. Comparing party identification categories we find that strong Republicans were more likely to vote than strong Democrats and that independents who leaned toward the Republican Party were more likely to vote than independents who leaned toward the Democratic Party. On the other hand, weak Republicans and weak Democrats were equally likely to vote. If strong Democrats had been as likely to vote as strong Republicans, and if independents who leaned Democratic had been as likely to vote as independents who leaned Republican, and if Democrats in these two groups had been as likely to vote for Gore as strong Democrats and independents who leaned Democratic and did vote, Gore's overall share of the vote would have increased 1.8 percentage points. Depending upon in which states these increased votes were cast, even this small increase could have provided Gore with an electoral-vote majority. Moreover, under similar assumptions, the overall share of the Democratic congressional vote would have increased 2.0 percentage points. Whether this increase would have led to Democratic control of the House would depend upon where these voters were distributed. Indeed, the Republicans won nine House districts by 3 points or less, so even a small increase in turnout could have given the Democrats control of this chamber.

In chapter 6 we will examine the issue preferences of the electorate. Our measure of issue preferences is based upon the respondents' positions on seven issues—reducing or increasing government services, decreasing or increasing defense spending, government job guarantees, government aid for blacks, two questions about government protection of the environment, and a question about the role of women in society. In 1980 there was no systematic relationship between issue preferences and turnout, although in 1984, 1988, 1992, and 1996 respondents with pro-Republican views were more likely to vote than those with pro-Democratic views. In 1984 and 1988 these biases cost the Democratic presidential candidates, Walter F. Mondale and Michael S. Dukakis, about 2 percentage points, and in 1992 they cost Clinton about 1 point. In 1996 these biases cost Clinton about 0.8 of a percentage point. But as Table 4-5 shows, in 2000 there was only a small tendency for respondents who were closer to Bush on the issues to vote more than those who were closer to Gore. The only substantial difference we find is that respondents who were slightly Republican on the issues were more likely to vote than those who were slightly Democratic; but as we will see in chapter 6, more than three out of five major-party voters in both groups voted for Gore. As a result, it would be difficult to argue that Gore would have gained many votes if relatively liberal Americans had turned out at the same rate as relatively conservative Americans.[73] Likewise, it would be difficult to demonstrate that differential turnout along issue lines affected the congressional elections.

In chapter 7 we study the retrospective evaluations of the electorate. Our measure of retrospective evaluations has three components: (1) an evaluation of Clinton's performance as president; (2) an assessment of how good a job the government was doing in solving the most important problem facing the country; and (3) an assessment of which party would do a better job of solving that problem.[74] In 1980 respondents who expressed negative views toward Carter and the Democrats were more likely to vote than those with positive views; given that negative views prevailed, these biases hurt Carter. In 1984 and 1988 respondents with positive views of the Republicans were more likely to vote than those with negative views, although in 1992 these biases were eliminated. In 1996 respondents with pro-Republican views were more likely to vote, and these biases probably cost Clinton about 0.7 of a percentage point and cost Democratic House candidates about 1 percentage point.

In 2000 there were no consistent biases between retrospective evaluations and voting participation. Respondents who were strongly negative toward Clinton and the Democrats were more likely to vote than those who were strongly positive; but since very few Americans had strongly pro-Democratic evaluations, this bias could not have cost the Democrats many votes. On the other hand, respondents who were moderately against the Democratic Party were much less likely to vote than those who were moderately positive toward the Democrats. And there were no significant differences in turnout between respondents who leaned toward the Republicans and those who leaned toward the Democrats. Given the absence of any systematic turnout biases, differential turnout had a negligible effect on the overall share of the vote.

Of these three variables, only turnout differences in party identification could have cost Gore the election and cost the Democrats control of the House. However, pointing to CBS News polls conducted before and after the election, Gerald M. Pomper argues that "if every citizen had actually voted, both the popular and electoral votes would have led to an overwhelming Gore victory."[75] He notes that a CBS poll issued on November 5 showed that Americans who expected not to vote favored Gore by a 42 percent to 28 percent margin over Bush. A CBS poll released on November 13 showed that Americans who regretted not having voted favored Gore by a 53 percent to 33 percent margin over Bush. This latter evidence is questionable, however, for although the electoral-vote outcome was not definitive, Gore was trailing Bush in the Florida popular vote.

Clearly, it seems unlikely that increased turnout would have altered the outcome of most presidential elections, although given the remarkably close results in 2000, this contest may be an exception. Given that in most contests increased turnout would not have affected the outcome, some analysts might argue that low turnout does not matter. A number of scholars have argued that in many elections the policy preferences of Americans who do not vote have been similar to those who do go to the polls. Turnout has been low in postwar elections, but in most of them the voters reflected the sentiments of the electorate as a whole.[76]

Despite this evidence, we cannot accept the conclusion that low turnout is unimportant. We are especially concerned that turnout is low among disadvantaged Americans. Some observers believe that turnout is low among the disadvantaged because political leaders structure policy alternatives in a way that provides disadvantaged Americans with relatively little choice. Frances Fox Piven and Richard A. Cloward, for example, acknowledge that the policy preferences of voters and nonvoters are similar, but they argue that this similarity exists because of the way that elites have structured policy choices. "Political attitudes would inevitably change over time," they argue, "if the allegiance of voters at the bottom became the object of partisan competition, for then politicians would be prodded to identify and articulate the grievances and aspirations of lower income voters to win their support, thus helping them to give form and voice to a distinctive political class."[77]

We cannot accept this argument either, mainly because it is highly speculative and there is little evidence to support it. The difficulty in supporting this view may result partly from the nature of survey research, because questions about public policy are usually framed along the lines of controversy as defined by mainstream political leaders. Occasionally, however, surveys pose radical policy alternatives, and they often ask open-ended questions that allow respondents to state their policy preferences. We find little concrete evidence that low turnout leads American political leaders to ignore the policy preferences of the American electorate.

Nevertheless, low turnout can scarcely be healthy for a democracy. Even if low turnout seldom affects electoral outcomes, it may undermine the legitimacy of political leaders. The large bloc of nonparticipants in the electorate may be potentially dangerous because this means that many Americans have weak ties to the established parties and leaders. The prospects for electoral instability, and perhaps political instability, thus increase.[78]

Does low turnout imply that a partisan realignment has occurred or is likely to occur? Low turnout in 1980 led scholars to question whether Reagan's victory presaged a pro-Republican realignment. As Pomper pointed out at the time, "Elections that involve upheavals in party coalitions have certain hallmarks, such as popular enthusiasm."[79] Indeed, past realignments have been characterized by increases in turnout. As Table 4-1 shows, turnout rose markedly from 1852 to 1860, a time when the Republican Party formed, replaced the Whigs, and gained control of the presidency. Turnout rose in the Bryan-McKinley contest of 1896, which is generally considered a realigning election. As both Table 4-2 and Figure 4-1 show, turnout rose markedly after 1924, increasing in 1928, and again in 1936, a period when the Democrats emerged as the majority party.

Of course, there is no reason that future party realignments must bear all the hallmarks of previous realignments. But it would be difficult to consider any alignment as stable when nearly half the politically eligible population does not vote.

Chapter 5

Social Forces and the Vote

$$\spadesuit\spadesuit\spadesuit$$

More than 105 million Americans voted for president in 2000. Although voting is an individual act, group memberships influence voting choices because individuals with similar social characteristics may share political interests. Group similarities in voting behavior may also reflect past conditions. The partisan loyalties of African Americans, for example, were shaped by the Civil War; black loyalty to the Republican Party, the party of Lincoln, lasted through the 1932 presidential election. The steady Democratic voting of southern whites, the product of these same historical conditions, lasted even longer, perhaps through 1960.

It is easy to see why group-based loyalties persist over time. Studies of preadult political learning suggest that partisan loyalties are often transmitted from generation to generation. And because religion, ethnicity, and to a lesser extent, social class are also transmitted from generation to generation, social divisions have considerable staying power. Moreover, the interaction of social group members with each other may reinforce similarities in political attitudes and behaviors.

Politicians often think in group terms. They recognize that to win they may need to mobilize social groups that have supported them in the past and that it is helpful to cut into their opponents' social bases of support. The Democrats think more in group terms than the Republicans do because since the 1930s the Democrats have been a coalition of minorities. To win, the Democratic Party needs to earn high levels of support from the social groups that have traditionally supported its broad-based coalition.

The 1992 election was unique, however. Bill Clinton earned high levels of support from only two of the groups composing the coalition forged by Franklin D. Roosevelt in the 1930s—African Americans and Jews. Most of the other New Deal coalition groups gave less than half of their votes to Clinton. Fortunately for him, in a three-way contest it took only 43 percent of the vote to win. The 1996 election was much more of a two-candidate fight, and Clinton won 49 percent of the popular vote. Clinton gained ground among the vast majority of the groups that we will analyze below, making especially large gains among union members (a traditional component of the New Deal coalition) and among Hispanics. In many respects, Democratic presidential losses during the past three decades can be attributed to the party's failure to hold the basic loyalties of the New Deal coalition groups. In winning in 1992 and 1996, Clinton only partly revitalized that coalition.

In 2000 Al Gore won only 1 percentage point less of the popular vote than Clinton had won in 1996, while George W. Bush won 7 points more than Bob Dole. The changes are reflected in the results when we analyze the vote by social groups. As we will see, for most groups Gore won about the same share of the vote as Clinton, but among most groups Bush won a larger share than Dole. As a result group differences in the vote were lower than in previous elections.

This chapter analyzes the voting patterns of groups in the 2000 presidential election. To put the 2000 election in perspective, we will examine the voting behavior of groups during the entire postwar period. By studying the social bases of party support since 1944, we discover the long-term trends that weakened the New Deal coalition and are thus better able to understand the distinctive character of Bush's victory.

HOW SOCIAL GROUPS VOTED IN 2000

Our basic results on how social groups voted in the 2000 election are presented in Table 5-1.[1] Among the 1,097 respondents who said how they voted, 50.1 percent said they had voted for Gore, 45.9 percent for Bush, 3.0 percent for Nader, .3 percent for Buchanan, and .7 percent for other candidates. The National Election Studies (NES) survey shows Gore winning 1.7 percent more than he actually won, and Bush winning 2.0 percent less. In the NES survey, Gore won 52.2 percent of the major-party vote; in fact, he won 50.3 percent. This is only a small bias, but readers should remember that these results slightly exaggerate the relative share of the Gore vote. The 2000 NES survey was very close, however, in its estimate of the vote for Ralph Nader and for Pat Buchanan, although the very small number of respondents who voted for these candidates (only 33 for Nader and only 3 for Buchanan) precludes any systematic analysis of the bases of their support.

Despite its slightly pro-Gore bias, the 2000 NES survey is the single best source of survey data, especially when we examine change over time. However, once we examine subgroups of the electorate, the number of respondents becomes rather small. Therefore, we often supplement these analyses by referring to the exit poll of 13,279 voters conducted by the Voter News Service (VNS) for the television networks.[2]

Race, Gender, Region, and Age

Political differences between African Americans and whites are far sharper than any other social cleavage.[3] According to the NES survey, 90 percent of blacks sup-

TABLE 5-1   How Social Groups Voted for President, 2000, by Social Group
(in percentage)

Social group	Bush	Gore	Nader	Total	(N)[a]
Total electorate	46	51	3	100	(1,087)
Electorate, by race					
African American	8	90	2	100	(125)
White	53	44	3	100	(876)
Hispanic (of any race)	33	59	8	100	(49)
Whites, by gender					
Female	50	48	2	100	(485)
Male	57	39	3	99	(390)
Whites, by region					
New England and					
Mid-Atlantic	48	48	4	100	(191)
North Central	48	50	2	100	(256)
South	68	29	2	99	(208)
Border	62	37	0	99	(61)
Mountain and Pacific	44	52	4	100	(160)
Whites, by birth cohort					
Before 1924	50	50	0	100	(58)
1924–1939	51	48	1	100	(164)
1940–1954	49	48	2	99	(252)
1955–1962	58	40	2	100	(154)
1963–1970	64	33	3	100	(124)
1971–1978	51	48	1	100	(73)
1979–1982	49	35	16	100	(37)
Whites, by social class					
Working class	57	40	2	99	(228)
Middle class	51	45	4	100	(561)
Farmers	69	31	0	100	(13)
Whites, by occupation					
Unskilled manual	60	38	2	100	(94)
Skilled manual	57	43	1	101	(134)
Clerical, sales, other					
white collar	52	46	2	100	(222)
Managerial	54	42	4	100	(149)
Professional and					
semiprofessional	47	48	5	100	(190)

TABLE 5-1   (continued)

Social group	Bush	Gore	Nader	Total	(N)[a]
Whites, by level of education					
Eight grades or less	53	47	0	100	(17)
Some high school	49	51	0	100	(51)
High school graduate	53	45	3	101	(260)
Some college	57	40	3	100	(260)
College graduate	52	45	3	100	(185)
Advanced degree	48	47	4	99	(99)
Whites, by annual family income					
Less than $15,000	71	29	0	100	(21)
$15,000 to $24,999	33	63	4	100	(52)
$25,000 to $34,999	63	35	1	99	(79)
$35,000 to $49,999	52	41	6	99	(82)
$50,000 to $64,999	58	39	3	100	(107)
$65,000 to $84,999	51	44	5	100	(137)
$85,000 to $104,999	45	53	2	100	(64)
$105,000 to $144,999	60	38	2	100	(52)
$145,000 and over	66	29	5	100	(38)
Whites, by union membership[a]					
Member	42	52	6	100	(150)
Nonmember	56	42	2	100	(722)
Whites, by religion					
Jewish	12	88	0	100	(25)
Catholic	54	45	1	100	(272)
Protestant	59	38	2	99	(464)
No preference	38	53	9	100	(104)
White Protestants, by whether born again					
Not born again	49	48	2	99	(237)
Born again	69	29	2	100	(223)
White Protestants, by religious commitment					
Medium or low	49	48	2	99	(217)
High	60	37	2	99	(161)
Very high	87	13	0	100	(77)

(Table continues)

TABLE 5-1   (continued)

Social group	Bush	Gore	Nader	Total	(N)[a]
White Protestants, by religious tradition					
Mainline	49	49	2	100	(193)
Evangelical	68	30	2	100	(189)
Whites, by social class and religion					
Working-class Catholics	59	41	0	100	(79)
Middle-class Catholics	53	45	2	100	(164)
Working-class Protestants	56	42	2	100	(117)
Middle-class Protestants	59	38	3	100	(300)

Note: Numbers are weighted. The sixteen respondents for whom the direction of vote was not ascertained and the ten voters who voted for other candidates have been excluded from the analysis.

[a] Whether respondent or family member in union.

ported Gore; among whites, only 44 percent did. The VNS exit poll also shows that 90 percent of blacks supported Gore; among whites, only 42 percent did. Even though blacks make up only about one-ninth of the electorate, and even though they have lower turnout than whites, about one-fifth of Gore's total vote came from black voters.[4] Put differently, of the nearly 51 million votes that Gore received, about 10 million came from black voters.

Because race is such a profound social division, we examine whites and blacks separately.[5] Among African Americans, as among whites, women were more likely to vote for Gore than men. According to the VNS survey, 94 percent of black women voted for Gore; among black men, 85 percent did. Unlike whites, however, blacks in the South were more likely to vote for Gore than those outside it. According to the VNS poll, 92 percent of southern blacks voted for Gore; outside the South, 88 percent did.

As Table 5-1 shows, among respondents (of either race) who identified as Hispanic, 59 percent voted for Gore. The VNS survey reports that 67 percent voted for Gore. The VNS survey suggests that Gore's support among Hispanics fell from Clinton's support in 1996, when Clinton won 72 percent of the Hispanic vote. Of course, Hispanics are not a homogeneous group. Cubans in South Florida usually vote Republican, for example.[6]

Gender differences in voting behavior have been pronounced in some European societies, but historically they have been weak in the United States.[7] But differences between men and women emerged in 1980, and they have grown ever since. For example, according to exit polls, in 1976 Jimmy Carter gained 50 percent of the female vote and 50 percent of the male vote, while Gerald R. Ford won 48 percent of the female vote and 48 percent of the male vote. But in every subsequent presidential election, women have been more likely to vote Democratic than men. The "gender gap" was 8 points in 1980, 6 points in 1984, 7 points in 1988, 4 points in 1992, and 11 points in 1996. According to the VNS survey, 54 percent of female voters supported Gore, while 42 percent of the male voters did, a record gap of 12 percentage points.

As the gender gap began to emerge, some feminists hoped that women would play a major role in defeating the Republicans. But, as we pointed out two decades ago, a gender gap does not necessarily help the Democrats.[8] For example, in the 1988 election George Bush and Michael S. Dukakis each won half the women's vote; but Bush won a clear majority of the male vote. Bush benefited from the gender gap in the 1988 election.

On the other hand, Bill Clinton clearly benefited from the gender gap in both 1992 and 1996. The gap may have been even more important in 1996 than 1992; exit polls suggest that Dole won a slight majority of the male vote, whereas women favored Clinton 54 percent to 38 percent over Dole. In 2000, however, George W. Bush benefited from the gender gap. As Table 5-1 shows, according to the NES survey, among white women, the vote was divided almost evenly, with 48 percent for Gore and 50 percent for Bush; among white men, only 39 percent voted for Gore, while 57 percent voted for Bush. The VNS exit poll reveals similar results. Among white women, 48 percent voted for Gore, while 49 percent voted for Bush; among white men, only 36 percent voted for Gore, while 60 percent voted for Bush.

As in previous elections, the gender gap was greater among voters with higher socioeconomic status. According to the NES survey, white women were 8 points more likely to vote for Gore than white men were. Among white women with advanced degrees ($N = 47$), 55 percent voted for Gore; among white men with advanced degrees ($N = 53$), 40 percent voted for Gore, a 15-point gap. Moreover, the VNS survey, based upon a sample twelve times as large as the NES survey, reveals a similar pattern. Women without high school diplomas were only 3 points more likely to vote for Gore than men; but female college graduates were 18 points more likely to vote for Gore than male college graduates.[9]

As in our analyses of the 1984, 1988, 1992, and 1996 NES surveys, we found clear differences between women who were married and those who were single.[10] Single women, in particular, may have believed they had been harmed by the policies of Ronald Reagan and George Bush, and that they had been aided by Clinton's policies. The Republican emphasis on "family values" may have cost them votes among single women. Among all women who had never been married ($N = 102$), 64 percent voted for Gore; among all women who were married ($N = 362$), 48 percent voted for Gore, a gap of 16 percentage points. Unlike in earlier years, this gap resulted mostly from the very large number of unmarried black women who voted for Gore, for unmarried white women were only 2 percentage points more likely to vote for Gore than married white women. Among all unmarried men ($N = 85$), 49 percent voted for Gore; among all married men ($N = 331$), 42 percent did, a gap of 7 points. But this gap, too, resulted mostly from the large number of unmarried black men who voted for Gore; unmarried white men were only 3 points more likely to vote for Gore than married white men.

The VNS exit polls also reveal that unmarried voters were more likely to support Gore than married voters. Among unmarried women, 63 percent voted for Gore; among married women, 48 percent did. As with the NES survey, the gap was not as large among men. Among unmarried men, 48 percent voted for Gore; among married men, 38 percent did. Because the data as presented did not include controls for race, we cannot determine the extent to which the "marriage gap" results from racial differences.

The VNS poll also reveals a very large gap according to sexual orientation. Even though controversies about sexual orientation did not play a part in the presidential campaign, the Republican emphasis on "family values" was unattractive to many gay voters, and the Clinton administration occasionally made overtures on policies favored by the gay community. The VNS poll asked respondents whether they were gay or lesbian. Among the four percent of the electorate who answered, "yes," 70 percent voted for Gore and only 25 percent for Bush.[11]

Our analysis in chapter 3 shows that overall regional differences were relatively small. There were, however, clearer regional differences among whites. As Table 5-1 reveals, among southern whites, Bush won 68 percent of the vote, while Gore won only 29 percent. The South and the border states were the only regions where the NES data show Bush winning a majority of the white vote. The VNS exit poll shows that Bush won 66 percent of the white vote in the South, while Gore won only 31 percent. However, the VNS poll shows that Bush carried a majority of the white vote in the Midwest and West, and shows Gore with a majority of the white vote only in the East.[12]

In recent years, young Americans have been more likely to identify with the Republican Party than have older Americans, and in the 1980, 1984, 1988, 1992, and 1996 elections the Democrats did better among whites who had reached voting age before or during World War II (born before 1924), although in 1996 these differences were relatively small. As Table 5-1 shows, in 2000 Gore did do better among these older voters than he did among others, although the differences were small in most cases and the number of older voters was small as well. George W. Bush did best among voters born between 1963 and 1970, but he also did relatively well among those born between 1955 and 1962, which was the strongest age group for Dole in 1996. These are the voters who entered the electorate in the early 1970s and early 1980s and who may have been influenced by the pro-Republican tide during the early Reagan years. The VNS survey shows that whites who were 60 years old and older were more likely to vote for Gore than any other age group: 46 percent voted for Gore and 52 percent for Bush. But there were very small differences among the other three age categories reported in the VNS survey. The NES survey shows Nader doing very well among the small group of voters born between 1979 and 1982. The VNS survey also shows

Nader doing best among voters between the ages of 18 and 29 (born between 1971 and 1982), gaining 5 percent of the vote among these youths. Of course, Nader's environmentalism appealed to young Americans, but to some extent his success results from their low levels of party identification.

Social Class, Education, Income, and Union Membership

Traditionally, the Democratic Party has done well among the relatively disadvantaged. It has done better among the working class, voters with lower levels of education, and the poor. Moreover, since the 1930s most union leaders have supported the Democratic Party, and union members have been a mainstay of the Democratic presidential coalition. In 2000 there were clear differences between union members and nonmembers, and the VNS survey revealed a weak tendency for the more affluent voters to support the Republicans. But differences between the better and less well educated were weak. Moreover, since World War II social class differences in voting behavior have been declining. In 2000 this relationship disappeared, at least among the white electorate.

In 1996 Clinton won a plurality of the vote among working-class whites and an absolute majority among whites who were unskilled manual workers. But in 2000 Bush won a majority of the votes among working-class whites and did best among whites who were unskilled manual workers. Moreover, whereas in 1992 and 1996 Clinton clearly fared better among the poor than among the affluent, the relationship between income and voting preferences was weak and inconsistent in 2000. The VNS survey also shows a weak relationship between income and voting preferences. Among respondents with family incomes below $15,000, 57 percent voted for Gore. Support for Gore declines until we reach respondents with family incomes above $50,000, but it levels off for the three highest income categories, with about 44 percent of the voters supporting Gore. Robert S. Erikson uses exit poll data from 1988 and 2000 to compare voters at high-, medium-, and low-income levels. He concludes that the relationship between income and the vote appears to have declined slightly, mainly because "high income voters were more attracted to Gore (despite his alleged populism) than to Dukakis in 1988."[13]

In 1996 Clinton had fared best among whites who had not graduated from high school, whereas Dole had fared best among those who were college graduates. Among whites with advanced degrees, Clinton picked up some support and won nearly half the major-party vote. In 2000 there was a weaker relationship between education and voting preferences. Gore did best among whites who had not graduated from high school, while Bush did best among whites with some college education. As in 1996 Democratic support grew somewhat among white voters with advanced degrees, and Gore won nearly half the major-party vote. The VNS survey reveals a similar pattern. Gore did best among all voters who had not graduated from high school, gaining 59 percent of the vote. Bush's two best groups were voters with some college and college graduates. But Bush's support fell among voters with advanced degrees, and Gore won 52 percent of the vote among these highly educated voters.

Some scholars of American politics, such as Walter Dean Burnham and Everett Carll Ladd Jr., argue that the Democrats now tend to fare better among upper and lower socioeconomic groups.[14] This pattern for education seems to support their thesis. The Democrats may be appealing to disadvantaged Americans because of the party's economic policies and better-educated Americans—especially better-educated women—may reject the interpretation of traditional values emphasized by the Republicans in recent elections.

According to the NES survey, Clinton made major gains among white union households between 1992 and 1996. But the NES survey suggests that Gore slipped some 12 percentage points from Clinton's 1996 total, while George W. Bush gained 16 points on Dole. The VNS surveys shows that Gore won 59 percent of the union vote, while Bush won 37 percent; among voters who were not in households with a union member, Gore won 44 percent of the vote, while Bush won 52 percent.[15] However, the exit polls show little variation in the Democratic share of the vote over the past three presidential elections. But those polls do show the Republican candidates gaining across these elections, from 24 percent for George Bush in 1992 to 30 percent for Dole in 1996 to 37 percent for George W. Bush in 2000.

Religion

Religious differences, which partly reflect ethnic differences between Protestants and Catholics, have also played an important role in American politics.[16] Catholics have tended to support the Democrats, and white Protestants, especially outside the South, have tended to favor the Republicans. In all of Franklin D. Roosevelt's elections, and in every election through 1968, Jews strongly supported the Democrats. Even though Jewish support for the Democrats fell after that, an absolute majority of Jews have voted Democratic in every election except 1980.

In 1996 the NES surveys showed that Clinton won a majority of the vote among white Catholics while gaining two out of five votes among white Protestants. Exit polls in 1996 showed Clinton winning 53 percent of the vote among Catholics, but only 36 percent among white Protestants. But in the 2000 NES survey Bush won a majority of the vote among both white Catholics and white Protestants, although he did better among Protestants. According to the VNS poll, Bush won 63 percent of the vote among white Protestants but only 47 percent among Catholics.

The Republican emphasis on traditional values also may have had a special appeal to religious groups. Bush himself emphasized these appeals at some points during the nomination campaign, especially in the South Carolina contest, but these themes were de-emphasized during both the convention and the general election campaign. All the same, Bush was more acceptable to traditional religious groups than Gore. Thus, we find substantial religious differences even when we study differences among white Protestants. For example, among white Protestants who said they had been "born again," 69 percent voted for Bush, while among those who said they had not had this religious experience, 49 percent did. As we saw in chapter 4, white born-again Protestants are more likely to live in the South. We found that among white Protestants in the South the differences between those who were born again and those who were not were relatively small. Among those who were born again ($N = 93$), 70 percent voted for Bush, while among those who were not ($N = 56$), 66 percent did. Outside the South, however, these differences were substantial. Among white Protestants who had been born again ($N = 129$), 67 percent voted for Bush, while among those who had not been born again ($N = 179$), only 45 percent did.

As we noted in chapter 4, David C. Leege and Lyman A. Kellstedt argue that religious commitment has an important effect on voting behavior.[17] Table 5-1 reveals that white Protestants with very high levels of religious commitment were much more likely to vote for Bush than those with less commitment. Among white Protestants with medium or low levels of commitment, Bush and Gore split the major-party vote. As we noted, religious commitment is higher in the South. Religious commitment was related to the vote both in the South and outside it, although the relationship was stronger outside the South. Among white Protestants in the South who pray several times a day, attend church at least once a week, and say that religion provides "a great deal" of guidance in their lives, and who believe that the Bible is literally true or "the word of God" ($N = 29$), 83 percent voted for Bush; among those with medium or low levels of religious commitment ($N = 61$), 66 percent did. Among white Protestants outside the South with very high levels of religious commitment ($N = 48$), 90 percent voted for Bush; among those with medium or low levels of commitment ($N = 156$), only 43 percent did.

Table 5-1 also shows that Bush did much better among white evangelicals than among white mainline Protestants. These differences were about the same in the South as outside it. Among white evangelicals in the South ($N = 93$), Bush won 73 percent of the vote, while among white mainline Protestants there ($N = 41$), he won 54 percent. Among white evangelicals outside the South ($N = 96$), Bush won 64 percent of the vote; among white mainline Protestants there ($N = 152$), he won 47 percent.

Historically, as noted above, Jews have supported the Democratic Party, and many Jews may have seen the Clinton administration as friendly toward Israel. And by naming Joseph Lieberman, an Orthodox Jew, as his running mate, Gore made an additional appeal to Jewish voters. Moreover, many Jews may have been alienated from the Republican Party because of its conservative social values. As Table 5-1 reveals, 88 percent of the Jewish voters supported Gore. However, as only 25 Jews were sampled, we must be cautious in accepting this result. Fortunately, we can turn to the VNS survey, which sampled about 500 Jews. That survey shows that 79 percent of the Jewish voters supported Gore, while only 19 percent voted for Bush. The NES survey also shows half of the white voters with no religious preference supported Gore, while only 36 percent voted for Bush.

In most surveys we can gain additional understanding by combining social class and religion. In all previous NES surveys, when we divide Catholics and Protestants into the two basic social class categories, we find that working-class Catholics are more likely to vote Democratic than any other group; middle-class Protestants have always been the most likely to vote Republican. In 2000 middle-class Protestants gave Bush the largest share of the major-party vote, while middle-class Catholics were the most Democratic group. The most striking conclusion is that the differences among these four groups are small, a finding that will be reinforced when we compare the 2000 results with previous election surveys.

HOW SOCIAL GROUPS VOTED DURING THE POSTWAR YEARS

How does the 2000 election compare with other presidential elections? Do the relationships in 2000 result from a long-term trend that has eroded the importance of social forces? To answer these questions we examine the voting behavior of social groups that have been an important part of the Democratic presidential coalition during the postwar years. Our analysis begins with the 1944 presidential election between Roosevelt and Thomas E. Dewey and uses a simple measure of social cleavages to assess the effect of social forces over time.

In his lucid discussion of the logic of party coalitions, Robert Axelrod analyzes six basic groups that make up the Democratic presidential coalition: the poor, southerners, blacks (and other nonwhites), union members (and members of their families), Catholics and other non-Protestants, such as Jews, and residents of the twelve largest metropolitan areas.[18] John R. Petrocik's more comprehensive study identifies fifteen coalition groups and classifies seven of them as predominantly Democratic: blacks, lower-status native southerners, middle- and upper-status southerners, Jews, Polish and Irish Catholics, union members, and lower-status border state whites.[19] A more recent study by Harold W. Stanley, William T. Bianco, and Richard G. Niemi analyzes seven pro-Democratic groups: blacks, Catholics, Jews, women, native white southerners, members of union households, and the working class.[20] Our analysis focuses on race, region, union membership, social class, and religion.[21]

The contribution that a social group can make to a party's coalition depends upon three factors: the relative size of the group in the total electorate, its level of turnout compared with that of the total electorate, and its relative loyalty to a political party.[22] The larger a social group, the greater its contribution can be. African Americans make up 12 percent of the electorate; the white working class makes up 30 percent. Thus, the potential contribution of blacks is smaller than that of the white working class. The electoral power of blacks is further diminished by their relatively low turnout. However, because blacks vote overwhelmingly Democratic, their contribution to a party can be greater than their size

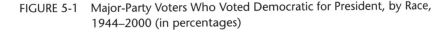

FIGURE 5-1 Major-Party Voters Who Voted Democratic for President, by Race, 1944–2000 (in percentages)

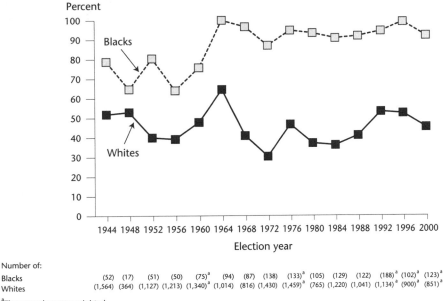

Number of:

Blacks	(52)	(17)	(51)	(50)	(75)[a]	(94)	(87)	(138)	(133)[a]	(105)	(129)	(122)	(188)[a]	(102)[a]	(123)[a]
Whites	(1,564)	(364)	(1,127)	(1,213)	(1,340)[a]	(1,014)	(816)	(1,430)	(1,459)[a]	(765)	(1,220)	(1,041)	(1,134)[a]	(900)[a]	(851)[a]

[a]These numbers are weighted.

would indicate. And the relative size of their contribution grows as whites desert the Democratic Party.

Race

Let us begin by examining racial differences, which we can trace back to 1944 by using the 1944 National Opinion Research Center (NORC) survey for that year.[23] Figure 5-1 shows the percentage of white and black major-party voters who voted Democratic for president from 1944 through 2000. Although most African Americans voted Democratic from 1944 through 1960, a substantial minority voted Republican. The political mobilization of blacks spurred by the civil rights movement and the Republican candidacy of Barry M. Goldwater in 1964 ended that Republican voting, and the residual Republican loyalties of older blacks were discarded between 1962 and 1964.[24]

While the Democrats made substantial gains among blacks, they lost ground among whites. From 1944 through 1964, the Democrats gained an absolute majority of the white vote in only two elections. Since then, they have never won an absolute majority of the white vote. However, in a two-candidate contest a Democrat can win with just under half the white vote, as the 1960 and 1976 elections demonstrate. In the three-way contests of 1992 and 1996, Clinton was able to win with only about two-fifths of the white vote.[25] Even in the two-candidate contest of 2000, Gore came very close to winning with just over two-fifths of the white vote.

The gap between the two trend lines in Figure 5-1 illustrates the overall difference in the Democratic vote between whites and blacks. Table 5-2 shows the overall level of "racial voting" in all fifteen elections, as well as four other measures of social cleavage.

From 1944 through 1964, racial voting ranged from a low of 12 percent to a high of 40 percent. But racial voting rose to 56 percent in 1968 (to 61 percent if those who voted for Wallace are included with Nixon voters) and did not fall to 40 points until 1992.[26] But racial voting was high in both 1996 and 2000.

Not only did African American loyalty to the Democratic Party increase sharply after 1960, but black turnout rose dramatically from 1960 to 1968 because southern blacks (about half the black population during this period) were reenfranchised. Moreover, the relative size of the black population increased somewhat during the postwar years. Between 1960, when overall turnout was at its highest, and 1996, when overall turnout reached its postwar low, turnout among whites dropped about 15 percentage points. But although black turnout fell in 1996, it was well above its levels before the Voting Rights Act of 1965.

From 1948 through 1960, African Americans never accounted for more than one Democratic vote out of twelve. In 1964, however, Johnson received about one out of seven of his votes from blacks, and blacks contributed a fifth of the Democratic totals in both 1968 and 1972. In the 1976 election, which saw Democratic gains among whites, the black total fell to just one in seven. In 1980 Jimmy Carter received about one in four of his votes from blacks, and in the next three elections about one Democratic vote in five came from blacks. In 1996 about one in six of Clinton's votes came from blacks, and in 2000, as we saw, about one in five of Gore's votes were cast by black voters.

Region

The desertion of the Democratic Party by white southerners is among the most dramatic changes in postwar American politics. As we saw in chapter 3, regional differences can be analyzed by using official election statistics. But official statistics are of limited usefulness in examining race-related differences in regional voting because election results are not tabulated by race. Survey data allow us to document the dramatic shift in voting behavior among white southerners.

As the data in Figure 5-2 reveal, white southerners were somewhat more Democratic than whites outside the South in the 1952 and 1956 contests between Dwight D. Eisenhower and Adlai E. Stevenson and in the 1960 contest between John F. Kennedy and Richard M. Nixon.[27] But in the next three elections, regional differences were reversed, with white southerners voting more Republican than whites outside the South. In 1976 and 1980, when the Democrats fielded Jimmy Carter of Georgia as their standard-bearer, white southerners and whites outside the South voted very much alike. In 1984 and 1988 white southerners were less

TABLE 5-2 Relationship of Social Characteristics to Presidential Voting, 1944–2000

	Election year														
	1944	1948	1952	1956	1960	1964	1968	1972	1976	1980	1984	1988	1992	1996	2000
Racial voting[a]	27	12	40	25	23	36	56	57	48	56	54	51	41	47	47
Regional voting[b]															
Among whites	—	—	12	17	6	-11	-4	-13	1	1	-9	-5	-10	-8	-20
Among entire electorate (NES surveys)	—	—	9	15	4	-5	6	-3	7	3	3	2	0	0	-10
Among entire electorate (official election results)	23	14	8	8	3	-13	-3	-11	5	2	-5	-7	-6	-7	-8
Union voting[c]															
Among whites	20	37	18	15	21	23	13	11	18	15	20	16	12	23	12
Among entire electorate	20	37	20	17	19	22	13	10	17	16	19	15	11	23	11
Class voting[d]															
Among whites	19	44	20	8	12	19	10	2	17	9	8	5	4	6	-6
Among entire electorate	20	44	22	11	13	20	15	4	21	15	12	8	8	9	2
Religious voting[e]															
Among whites	25	21	18	10	48	21	30	13	15	10	16	18	20	14	8
Among entire electorate	24	19	15	10	46	16	21	8	11	3	9	11	10	7	2

Note: All calculations are based on major-party voters.

[a] Percentage of blacks who voted Democratic minus percentage of whites who voted Democratic.
[b] Percentage of southerners who voted Democratic minus percentage of voters outside the South who voted Democratic.
[c] Percentage of members of union households who voted Democratic minus percentage of members of households with no union members who voted Democratic.
[d] Percentage of working class that voted Democratic minus percentage of middle class that voted Democratic.
[e] Percentage of Catholics who voted Democratic minus percentage of Protestants who voted Democratic.

FIGURE 5-2   White Major-Party Voters Who Voted Democratic for President, by
Region, 1952–2000 (in percentages)

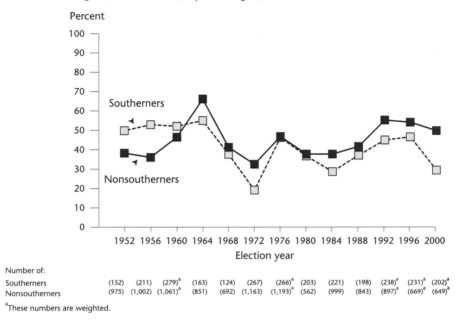

Number of:

Southerners	(152)	(211)	(279)[a]	(163)	(124)	(267)	(266)[a]	(203)	(221)	(198)	(238)[a]	(231)[a]	(202)[a]
Nonsoutherners	(975)	(1,002)	(1,061)[a]	(851)	(692)	(1,163)	(1,193)[a]	(562)	(999)	(843)	(897)[a]	(669)[a]	(649)[a]

[a]These numbers are weighted.

likely to vote Democratic than whites from any other region. In 1992 both Bill
Clinton and Al Gore were from the South. Even so, both George Bush in 1992
and Bob Dole in 1996 did better among white southerners than among whites
from any other region. In 2000 the Democrats ran a southern presidential candidate, but with Lieberman of Connecticut as his running mate. As our figure
reveals, George W. Bush and Dick Cheney did much better than the Democratic
team among southern whites.

Regional differences among whites from 1952 through 2000 are presented in
Table 5-2. The negative signs for 1964, 1968, 1972, 1984, 1988, 1992, 1996, and
2000 reveal that the Democratic candidate fared better among white major-
party voters outside the South than he did in the South. As we saw in chapter 3,
Wallace had a strong regional base in the South. If we include Wallace voters
with Nixon voters, regional differences among whites increase markedly, moving from −4 to −12.

Table 5-2 also presents regional voting for the entire electorate. Here, however, we present two sets of estimates: (1) NES results from 1952 through 2000,
and (2) results based upon official election statistics. Both sets of statistics show
that regional differences in voting have declined, but the NES somewhat overestimated the Democratic advantage in the South in 1956 and somewhat under-
estimated the Republican advantage in 1964 and 1972. In 1968, 1984, and 1988
the NES survey registered a slight Democratic advantage in the South, while the

official election statistics showed that the Democrats actually fared better outside the South. In 1992 and 1996 the NES surveys show the Republicans and Democrats faring equally in both regions, whereas the official election statistics demonstrate that the Republicans actually fared better in the South.

The mobilization of southern blacks and the defection of southern whites from the Democratic Party dramatically transformed the Democratic coalition in the South. Democratic presidential candidates from 1952 through 1960 never received more than one out of fifteen of their votes in the South from black voters. In 1964 nearly three out of ten of Johnson's southern votes came from black voters, and in 1968 Hubert H. Humphrey received nearly as many votes from southern blacks as from southern whites. In 1972, according to these data, George S. McGovern received more votes from southern blacks than from southern whites.

African American votes were crucial to Carter's success in the South in 1976. He received about one out of three of his southern votes from blacks in 1976 and again in 1980. In 1984 Mondale received about four in ten of his southern votes from blacks, and in 1988 about one in three votes that Michael S. Dukakis received in the South came from blacks. About a third of Clinton's southern votes in 1992 came from black voters, and in 1996 about three in ten of his votes came from black voters. In 2000 about four in ten of the southern votes received by Gore came from black voters.[28]

Union Membership

Figure 5-3 shows the percentage of white union members and nonmembers who voted Democratic for president from 1944 through 2000. In all six elections from 1944 through 1964, a majority of white union members (and their families) voted Democratic. For1968 our figure shows Humphrey receiving a slight majority of the white union vote, although his total would be cut to 43 percent if Wallace voters were included. The Democrats won about 61 percent of the union vote in 1976, when Carter defeated Ford. In 1988 Dukakis appears to have won a slight majority of the union vote, although he fell well short of Carter's 1976 tally. In 1992 Clinton won nearly half the white union vote, although he won about three-fifths of their major-party vote. In 1996, according to the NES survey, Clinton made major gains among union voters, winning 64 percent of the white union voters and 71 percent of their major-party vote. Gore won a majority of the white union vote, but he was well below Clinton's 1996 tally.[29] Conversely, the Republicans have won a majority of the white union vote in only one of these fifteen elections, Nixon's 1972 landslide over McGovern.

Differences between union members and nonmembers are presented in Table 5-2. Because Wallace did better among union members than nonmembers, including Wallace voters with Nixon voters reduces union voting from 13 to 10 percentage points. Union voting was highest in 1948, a year when

FIGURE 5-3   White Major-Party Voters Who Voted Democratic for President, by Union Membership, 1944–2000 (in percentages)

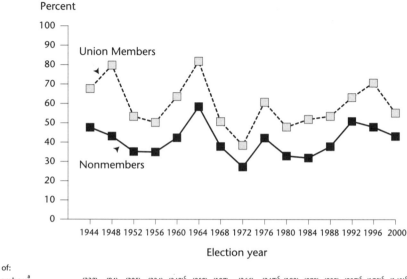

Number of:
Union members[a]   (332) (94) (305) (334) (342)[c] (259) (197) (366) (347)[c] (193) (278) (209) (207)[c] (175)[c] (141)[c]
Nonmembers[b]   (1,215) (266) (815) (877) (979)[c] (755) (617) (1,049) (1,099)[c] (569) (941) (828) (925)[c] (723)[c] (706)[c]

[a]Union members or in household with union member.
[b]Not a union member and not in household with union member.
[c]These numbers are weighted.

Harry S. Truman's opposition to the Taft-Hartley Act gained him strong union support. Union voting were low in 1992 and 2000, when white union members were only 12 percentage points more likely to vote Democratic than nonmembers. We have also included results for the entire electorate, but because blacks are as likely to live in union households as whites, including blacks has little effect on the results.

The percentage of the total electorate composed of white union members and their families declined during the postwar years. Members of white union households made up 25 percent of the electorate in 1952; by 2000 they made up 13 percent. Turnout among white union households has declined at about the same rate as turnout among nonunion whites. In addition, in many elections since 1964 the Democratic share of the union vote has been relatively low. All of these factors, as well as increased turnout by blacks, have reduced the total contribution of white union members to the Democratic presidential coalition. Through 1960 a third of the total Democratic vote came from white union members and members of their families. Between 1964 and 1984 only about one Democratic vote in four came from white union members. In 1988, 1992, and 1996 only about one Democratic vote in five came from white union members, and in 2000 only about one Gore vote in six came from white union members.

Social Class

The broad cleavage in political behavior between manually employed workers (and their dependents) and nonmanually employed workers (and their dependents) is especially valuable for studying comparative voting behavior.[30] In every presidential election from 1936 through 1996, the working class voted more Democratic than the middle class. But as Figure 5-4 shows, the percentage of working-class whites who voted Democratic has varied considerably from election to election. It reached its lowest level in 1972. Carter regained a majority of the working-class vote in 1976, but he lost it four years later. The Democrats failed to win a majority of the working-class vote in 1984 and 1988. Clinton won only about two-fifths of the working-class vote in 1992, although he did win a clear majority of the major-party vote among working-class whites. In 1996 he won half the working-class vote and a clear majority of the major-party vote among working-class whites. In 2000 Gore won only 40 percent of the vote among working-class whites.

Although levels of class voting have varied since 1944, they have clearly followed a downward trend, as Table 5-2 reveals.[31] Class voting is even lower in 1968, falling to 6 points if Wallace voters are included with Nixon voters, because 15 percent of the white working class supported Wallace, while only 10 percent of white middle-class voters did. Class voting in 1972 reached a very low level, mainly because many working-class whites deserted McGovern. But only in 2000 do we find that middle-class voters were more likely to vote Democratic than working-class voters. We should bear in mind that in 2000 there was no measure of the head of household's occupation or of the spouse's occupation, but our analysis of the 1996 data suggests that this limitation probably does not account for the negative level of class voting in the 2000 contest.[32]

Class voting trends are affected substantially if African Americans are included in the analysis. Blacks are disproportionately working class, and as we have seen, they vote overwhelmingly Democratic. In all the elections between 1976 and 1996, class voting is somewhat higher when blacks are included in the analysis. In 2000 class voting is positive (although very low) when blacks are included in our estimates. Therefore, the overall trend toward declining class voting is dampened somewhat when blacks are included in the analysis. However, black workers voted Democratic because they were black, not because they were working class. In most NES surveys differences between working- and middle-class blacks were small. In 2000 working-class blacks were 8 points more likely to vote for Gore than middle-class blacks, but even among the forty-eight middle-class black voters, 83 percent voted for Gore. It seems reasonable, therefore, to focus on the decline of class voting among the white electorate.

During the postwar years the proportion of the electorate made up of working-class whites has remained relatively constant, while that of middle-class whites has grown.[33] The percentage of whites in the agricultural sector has declined dramatically. Turnout fell among both the middle and working classes

FIGURE 5-4   White Major-Party Voters Who Voted Democratic for President, by
Social Class, 1944–2000 (in percentages)

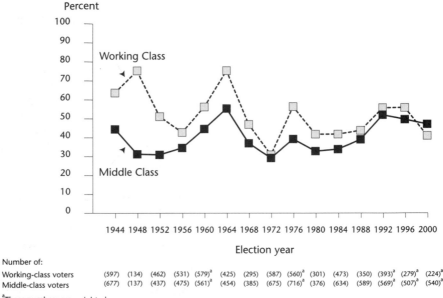

Number of:														
Working-class voters	(597)	(134)	(462)	(531)	(579)ᵃ	(425)	(295)	(587)	(560)ᵃ	(301)	(473)	(350)	(393)ᵃ	(279)ᵃ	(224)ᵃ
Middle-class voters	(677)	(137)	(437)	(475)	(561)ᵃ	(454)	(385)	(675)	(716)ᵃ	(376)	(634)	(589)	(569)ᵃ	(507)ᵃ	(540)ᵃ

ᵃThese numbers are weighted.

after 1960, but it fell more among the working class. As we saw in chapter 4, only
64 percent of the white working class claimed to have voted in 2000, while 79
percent of the middle class did. Declining turnout and defections from the
Democratic Party by working-class whites, along with increased turnout by
blacks, have reduced the total contribution of the white working class to the
Democratic presidential coalition.

In 1948 and 1952 about half the total Democratic vote came from working-
class whites, and from 1956 through 1964 more than four out of ten Democratic
votes came from this social group. In 1968 their contribution fell to just over a
third and then to under a third in 1972. In 1976, with the rise in class voting, the
white working class provided nearly two-fifths of Carter's total support, but it
provided just over a third in 1980. In 1984 over a third of Mondale's support
came from working-class whites, and in 1988 Dukakis gained just over two out
of five of his votes were from this group. In both 1992 and 1996 three out of ten
of Clinton's total votes came from working-class whites. In 2000 only about a
fifth of Gore's total vote came from the white working class.

The middle-class contribution to the Democratic presidential coalition
amounted to fewer than three out of five votes in 1948 and 1952, and just under
one-third in 1956, stabilizing at just over one-third in the next five elections.
In 1980 a third of Carter's support came from middle-class whites. In 1984
Mondale received just under two out of five votes from middle-class whites, and

in 1988 Dukakis gained more than two out of five. In 1992 more than two out of five of Clinton's total votes came from middle-class whites, and in 1996 nearly half of his vote came from this group. In 2000 Gore received two-fifths of his total votes from middle-class whites. In each of the past five presidential elections, the Democrats have received a larger share of their total vote from middle-class whites than from working-class whites. The increasing middle-class contribution results from two factors: first, the middle class is growing; and, second, class differences are eroding. The decline in class differences in voting behavior may be part of a widespread phenomenon that is occurring in advanced industrial societies.[34]

Of course, our argument that class-based voting has declined depends on the way we have defined social class. Different definitions may yield different results. For example, in a major study using a far more complex definition that divides the electorate into seven social class categories, Jeff Manza and Clem Brooks, using the NES data from 1952 through 1996, conclude that class differences are still important.[35] But their findings actually support our conclusion that the New Deal coalition has eroded. They find, for example, that professionals were the most Republican class in the 1950s, but that by the 1996 election they had become the most Democratic.

Religion

Voting differences among the major religious groups have also declined during the postwar years. Even so, as Figure 5-5 reveals, in every election since 1944, Jews have been more likely to vote Democratic than Catholics, and Catholics have been more likely to vote Democratic than Protestants.

A large majority of Jews voted Democratic in every election from 1944 through 1968, and although the Jewish vote dropped during Nixon's 1972 landslide, even McGovern won a majority of the Jewish vote. In 1980 many Jews (like many gentiles) were dissatisfied with Carter's performance as president, and some of them resented the pressure he had exerted on Israel to accept the Camp David peace accord, which returned the Sinai Peninsula—captured by Israel in 1967—to Egypt. A substantial minority of Jews voted for John B. Anderson, but Carter still outpolled Reagan among Jewish voters. Both Mondale in 1984 and Dukakis (whose wife, Kitty, is Jewish) in 1988 won a clear majority of the Jewish vote. The Jewish vote for Clinton surged in 1992, with Clinton winning nine out of ten of the major-party voters, and Clinton won overwhelming Jewish support in his 1996 reelection. With Lieberman as his running mate, Gore, too, won overwhelming Jewish support in 2000.

A majority of the white Catholics voted Democratic in six of the seven elections from 1944 through 1968. The percentage of Catholics voting Democratic surged in 1960, when the Democrats fielded a Catholic candidate, and it was still very high in Johnson's landslide four years later. Since then, Democratic voting among Catholics has declined precipitously. In 1968 a majority of the white

FIGURE 5-5   White Major-Party Voters Who Voted Democratic for President,
by Religion, 1944–2000 (in percentages)

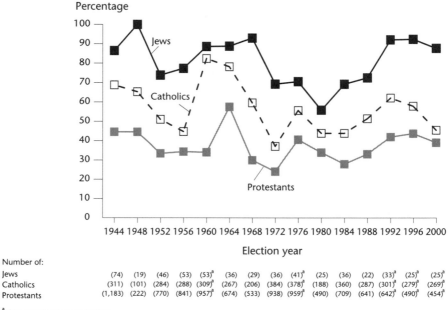

Number of:														
Jews	(74)	(19)	(46)	(53)	(53)[a]	(36)	(29)	(36)	(41)[a]	(25)	(36)	(22)	(33)[a]	(25)[a]	(25)[a]
Catholics	(311)	(101)	(284)	(288)	(309)[a]	(267)	(206)	(384)	(378)[a]	(188)	(360)	(287)	(301)[a]	(279)[a]	(269)[a]
Protestants	(1,183)	(222)	(770)	(841)	(957)[a]	(674)	(533)	(938)	(959)[a]	(490)	(709)	(641)	(642)[a]	(490)[a]	(454)[a]

[a]These numbers are weighted.

Catholics voted Democratic, although Humphrey's total among white Catholics
would be reduced from 60 to 55 percent if Wallace voters were included. In 1976
Carter won a majority of the vote among white Catholics, but the Democrats did
not win a clear majority of the major-party vote among white Catholics again
until Clinton's election in 1992. In his 1996 reelection, Clinton won just over half
the white Catholic vote, and a clear majority of the major-party vote. But in 2000
George W. Bush outpolled Al Gore among white Catholic voters.

Our simple measure of religious voting shows considerable change from election to election, although there was a clear downward trend through 1980 (see
Table 5-2). Even though white Protestants were more likely to vote for Wallace in
1968 than white Catholics were, including Wallace in our totals has little effect
on religious voting (it falls from 30 to 29 points). Religious differences were small
in the 1980 Reagan-Carter contest, but since then they have varied. However, the
lowest level of religious voting over this fifty-six-year period was recorded in the
2000 election.

Including African Americans in our calculations substantially reduces religious
voting. Blacks are much more likely to be Protestant than Catholic, and including
blacks adds a substantial number of Protestant Democrats. The effect of including blacks is greater from 1968 on because black turnout has been higher. In 2000
religious voting is reduced from 8 to 2 points if blacks are included.

The Jewish contribution to the Democratic coalition has declined, partly because Jews did not vote overwhelmingly Democratic from 1972 through 1988, and partly because the percentage of Jews in the electorate has declined. From 1972 through 1988 Jews made up only about a twentieth of the Democratic presidential coalition. Despite the upsurge in Jewish Democratic voting in 1992, the NES surveys show that Clinton received only 4 percent of his total vote from Jews and show him receiving a similar proportion in 1996. In both cases, the exit polls show Clinton receiving a somewhat larger share of his vote from Jewish voters— 7 percent in 1992 and 5 percent in 1996. In 2000, according to the NES survey, Gore received 4 percent of his vote from Jewish voters, although, once again, the major exit poll shows him receiving a somewhat larger share—a total of 7 percent. But although Jews make up only 2.3 percent of the population, three-fourths of the nation's Jews live in seven large states (New York, California, Florida, New Jersey, Pennsylvania, Massachusetts, and Illinois), which will combine for 182 electoral votes in the 2004 and 2008 elections.[36]

White Catholics make up just over a fifth of the electorate, and this proportion has remained relatively constant over the postwar years. However, since 1960 turnout has declined more among white Catholics than among white Protestants. As Figure 5-5 shows, the proportion of Catholics voting Democratic has declined since the 1960 and 1964 elections, although it rose between 1984 and 1992. In 2000, however, there was a marked decline in Democratic voting among white Catholics. In the six elections from 1980 through 2000 the Democrats won an absolute majority of the white Catholic vote in only one election, Clinton's 1996 reelection.

According to our estimates, based upon NES surveys, Truman received about a third of his total vote from white Catholics. Stevenson won three-tenths of his vote from white Catholics in 1952, but received only a fourth of his vote from Catholics in 1956. In 1960 Kennedy received 37 percent of his vote from white Catholics, but the Catholic contribution fell to just below three out of ten votes when Johnson defeated Goldwater in 1964. In 1968 three-tenths of Humphrey's total vote came from white Catholics, but only a fourth of McGovern's vote came from white Catholics. Just over a fourth of Carter's vote came from white Catholics in his 1976 victory, but in his 1980 loss to Reagan just over a fifth of his vote came from this source. Mondale received just under three out of ten votes from white Catholics, and in 1988 Dukakis received a fourth of his vote from this group. According to our analysis, based upon the NES surveys, just under a fourth of Clinton's vote in 1992 came from white Catholics and just over a fourth came from white Catholics in 1996. The NES surveys suggest that just over a fifth of Gore's vote came from white Catholics, while our estimates based upon the VNS surveys suggest that just over a fourth of his vote came from Catholics.

As the data in Figure 5-6 reveal, in all the elections from 1944 through 1996 the effects of social class and religion have been cumulative. In every one of these fourteen elections, working-class Catholics have been more likely to vote

FIGURE 5-6   White Major-Party Voters Who Voted Democratic for President, by
Social Class and Religion, 1944–2000 (in percentages)

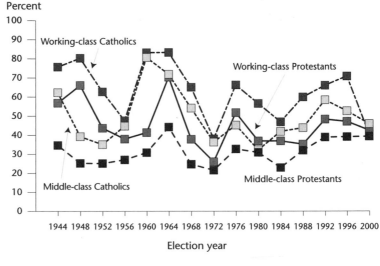

Number of:															
Working-class Catholics	(152)	(61)	(158)	(168)	(179)[a]	(126)	(83)	(176)	(163)[a]	(76)	(156)	(100)	(100)[a]	(86)[a]	(79)[a]
Middle-class Catholics	(130)	(28)	(94)	(96)	(109)[a]	(121)	(96)	(176)	(179)[a]	(96)	(177)	(164)	(166)[a]	(167)[a]	(161)[a]
Working-class Protestants	(405)	(59)	(279)	(329)	(374)[a]	(280)	(198)	(383)	(367)[a]	(197)	(286)	(218)	(234)[a]	(159)[a]	(115)[a]
Middle-class Protestants	(479)	(91)	(302)	(336)	(405)[a]	(287)	(254)	(430)	(457)[a]	(226)	(359)	(349)	(303)[a]	(256)[a]	(292)[a]

[a]These numbers are weighted.

Democratic than any other group. In every one of these elections, middle-class
Protestants have been the least likely to vote Democratic. But in 2000 middle-
class Catholics were the most likely to vote Democratic. As in all the previous
elections, however, middle-class Protestants were the least likely to vote
Democratic. They are more constant over time than any other group. An
absolute majority voted Republican in every election from 1944 through 1988,
and George Bush won nearly half of their vote in the three-way contest of 1992.
In 1996 Dole won a majority of the major-party vote among middle-class
Protestants and won three-fifths of the major-party vote. George W. Bush won
three-fifths of the middle-class Protestant vote in 2000.

The relative importance of social class and religion can be assessed by comparing the voting behavior of middle-class Catholics and working-class
Protestants. Religion was more important than social class in predicting voting choices in 1944, 1956, 1960 (by a considerable margin), 1968, 1972, 1984,
1988, 1992, 1996, and 2000. Social class was more important than religion in
1948 (by a considerable margin), 1952, 1976, and 1980. And class and religion
were equally important in 1964. However, all of these trend lines have been
converging, suggesting that traditional sources of social cleavage are declining
in importance.

WHY THE NEW DEAL COALITION BROKE DOWN

Except for race, which increased in importance after 1960, all of the factors we have examined have declined in importance during the postwar years. The decline in regional differences directly parallels the increase in racial differences. As the national Democratic Party strengthened its appeals to African Americans during the 1960s, party leaders endorsed policies opposed by southern whites, and many of these voters deserted the Democratic Party. The migration of northern whites to the South may have also reduced regional differences.

The Democratic Party's appeals to blacks also may have weakened its hold on other white groups that traditionally supported it. Robert Huckfeldt and Carol Weitzel Kohfeld clearly demonstrate that Democratic appeals to blacks weakened the party's support among working-class whites.[37] But the erosion of Democratic support among union members, the working class, and Catholics results from other factors as well. During the postwar years, these groups have changed. Although union members do not hold high-paying professional and managerial jobs, they have gained substantial economic advantages. Differences in income between the working class and the middle class have diminished. And Catholics, who often came from more recent immigrant groups than Protestants, have become increasingly middle class as the proportion of second- and third-generation immigrants has become larger, a trend only partly offset by the growing number of white Catholic Hispanics. During the 1950s and 1960s white Catholics were more likely to be working class than white Protestants. In 1976, 1980, and 1984 they were just as likely as white Protestants to be middle class, and in the past four elections they were somewhat more likely to be middle class than were white Protestants.

Not only have these groups changed economically and socially, but the historical conditions that led union members, the working class, and Catholics to become Democrats have receded further into the past. While the transmission of party loyalties from generation to generation gives historically based coalitions some staying power, the ability of the family to transmit party loyalties has decreased as the strength of party identification has weakened.[38] Moreover, with the passage of time, the proportion of the electorate that directly experienced the Roosevelt years has progressively declined. By 2000 only one voter in fourteen had entered the electorate before or during World War II. New policy issues, often unrelated to the traditional political conflicts of the New Deal, have tended to erode party loyalties among traditional Democratic groups. Edward G. Carmines and James A. Stimson provide strong evidence that race-related issues have been crucial in weakening the New Deal coalition.[39]

Despite the breakdown of the New Deal coalition, the Democrats managed to win the presidency in 1992 and 1996, and came very close to holding the presidency in 2000. In his 1992 victory Clinton boosted his share of the major-party vote among union members, the white working class, Catholics, and even white southerners. Clinton focused his appeals to middle America, and in both 1992 and 1996 he paid as low a price as possible to gain the black vote. Clinton's Democratic win in 1992 was the first Democratic victory in which blacks made up more than 15 percent of the Democratic coalition. In 1996 he once again won with over 15 percent of his vote coming from blacks. But 1992, and to a lesser extent 1996, were three-candidate contests in which the white vote was split among three candidates. Our calculations suggest that it would be difficult for the Democrats to win a two-candidate contest in which blacks made up a fifth or more of their total coalition. Gore came close to a victory (and won more popular votes than Bush) with a fifth of his votes coming from blacks, but the total share of his votes coming from blacks was large because he lost ground among white southerners, white union members, the white working class, and white Catholics.

Clinton's victory in 1992 seemed to provide an opportunity to forge a new Democratic coalition, which might have been partly based upon some of the components of the old New Deal coalition. But after the Democratic losses of the House and the Senate in the 1994 midterm election, Clinton developed a more reactive strategy that focused on moving to the political center. In some respects he partly revitalized the New Deal coalition, primarily because of the efforts of union leaders to end the Republican control of Congress. But in 2000, despite Gore's populist appeals, union voting and religious voting were low, and the white middle class actually voted somewhat more Democratic than the white working class. Perhaps, as James W. Ceaser and Andrew E. Busch argued after the 1992 election, new coalitions will be formed on common issue positions rather than on the type of demographic groups that both politicians and political scientists employ.[40] Turning to the issue preferences of the electorate provides an opportunity to see how a Democratic coalition can be formed and may also suggest strategies that the Republicans can follow to hold the presidency.

Chapter 6

Candidates, Issues, and the Vote

◆◆◆

In chapter 5, we discussed the relationship between various social forces and the vote. The impact of such forces on the vote is indirect. Even though the Democratic New Deal coalition was constructed from members of different groups, people who were members of these groups did not vote Democratic simply because they were African Americans, white southerners, union members, Catholics, or Jews. Rather, they usually voted Democratic because that party offered symbolic and substantive policies and candidates that appealed to the concerns of members of these groups, and because the party's platforms and candidates were consistent, encouraging many voters to develop long-term partisan loyalties. The long-term decline in class voting, for example, is evidence of the decreasing importance members of the working and middle classes assign to the differences between the parties on concerns that divide blue-collar and white-collar workers. That race is the sharpest division in American politics today does not mean that blacks vote Democratic simply because they are black; as Supreme Court Justice Clarence Thomas and Rep. J. C. Watts, Jr. R-Okla., demonstrate, African Americans may also be conservative ideologically and may identify with and vote for Republicans.

In this and the following two chapters, we examine some of the concerns that underlie voters' choices for president, connecting the indirect relationship between group membership and the vote. Even though, as we shall see, scholars and politicians disagree among themselves about what factors voters employ, and how they employ them, there is general consensus on several points. First, voters' attitudes or preferences determine their choices. There may be disagreement over exactly which attitudes shape behavior, but most scholars agree that voters deliberately choose to support the candidate they believe will make the best president. There is also general agreement that the most important attitudes in shaping the vote are attitudes toward the candidates, the issues, and the parties.[1]

In this chapter, we first look briefly at the relationship between one measure of candidate evaluation and the vote, the "feeling thermometers" that the National

Election Studies (NES) uses to measure affect toward the candidates. In this brief analysis we ignore two of the major components underlying these evaluations: voters' perceptions of the candidates' personal qualities, and voters' perceptions of the candidates' professional qualifications and competence to serve as president.[2] As we will see, there is a very powerful relationship between these evaluations of candidates and the vote. It might seem obvious that voters support the candidate they like best, but the presence of a third candidate illustrates the complicated nature of voters' decision making.[3] In several recent elections, including that in 2000, it appears that some people may not have voted for the candidate they rated the highest, supporting instead one they thought had a better chance of winning in the hope of blocking the election of the candidate they liked least. Voters who do not vote for their first preference for these reasons are called "sophisticated" or "strategic" voters.[4]

We see the simple measure of attitudes toward the candidates as the most direct influence on the vote itself; attitudes toward the issues and the parties help to shape attitudes toward the candidates and thus the vote. In that light, we then turn to the first part of our investigation of the role of issues. After analyzing what problems most concerned the voters in 2000, we discuss the two basic forms of issue voting, which are referred to as voting based on "prospective" and "retrospective" issues. In this chapter we investigate the impact of prospective issues. We consider one of the controversies about issue voting: how much information the public has about issues and candidates' positions on them. Our analyses provide an indication of the significance of prospective issues in 2000, and we can compare their impact as shown in earlier election surveys. Chapter 7 examines retrospective issues and the vote, and chapter 8 examines partisan identification and assesses the significance of parties and issues, together, on voting in 2000 and in earlier elections.

ATTITUDES TOWARD THE CANDIDATES

Overall Ratings of the Candidates

While relatively few people voted for Ralph Nader, a substantial number preferred him to the two major-party nominees. Voters, therefore, faced three major choices in the 2000 election, as they did in four other elections for which there are National Election Studies (NES) surveys—1968, 1980, 1992, and 1996.[5] It seems reasonable to assume that voters support the candidate they believe would make the best president. This close relationship can be demonstrated by analyzing the "feeling thermometer." In Figure 6-1, we reproduce the drawing shown to each in-person respondent and explained to each respondent interviewed by telephone. This measure produces a scale that runs from 0 through 100 degrees, with zero indicating "very cold," or most negative feelings, 50 indicating neutral feelings, and 100 indicating the "very warm," or most positive, evaluation.

FIGURE 6-1   The "Feeling Thermometer" Shown to Respondents When They Were Asked to Rate Candidates and Groups

100°	Very warm or favorable feeling
85°	Quite warm or favorable feeling
70°	Fairly warm or favorable feeling
60°	A bit more warm or favorable than cold feeling
50°	No feeling at all
40°	A bit more cold or unfavorable feeling
30°	Fairly cold or unfavorable feeling
15°	Quite cold or unfavorable feeling
0°	Very cold or unfavorable feeling

Source: 2000 National Election Studies, Pre-Election Survey, Respondent Booklet.

Voters usually know less about the third candidate than about the nominees of the two major parties. Therefore, fewer respondents ranked third candidates on the thermometer scales, and more rated them at the exact neutral point. For example, in the preelection measurement in 1980, 14 percent did not rate John B. Anderson, about three times as many as did not rate Jimmy Carter or Ronald Reagan; in the postelection survey 9 percent failed to rate Anderson, but only 2 percent or less failed to rate Carter or Reagan. More than 27 percent of the respondents in the preelection survey and 34 percent in the postelection survey rated Anderson at exactly the neutral point, twice as many as rated Reagan at 50 degrees, and more than twice as many as rated Carter at 50 degrees. Perot ran an extremely expensive media advertising campaign in 1992, with heavier than usual media coverage of his candidacy. Still, in 1992, 7 percent did not rate Perot on the preelection feeling thermometer compared to 2 percent not rating Clinton and 1 percent George Bush; 24 percent rated Perot at 50 degrees, compared to the 15 percent so rating Clinton and the 14 percent so rating Bush. In 1996 only 3 percent did not rate Perot on the preelection feeling thermometer, compared to less than 2 percent failing to rate Dole and less than 1 percent failing to rate the now-incumbent Clinton. However, a full 30 percent rated Perot at exactly 50 degrees that year, whereas the comparable Dole and Clinton figures were 17 and 7 percent, respectively. In 2000, 27 percent did not rate Nader in the preelection survey, compared to 4 percent for George W. Bush and 2 percent for Gore. In the postelection survey, the comparable figures were 25 percent, 1 percent, and 1 percent, respectively. In addition, 22 percent of respondents in the preelection survey and 25 percent in the postelection survey scored Nader at exactly 50 degrees, compared to 17 and 11 percent for Bush and 15 and 10 percent for Gore in the two surveys.

Were Voters "Sophisticated"?

The comparative ranking of the candidates on these scales is usually a very accurate reflection of the vote. Table 6-1 reports the candidate ranked highest by voters in the 2000 preelection and postelection surveys and the candidate they supported. Included as well are comparable figures from the 1968, 1980, 1992, and 1996 NES postelection surveys. In all five cases, those who rated a major-party nominee highest overwhelmingly voted for that candidate. The lowest proportion were the 93 percent who rated Gore first in 2000 and who rated George Bush first in 1992. In all cases, however, the third candidate fared more poorly. Nader was perhaps surprisingly well evaluated. Ignoring ties, 15 percent rated him higher than either George W. Bush or Gore in the preelection survey, and about 11 percent did so in the postelection survey. A very large percentage of these people, however, voted for Gore and some backed Bush. Nader held only one in five of those who most preferred him in the preelection survey, and three in ten who ranked him first in the postelection survey (see Table 6-1). These results strongly suggest that many who preferred Nader voted strategically for Gore or even Bush. Wallace, Anderson, and Perot (in both 1992 and 1996) all fared much better than Nader, but they, too, appear to have lost votes due to strategic voting.

The most obvious problem facing an independent or third-party candidate is how to attract a following, but there is a second obstacle as well. People find it hard to justify voting for their preferred candidate if they believe he or she has very little chance of winning. Many people are unwilling to "waste" their vote. Third-party candidates are aware of this fact and try to counter the logic. Perot in 1992 employed the slogan, "Don't waste your vote on politics as usual," while as we saw in chapter 2, Nader pointed out in 2000 that when you vote for the lesser of two evils, the winner will still be evil. The logic against "wasted votes" is commonly faced by third parties in many elections, especially those in which the leading candidate or party takes all offices or seats. Thus there is strong evidence that some voters in Canada and Britain, which use winner-take-all systems, abandon the party they prefer to prevent the party they like least from winning.[6] Moreover, some voters in U.S. presidential nomination contests also vote for candidates who are not their first choice.[7]

Nader, as candidate of the Green Party, presented another consideration. The Green Party would receive federal funding for the 2004 campaign if he secured at least 5 percent of the vote. As his likely vote seemed close to the 5 percent threshold, he thereby offered his supporters something very specific to "win"— future financial support (and consequently enhanced credibility and media attention). In that way, he argued, potential Nader voters would not be wasting their vote. This argument was harder to make in this particular case, however, because there were many crucial states in which the Bush-Gore contest was extremely close. In fact, there was even use of the Internet to trade Gore votes in safe Republican or safe Democratic states for Nader votes in highly competitive

TABLE 6-1   Candidate Thermometer Rankings and the Vote, 1968, 1980, 1992, 1996, and 2000 (in percentages)

First place in thermometer rating

A. Voted for in 1968	Nixon	Humphrey	Wallace	Total	(N)
Nixon	96	2	2	100	(418)
Humphrey	2	97	1	100	(353)
Wallace	15	1	84	100	(107)
N-H tie	39	60	2	100	(67)
W-N tie	[4]	—	[5]	—	(9)
W-H tie	—	[3]	—	—	(3)
3-way tie	[3]	[4]	[2]	—	(9)

B. Voted for in 1980	Reagan	Carter	Anderson	Total	(N)
Reagan	97	2	1	100	(409)
Carter	3	97	—	100	(253)
Anderson	18	25	57	100	(111)
R-C tie	40	60	—	100	(40)
A-R tie	88	3	9	100	(34)
A-C tie	7	67	26	100	(27)
3-way tie	24	64	12	100	(25)

C. Voted for in 1992	Bush	Clinton	Perot	Total	(N)[a]
Bush	93	2	6	101	(485)
Clinton	2	95	3	100	(685)
Perot	10	13	77	100	(258)
B-C tie	49	42	8	99	(72)
P-B tie	45	2	52	99	(48)
P-C tie	5	57	38	100	(76)
3-way tie	20	44	37	101	(27)

D. Voted for in 1996	Dole	Clinton	Perot	Total	(N)[a]
Dole	97	3	0	100	(342)
Clinton	3	95	2	100	(533)
Perot	33	6	61	100	(84)
D-C tie	45	49	5	99	(73)
P-D tie	88	9	3	100	(34)
P-C tie	—	48	52	100	(23)
3-way tie	35	29	35	99	(17)

(Table continues)

TABLE 6-1   (continued)

First place in thermometer rating

E. Voted for in 2000:

Preelection Survey	Bush	Gore	Nader	Total	(N)[a]
Bush	95	5	—	100	(328)
Gore	7	93	—	100	(310)
Nader	22	58	19	99	(113)
B-G tie	68	32	—	100	(38)
G-N tie	3	97	—	100	(32)
N-B tie	92	8	—	100	(25)
3-way tie	35	65	—	100	(17)

F. Voted for in 2000:

Postelection Survey	Bush	Gore	Nader	Total	(N)[a]
Bush	97	3	—	100	(407)
Gore	2	97	1	100	(371)
Nader	15	56	29	100	(96)
B-G tie	39	61	—	100	(28)
G-N tie	—	93	7	100	(30)
N-B tie	82	9	9	100	(11)
3-way tie	[3]	[4]	—	100	(7)

Note: The thermometer ratings for 1968, 1980, 1992, and 1996 are based on the postelection interviews. The numbers in brackets are the number of cases when there are fewer than ten total cases.

[a] Numbers are weighted.

states. But there is little evidence that any appreciable number of such trades occurred. We cannot tell whether the 5 percent threshold would have made a more effective appeal had the presidential race not been so tightly contested.

In July 1992 Perot justified his temporary withdrawal partly on the grounds that he could not win. Perot had just taken the (plurality) lead in the polls, but he argued that his candidacy might lead to a deadlock in which no candidate won a majority of the electoral vote. The U.S. House of Representatives would then need to elect the president, and the House had not chosen a president since it picked John Quincy Adams in 1825 (under the cloud of an alleged "corrupt bargain"). Having the House choose the president, Perot argued, would be "disruptive."

Perot in 1992 was a very successful candidate, at least in terms of the popular vote. In a three-candidate race, a candidate opposed by a majority may, by virtue of the rules governing presidential elections, nonetheless win. William H. Riker argues that Woodrow Wilson, the Democratic standard-bearer in 1912, was such a candidate. A majority may have preferred William Howard Taft, the Republican incumbent, to Wilson, and a majority may have preferred Theodore Roosevelt, a

TABLE 6-2　Comparative Thermometer Ratings of the Candidates, 2000
(Head-to-Head Comparisons, in percentages)

	Bush versus Gore		Bush versus Nader		Gore versus Nader	
A. Preelection Survey, Candidate Rated First						
Bush	41	Bush	50	Gore	51
Tie	13	Tie	13	Tie	14
Gore	46	Nader	37	Nader	35
Total %	100	Total %	100	Total %	100
$(N)^a$	(1,745)	$(N)^a$	(1,240)	$(N)^a$	(1,247)
B. Postelection Survey, Candidate Rated First						
Bush	45	Bush	56	Gore	51
Tie	8	Tie	11	Tie	14
Gore	48	Nader	33	Nader	35
Total %	101	Total %	100	Total %	100
$(N)^a$	(1,528)	$(N)^a$	(1,257)	$(N)^a$	(1,257)

[a] Numbers are weighted.

former Republican president running under the Progressive, or "Bull Moose," Party label, to Wilson. With the vote for the other two candidates split, Wilson won with a plurality vote (approximately the same as Bill Clinton's in 1992), which became an electoral college majority by virtue of the states' winner-take-all rules.[8]

As there were no studies of the attitudes of American voters in 1912, we will never know whether Riker's conjectures about that election are correct. By using the feeling thermometers employed in the 2000 NES survey, however, we can at least indirectly determine how Bush would have done in a two-candidate race against Gore or Nader. Because these thermometer scores are so strongly related to the vote, they can be used to run three mock elections: one pairing Bush against Gore, another pairing Bush against Nader, and a third pairing Gore against Nader. These pairings are reported in Table 6-2.

In both surveys, Gore was preferred to Bush by a small plurality.[9] If those who reported a tie between Gore and Bush ended up giving at least one in three of their votes to Gore, he would have won a majority in each case. Nader received few actual votes, but he had a much larger number of respondents who ranked him higher than Bush and than Gore. Still, he would have received only about one vote in three in either two-candidate pairings, and Gore would have defeated him (making it irrelevant how Bush and Nader would have fared against each other) unless all the people who tied Gore and Nader voted for Nader. Our main conclusion, therefore, is that Gore would likely have been the majority winner in either two-candidate contest, although his lead against Bush would certainly have been small. Most social choice theorists would agree with Condorcet that if there is an outcome that would be preferred by a majority over any other alternative in head-to-head comparisons, that outcome should be selected. In this sense, Gore probably met the Condorcet criterion.[10] Likewise, Nixon was very likely the Condorcet winner in 1968, Reagan was the Condorcet winner in 1980, and Clinton was likely to have been so in 1992 and assuredly so in 1996.[11] Moreover, the Voter News Service (VNS) exit poll also suggests Gore may have been the Condorcet winner, since Nader voters preferred Gore to Bush.[12] If Gore had won even a slight edge among the 97,488 Floridians who voted for Nader, he would easily have overcome Bush's 537-vote edge, thereby winning a clear majority of the electoral vote.

RETROSPECTIVE AND PROSPECTIVE EVALUATIONS

Underlying these evaluations of the candidates are the public's attitudes toward the issues and toward the parties (as well as more specific evaluations of the candidates). We begin by considering the role of issues in elections. Public policy concerns enter into the voting decision in two very different ways. In an election in which an incumbent is running, two questions become important: How has the incumbent president done on policy? And how likely is it that his opponent (or opponents) would do any better? Voting based on this form of policy appraisal is called retrospective voting and will be analyzed in chapter 7.

The second form of policy-based voting involves examining the candidates' policy platforms and assessing which candidate's policy promises conform to what the voter believes the government should be doing. Policy voting, therefore, involves comparing sets of promises and voting for the set that is most like the voter's own preferences. Voting based on these kinds of decisions may be referred to as prospective voting, for it involves examining the promises of the candidates about future actions. In this chapter, we examine prospective evaluations of the two major-party candidates and how these evaluations relate to voter choice.

The past eight elections show some remarkable similarities in prospective evaluations and voting. Perhaps the most important similarity is the perception of where the Democratic and Republican candidates stood on issues. In these elections, the public saw clear differences between the major-party nominees. In all cases, the public saw the Republican candidates as conservative on most issues, and most citizens scored the GOP candidates as more conservative than the voters themselves. And in all eight elections the public saw the Democratic candidates as being liberal on most issues, and most citizens viewed the Democratic candidates as more liberal than the voters themselves. As a result, many voters perceived a clear choice based on their understanding of the candidates' policy positions. The candidates presented, in the 1964 campaign slogan of Republican nominee Barry M. Goldwater, "a choice, not an echo." The *average* citizen, however, faced a difficult choice. For many, the Democratic nominees were considered to be as far to the left as the Republicans were to the right. On balance, the net effect of prospective issues was to give neither party a clear advantage.

One of the most important differences among these elections was the mixture of issues that concerned the public. Each election presented its own mixture of policy concerns. Moreover, the general strategies of the candidates on issues differed in each election.[13] In 1980 Jimmy Carter's incumbency was marked by a general perception that he was unable to solve pressing problems. Reagan attacked that weakness both directly (for example, by the question he posed to the public during his debate with Carter, "Are you better off today than you were four years ago?") and indirectly. The indirect attack was more future oriented. Reagan set forth a clear set of proposals designed to convince the public that he would be more likely to solve the nation's problems because he had his own proposals to end soaring inflation, to strengthen the United States militarily, and to regain respect and influence for the United States abroad.

In 1984 the public perceived Reagan as a far more successful president than Carter had been. He chose to run a campaign focused primarily on the theme of how much better things were by 1984 (as illustrated by his advertising slogan, "It's morning in America"). Walter F. Mondale attacked that claim by arguing that Reagan's policies were unfair and by pointing to the rapidly growing budget deficit. Reagan's counter to Mondale's pledge to increase taxes to reduce the deficit was that he, Reagan, would not raise taxes and that Mondale would do so only to spend them on increased government programs (or, in his words, Mondale was another "tax and spend, tax and spend" Democrat).

The 1988 campaign was more similar to the 1984 than to the 1980 campaign. Bush continued to run on the successes of the Reagan-Bush administration and promised no new taxes. ("Read my lips," he said. "No new taxes!") Michael S. Dukakis initially attempted to portray the election as one about "competence" rather than "ideology," arguing that he had demonstrated his competence as governor of Massachusetts. By competent management, he would be able to solve the budget and trade deficit problems, for example. Bush, by implication, was less competent. Bush countered that it really was an election about ideology, that Dukakis was just another liberal Democrat from Massachusetts.

The 1992 election presented yet another type of campaign. Bush initially hoped to be able to run as the president who presided over the "new world order," the post-Soviet world, and he used the success of the Persian Gulf War to augment his claim that he was a successful world leader. Clinton attacked the Bush administration on domestic issues, however, barely discussing foreign affairs at all. He sought to keep the electorate focused on the current economic woes, seeking to get the nation moving again. He argued for substantial reforms of the health care system and raised a number of other issues he expected to appeal to Democrats and to serve as the basis for action, should he become the first Democrat in the White House in twelve years. At the same time, he sought to portray himself not as another "tax and spend," liberal Democrat, but as a moderate, "New Democrat."

In 1996 Clinton ran a campaign typical of a popular incumbent, focusing on what led people to approve of his handling of the presidency and avoiding the mention of too many specific new programs. While he had a catchy slogan (handed to him by Dole), "building a bridge to the 21st century," his policy proposals were a lengthy series of relatively inexpensive, limited programs. Dole, having difficulties deciding whether to emphasize Clinton's personal failings in the first term or to call for different programs for the future, decided to put a significant tax cut proposal at the center of his candidacy under either of those campaign strategies.

In 2000 the candidates debated a broad array of domestic issues—education, health care, social security, and taxes the most prominent among them—often couched in terms of a newfound "problem," federal governmental budget surpluses. Typically, these issues (except for taxes) have favored Democratic contenders, and Republicans often avoided detailed discussions of all except taxes, on the grounds that doing so would make the issues more salient to voters and would highlight the Democratic advantages. Bush, however, spoke out on education and such issues, believing he could undercut the traditional Democratic advantage. For his part, Gore was advantaged by the belief (backed by public opinion polls) that the public was less in favor of tax cuts than usual and more in favor of allocating budget surpluses to buttress popular domestic programs.

THE CONCERNS OF THE ELECTORATE

The first question to ask about prospective voting is what kinds of concerns moved the public. The NES surveys ask, "What do you personally feel are the most important problems facing this country?" In Table 6-3 we have listed the percentage of responses to what respondents claimed was the single most important problem in broad categories of concerns over the eight most recent elections.

In the past four elections, the public was far more concerned about domestic issues than about foreign or defense policies. This lack of concern for foreign policy might have been due to the end of the Cold War, but it also was low in 1976 during the Cold War. Perhaps, then, the low levels reflect the absence of candidate discussion of foreign affairs during the 2000 campaign—which of course was possible in recent years because the Cold War had ended and there were no other troubling international "hot spots" during the campaign period.

The great majority of responses, therefore, concerned domestic issues. In the past eight elections, two major categories of domestic issues dominated. From 1976 through 1992, in good times and bad, by far the more commonly cited issue was a concern about the economy. In 1972, 1996, and 2000 the most frequently cited problems were in the social issues category, and an absolute majority cited some social welfare (such as welfare reform, the environment, or health care) or public order (such as crime, terrorism, or drugs) problem. In 1992 and 1996 nine out of ten respondents named either an economic or a social problem, and in

TABLE 6-3 Most Important Problem as Seen by the Electorate, 1972–2000 (in percentages)

Problem	1972	1976	1980	1984	1988	1992	1996	2000
Economics	*27*	*76*	*56*	*49*	*45*	*64*	*29*	*19*
Unemployment/recession	9	33	10	16	5	23	7	5
Inflation/prices	14	27	33	5	2	—[a]	—[a]	1
Deficit/government spending	1	9	3	19	32	16	13	4
Social issues	*34*	*14*	*7*	*13*	*38*	*28*	*56*	*67*
Social welfare	7	4	3	9	11	17	33	45
Public order	20	8	1	4	19	10	23	21
Foreign and defense	*31*	*4*	*32*	*34*	*10*	*3*	*5*	*10*
Foreign	4	3	9	17	6	2	3	6
Defense	1	1	8	17	3	1	2	4
Functioning of government (competence, corruption, trust, power, etc.)	*4*	*4*	*2*	*2*	*1*	*2*	*5*	*5*
All others	*4*	*3*	*3*	*3*	*6*	*2*	*4*	*0*
Total	100	101	100	101	100	100	100	101
(N)	(842)	(2,337)	(1,352)	(1,780)	(1,657)	(2,003)	(794)	(907)
"Missing"	(63)	(203)	(56)	(163)	(118)	(54)	(27)	(31)
Percentage missing	7	7	4	7	7	2	4	3

Notes: Foreign in 1972 includes 25 percent who cited Vietnam. Foreign in 1980 includes 15 percent who cited Iran. Questions asked of randomly selected half sample in 1972, 1996, and 2000. Weighted *N* in 1976, 1992, 1996, and 2000. The main categories are in italics. All of the subcategories are not included. The total percentages for the subcategories, therefore, will not equal the percentages for the main categories. In 1984 total *N* is 1,943 because 46 respondents were not asked this question, being given a shortened postelection questionnaire. In 1992 the total *N* is 2,057, because 431 respondents either had no postelection interview or were given a shortened form via telephone.

[a] Less than 1 percent of responses.

2000, 86 percent did. From 1972 through 2000 very few cited problems in the "functioning of government" category, such as "gridlock," term limits, other reforms, or government corruption. Finally, in 2000 only 3 percent cited no problem at all.

While the economy and social issues have been by far the dominant concerns of the public over the past three decades, the particular concerns of the public have varied from election to election. In the economy, for example, inflation was a common concern throughout the 1970s, but by 1984, it all but dropped from sight, becoming a literal "asterisk in the polls" in 1992 and 1996, and little more than that in 2000. Unemployment has varied as a concern in rough accord with the actual level of unemployment in the nation. Not surprisingly, concern over the federal budget deficit has also tracked closely the rate of growth (or, in 2000, decline) in the actual deficit. Similarly, in the social issues category, the particular concerns have varied from year to year, most easily understood as following the headlines in the news media and the issues the candidates chose to emphasize in the campaigns. Thus in 1992, not only was Perot's (and Clinton's) focus on the deficit apparent in the public, but so too was Clinton's emphasis on the "health care crisis." By 1996 those concerns had waned somewhat, replaced by crime, education, and welfare policy, while education, health care, and the environment loomed large in 2000.

The concerns of the electorate are the backdrop of the campaign. For example, the decline in concern about the economy was good news for the incumbent. Still, being concerned about a problem does not directly indicate which candidate the voter intends to back. A vote, after all, is a choice among alternatives. To investigate these questions we must look at the voters' issue preferences and their perceptions of where candidates stood on the issues.

ISSUE POSITIONS AND PERCEPTIONS

Since 1972 the NES surveys have included a number of issue scales designed to measure the preferences of the electorate and voters' perceptions of the positions the candidates took on the issues.[14] The questions are therefore especially appropriate for examining prospective issue evaluations. We hasten to add, however, that voters' perceptions of where the incumbent party's nominee stands may well be based in part on what the president has done in office, as well as on the campaign promises he made as the party's nominee. The policy promises of the opposition party candidate may also be judged partly by what his party did when it last held the White House. Nevertheless, the issue scales generally focus on prospective evaluations and are very different from those used to make the retrospective judgments examined in chapter 7.

The issue scales will be used to examine several questions: What alternatives did the voters believe the candidates were offering? To what extent did the voters have issue preferences of their own and relatively clear perceptions of candidates'

FIGURE 6-2   Example of a 7-Point Issue Scale: Jobs and Standard of Living
              Guarantees

Question asked by interviewers:

> Some people feel the government in Washington should see to it that every person has
> a job and a good standard of living. Suppose these people are at one end of a scale,
> at point 1. Others think the government should just let each person get ahead on their
> own. Suppose these people are at the other end, at point 7. And, of course, some other
> people have opinions somewhere in between at points 2, 3, 4, 5, or 6.
>
> Where would you place yourself on this scale, or haven't you thought much about this?
>
> Where would you place Al Gore on this issue?
>
> [Where would you place] George W. Bush?

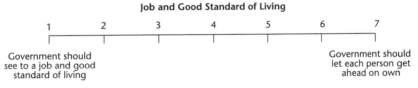

Source: 2000 National Election Studies, Pre-Election Survey, Respondent Booklet.

positions? Finally, how strongly were voters' preferences and perceptions related
to their choice of candidates?

Figure 6-2 presents the text of one of the 7-point issue scale questions, along
with an example of an illustration presented to respondents as they considered
their responses. Figure 6-3 shows the 7-point issue scales used in the 2000 NES
survey. The figure presents the average (median) position of the respondents
(labeled "s" for self) and the average (median) perception of the positions of
Gore and Bush.[15] Issues asked in 2000 probe the respondents' own preferences
and perceptions of the major-party nominees on whether government spending
should be reduced or increased in providing for greater social services; whether
defense spending should be increased or decreased; the jobs scale as shown in
Figure 6-2; whether the government should provide aid to blacks or whether
they should get ahead on their own; whether environmental protections should
or should not come at the expense of jobs; whether government regulations of
the environment should be increased or decreased; and whether women should
play a role equal with men in society or whether they should stay at home ("a
woman's place is in the home").[16]

These issues were selected because they were controversial and generally
measured longstanding partisan divisions. As a result, the average citizen comes
out looking reasonably moderate on these issues—in five out of seven cases,
between the positions corresponding to the average placements of the two candidates. On many issues in 2000, the typical citizen is very near the center of the
scale, especially on the defense spending, jobs and standard of living, and aid to
minorities. These average citizen stances are quite similar from one election to

FIGURE 6-3   Median Self-Placement of the Electorate and the Electorate's
Placement of Candidates on Issue Scales, 2000

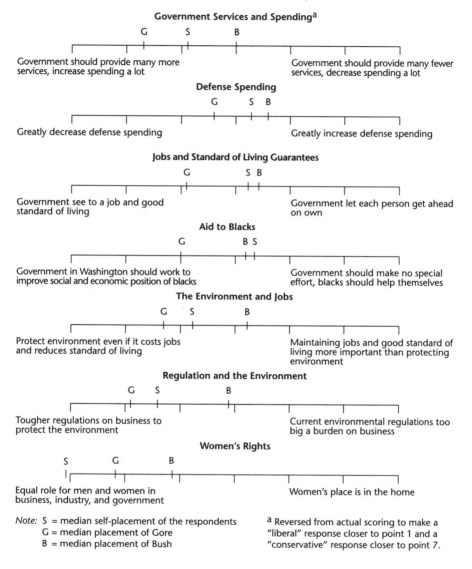

Note: S = median self-placement of the respondents
        G = median placement of Gore
        B = median placement of Bush

[a] Reversed from actual scoring to make a
"liberal" response closer to point 1 and a
"conservative" response closer to point 7.

the next (although self placement on the jobs scale was rather more conservative in Reagan's initial victory in 1980 and again in George W. Bush's victory in 2000). The average citizen on the government spending and services scale has typically been just to the left of the middle, rather like the position in 2000. In 1996 the average response was a noticeable step to the right, perhaps reflecting the new welfare bill, the "Republican revolution" of 1994, and/or Clinton's claim in the

1996 State of the Union address that the "era of big government is over." For whatever reason or reasons, that step to the right in 1996 was reversed in 2000, reflecting an unusual degree of change over time in the past two elections. In those surveys in which the same women's rights scale as in 2000 was used (all but 1984), most citizens place themselves about as far to the "equal role" end as possible, just as in 2000. The two environmental scales were new to 1996. The average citizen placement was a full point to the environmental side of the middle in that year, suggesting that the reaction against House initiatives in the 104th Congress designed to cut support for the environment reflected beliefs in the public at large. The average position of the electorate was very similar in 2000.

The public has seen the Democratic candidate as more liberal and the Republican candidate as more conservative than the position of the average member of the public on every issue scale used between 1980 and 2000. The result is that the typical citizen sees the candidates as taking very different positions. In 2000 the candidates were placed about 1.3 units apart, approximately one-quarter of the maximum difference possible. The differences were least on the women's rights and the defense spending scales. Conversely, the difference between the two candidates was 1.6 on the government spending and services scale, reflecting the core of the longstanding partisan divide, and it was 1.8 for the scale measuring regulation and the environment, combining partisan differences with an issue Gore had long championed personally. While these differences are substantial, they are less than the differences in several preceding elections. In 1996, for example, which featured many of the same issue scales, the average difference perceived between Clinton and Dole was 1.7 points, noticeably further apart than Gore and Bush were seen to be. Still, the differences between Gore and Bush were seen to be substantial.

While voters saw clear differences between the candidates, the average voter faced a difficult choice. Gore was seen to be about as far to the left of the average respondent as Bush was seen to be to the right. On average Gore was 0.83 units to the left and Bush 0.78 units to the right of the average citizen. While Bush held a slight advantage, the key word is slight. Gore was in an especially favorable position on the environment scales, but that was balanced by a large Bush advantage on the jobs and the aid to minorities scales, where Bush was very close to the average respondent and Gore was more than a point to the left. Of course, these data are averages, not where specific individuals stand and see the candidates. To consider a voter's choices, we must look beyond these averages.

ISSUE VOTING CRITERIA

The Problem

Since voting is an individual action, we must look at the preferences of individuals to see whether prospective issues influenced their votes. In fact, the question of prospective voting is controversial. Angus Campbell and the other authors of the classic study of the American electorate, *The American Voter,* point out that the public is often ill informed about public policy and may not be able to vote on the basis of issues.[17] They asked what information voters would need before an issue could influence the decision of how to vote, and they specified three conditions. First, the voters must hold an opinion on the issue; second, they must see what the government is doing on the issue; and third, they must see a difference between the policies of the two major parties. According to the authors' analysis, only about one-quarter to one-third of the electorate in 1956 could meet these three conditions.

Although it is impossible to replicate the analysis in *The American Voter,* we can adapt the authors' procedures to the 2000 electorate. In some ways, more recent NES data focus more directly on the actual choice citizens must make—a choice among the candidates. The first criterion is whether respondents claim to have an opinion on the issue. This is measured by whether they placed themselves on the issue scale. Second, the respondents should have some perception of the positions taken by the candidates on an issue. This was measured by whether they could place both major-party candidates on that issue.[18] Although some voters might perceive the position of one candidate and vote on that basis, prospective voting involves a comparison among alternatives, so the expressed ability to perceive the stands of the contenders seems a minimal requirement of prospective issue voting. Third, the voter must see a difference between the positions of the candidates. Failing to see a difference means that the voter perceived no choice on the issue.

A voter might be able to satisfy these criteria but misperceive the offerings of the candidates. This leads to a fourth condition, which we are able to measure more systematically than was possible in 1956: Does the respondent accurately perceive the relative positions of the two major-party candidates—that is, see Bush as more "conservative" than Gore? This criterion does not demand that the voter have an accurate perception of what the candidate proposes, but it does expect the voter to see that Gore, for instance, favored more spending on social services than Bush did.[19]

The Data

In Table 6-4 we report the percentages of the sample that met the four criteria on the seven issue scales used in 2000. We also show the average proportion that met these criteria for all scales and compare those averages to comparable averages for all issue scales used in the seven preceding elections.[20] As can be seen in column I of Table 6-4, most people felt capable of placing themselves on the issue scales, and this capability was common to all election years.[21]

For all seven issues, fewer people could place both the candidates and themselves on an issue scale than could place just themselves, as can be seen in column II of Table 6-4. Nonetheless, seven in ten respondents met these two crite-

TABLE 6-4   Four Criteria for Issue Voting, 2000, and Comparisons with 1972–1996 Presidential Elections (in percentages)

Issue scale	Percentage of Sample Who			
	I Placed self on scale	II Placed both candidates on scale[a]	III Saw differences between Gore and Bush	IV Saw Gore more "liberal" than Bush
Government spending/services	83	73	61	51
Defense spending	80	66	52	39
Jobs and standard of living	89	72	57	44
Aid to blacks	91	70	52	43
Jobs and the environment	91	67	51	40
Regulation and the environment	77	60	46	39
Women's rights	97	73	39	29
Average[b]				
2000 (7)	87	69	51	41
1996 (9)	89	80	65	55
1992 (3)	85	71	66	52
1988 (7)	86	66	52	43
1984 (7)	84	73	62	53
1980 (9)	82	61	51	43
1976 (9)	84	58	39	26
1972 (8)	90	65	49	41

Note: Columns II, III, and IV compare the Democratic and Republican nominees (Anderson, Perot, and Nader excluded in 1980, 1992, 1996, and 2000, respectively).

[a] Until 1996, respondents who could not place themselves on a scale were not asked to place the candidates on that issue scale. While they were asked to do so in 1996 and 2000, we have excluded them from further calculations to maintain comparability with prior surveys.
[b] Number in parentheses is the number of issue scales included in the average for each election year survey.

ria in 2000. Notice that there was relatively little variation across issues: 60 to 73 percent met these criteria on each issue scale. The relatively consistent ability to satisfy the criteria is similar to that obtained in 1984 and thereafter, but different from findings in earlier elections. In 1980, for instance, there were three issue scales on which fewer than half of the respondents placed themselves and both candidates. The average of nearly 70 percent who met these two conditions in

2000 is noticeably less than 1996, considerably greater than 1976, and otherwise at a level similar to the other elections, especially 1992.

As can be seen in column III of Table 6-4, only half of the sample met the first two criteria and also saw a difference between the positions of Bush and Gore. The 2000 result is considerably lower than the high-water-mark elections of 1984, 1992, and 1996, substantially greater than 1976, and quite like the marks achieved in 1972, 1980, and 1988. What are we to conclude about these differences in the ability of the electorate to satisfy the criteria and thus to be able to vote on the basis of issues? It seems highly unlikely that the ability of the public to comprehend the electoral process varies so greatly from election to election. Note that there is very little difference among elections in self-placement on issue scales. Rather, the differences are due to perceptions of the candidates' positions. The differences between the election of 1976 and the elections of 1984, 1992, and 1996 in particular first appear in the ability to place both candidates on the scales. Perhaps relatively few people could place both candidates in 1976 because Gerald R. Ford had not run for president before and had been the incumbent for only two years, and Jimmy Carter was a relatively unknown challenger. Perhaps other elections had higher scores because the incumbent party's candidate had served four or more years in the presidency or the vice presidency. The differences become especially pronounced, however, in the electorate's ability to characterize the candidates' positions. In 1984 the candidates adopted particularly distinctive positions on issues, and this relative clarity was perceived by the electorate. The same seems to be true in 1996. In 2000, as in 1972, 1980, and 1988, the candidates were only slightly less distinct, and the electorate saw the differences only slightly less clearly. In 1976, by contrast, Ford and Carter were generally described as moderates, albeit moderately conservative and moderately liberal, respectively. The electorate reacted to the relative lack of differences.

In sum, we agree with Morris P. Fiorina's argument that failure to satisfy the criteria for issue voting does not mean that the electorate has ill-formed preferences and perceptions.[22] Rather, the electorate's ability to perceive differences between the candidates varies because political conditions differ from election to election, and these differences result mainly from differences in the strategies candidates follow. Thus the "quality" of the responses to these issue questions is based in part on how clearly the candidates articulate their issue positions and on how distinctly the alternative policy platforms are presented to the public.

The data in column IV reflect the ability of the electorate to discern distinctions between the candidates' policy offerings. Averaging these issues together, we see that in 2000 only four in ten of the respondents satisfied all four issue-voting conditions, the final one being that they saw Gore as more liberal than Bush. The 2000 data trail the findings for 1984, 1992, and 1996 in these terms, and is quite similar to 1972, 1980, and 1988. In this case once again, the 1976 election stands out in very sharp contrast, as barely more than one in four voters could assess the relative positions of the two candidates.

The data in Table 6-4 suggest that the potential for prospective issue voting was about moderate in 2000. Therefore, we might expect these issues to be reasonably closely related to voter choice, as it was in the elections, such as 1972, 1980, and 1988, that most resembled 2000 in these terms. We will examine voter choice on these issues in two ways. First, how often did people vote for the closer candidate on each issue? Second, how strongly related to the vote is the set of all issues taken together?

APPARENT ISSUE VOTING IN 2000

Issue Criteria and Voting on Each Issue

The first question is to what extent did people who were closer to a candidate on a given issue actually vote for that candidate? That is, how strong is apparent issue voting?[23] In Table 6-5 we report the proportion of major-party voters who voted for Gore by where they placed themselves on the issue scales. We divided the seven points into the set of positions that were closer to where the average citizen placed Bush and Gore (see Figure 6-2).[24]

As can be seen in Table 6-5, there is a clear relationship between the voters' issue positions and the candidate they supported on six of the seven scales—all but the women's rights issue. Those who adopted positions at the "liberal" end of each scale were very likely to vote for Gore. If we define liberal as adopting position 1 or 2, he received about two out of three votes or more on six of those seven scales. Gore rarely received two out of five votes from those at the conservative end of the scales, while those with moderate views on each issue fell in between these two extremes of support. The pattern of support we would expect from voting on the basis of these issues is particularly clear on those issues that have long defined the traditional cleavages between the two parties (the top four scales on the table and probably regulation and the environment). Over these issues and, indeed, nearly all of the issues, then, there are substantial relationships between the public's opinions and their perceptions of candidates on prospective issues.

The information on issues can be summarized, as it is in Table 6-6, to illustrate what happened when voters met the various conditions for issue voting. In the first column of Table 6-6, we report the percentage of major-party voters who placed themselves closer to the average perception of Bush or Gore and who voted for the closer candidate. To be more specific, the denominator is the total number of major-party voters who placed themselves closer to the electorate's perception of Bush or of Gore. The numerator is the total number of major-party voters who were both closer to Gore and voted for him plus the total number of major-party voters who were both closer to Bush and voted for him.

If voting were unrelated to issue positions, we would expect 50 percent of voters to vote for the closer candidate on average. In 2000, 60 percent voted for the closer candidate. This is a higher percentage on average than in 1976, but it is

TABLE 6-5 Major-Party Voters Who Voted for Gore, by Seven-Point Issue Scales, 2000 (in percentages)

Issue scale	1	2	3	Closer to median perception of Gore	4	5	6	7	Closer to median perception of Bush	(N)
Government spending/services[a] (N)[b]	73 (56)	70 (63)	75 (93)		50 (153)	17 (56)	16 (30)	8 (25)		(476)
Defense spending (N)	60 (12)	74 (18)	80 (39)		65 (120)	47 (138)	37 (92)	29 (44)		(463)
Jobs and standard of living (N)	68 (33)	83 (22)	75 (59)		67 (88)	53 (112)	34 (109)	41 (70)		(493)
Aid to blacks (N)	75 (19)	71 (21)	68 (48)		63 (139)	42 (85)	43 (98)	46 (94)		(504)
Jobs and the environment (N)	74 (50)	60 (78)	53 (88)		47 (161)	42 (70)	36 (32)	71 (21)		(500)
Regulation and the environment (N)	71 (90)	63 (82)	61 (86)		42 (109)	32 (42)	28 (30)	13 (19)		(458)
Women's rights (N)	63 (317)	39 (82)	46 (37)		33 (53)	37 (16)	80 (11)	47 (14)		(530)

[a] Reversed from actual scoring to make a "liberal" response closer to 1 and a "conservative" response closer to 7.
[b] Numbers in parentheses are the totals on which percentages are based. Numbers are weighted.

TABLE 6-6   Apparent Issue Voting, 2000, and Comparisons with 1972–1996 (in percentages)

Issue scale	Placed self on issue scale	Met all four issue voting criteria	Placed self but failed to meet all three other criteria
	Percentage of voters who voted for closer candidate and		
Government spending/services	68	79	54
Defense spending	63	67	42
Jobs and standard of living	57	74	42
Aid to blacks	54	68	37
Jobs and the environment	57	68	38
Regulation and the environment	65	77	44
Women's rights	58	43	25
Averages[a]			
2000 (7)	60	68	40
1996 (9)	63	74	41
1992 (3)	62	70	48
1988 (7)	62	71	45
1984 (7)	65	73	46
1980 (9)	63	71	48
1976 (9)	57	70	50
1972 (8)	66	76	55

Note: An "apparent issue vote" is a vote for the candidate closer to one's position on an issue scale. The closer candidate is determined by comparing self-placement to the median placements of the two candidates on the scale as a whole. Respondents who did not place themselves or who were equidistant from the two candidates are excluded from the calculations.

[a] Number in parentheses is the number of issue scales included in the average for each election year survey.

about the same as in other elections. These figures do not tell the whole story, however, for those who placed themselves on an issue but failed to meet some other criterion were unlikely to have cast a vote based on that issue. In the second column of Table 6-6, we report the percentage of those who voted for the closer candidate on each issue among voters who met all four conditions on that issue. The third column reports the percentage that voted for the closer candidate among voters who failed to meet at least one of the three remaining conditions.

Those respondents who met all four conditions were much more likely to vote for the closer candidate on any issue. Indeed, there is relatively little difference, on average, across all eight elections. In each case, about seven of ten such voters supported the closer candidate, although 1972 and 1996 were unusually high and 2000 was, by a very small amount, the lowest. For those respondents who failed to meet the last three of the conditions on issue voting, in contrast, voting was essentially random with respect to the issues.

The strong similarity of all eight election averages in the second and third columns suggests that issue voting seems more prevalent in some elections than others because elections differ in the number of people who clearly perceive differences between the candidates. In all elections, at least seven in ten who satisfied all four conditions voted consistently with their issue preferences; in all elections, those who did not satisfy all the conditions on perceptions of candidates voted essentially randomly with respect to individual issues. As we saw earlier, the degree to which such perceptions vary from election to election depends more on the strategies of the candidates than on the qualities of the voters. Therefore, the relatively low percentage of apparent issue voting in 1976, for instance, results from the perception of small differences between the two rather moderate candidates. The larger magnitude of apparent issue voting in 2000, as in most other elections, results from the greater clarity with which most people saw the positions of Bush and Gore.

The Balance of Issues Measure

Prospective issue voting means that voters compare the full set of policy proposals made by the candidates. As we have noted, nearly every issue is strongly related to the vote so we might expect the set of all issues to be even more strongly so. To examine this relationship, we constructed an overall assessment of the issue scales, what we call the balance of issues measure. We did so by giving individuals a score of +1 if their positions on an issue scale were closer to the average perception of Bush, a −1 if their positions were closer to the average perception of Gore, and a score of 0 if they had no preference on an issue. The scores for all seven issue scales were added together, creating a measure that ranged from −7 to +7. For instance, respondents who were closer to the average perception of Gore's positions on all seven scales received a score of −7. A negative score indicated that the respondent was, on balance, closer to the public's perception of Gore, while a positive score indicated the respondent was, overall, closer to the public's perception of Bush.[25] We collapsed this 15-point measure into seven categories, running from strongly Democratic through neutral to strongly Republican.[26] The results are reported in Table 6-7.

As can be seen in Table 6-7 A, one in twenty respondents was strongly Democratic; one in seven was strongly Republican. Three in ten were moderately or slightly Democratic, somewhat fewer than the four in ten in the two comparable Republican categories. Thus the balance of issues measure tilted in the Republican direction. As we will see in the next section, two other issues we analyze were skewed slightly in the Democratic direction, and as a result, we conclude that prospective issues favored neither party overall.

TABLE 6-7 Distribution of the Electorate on the Net Balance of Issues Measure and Major-Party Vote, 2000 (in percentages)

				Net balance of issues				
	Strongly Democratic	Moderately Democratic	Slightly Democratic	Neutral	Slightly Republican	Moderately Republican	Strongly Republican	Total (N)
A. Distribution of Responses								
	5	10	20	9	24	17	14	99 (969)
B. Major-Party Voters Who Voted for Gore								
Percent	97	74	67	64	61	36	18	54%
(N)	(34)	(51)	(91)	(54)	(125)	(93)	(91)	(539)

Note: Numbers are weighted.

The balance of issues measure was strongly related to the vote, as the findings for the individual issues would suggest (see Table 6-7 B). Gore won the vast majority of the votes from those in the strongly Democratic category, and three of four from the moderately and two of three from the slightly Democratic categories. He won six in ten votes from those in the neutral and the slightly Republican categories. His support dropped off dramatically from that point. Indeed, decline in Democratic voting across the net balance of issues categories in 2000 is as strong as in 1972 and nearly as strong as in 1984 and 1996, the three strongest cases in the past eight elections.

The Issues of Abortion and Gun Control

We give special attention to the public policy controversies about abortion and gun control for two reasons. First, both are especially divisive issues. The Republican national platform has taken a strong "pro-life" stand since 1980, while the Democratic Party has become increasingly "pro-choice." Indeed, abortion is one of the most contentious issues in government at all levels, between the two parties, and within the public. President Clinton's views did not satisfy the strongest of pro-choice advocates, but he did veto a controversial measure to outlaw so-called "partial birth abortions," because, he said, it did not include safeguards for the life and health of the mother. His appointments to the Supreme Court strengthened the pro-choice end of the spectrum, and another four years of the Clinton-Gore administration through election of Gore might have given him a sufficient number of appointments to all but end the possibility of reversing the *Roe v. Wade* decision. George W. Bush took a consistently less pro-life stance than had Ronald Reagan, but like his father, he was clearly far closer to that end of the spectrum than was his Democratic opponent.

Gun control policies have also divided the two parties, as well as dividing interest groups and citizens. The Republican Party has tended to emphasize the importance of the Second Amendment to the Constitution, which bars infringement of the right to bear arms. The Democratic Party and the Clinton-Gore administration were active in seeking ways to limit easy access to weapons. They championed the eventual passage of the Brady Bill, for example, a measure named for James Brady, Reagan's press secretary who was wounded in an assassination attempt, and who, along with his wife, have actively sought passage of the bill named in his honor.

The second reason for examining these issues is that they include other policy questions about which respondents were asked their own views as well as what they thought Bush's and Gore's positions were. With respect to abortion, respondents were given the following four alternatives:

1. By law, abortion should never be permitted.
2. The law should permit abortion only in the case of rape, incest, or when the woman's life is in danger.

3. The law should permit abortion for reasons *other than* rape, incest, or danger to the woman's life, but only after the need for the abortion has been clearly established.
4. By law, a woman should always be able to obtain an abortion as a matter of personal choice.

The electorate's responses were clearly toward the pro-choice end of the measure. Among the major-party voters who chose among these four alternatives, 40 percent said that abortion should be a matter of personal choice. Seventeen percent were willing to allow abortions for reasons other than rape, incest, or danger to the woman's life, while 31 percent said abortion should be allowed only under those conditions. Only 12 percent said that abortion should never be permitted.

Among major-party voters, there was a strong relationship between a voter's opinion and the way he or she voted. Table 6-8 presents the percentage of major-party voters who voted for Gore according to their view on the abortion issue. While two in three of those who believed that abortion should be a matter of personal choice supported Gore, six in ten who thought it should never be permitted or permitted only in the cases of rape, incest, or danger to the health of the woman voted against him.

Because the survey asked respondents what they thought Gore's and Bush's positions were, we can see if the basic issue-voting criteria apply. If they do, we can expect to find a very strong relationship between the respondents' positions and how they voted if they met three additional conditions, beyond having an opinion on this issue themselves. First, they had to have an opinion about where the candidates stood on the issue. Second, they had to see a difference between the positions of the two major-party nominees. Third, to cast a policy-related vote reflecting the actual positions of the candidates, they had to recognize that Gore held a more pro-choice position than Bush. In 1992 seven out of ten major-party voters met all these conditions, and in 1996 two out of three did. In 2000, however, only half of the major-party voters met all of these conditions.

Among voters who met all of these conditions, there was a very strong relationship between policy preferences and voting. We see this relationship by reading across the second row of Table 6-8. Among major-party voters who thought that abortions should never be allowed, only one in four supported Gore. Among those who thought that the decision to have an abortion should be a matter of personal choice, more than three out of four voted for him. The final row of Table 6-8 shows the relationship of issue preferences and the vote among voters who did *not* see Gore as more pro-choice than Bush. Among such voters, there is a much weaker relationship. In fact, voters who were pro-choice were more likely to vote for Bush than those who held a right-to-life position. Similar results are found in 1992 and 1996.[27]

In 2000, for the first time, respondents were asked about their preferences and their perceptions of candidate stances on the issue of gun control. In this case, researchers used a five-point scale, which asked whether purchase of guns should

TABLE 6-8 Percentage of Major-Party Voters Who Voted for Gore, by Opinion about Abortion and What They Believe Bush's and Gore's Positions Are, 2000

	Respondent's position on abortion							
	Abortion should never be permitted		Abortion should be permitted only in the case of rape, incest, or health of the woman		Abortion should be permitted for other reasons, but only if a need is established		Abortion should be a matter of personal choice	
	%	(N)	%	(N)	%	(N)	%	(N)
All major-party voters	40	(123)	39	(319)	49	(170)	67	(414)
Major-party voters who placed both candidates, who saw a difference between them, and who saw Gore as more "pro-choice" than Bush	24	(72)	23	(149)	48	(86)	77	(205)
Major-party voters who did not meet all three of these conditions	64	(50)	54	(168)	50	(84)	58	(206)

Note: Numbers in parentheses are the totals on which the percentages are based. Numbers are weighted.

TABLE 6-9 Percentage of Major-Party Voters Who Voted for Gore, by Opinion about Gun Control and What They Believe Bush's and Gore's Positions Are, 2000

	Respondent's position on gun control											
	Purchase should be a lot more difficult		Purchase should be somewhat more difficult		Keep rules about the same		Purchase should be somewhat easier		Purchase should be a lot easier	
	%	(N)	%	(N)	%	(N)	%	(N)	%	(N)
All major-party voters	68	(491)	54	(113)	35	(404)	22	(21)	34	(19)
Major-party voters who placed both candidates, who saw a difference between them, and who saw Gore as more for gun control than Bush	83	(243)	61	(64)	24	(244)	20	(20)	30	(16)
Major-party voters who did not meet all three of these conditions	53	(248)	46	(48)	51	(159)	—		—	

Note: Numbers in parentheses are the totals on which the percentages are based. Numbers are weighted. "—" denotes fewer than 5 observations.

be a lot more difficult than now, or somewhat more difficult, whether the rules should be kept the same, or whether they should be made somewhat easier or a lot easier. Table 6-9 presents information about this issue scale comparable to that for the abortion scale in Table 6-8.

Most evident in the table is that very few major-party voters thought purchasing of guns should be made easier. So few are there in these two categories that the scale effectively reduces to three options; two for making purchases harder and one for maintaining current rules. About six in ten prefer to make purchases more difficult, with four in ten desiring to maintain the status quo.

The second thing to notice is that preferences on this issue are strongly related to the major-party vote. Gore won two in three votes from those believing purchases should be much harder, while he carried a slight majority of those who felt purchases should be somewhat harder, and he won only one in three votes from the remainder. The third observation is that satisfying the conditions for casting an issue vote greatly strengthens the relationship between voting for Gore and stance on gun control. Among this set of voters, Gore won the votes of greater than four in five who wanted purchases to be a lot more difficult and three in five votes of those wanting purchases to be somewhat more difficult. Among the remaining voters, he won only one vote in four. Among voters who failed to meet all of these issue voting conditions, the vote was similar in every category of response.

The results for abortion and gun control and, indeed, for all prospective issues do not prove that policy preferences shape voting decisions. Some voters may project the position they themselves favor onto the candidate they favor. But it does appear that unless all the basic conditions for issue voting are present, issue voting does not occur. When the conditions are present, there can be a strong relationship between the position voters hold and their choice between the major-party candidates.

CONCLUSION

The findings suggest that for major-party voters prospective issues were quite important in the 2000 election, slightly less strongly so than in 1996, but nearly at that high-water-mark election. Even so, studying prospective issues alone cannot account for Gore's narrow victory in the popular vote. Those for whom prospective issues gave a clear choice voted consistently with those issues. Most people, however, were located between the candidates as the electorate saw them. Indeed, on most issues, the majority of people were relatively moderate, and the candidates were seen as more liberal and more conservative, respectively.

This line of reasoning suggests that voters took prospective issues into account in 2000 but that they also considered other factors. In the next chapter, we will see that the second form of policy voting, that based on retrospective evaluations, was among those other factors, as it has been in all seven of the previous presidential elections.

Chapter 7

Presidential Performance
and Candidate Choice

◆◆◆

In the aftermath of this very close election, many Democrats, as well as pundits, criticized Al Gore for his failure to campaign on the successes of the Clinton-Gore administration. They believed that, by doing so, he could have reminded voters of the positive performance of the American economy in the late 1990s. These criticisms were easy to understand because there has often been a close correspondence between the performance of the economy and the electoral fortunes of the party of the incumbent president, both directly and indirectly; a strong economy has enhanced the approval ratings of the incumbent, thereby strengthening that party's support among the public. Indeed, in 1988 George W. Bush's father was aided in his bid to rise from vice president to president by the strong economy during the Reagan-Bush administration. In 1992, by contrast, voters concluded that it was time to "throw the rascals out," voting against George Bush as incumbent and electing Bill Clinton.[1]

In this chapter, we will look at the evidence to see if, in spite of lesser emphasis by Gore, voters may have concluded in 2000, as they had in 1996 and 1984, that "one good term deserves another." Such appeals to the performance of the incumbent administration, appeals about the successes or failures of earlier administrations, and assessments of what previous performance indicates about the future are attempts to benefit from retrospective evaluations.

Retrospective evaluations are concerns about policy, but they differ significantly from the prospective evaluations we considered in the last chapter. Retrospective evaluations are, as the name suggests, concerned about the past. While the past may be prologue to the future, retrospective evaluations also focus on outcomes, with what actually happened, rather than on the policy means for achieving outcomes—the heart of prospective evaluations.

In this chapter, we focus primarily on prosperity and the public's approval of the incumbent. We shall see that such assessments by the public played a strong role in shaping not only the candidates' strategies but also voters' attitudes toward the candidates and the parties and voters' choices on Election Day. We also shall see, however, that the strength of these relationships was somewhat weaker than in some prior elections, perhaps supporting the arguments of those who claimed that Gore should have emphasized his ties to the administration. We cannot, however, know whether doing so would have strengthened those relationships nor can we know if doing so would have cost Gore support by raising the personal failings of the incumbent administration, as Gore worried would happen.

WHAT IS RETROSPECTIVE VOTING?

An individual who voted for the incumbent party's candidate because the incumbent was, in the voter's opinion, a successful president is said to have cast a retrospective vote. A voter who votes for the opposition because, in the voter's opinion, the incumbent has been unsuccessful has also cast a retrospective vote. In other words, retrospective voting decisions are based on evaluations of the course of politics over the last term in office and on evaluations of how much the incumbent should be held responsible for what good or ill occurred. V. O. Key Jr. popularized this argument by suggesting that the voter might be "a rational god of vengeance and of reward."[2]

Obviously, the more closely the candidate of one party can be tied to the actions of the incumbent, the more likely it is that voters will decide retrospectively. The incumbent president cannot escape such evaluations, and the incumbent vice president is usually identified with (and often chooses to identify himself with) the administration's performance. As a result, the electorate has often been able to play the role of Key's "rational god," because an incumbent president or vice-president stood for elections in twenty-two of the twenty-six presidential elections since 1900 (all but 1908, 1920, 1928, and 1952).

The perspective offered by Key has three aspects. First, retrospective voters are oriented toward outcomes rather than the policy means to achieve them. Second, these voters evaluate the performance of the incumbent only, all but ignoring the opposition. Finally, they evaluate what has been done, paying little attention to what the candidates promise to do in the future.

Anthony Downs presents a different picture of retrospective voting.[3] He argues that voters look to the past to understand what the incumbent party's candidate will do in the future. According to Downs, parties are basically consistent in their goals, methods, and ideologies over time. Therefore, the past performance of both parties' candidates, but especially that of the incumbent, may prove relevant for making predictions about their future conduct. Because it takes time and effort to evaluate campaign promises and because promises are just words, voters find it faster, easier, and safer to use past performance to project the administration's actions for the next four years. Downs also emphasizes that retrospective evaluations are used in making comparisons among the alternatives standing for election. Key sees a retrospective referendum on the incumbent's party alone. Downs believes that retrospective evaluations are used to compare the candidates as well as to provide a guide to the future. In 1996, for example, Clinton attempted to tie Dole to the performance of congressional Republicans since they had assumed the majority in 1994 (an attempt made easier by virtue of Dole's having served as majority leader in the Senate throughout most of the preceding two years). Clinton pointedly referred to the 104th Congress as the "Dole-Gingrich" Congress.

Morris P. Fiorina advances another view of retrospective voting, one that is in many respects an elaboration and extension of Downs's thesis. For our purposes, Fiorina's major addition to the Downsian perspective is his argument that party identification plays a central role. He argues that "citizens monitor party promises and performances over time, encapsulate their observations in a summary judgment termed 'party identification,' and rely on this core of previous experience when they assign responsibility for current societal conditions and evaluate ambiguous platforms designed to deal with uncertain futures."[4] We will return to Fiorina's views on partisanship in the following chapter.

Retrospective voting and voting according to issue positions, as analyzed in chapter 6, differ significantly. The difference lies in how concerned people are with societal outcomes and how concerned they are with the means to achieve desired outcomes. For example, everyone prefers economic prosperity. The disagreement among political decision makers lies in how best to achieve it. At the voters' level, however, the central question is whether people care only about achieving prosperity or whether they care, or even are able to judge, how to achieve this desired goal. Perhaps they looked at high inflation and interest rates in 1980 and said, "We tried Carter's approach, and it failed. Let's try something else—anything else." They may have noted the long run of relative economic prosperity from 1983 to 1988 and said, "Whatever Reagan did, it worked. Let's keep it going by putting his vice president in office." In 1996 they may have agreed with Clinton that he had presided over a successful economy, and they were sufficiently convinced that they should remain with Clinton's programs.

Economic policies and foreign affairs issues are especially likely to be discussed in these terms because they share several characteristics. First, the outcomes are clear, and most voters can judge whether they approve of the results. Inflation and unemployment are high or low; the economy is growing or it is not. The country is at war or at peace; the world is stable or unstable. Second, there is often near consensus on what the desired outcomes are; no one disagrees with peace or prosperity, with world stability or low unemployment. Third, the means to achieve these ends are often very complex, and information is hard to understand; experts as well as candidates and parties disagree over the specific ways to achieve the desired ends.

As issues, therefore, peace and prosperity differ sharply from policy areas such as abortion and gun control, in which there is vigorous disagreement over ends among experts, leaders, and the public. On still other issues, people value both ends *and* means. The classic cases often involve the question of whether it is appropriate for government to take action in that area at all. Reagan was fond of saying, "Government isn't the solution to our problems, government *is* the problem." For instance, should the government provide national health insurance? Few disagree with the end of better health care, but they do disagree over the appropriate means to achieve it. The choice of means involves some of the basic philosophical and ideological differences that have divided the Republicans from the Democrats for decades.[5] For example, in 1984 and 1988 the Democratic nominees agreed with Reagan that we were in a period of economic prosperity and that prosperity is a good thing. What Walter F. Mondale emphasized in 1984 was that Reagan's policies were unfair to the disadvantaged. Mondale, like Michael S. Dukakis in 1988, and Clinton and H. Ross Perot in 1992, also claimed that Reagan's and Bush's policies, by creating such large deficits, were sowing the seeds for future woes. Clearly, then, disagreement was not over the ends, but over the means and the consequences that would follow from using different means to achieve the shared ends.

Two basic conditions must be met before retrospective evaluations can affect voting choices. First, individuals must connect their concerns (especially the problems they feel to be the most important) with the incumbent and the actions he took in office. For example, this condition would not be present if a voter blamed earlier administrations with sowing the seeds that grew into the huge deficits of the 1980s, blamed a profligate Congress, or even believed that the problems were beyond anyone's control. Second, individuals, in the Downs-Fiorina view, must compare their evaluations of the incumbent's past performance with what they believe the nominee of the opposition party would do. For example, if they had thought Clinton's performance on the economy weak, voters might have compared Dole's programs and concluded they would not be any better or might even make things worse.

In this second condition, a certain asymmetry exists, one that benefits the incumbent. Even if the incumbent's performance has been weak in a certain area, the challenger still has to convince voters that he could do better. It is even more difficult for a challenger to convince voters who think the incumbent's performance has been strong that the challenger would be even stronger. This asymmetry that had advantaged Republican candidates in the 1980s worked to Dole's disadvantage in 1996 and to Bush's in 2000.

We examine next some illustrative retrospective evaluations and study their impact on voter choice. In chapter 6 we looked at issue scales designed to measure the public's evaluations of candidates' promises. Of course, the public can evaluate not only the promises of the incumbent party but also its actions. We will compare promises with performance in this chapter, but one must remember that the distinctions are not as sharp in practice as they are in principle.[6] Of course, the Downs-Fiorina view is that past actions and projections about the future are necessarily intertwined.

EVALUATIONS OF GOVERNMENTAL PERFORMANCE

What do you consider the most important problem facing the country, and how do you feel the government in Washington has been handling the problem? These questions are designed to measure retrospective judgments. Table 7-1 compares the respondents' evaluations of governmental performance on the problem that each respondent identified as the single most important one facing the country. We are able to track such evaluations for the past eight elections.[7] The most striking findings in Table 7-1 A are that in 2000 few thought the government was doing a good job, but that there was a nearly even division between those who thought the government was doing poorly and those who felt it was doing only fairly. This makes 2000 look most like 1976, 1984, and 1996—two elections that did return the incumbent party and one that (barely) did not. In contrast, 1980 and 1992 were elections with even more negative opinions and in which the incumbent party was soundly defeated.[8]

If the voter is a rational god of vengeance and reward, we can expect to find a strong relationship between the evaluation of government performance and the vote. Such is indeed the case for all elections, as seen in Table 7-1 B. From seven to nine out of ten major-party voters who thought the government was doing a good job on the most important problem voted for the incumbent party's nominee in each election. In 1996 those who thought the government was doing a good job with the most important problem supported Clinton even more strongly than they had supported incumbents in previous elections. Gore, however, received considerably less support from those (relatively few) who felt the government was doing a good job. His 70 percent from that group was similar to that received by Gerald R. Ford in 1976 and Bush in 1992—two elections in which the incumbent lost. Gore did hold three in five of those who thought the government did only a fair job—a higher percentage than in 1976 and 1992.

According to Downs and Fiorina, it is important to know not only how things have been going but also to assess how that evaluation compares with the alternative. In recent elections, respondents have been asked which party would do a better job of solving the problem they named as the most important. Table 7-2 A shows the responses to this question. This question is clearly future oriented, but it may call for judgments about past performance, consistent with the Downs-Fiorina view. It does not ask the respondent to evaluate policy alternatives, and thus responses are most likely based on a retrospective comparison of how the incumbent party had handled things with a prediction about how the opposition would fare. We therefore consider this question to be a measure of comparative retrospective evaluations.

By comparing Tables 7-1 A and 7-2 A, we can see that in 2000 about one in four of the respondents thought the Democratic Party would be better at handling the most important problem, but this was a far larger proportion of respondents than thought the government was already doing a good job with it.

TABLE 7-1 Evaluation of Governmental Performance on Most Important Problem and Major-Party Vote, 1972–2000

Governmental performance	1972[a]	1976	1980	1984	1988	1992	1996[a]	2000[a]
A. Evaluation of Governmental Performance on Most Important Problem (in percentages)								
Good job	12	8	4	16	8	2	7	10
Only fair job	58	46	35	46	37	28	44	44
Poor job	30	46	61	39	56	69	48	47
Total	100%	100%	100%	101%	101%	99%	99%	101%
(N)	(993)	(2,156)[b]	(1,319)	(1,797)	(1,672)	(1,974)[b]	(752)[b]	(856)[b]

B. Percentage of Major-Party Vote for Incumbent Party's Nominee

	Nixon[a]	Ford	Carter	Reagan	Bush	Bush	Clinton[a]	Gore[a]
Good job	85	72	81	89	82	70	93	70
(N)	(91)	(128)[b]	(43)	(214)	(93)	(27)[b]	(38)[b]	(58)[b]
Only fair job	69	53	55	65	61	45	68	60
(N)	(390)	(695)[b]	(289)	(579)	(429)	(352)[b]	(238)[b]	(239)[b]
Poor job	46	39	33	37	44	39	44	37
(N)	(209)	(684)[b]	(505)	(494)	(631)	(841)[b]	(242)[b]	(230)[b]

Note: Numbers in parentheses are totals upon which percentages are based.

[a] These questions were asked of a randomly selected half of the sample in 1972, 1996, and 2000. In 1972 respondents were asked whether the government was being a) very helpful, b) somewhat helpful, or c) not helpful at all in solving this most important problem.
[b] Numbers are weighted.

TABLE 7-2 Evaluation of Party Seen as Better on Most Important Problem and Major-Party Vote, 1972–2000

Party better	1972[a]	1976	1980	1984	1988	1992	1996[a]	2000[a]
A. Distribution of Responses on Party Better on Most Important Problem (in percentages)								
Republican	28	14	43	32	22	13	22	23
No difference	46	50	46	44	54	48	54	50
Democratic	26	37	11	25	24	39	24	27
Total	100%	101%	100%	101%	100%	100%	100%	100%
(N)	(931)	(2,054)[b]	(1,251)	(1,785)	(1,655)	(1,954)[b]	(746)[b]	(846)[b]
B. Percentage of Major-Party Voters Who Voted Democratic for President								
Republican	6	3	12	5	5	4	15	9
(N)	(207)	(231)[b]	(391)	(464)	(295)	(185)[b]	(137)[b]	(143)[b]
No difference	32	35	63	41	46	45	63	52
(N)	(275)	(673)[b]	(320)	(493)	(564)	(507)[b]	(250)[b]	(227)[b]
Democratic	75	89	95	91	92	92	97	94
(N)	(180)	(565)[b]	(93)	(331)	(284)	(519)[b]	(133)[b]	(153)[b]

Note: Numbers in parentheses are the totals upon which percentages are based.

[a]These questions were asked of a randomly selected half of the sample in 1972, 1996, and 2000. In 1972 respondents were asked which party would be more likely to get the government to be helpful in solving the most important problem.

[b]Numbers are weighted.

Half thought neither party would do a better job, while a bit less than one in four thought the Republicans would be better at handling the most important problem. Indeed, responses in 2000 were very similar to those in 1988 and 1996, years in which the incumbent party's candidate won solid, but not landslide, victories. One similarity runs across all eight elections: the most frequent answer to the question of which party would do a better job handling the most important problem was *neither*.

As Table 7-2 B reveals, the relationship between the party seen as better on the most important problem and the vote is very strong—stronger than that found in Table 7-1 B, which examines voters and their perception of the government's handling of the problem. Gore won nineteen out of twenty votes from those who thought his party would do better. He won only one in eleven votes from those respondents who thought the opposition party would do better, while the half of the electorate that saw no difference between the parties split their vote evenly. It appears that one way of winning a vote is to convince the voter that your party will be better at handling whatever issue it is that concerns the voter the most. If neither candidate convinces the voter that his party is better, the voter apparently looks to other factors, although in all eight elections voters who saw no difference were more likely to stay with the incumbent party, albeit barely so in 2000.

The data presented in Tables 7-1 and 7-2 have an important limitation. The first survey question refers to "the government" and not to the incumbent president. (Is it the president, Congress, both, or even others—such as the bureaucracy or the courts—who are handling the job poorly, and what about the vice president?) The second question refers to the "political party" and not the candidate, and it is the performance of the incumbent that most directly relates to the choice between candidates. So we will look more closely at the incumbent and at people's evaluations of comparable problems where there are data to permit such comparisons.

ECONOMIC EVALUATIONS AND THE VOTE FOR THE INCUMBENT

More than any other, economic issues have received attention as suitable retrospective issues. The impact of economic conditions on congressional and presidential elections has been studied extensively.[9] Popular evaluations of presidential effectiveness, John E. Mueller has pointed out, are strongly influenced by the economy. Edward R. Tufte suggests that because the incumbent realizes his fate may hinge on the performance of the economy, he may attempt to manipulate it, leading to what is known as a "political business cycle."[10] A major reason for Carter's defeat in 1980 was the perception that economic performance had been weak during his administration. Reagan's rhetorical question in the 1980 debate with Carter, "Are you better off than you were four years ago?" indicates that politicians realize the power such arguments have with the electorate. Reagan owed his sweeping reelection victory in 1984 largely to the perception that economic performance by the end of his first term had become, after a deep recession in the middle, much stronger.

If people are concerned about economic outcomes, they might start by looking for an answer to the sort of question Reagan asked. Table 7-3 A presents respondents' perceptions of whether they were financially better off than they had been one year earlier. From 1972 to 1980 about a third of the sample felt they were better off. Over that period, however, more and more of the remainder felt they were worse off. By 1980, "worse now" was the most common response. But in 1984 many felt the economic recovery, and more than two of five said they were better off than in the previous year; only a little more than one in four felt worse off. Of course, 1984 was only two years after a deep recession. Therefore, many may have seen their economic fortunes improve considerably over the prior year or so. In 1988 that recovery had been sustained, and the distribution of responses to this question in 1988 was very similar to that of 1984. By 1992 there was a return to the feelings of the earlier period, and responses were nearly evenly divided between better, the same, and worse off. In 1996 the responses were like those of the 1984 and 1988 elections—and even slightly more favorable than in those years. In 2000 about a third felt better off, similar to responses through 1980. However, far fewer felt worse off in 2000 than in any of the seven preceding elections. Over half responded in 2000 that they were about the same as a year ago.

In Table 7-3 B responses to this question are related to the two-party presidential vote. We can see that the relationship between the respondents' financial situations and their vote is often not particularly strong. Even so, through 1996 those who felt their financial status had become worse off in the last year were always the least likely to support the incumbent. Moreover, the relationship between this variable and the vote became considerably stronger in 1984 and only slightly less so in 1988, 1992, and 1996. In 2000 Gore essentially held the same support as Clinton had received four years earlier, dropping only among those who responded that their fortunes had improved.

People may "vote their pocketbooks," but people are even more likely to vote retrospectively based on their judgments of how the economy as a whole has been faring. In 1980 about 40 percent of the respondents thought their own financial situation was worse than the year before, but responses to the 1980 NES survey show that twice as many (83 percent) thought the national economy was worse off than the year before. In the first four columns of Table 7-4 A, we see that there was quite a change in the perceptions of the fortunes of the national economy over the past six elections. In 1984 the improved status of personal finances almost matched perceptions of the status of the economy as a whole. In 1988 the personal financial situation was quite like that in 1984, but perceptions of the national economy were clearly more negative. In 1992 the public gave the nation's economy a far more negative assessment than they gave of their personal financial situations, illustrating that one's perceptions of personal fortunes may

TABLE 7-3 Assessments of Personal Financial Situation and Major-Party Vote, 1972–2000

"Would you say that you (and your family here) are better off or worse off financially than you were a year ago?"

Response	1972[a]	1976	1980	1984	1988	1992	1996	2000
A. Distribution of Responses (in percentages)								
Better now	36	34	33	44	42	31	46	33
Same	42	35	25	28	33	34	31	53
Worse now	23	31	42	27	25	35	24	14
Total	101%	100%	100%	99%	100%	100%	101%	100%
(N)	(955)	(2,828)[b]	(1,393)	(1,956)	(2,025)	(2,474)[b]	(1,708)[b]	(907)[b]
B. Percentage of Major-Party Voters Who Voted for the Incumbent Party Nominee for President								
Better now	69	55	46	74	63	53	66	56
(N)	(247)	(574)[b]	(295)	(612)	(489)	(413)[b]	(462)[b]	(164)[b]
Same	70	52	46	55	50	45	52	51
(N)	(279)	(571)[b]	(226)	(407)	(405)	(500)[b]	(348)[b]	(291)[b]
Worse now	52	38	40	33	40	27	47	45
(N)	(153)	(475)[b]	(351)	(338)	(283)	(453)[b]	(225)[b]	(56)[b]

Note: Numbers in parentheses are the totals upon which percentages are based.

[a] These questions were asked of a randomly selected half sample in 1972 and 2000.

[b] Numbers are weighted.

TABLE 7-4   Public's View of the State of the Economy and Major-Party Vote, 1980–2000

"Would you say that over the past year the nation's economy has gotten ..."

Response	1980	1984	1988	1992	1996	2000[b]
A. Distribution of Responses (in percentages)						
Better	4	44	19	4	40	39
Stayed same	13	33	50	22	44	44
Worse	83	23	31	73	16	17
Total	100%	100%	100%	99%	100%	100%
N	(1,580)	(1,904)	(1,956)	(2,465)[a]	(1,700)[a]	(1,787)[a]

B. Percentage of Major-Party Voters Who Voted for the Incumbent Party Nominee for President

	1980	1984	1988	1992	1996	2000
Better	58	80	77	86	75	69
N	(33)	(646)	(249)	(62)[a]	(458)[a]	(408)[a]
Stayed same	71	53	53	62	45	45
N	(102)	(413)	(568)	(318)[a]	(443)[a]	(487)[a]
Worse	39	21	34	32	33	31
N	(732)	(282)	(348)	(981)[a]	(130)[a]	(154)[a]

Note: Numbers in parentheses are the totals upon which percentages are based.

[a] Numbers are weighted.
[b] Combines standard and experimental prompts that contained different word ordering.

be very different from those of the economy as a whole. That was not the case in 1996 and 2000, when respondents gave broadly similar assessments of their personal fortunes as those of the nation—making the past two elections look most like 1984.

In Table 7-4 B, we show the relationship between responses to these items and the two-party vote for president. As we can see, this relationship between these measures and the vote is always strong. Moreover, comparing Tables 7-3 B and 7-4 B shows that, in general, the vote is more closely associated with perceptions of the nation's economy than it is with perceptions of one's personal economic well being. What made 2000 different from 1996, to Gore's disadvantage, was that the relationship between this variable and the vote was weaker than in 1996, and, indeed, at its weakest in 2000 compared to the preceding four elections. Still, while that relationship was weaker in 2000 than in preceding elections, it was still very strongly related to the vote.

To this point, we have looked at personal and national economic conditions and the role of the government in shaping them. We have not yet looked at the extent to which such evaluations are attributed to the incumbent. In Table 7-5 we report responses to the question of whether people approved of the incumbent's handling of the economy from the 1980 through 2000 elections. While a majority approved of Reagan's handling of the economy in both 1984 and 1988,

TABLE 7-5   Evaluations of the Incumbent's Handling of the Economy and Major-Party Vote, 1980–2000

	Approval of incumbent's handling of the economy					
	1980[a]	1984[b]	1988[b]	1992[b]	1996[b]	2000[b]
A. Distribution of Responses (in percentages)						
Positive view	18	58	54	20	66	77
Balanced view	17	—	—	—	—	—
Negative view	65	42	46	80	34	23
Total	100%	100%	100%	100%	100%	100%
(N)	(1,097)	(1,858)	(1,897)	(2,425)[c]	(1,666)[c]	(1,686)[c]
B. Percentage of Major-Party Voters Who Voted for the Incumbent Party Nominee						
Positive view	88	86	80	90	79	67
(N)	(130)	(801)	(645)	(310)[c]	(688)[c]	(768)[c]
Balanced view	60	—	—	—	—	—
(N)	(114)					
Negative view	23	16	17	26	13	11
(N)	(451)	(515)	(492)	(1,039)[c]	(322)[c]	(233)[c]

[a] In 1980 the questions asked whether the respondent approved or disapproved of Carter's handling of inflation [unemployment]. A positive [negative] view was approve [disapprove] on both; balanced responses were approve on one, disapprove on the other.
[b] In 1984, 1988, 1992, 1996, and 2000 responses were whether the respondent approved of [the president's] handling of the economy.
[c] Numbers are weighted.

less than one in five held positive views of economic performance in the Carter years. In 1992 evaluations of Bush were also very negative. In 1996 evaluations of Clinton's handling of the economy were stronger than those of incumbents in the previous surveys. By 2000 evaluations of Clinton's handling of the economy were even stronger, with three of every four respondents approving.

The bottom-line question is whether these views are related to voter choice. As the data in Table 7-5 B show, the answer is yes. Those who held positive views of the incumbent's performance on the economy were very likely to vote for that party's candidate. However, while four of five backed Clinton in 1996, that percentage declined to two of three in 2000, a high proportion in absolute terms but the lowest proportion by far in any of these elections. Large majorities of those with negative views voted to change parties. Bush's loss to Clinton among major-party voters in 1992, therefore, is attributable primarily to the heavily negative views of his stewardship of the economy, just as was Carter's loss to Reagan in 1980. In 1996 Clinton benefited primarily from the positive assessments of his handling of the economy. In 2000 Gore suffered, in relative terms, by receiving less support from those who approved—and from those who disapproved.

EVALUATIONS OF THE INCUMBENT

Fiorina distinguishes between "simple" and "mediated" retrospective evaluations. By simple Fiorina means evaluations of the direct effects of social outcomes on the person, such as one's financial status, or direct perceptions of the nation's economic well being. Mediated retrospective evaluations are evaluations seen through or mediated by the perceptions of political actors and institutions.[11] Approval of Clinton's handling of the economy or the assessment of which party would better handle the most important problem facing the country are examples.

As we have seen, the more politically mediated the question, the more closely responses align with voting behavior. Perhaps the ultimate in mediated evaluations is the presidential approval question: "Do you approve or disapprove of the way [the incumbent] is handling his job as president?" From a retrospective voting standpoint, this evaluation is a summary of all aspects of his service in office. Table 7-6 reports the distribution of overall evaluations and their relationship to major-party voting in the past eight elections.[12]

As can be seen in Table 7-6 A, incumbents Nixon, Ford, Reagan, and Clinton enjoyed widespread approval, whereas only two respondents in five approved of Carter's and of Bush's handling of the job. This presented Carter in 1980 and Bush in 1992 with a problem. Conversely, highly approved incumbents, such as Reagan in 1984—and his vice president as beneficiary in 1988—had a major advantage. Clinton dramatically reversed any negative perceptions of his incumbency held in 1994, such that by 1996 he received the highest level of approval since Nixon's landslide reelection in 1972.

Between 1996 and 2000 Clinton suffered through scandals, culminating in his impeachment in 1998. Such events might be expected to lead to substantial declines in his approval ratings, but instead they remained high—higher even than Reagan's at the end of his presidency. As can be seen in Table 7-6 B, there is a very strong relationship between approval of the incumbent and the vote for that incumbent (and, as in 1988, his vice president). Once again, Gore was relatively less successful in holding support of those who approved, even though he received three votes in four of approvers, the same as Ford in 1976 and only slightly less than Bush in 1988. Nonetheless, approval is strongly related to the vote among major-party voters in all eight elections.

THE IMPACT OF RETROSPECTIVE EVALUATIONS

Our evidence strongly suggests that retrospective voting has been widespread in all recent elections. Moreover, as far as data permit us to judge, the evidence is clearly on the side of the Downs-Fiorina view. Retrospective evaluations appear to be used to make comparative judgments. Presumably, voters find it easier, less time consuming, and less risky to evaluate the incumbent party on what its

TABLE 7-6 Distribution of Responses on President's Handling of Job and Major-Party Vote, 1972–2000

"Do you approve or disapprove of the way [the incumbent] is handling his job as president?"

	1972	1976	1980	1984	1988	1992	1996	2000
A. Distribution of Responses (in percentages)								
Approve	71	63	41	63	60	43	68	67
Disapprove	29	37	59	37	40	57	32	33
Total	100%	100%	100%	100%	100%	100%	100%	100%
(N)	(1,215)	(2,439)[a]	(1,475)	(2,091)	(1,935)	(2,419)[a]	(1,692)[a]	(1,742)[a]
B. Percentage of Major-Party Voters Who Voted for the Incumbent Party's Nominee								
Approve	83	74	81	87	79	81	84	74
(N)[b]	(553)	(935)[a]	(315)	(863)	(722)	(587)[a]	(676)[a]	(662)[a]
Disapprove	14	9	18	7	12	11	4	13
(N)	(203)	(523)[a]	(491)	(449)	(442)	(759)[a]	(350)[a]	(366)[a]

Note: Question was asked of a randomly selected half sample in 1972.

[a] Numbers are weighted.

[b] Numbers in parentheses are the totals upon which percentages are based.

president did in the most recent term or terms in office than on the nominees' promises for the future. But few people base their votes on judgments of past performance alone. Most use past judgments as a starting point for comparing the major contenders. When the incumbent's performance in 1980 and 1992 was compared with the anticipated performance of the opponent, most respondents felt the incumbent had not done very well, but a surprisingly large number did not believe that the opposition party would do any better (see Table 7-2). In 1972, 1984, 1988, 1996, and 2000 many voters felt the incumbent had done well, and few thought the challenger's party would do better. The 2000 election was most like the 1984, 1988, and 1996 elections. Evaluations were generally positive and, in the case of overall approval, unusually so. Even though few respondents thought the government had done a good job handling the most important problem, many more thought the Democrats would do just as well as or better than the Republicans.

We can strengthen the overall assessment of retrospective voting in the past few elections by forming a combined index of retrospective evaluations common to the seven most recent presidential election surveys. Our measure is constructed by combining the presidential approval measure with the evaluation of the job the government has done on the most important problem and with the assessment of which party would better handle that problem.[13] This creates a 7-point scale ranging from strongly opposed to the job the incumbent and his party have done to strongly supportive of that performance. For instance, those who approved of Clinton's job performance, thought the government was doing a good job, and thought the Democratic Party would better handle the problem are scored as strongly supportive of the incumbent party's nominee in their retrospective evaluations in 1996 and 2000. In Figures 7-1 and 7-2 we present the results for the four most recent elections; the results for the 1976, 1980, and 1984 elections are presented in an earlier edition. [14]

In Figure 7-1 we report the distribution of responses on this combined measure. As these figures make clear, respondents had rather positive evaluations of the incumbent and his party in 2000. The most common category was slightly pro-incumbent, followed by all other categories, with the smallest percentage in the two extreme categories. This set of responses corresponds most closely to 1988 and 1996 (and to 1984) although responses in 1988 were more uniformly distributed over the seven categories. The 2000 responses were most unlike 1992 (and 1976 and 1980). In short, evaluations in 2000 were like those in elections won by incumbents and unlike those in which they lost.

As Figure 7-2 shows, respondents who have positive retrospective evaluations of the incumbent party are much more likely to vote for that party than those who disapprove of the incumbent party's performance. What is most striking about the figure is how similar and how very strong the relationship is in every election year. In this case, the support for Gore is, however, much like that of 1976, another year in which the incumbent party lost in a very close contest. No one in the category least favorable to the incumbent supported him, while the

FIGURE 7-1   Distribution of Electorate on Summary Measure of Retrospective
Evaluations, 1988–2000

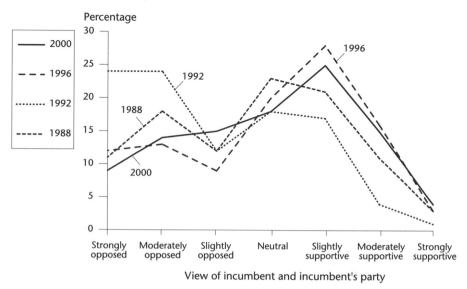

Note: The total number of cases: 1988 — 1,409; 1992 — 1,987 (weighted); 1996 — 758 (weighted);
2000 — 857 (weighted). Questions asked of a random half sample in 1996 and 2000.

vast majority in the most favorable two categories voted for him, and there was
a sharp increase in going from slightly against to slightly in favor of the incumbent. Indeed, the largest changes were right around the neutral point.

In sum, it would seem reasonable to conclude that the 1980 election was a
clear and strong rejection of Carter's incumbency. In 1984 Reagan won in large
part because he was seen as having performed well and because Mondale was
unable to convince the public that he would do better. In 1988 George Bush won
in large part because Reagan was seen as having performed well—and people
thought Bush would stay the course. In 1992 Bush lost because of the far more
negative evaluations of his administration and of his party than had been
obtained in any other recent elections except 1980. In 1996 Clinton won reelection in large part for the same reasons that Reagan won in 1984: he was seen as
having performed well on the job, and he was able to convince the public that his
opponent would not do any better. In 2000 Gore essentially tied George W. Bush,
because there was a slightly proincumbent set of evaluations, combined with a
very slight asymmetry against the incumbent in translating those evaluations
into voting choices.

There is obviously more to the differences among these elections than retrospective evaluations. As you may recall from chapter 6, prospective issues, especially our balance of issues measure, have been increasingly strongly related to the

FIGURE 7-2   Percentage of Major-Party Voters Who Voted for Incumbent, by
Summary Measure of Retrospective Evaluations, 1988–2000

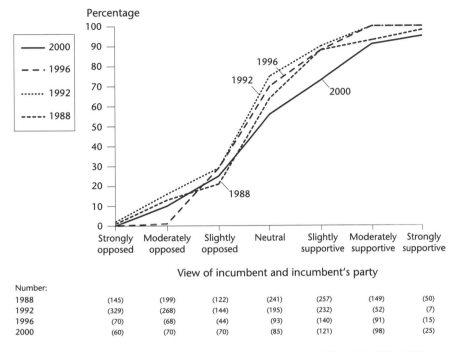

Number:							
1988	(145)	(199)	(122)	(241)	(257)	(149)	(50)
1992	(329)	(268)	(144)	(195)	(232)	(52)	(7)
1996	(70)	(68)	(44)	(93)	(140)	(91)	(15)
2000	(60)	(70)	(70)	(85)	(121)	(98)	(25)

Note: Numbers in 1992, 1996, and 2000 are weighted. Questions asked of a random half sample in 1996 and 2000.

vote over the past few elections. Table 7-7 reports the impact of both types of policy evaluation measures on the major-party vote in 2000. Both policy measures were collapsed into three categories: pro-Democratic, neutral, and pro-Republican. Reading across each row, we see that retrospective evaluations are very strongly related to the vote, even when one controls for prospective issues. Reading down each column, we see that prospective issues are modestly positively related to the vote (except for the relatively few respondents with neutral retrospective evaluations). Together, the two kinds of policy measures take us a long way toward understanding voting choices. More than nine in ten of those with pro-Republican stances on the two measures, for example, voted for Bush, while nineteen in twenty of those with pro-Democratic stances voted for Gore, and this accounting of voting choices is stronger when considering both forms of policy evaluations than when looking at either one individually. Analyses of the 1976 and 1980 elections, by contrast, showed little relationship between prospective issues and the vote, once retrospective issues were taken into account. For 1984 we found that prospective issues had some effect, while the relationship in 1988 and in 1996 was stronger still.[15]

TABLE 7-7　Percentage of Major-Party Voters Who Voted for Gore, by Balance of Issues and Summary Retrospective Measures, 2000

| | Summary Retrospective[b] | | | | | | | |
| | Republican | | Neutral | | Democratic | | Total | |
Balance of Issues[a]	(%)	(N)	(%)	(N)	(%)	(N)	(%)	(N)
Republican	8	(76)	58	(18)	78	(59)	41	(153)
Neutral	16	(4)	94	(8)	72	(19)	70	(30)
Democratic	21	(24)	45	(19)	95	(48)	65	(91)
Total	11	(104)	59	(45)	84	(125)	52	(274)

Note: Numbers in parentheses are the totals on which percentages are based. The numbers are weighted.

[a] The neutral category is a score of 0 on the full measure, while the Republican [Democratic] category is any score greater than 0 [less than 0] on the full measure.

[b] The neutral category is the same as on the full scale, while the Republican [Democratic] category is the combination of all three Republican [Democratic] categories on the full measure.

CONCLUSION

In this and the previous chapter, we have found that both retrospective and prospective evaluations were strongly related to the vote. Indeed, in 1992 dissatisfaction with Bush's performance and with his and his party's handling of the most important problem—often an economic concern—goes a long way in explaining his defeat, while satisfaction with Clinton's performance and the absence of an advantage for the Republicans in being seen as able to deal with the most important concerns of voters goes a long way in explaining his 1996 victory. In 2000 prospective issues favored neither candidate because essentially the same number of major-party voters were closer to Bush as were closer to Gore. The Democrat had a modest advantage on retrospective evaluations, but Bush won greater support among those with pro-Republican evaluations than did Gore among those with pro-Democratic evaluations. The result was another even balance and, as a result, a tied outcome. Even so, our explanation remains incomplete. Most important, we have not accounted for why people hold the views they expressed on these two measures. We cannot provide a complete account of the origins of people's views, but there is one important source we can examine: party identification, a variable we have used in previous chapters, provides a powerful means for the typical citizen to reach preliminary judgments. As we will see, partisanship is strongly related to these judgments, especially to retrospective evaluations.

Moreover, party identification plays a central role in debates about the future of American politics. Will there be a partisan realignment? A dealignment? Or will the federal government continue under divided government, perhaps in a situation some have called a split-level realignment (albeit in a split different than originally considered, especially with Republican majorities in Congress)? Many political scientists believe that change in the political system of this magnitude can come only if there are changes in party loyalties in the electorate as well as in their voting behavior. Therefore, to understand voter choice better and to assess future partisan prospects, we must examine the role of party loyalties.

Chapter 8

Party Loyalties, Policy Preferences, and the Vote

✦✦✦

Most Americans identify with a political party. Their party identification influences their political attitudes and, ultimately, their behavior. In the 1950s and 1960s the authors of *The American Voter*, along with other scholars, began to emphasize the role of party loyalties.[1] Although today few people would deny that partisanship is central to political attitudes and behavior, many scholars question the interpretation of the evidence gathered during this period. We ask two questions: What is party identification? And how does it actually structure other attitudes and behavior? We then examine the role that party identification played in the 2000 presidential election.

According to Angus Campbell and the other authors of *The American Voter*, party identification is "the individual's affective orientation to an important group-object in his environment," in this case the political party.[2] In other words, an individual sees that there are two major political parties that play significant roles in elections and develops an affinity for one of them. Partisanship, therefore, represents an evaluation of the two parties, but its implications extend to a wider variety of political phenomena. Campbell and his colleagues measured partisanship by asking individuals which party they identified with and how strong that identification was.[3] If an individual did not identify with one of the parties, he or she may have either "leaned" toward a party or been a "pure" independent. Individuals who could not answer the party identification questions were classified as "apolitical."[4] Most Americans develop a preference for either the Republican or the Democratic Party. Very few identify with any third party. The remainder are mostly independents, who are not only unattached to a party but also relatively unattached to politics in general. They are less interested, less informed, and less active than those who identify with a party.

Partisan identification in this view becomes an attachment or loyalty not unlike that between the individual and other groups or organizations in society, such as a religious body, a social class, or even a favorite sports team. As with loyalties to many of these groups, partisan affiliation often begins early. One of the first political attitudes children develop is partisan identification, and it develops well before they acquire policy preferences and many other political orientations. Furthermore, as with other group loyalties, once an attachment to a party develops, it tends to endure. Some people do switch parties, of course, but they usually do so only if their social situation changes, if there is an issue of overriding concern that sways their loyalties, or if the political parties themselves change substantially.

Party identification, then, stands as a base or core orientation to electoral politics. It is formed at an early age and endures for most people throughout their lives.[5] Once formed, this core orientation, predicated on a general evaluation of the two parties, affects many other specific orientations. Democratic loyalists tend to rate Democratic candidates and officeholders more highly than Republican candidates and officeholders, and vice versa. In effect, one is predisposed to evaluate the promises and performance of one's party leaders relatively more favorably. It follows, therefore, that Democrats are more likely to vote for Democratic candidates than are Republicans, and vice versa.

PARTY IDENTIFICATION: AN ALTERNATIVE VIEW

In *The Responsible Electorate*, published in 1966, V. O. Key Jr. argued that party loyalties contributed to electoral inertia and that many partisans voted as "standpatters" from election to election.[6] That is, in the absence of any information to the contrary, or if the attractions and disadvantages of the candidates are fairly evenly balanced, partisans are expected to vote for the candidate of their party. Voting for their party's candidates is their "standing decision," until and unless voters are given good reasons not to. More recently, scholars have reexamined the bases of such behavior. In this new view, citizens who consider themselves Democrats have a standing decision to vote for the Democratic nominee because of the past positions of the Democrats and the Republicans and because of the parties' comparative past performances while in office. In short, this view of partisan identification presumes that it is a "running tally" of past experiences (mostly in terms of policy and performance), a sort of summary expression of political memory, according to Morris P. Fiorina.[7]

Furthermore, when in doubt about what, for example, a Democratic candidate is likely to do on civil rights in comparison to the Republican opponent, it is reasonable to assume the Democrat will be more liberal than the Republican—unless the candidates indicate otherwise. Because the political parties tend to be consistent on the basic historical policy cleavages, summary judgments of parties and their typical candidates will not change radically or often.[8]

As a result, a citizen's running tally serves as a good first approximation, changes rarely, and can be an excellent device for saving time and effort that would be spent gathering information in the absence of this "memory."

Many of the major findings used in support of the conventional interpretation of party identification are completely consistent with this more policy-oriented view. We do not have the evidence to assert that one view is superior to the other. Indeed, the two interpretations are not mutually exclusive. Moreover, they share the important conclusion that party identification plays a central role in shaping voters' decisions.

In terms of the account of voting discussed in chapter 6, both views agree that partisan identifications are long-term forces in politics. Both agree that, for most people, such identifications are formed early in life; children often develop a partisan loyalty, which they usually learn from their parents, although these loyalties are seldom explicitly taught. Partisan identifications also are often closely associated with social forces, as discussed in chapter 5, especially when a social group is actively engaged in partisan politics. An important illustration of this point is the affiliation of many labor unions with the New Deal Democratic coalition, which often reinforced the tendency of those who were in labor unions to identify with the Democratic Party. Finally, both views agree that partisanship is closely associated with more immediate evaluations, including prospective and retrospective evaluations of the issues and candidates, as analyzed in chapters 6 and 7.

The two views disagree over the nature of the linkage between partisanship and other attitudes, such as those toward the candidates and issues. The standard view argues that partisanship, as a long-term loyalty, affects the evaluations of issues and candidates by voters, but that it in turn is largely unaffected by such evaluations, except in such dramatic circumstances as realigning elections. In this sense, partisanship is a "filter" through which the concerns relevant to the particular election are viewed. In the alternative view, partisanship as a running tally may affect, but is also affected by, more immediate concerns. Indeed, Fiorina's definition of partisanship makes clear that the running tally includes current as well as past assessments. Distinguishing empirically between these two views is therefore quite difficult. Although the alternative view may see partisan identification as being affected by retrospective and prospective assessments of the issues and candidates in the current election, such assessments rarely change an individual's identification relatively, due to past experiences and the impact of initial socialization. We shall analyze the role of partisan identification in 2000 and other recent elections in ways consistent with both major views of partisan identification.

PARTY IDENTIFICATION IN THE ELECTORATE

If partisan identification is a fundamental orientation for most citizens, then the distribution of partisan loyalties is crucial. The National Election Studies (NES) have monitored the party loyalties of the American electorate since 1952. In

TABLE 8-1   Party Identification in Presidential Years, Preelection Surveys, 1980–2000

Party identification	1980	1984	1988	1992	1996	2000
Strong Democrat	18%	17%	18%	17%	18%	19%
Weak Democrat	24	20	18	18	20	15
Independent, leans Democratic	12	11	12	14	14	15
Independent, no partisan leanings	13	11	11	12	8	12
Independent, leans Republican	10	13	14	13	12	13
Weak Republican	14	15	14	15	16	12
Strong Republican	9	13	14	11	13	12
Total	100%	100%	101%	100%	101%	98%
(*N*)	(1,577)	(2,198)	(1,999)	(2,450)[a]	(1,696)[a]	(1,777)[a]
Apolitical	2%	2%	2%	1%	1%	1%
(*N*)	(35)	(38)	(33)	(23)	(14)	(21)

[a] Numbers are weighted.

Table 8-1 we show the basic distributions of partisan loyalties in presidential election years from 1980 through 2000. As the table shows, most Americans identify with a political party. In 2000 about three in five claimed to think of themselves as a Democrat or as a Republican, and one-quarter more, who initially said they were independent or had no partisan preference, nonetheless said they felt closer to one of the major parties than to the other.[9] About one in eight was purely independent of party, and barely one in one hundred was classified as "apolitical." One of the largest changes in partisanship in the electorate began in the mid-1960s, when more people claimed to be independents.[10] This growth stopped, however, in the late 1970s and early 1980s. There was very little change in partisan loyalties between the 1984 and 1992 surveys.

There were signs in 1996 of reversals of the trends in party identification toward greater independence. All partisan groups increased slightly in 1996 compared to 1992, and the 8 percent of "pure" independents (that is, those with no partisan leanings) was the lowest percentage since 1968. That dip in independence stopped, however, so that the percentages of independents in 2000 rebounded to the same levels as in 1992.

Table 8-1 also shows that more people think of themselves as Democrats than as Republicans. Over the past forty years, the balance between the two parties has favored the Democrats by a range of about 55/45 to about 60/40. While the results from the past five presidential election years still fall within that range, they show a clear shift toward the Republicans. In 1980, 35 percent of partisans were Republicans; in 1984, 42 percent were; by 1988, 44 percent were; in 1992 and in 1996, 43 percent of partisans were; and in 2000, 42 percent were

Republicans. Including independents who leaned toward a party would increase the percentage of Republicans to 38 percent in 1980, 45 percent in 1984, and 47 percent in 1988. That figure dropped to 44 percent in 1992 and 1996, and then 43 percent in 2000. Thus the Democratic advantage in loyalties in the electorate has narrowed, with only a slight rebound recently, and that edge is made even smaller in practice by the tendency of the Republicans to have higher turnout than the Democrats (see chapter 4).

The partisan loyalties of the American electorate can also be analyzed through other surveys. Among these, the most useful are the General Social Surveys (GSS) conducted by the National Opinion Research Council (NORC). These surveys, usually based on about 1,500 respondents who are interviewed in person, employ the standard party identification questions developed by the authors of *The American Voter* to measure long-term attachments to the political parties. The GSS have been conducted in most years since 1972.[11] Like the NES surveys, the GSS reveal some Republican gains. From 1972 through 1982, the percentage of party identifiers supporting the Republicans never rose above 37 percent, and even if independent leaners are included as partisans, support for the GOP never rose beyond 38 percent. The GOP made gains in 1983, and in 1984 the percentage of party identifiers who were Republican rose to 40 percent. Republican strength peaked in the 1990 General Social Survey. Forty-eight percent of all party identifiers were Republicans, and if independents who leaned toward a party are included 49 percent were Republicans. But the Republicans made no further gains, even in the 1991 survey conducted during and shortly after the Persian Gulf War. In the most recent survey, based upon 2,800 respondents and conducted in February, March, and April of 2000, 43 percent of all party identifiers were Republican; the total remains at 43 percent even when independent leaners are included. The most recent survey reveals weak partisan loyalties among the electorate. Only 25 percent were strong party identifiers, and only 57 percent were strong or weak party identifiers. Twenty percent were independents who leaned toward neither political party.

Our analysis of the NES surveys reveals that the shift toward the Republican Party is concentrated among white Americans. As we saw in chapter 5, the sharpest social division in U.S. electoral politics is race, and this division has been reflected in partisan loyalties for decades. Moreover, the racial gap appears to be widening. Although the distribution of partisanship in the electorate as a whole has changed only slightly since 1984, this stability masks a growth in Republican identification among whites, and, of course, a compensating growth of already strong Democratic loyalties among African Americans. In Table 8-2 we report the party identification of whites between 1952 and 2000, and in Table 8-3 we report the partisan identification of blacks. As the tables show, black and white patterns in partisan loyalties have been very different throughout this period. There was a sharp shift in black loyalties in the mid-1960s. Before then, about 50 percent of African Americans were strong or weak Democrats; since that time, 60 to 70 percent—and even higher—of blacks have considered themselves Democrats.

The party loyalties of whites have changed more slowly. Still, the percentage of self-professed Democrats among whites declined over the Reagan years, while the percentage of Republicans increased. In the past five elections partisanship by race has changed with shifts among whites. If independent leaners are included, there was close to an even balance among whites between the two parties in 1984. By 1988 the numbers of strong and weak Democrats and strong and weak Republicans were virtually the same, with more strong Republicans than strong Democrats for the first time. Adding in the two groups of independent leaners gives Republicans a clear advantage in identification among whites. In 1992, however, this advantage disappeared. There were slightly more strong and weak Democrats than strong and weak Republicans. In 1996 all four of the partisan categories were larger, by 1 to 3 points, than in 1992. The result was that the balance of Republicans to Democrats changed very slightly, and the near parity of identifiers with the two parties among whites remained. By 2000 the parity was even more striking. Perhaps most surprising of all is that, among white voters, each of the seven partisanship identification categories received strikingly close to one-seventh of the responses.

Although the increased Republicanism of the white electorate is partly the result of long-term forces, such as generational replacement, the actual movement between 1964 and 1988 appears to be the result of two shorter-term increases in Republican identification. There was a 5-percentage-point movement toward the GOP from 1964 through 1968, and a 10-point movement toward the GOP between 1982 and 1988. This movement waned modestly in the 1990s, as we saw. In 2000 the Republican categories, like the Democratic categories, had declined about equally, while the pure independent category had increased from 8 to 13 percent of the white electorate between 1996 and 2000.

Party identification among blacks is very different. In 2000 there were very few black Republicans. Indeed, in spite of George W. Bush's record of bipartisan and multiracial support in Texas, his appeal did not extend to attracting blacks to his party nationwide. The degree of Republican identification among blacks declined to its lowest level since the Reagan era.

These racial differences in partisanship are long standing, and over time, changes have increased this division. Between 1952 and 1962, blacks were primarily Democratic, but about one in seven supported the Republicans. Black partisanship shifted massively and abruptly even further toward the Democratic Party in 1964. In that year, over half of all black voters considered themselves *strong* Democrats. Since then, well over half have identified with the Democratic Party. Black Republican identification fell to barely a trace in 1964 and has edged up only slightly since then.

The abrupt change in black loyalties in 1964 reflects the two presidential nominees of that year. President Lyndon B. Johnson's advocacy of civil rights legislation appealed directly to black voters, and his Great Society and War on Poverty programs in general made an only slightly less direct appeal. Sen. Barry M. Goldwater, Ariz., the Republican nominee, voted against the 1964 Civil Rights

TABLE 8-2   Party Identification among Whites, 1952–2000

Party identification[a]	1952	1954	1956	1958	1960	1962	1964	1966	1968	1970	1972
Strong Democrat	21%	22%	20%	26%	20%	22%	24%	17%	16%	17%	12%
Weak Democrat	25	25	23	22	25	23	25	27	25	22	25
Independent, leans Democratic	10	9	6	7	6	8	9	9	10	11	12
Independent, no partisan leaning	6	7	9	8	9	8	8	12	11	13	13
Independent, leans Republican	7	6	9	5	7	7	6	8	10	9	11
Weak Republican	14	15	14	17	14	17	14	16	16	16	14
Strong Republican	14	13	16	12	17	13	12	11	11	10	11
Apolitical	2	2	2	3	1	3	1	1	1	1	1
Total	99%	99%	99%	100%	100%	101%	99%	101%	100%	99%	99%
(N)	(1,615)	(1,015)	(1,610)	(1,638)[b]	(1,739)[b]	(1,168)	(1,394)	(1,131)	(1,387)[b]	(1,395)	(2,397)

[a] The percentage supporting another party has not been presented; it usually totals less than 1 percent and never totals more than 1 percent.
[b] Numbers are weighted.

TABLE 8-3   Party Identification among Blacks, 1952–2000

Party identification[a]	1952	1954	1956	1958	1960	1962	1964	1966	1968	1970	1972
Strong Democrat	30%	24%	27%	32%	25%	35%	52%	30%	56%	41%	36%
Weak Democrat	22	29	23	19	19	25	22	31	29	34	31
Independent, leans Democratic	10	6	5	7	7	4	8	11	7	7	8
Independent, no partisan leaning	4	5	7	4	16	6	6	14	3	12	12
Independent, leans Republican	4	6	1	4	4	2	1	2	1	1	3
Weak Republican	8	5	12	11	9	7	5	7	1	4	4
Strong Republican	5	11	7	7	7	6	2	2	1	0	4
Apolitical	17	15	18	16	14	15	4	3	3	1	2
Total	100%	101%	100%	100%	101%	100%	100%	100%	101%	100%	100%
(N)	(171)	(101)	(146)	(161)[c]	(171)[c]	(110)	(156)	(132)	(149)	(157)	(267)

[a] The percentage supporting another party has not been presented; it usually totals less than 1 percent and never totals more than 1 percent.
[b] Less than 1 percent.
[c] Numbers are weighted.

1974	1976	1978	1980	1982	1984	1986	1988	1990	1992	1994	1996	1998	2000
15%	13%	12%	14%	16%	15%	14%	14%	17%	14%	12%	15%	15%	15%
20	23	24	23	24	18	21	16	19	17	19	19	18	14
13	11	14	12	11	11	10	10	11	14	12	13	14	15
15	15	14	14	11	11	12	12	11	12	10	8	11	13
9	11	11	11	9	13	13	15	13	14	13	12	12	14
15	16	14	16	16	17	17	15	16	16	16	17	18	14
9	10	9	9	11	14	12	16	11	12	17	15	11	14
3	1	3	2	2	2	2	1	1	1	1	1	2	1
99%	100%	101%	101%	100%	101%	101%	99%	99%	100%	100%	100%	101%	100%
(2,246)	(2,490)[b]	(2,006)	(1,405)	(1,248)	(1,931)	(1,798)[b]	(1,693)	(1,663)	(2,702)[b]	(1,510)[b]	(1,451)[b]	(1,091)[b]	(1,404)[b]

1974	1976	1978	1980	1982	1984	1986	1988	1990	1992	1994	1996	1998	2000
40%	34%	37%	45%	53%	32%	42%	39%	40%	40%	38%	43%	48%	47%
26	36	29	27	26	31	30	24	23	24	23	22	23	21
15	14	15	9	12	14	12	18	16	14	20	16	12	14
12	8	9	7	5	11	7	6	8	12	8	10	7	10
—[b]	1	2	3	1	6	2	5	7	3	4	5	3	4
—[b]	2	3	2	2	1	2	5	3	3	2	3	3	3
3	2	3	3	0	2	2	1	2	2	3	1	1	0
4	1	2	4	1	2	2	3	2	2	3	0	2	1
100%	99%	100%	100%	100%	99%	99%	101%	101%	100%	100%	100%	99%	100%
(224)[c]	(290)[c]	(230)	(187)	(148)	(247)	(322)	(267)	(270)	(317)[c]	(203)[c]	(200)[c]	(149)[c]	(225)[c]

Act, a vote criticized even by many of his Republican peers. Party stances have not changed appreciably since then, although the proportion of blacks who were strong Democrats declined somewhat after 1968.

In 1964 as well the proportion of blacks considered apolitical dropped from the teens to very small proportions, similar to those among whites. This shift resulted from the civil rights movement, the contest between Johnson and Goldwater, and the passage of the Civil Rights Act. The civil rights movement stimulated many blacks, especially in the South, to become politically active. Furthermore, the 1965 Voting Rights Act enabled many of them to vote for the first time.

PARTY IDENTIFICATION AND THE VOTE

As we saw in chapter 4, partisanship is related to turnout. Strong supporters of either party are more likely to vote than weak supporters, and independents who lean toward a party are more likely to vote than independents without partisan leanings. Republicans are somewhat more likely to vote than Democrats. Although partisanship influences whether people go to the polls, it is more strongly related to *how* people vote.

Table 8-4 reports the percentage of white major-party voters who voted for the Democratic candidate across all categories of partisanship since 1952. Clearly, there is a strong relationship between partisan identification and choice of candidate. In every election except 1972 the Democratic nominee has received more than 80 percent of the vote of strong Democrats and majority support from both weak Democratic partisans and independent Democratic leaners. In 1996 these figures were higher than in any other election in this period. While they fell somewhat in 2000, especially in the independent-leaning Democrat category, Al Gore still held the support of his partisans to an impressive extent. But so, too, did Bush. Since 1952 strong Republicans have given the Democratic candidate less than one vote in ten. In 1988 more of the weak Republicans and independents who leaned toward the Republican Party voted for Michael S. Dukakis than had for Walter F. Mondale, but, even so, only about one in seven voted Democratic. In 1992 Clinton won an even larger percentage of the two-party vote from these Republicans, and he increased his support among Republicans again in 1996. George W. Bush held essentially the same level of support among the three white Republican categories as his father had in 1988 and 1992. The pure independent vote, which fluctuates substantially, has tended to be Republican. John F. Kennedy won 50 percent of that vote in 1960, but Bill Clinton won nearly two-thirds of the pure independents' two-party votes in 1992, and nearly three-fifths of the white independent vote in 1996. Gore, however, was able to carry only two in five such votes. Thus, at least among major-party voters, Gore won the popular vote by a tiny margin because he held his own white party identifiers to about the same degree as Bush did white

TABLE 8-4   Percentage of White Major-Party Voters Who Voted Democratic for President, by Party Identification, 1952–2000

Party identification	1952	1956	1960	1964	1968	1972	1976	1980	1984	1988	1992	1996	2000
Strong Democrat	82	85	91	94	89	66	88	87	88	93	96	98	96
Weak Democrat	61	63	70	81	66	44	72	59	63	68	80	88	81
Independent, leans Democratic	60	65	89	89	62	58	73	57	77	86	92	91	72
Independent, no partisan leanings	18	15	50	75	28	26	41	23	21	35	63	58	44
Independent, leans Republican	7	6	13	25	5	11	15	13	5	13	14	26	15
Weak Republican	4	7	11	40	10	9	22	5	6	16	18	21	16
Strong Republican	2	—[a]	2	9	3	2	3	4	2	2	2	3	1

Note: To approximate the numbers upon which these percentages are based, see Table 8-2. Actual *N*s will be smaller than those that can be derived from Table 8-2 because respondents who did not vote (or voted for a non-major-party candidate) have been excluded from these calculations. Numbers also will be lower since the voting report is provided in the postelection interviews that usually contain about 10 percent fewer respondents than the preelection interviews in which party identification is measured.

[a]Less than 1 percent.

Republicans. Bush's slight edge among pure independents and his ability to hold on to GOP leaners better than Gore held on to Democratic leaners was more than offset by the tremendous advantage Gore received from black voters.

While virtually all blacks vote Democratic, among whites partisanship leads to loyalty in voting. Between 1964 and 1980 the relationship between party identification and the vote was declining, but in 1984 the relationship between party identification and the presidential vote was higher than in any of the five elections from 1964 through 1980. The relationship remained strong in 1988 and continued to be quite strong in the two Clinton and the Gore-Bush elections, at least among major-party voters.[12] Nonetheless, the partisan basis of the vote in congressional elections, while strengthening somewhat, remained weaker than it had been in the 1950s and early 1960s. Thus, the question of whether the parties are gathering new strength cannot be answered definitively from the 2000 election data, but these data suggest some resurgence of partisanship in influencing the vote.[13]

Partisanship is related to the way people vote. The question, therefore, is why do partisans support their party's candidates? As we shall see, party identification affects behavior because it helps structure (and, according to Fiorina, is structured by) the way voters view both policies and performance.

POLICY PREFERENCES AND PERFORMANCE EVALUATIONS

In their study of voting in the 1948 election, Bernard R. Berelson, Paul F. Lazarsfeld, and William N. McPhee discovered that Democratic voters attributed to their nominee, incumbent Harry S. Truman, positions on key issues that were consistent with their beliefs—whether those beliefs were liberal, moderate, or conservative.[14] Similarly, Republicans tended to see their nominee, Gov. Thomas E. Dewey of New York, as taking whatever positions they preferred. Research since then has emphasized the role of party identification not only in the projection onto the preferred candidate of positions similar to the voter's own views, but in shaping the policy preferences in the public as well.[15] We use four examples to illustrate the strong relationship between partisan affiliation and perceptions, preferences, and evaluations of candidates.

First, most partisans evaluate the job done by a president of their party more highly than do independents and, especially, more highly than do those who identify with the other party. Figure 8-1 shows the percentage of each of the seven partisan groups that approves of the way the incumbent has handled his job as president (as a proportion of those approving or disapproving) in the past eight presidential elections. Strong Republicans have given overwhelming approval to all Republican incumbents, just as strong Democrats overwhelmingly approved of Clinton's handling of the presidency in 2000. In 1980, on the other hand, "only" three strong Democrats in four approved of Carter. In 2000 the other two Democratic categories gave Clinton very high marks as well, far higher than com-

FIGURE 8-1 Approval of Incumbent's Handling of Job by Party Identification, 1972–2000

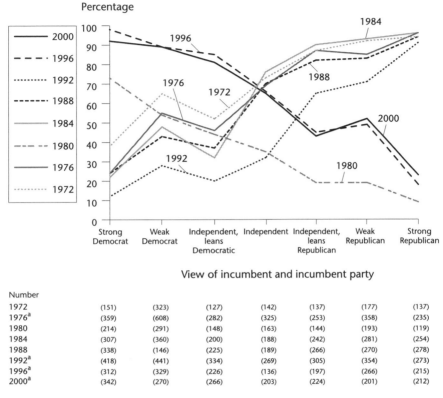

Percentage

View of incumbent and incumbent party

Number

1972	(151)	(323)	(127)	(142)	(137)	(177)	(137)
1976[a]	(359)	(608)	(282)	(325)	(253)	(358)	(235)
1980	(214)	(291)	(148)	(163)	(144)	(193)	(119)
1984	(307)	(360)	(200)	(188)	(242)	(281)	(254)
1988	(338)	(146)	(225)	(189)	(266)	(270)	(278)
1992[a]	(418)	(441)	(334)	(269)	(305)	(354)	(273)
1996[a]	(312)	(329)	(226)	(136)	(197)	(266)	(215)
2000[a]	(342)	(270)	(266)	(203)	(224)	(201)	(212)

[a] Numbers are weighted.

parable Republicans gave Bush in 1992, and even modestly higher than Republicans gave Reagan in 1988. In all but 1980 and 1992, independents have approved of the incumbent. Until 1996 that meant they approved of a Republican incumbent, but in 1996 and 2000, they approved of a Democratic incumbent. In both 1996 and 2000, about half of the independents who leaned Republican and the weak Republicans approved of Clinton, which is not unlike the percentages received by popular Republican incumbents from weak Democrats and Democratic-leaning independents in 1972, 1984, 1988, and even 1976. Strong partisans, however, rarely approve of an incumbent from the other party. Thus, there is clearly a strong relationship between partisanship and presidential approval. Still, the relationship may be strong, but it is far from complete.

Our second illustration extends the connection we have drawn between partisanship and approval of the incumbent. In this case, we examine the relationship between partisanship and approval of the incumbent's handling of the economy, in particular. Table 8-5 shows the relationship among all seven partisan

TABLE 8-5   Approval of Incumbent's Handling of the Economy among Partisan Groups, 1984, 1988, 1992, 1996, and 2000

Attitude toward handling of the economy	Party identification							
	Strong Democrat	Weak Democrat	Independent, leans Democrat	Independent	Independent, leans Republican	Weak Republican	Strong Republican	Total
1984								
Approve	17%	41%	32%	68%	84%	86%	95%	58%
Disapprove	83	59	68	32	16	14	5	42
Total	100%	100%	100%	100%	100%	100%	100%	100%
(N)	(309)	(367)	(207)	(179)	(245)	(277)	(249)	(1,833)
1988								
Approve	19%	35%	32%	57%	76%	79%	92%	54%
Disapprove	81	65	68	43	24	21	8	46
Total	100%	100%	100%	100%	100%	100%	100%	100%
(N)	(337)	(332)	(229)	(185)	(262)	(262)	(269)	(1,876)
1992[a]								
Approve	3%	9%	6%	9%	31%	34%	66%	20%
Disapprove	97	91	94	91	69	66	34	80
Total	100%	100%	100%	100%	100%	100%	100%	100%
(N)	(425)	(445)	(340)	(267)	(310)	(347)	(266)	(2,401)
1996[a]								
Approve	96%	82%	76%	58%	46%	49%	30%	66%
Disapprove	4	18	24	42	54	50	70	34
Total	100%	100%	100%	100%	100%	100%	100%	100%
(N)	(310)	(325)	(228)	(131)	(188)	(263)	(209)	(1,655)
2000[a]								
Approve	95%	90%	84%	73%	60%	70%	47%	77%
Disapprove	5	10	16	27	40	30	53	23
Total	100%	100%	100%	100%	100%	100%	100%	100%
(N)	(342)	(265)	(264)	(198)	(206)	(184)	(200)	(1,659)

[a] Numbers are weighted.

categories and the approval of the handling of the economy by Reagan in 1984 and 1988, Bush in 1992, and Clinton in 1996 and 2000.[16]

In 1984 and 1988 more than three-quarters of each of the three Republican groups approved of Reagan's handling of the economy, while more than half—and often more than two-thirds—of the three Democratic groups disapproved. Independents generally approved of Reagan's economic efforts, albeit more strongly in 1984 than in 1988. The 1992 election was dramatically different, with overwhelming disapproval of Bush's handling of the economy among the three Democratic groups and the pure independents. Even two-thirds of the weak and Republican-leaning independents disapproved. Only strong Republicans typically approved, and even then one in three did not. The relationship in 1996 is most like that of 1984. In part this is because approval of Reagan's handling of the economy was high that year—though approval of Clinton's handling of the economy was even higher. The relationship in 1996, while strong, is not quite as strong as in 1984, most notably because Democrats gave Reagan lower marks in 1984 than Republicans gave Clinton in 1996. In 2000 Clinton received even higher approval levels for his handling of the economy. As a result, the vast majority of Democrats and even three in four of the pure independents approved of his economic performance. This is by far the highest economic-approval marks independents have given. But then, most Republicans also approved, and nearly half of strong Republicans did so in 2000. As with overall approval, these figures for 2000 were more favorable for Gore's candidacy than the figures for the incumbent party in any other election have been.

The third example of the impact of partisanship on attitudes and beliefs is its relationship to positions on policy issues. In Table 8-6, we report this relationship among the seven partisan categories and our balance of issues measure developed in chapter 6, collapsed into a threefold, pro-Republican, neutral, pro-Democratic grouping.[17] As we saw in chapter 6, these issues favored the Republicans in 1972, 1976, and 1980, worked slightly to the Democratic advantage in 1984, 1988, and 1992, then once again favored the Republicans in 1996 and 2000. In all cases, the balance of issues measure has only moderately favored one party over the other.

As the table shows, there has regularly been a clear and moderately strong relationship between partisanship and the balance of issues measure, but it is one that, by 2000, had strengthened considerably. Until 1984 the relationship had been stronger among Republicans than among Democrats. In 1984 and 1988 (and also 1992, but recall that measure depends upon only three issues and is therefore less useful), the relationship was, if anything, stronger among Democrats than Republicans. That change very likely was due to the changing political context. In 1980, for example, more people, Democrats as well as Republicans, were closer to the median position of Reagan than of Carter on such important issues as defense spending and cutting income taxes. Reagan pushed increases in defense spending and cuts in income taxes through Congress in his first term, and he slowed the increases in spending for many

TABLE 8-6   Balance of Issues Positions among Partisan Groups, 1976–2000

Issue positions closer to[a]	Party identification							
	Strong Democrat	Weak Democrat	Independent, leans Democrat	Independent	Independent, leans Republican	Weak Republican	Strong Republican	Total
1976								
Democratic candidate	28%	27%	22%	15%	12%	9%	3%	18%
Neutral[b]	32	26	37	29	27	23	27	29
Republican candidate	39	47	40	55	61	67	69	53
Total	99%	100%	99%	99%	100%	99%	99%	100%
(N)	(422)	(655)	(336)	(416)	(277)	(408)	(254)	(2,778)
1980								
Democratic candidate	26%	23%	27%	20%	12%	10%	9%	19%
Neutral	34	37	33	43	40	43	31	37
Republican candidate	40	40	40	37	48	48	60	43
Total	100%	100%	100%	100%	100%	101%	100%	99%
(N)	(245)	(317)	(161)	(176)	(150)	(202)	(127)	(1,378)
1984								
Democratic candidate	57%	49%	59%	35%	23%	29%	14%	39%
Neutral	32	37	28	48	46	40	39	38
Republican candidate	11	14	13	17	32	32	47	23
Total	100%	100%	100%	100%	101%	101%	100%	100%
(N)	(331)	(390)	(215)	(213)	(248)	(295)	(256)	(1,948)

1988								
Democratic candidate	49%	36%	50%	33%	21%	21%	11%	32%
Neutral	34	40	38	48	46	43	35	40
Republican candidate	17	24	12	19	33	36	53	29
Total	100%	100%	100%	100%	100%	100%	99%	101%
(N)	(355)	(359)	(240)	(215)	(270)	(281)	(279)	(1,999)
1992[b]								
Democratic candidate	40%	36%	30%	26%	13%	13%	9%	25%
Neutral	55	57	65	70	74	77	74	67
Republican candidate	5	7	4	5	13	11	17	9
Total	100%	100%	99%	101%	100%	101%	100%	101%
(N)	(380)	(389)	(313)	(235)	(283)	(335)	(238)	(2,192)
1996[b]								
Democratic candidate	44%	27%	35%	17%	13%	9%	1%	22%
Neutral	27	36	34	43	27	23	14	29
Republican candidate	30	37	31	40	60	68	85	49
Total	101%	100%	100%	100%	100%	100%	100%	100%
(N)	(313)	(333)	(229)	(140)	(195)	(268)	(217)	(1,696)
2000[b]								
Democratic candidate	30%	26%	25%	20%	8%	10%	2%	19%
Neutral	47	48	46	49	40	33	25	43
Republican candidate	23	25	29	31	51	57	73	38
Total	100%	101%	100%	100%	99%	100%	100%	100%
(N)	(188)	(161)	(157)	(113)	(134)	(101)	(99)	(953)

[a] The neutral category consists of scores of −1, 0, or 1 on the full measure, while the Republican [Democratic] category is any score greater than 1 [less than −1] on the full measure.

[b] Numbers are weighted.

domestic programs as well. By 1984, therefore, the electorate no longer favored as great an increase in defense spending and were more amenable to increased spending on some domestic programs. Thus, in the next three elections, issues tended to divide the electorate along party lines, with Democrats closer to their party's nominee. The result was a sharper and more balanced relationship between partisanship and the balance of issues measure. The increased polarization of the parties in Congress and among candidates generally accelerated in the 1994 congressional elections. This division between the two parties appears to have translated to partisan affiliation in the public as well. In 1996, while the balance of issue measure favored the Republicans, its relationship to party identification was stronger. It was almost as strong in 2000 and was moderately strong on both sides of the competition. Prospective issues appear to be increasingly polarized by party, strikingly so by 2000. Partisan polarization characterizes not only prospective issues but also most other factors we have examined, but, as we have shown, increasingly polarization on prospective issues has gone hand in hand with the increase in impact of prospective issues on the vote.

Finally, we find a strong relationship between party identification and our measure of retrospective evaluations in the past seven presidential elections.[18] Table 8-7 shows the basic relationship from 1976 through 2000, collapsing the summary retrospective measure into the three categories of pro-Democratic, neutral, and pro-Republican. In all years except 1992, a majority in each Republican category tended to evaluate Republican performance favorably. In all years but 1980, more than three in five Democratic identifiers assessed the Democratic Party favorably. Even in the unfavorable years of 1980 for the Democrats and 1992 for the Republicans, party identifiers were far more likely than the rest of the public to favor their party. In 2000 the relationship was again very strong, with large majorities of partisan affiliates favoring their party on retrospective evaluations. This relationship, therefore, has consistently been among the strongest, and it suggests that Clinton was victorious in 1996 in large part because the public thought he and the Democrats had done well, and were at least as likely as the Republicans to do well in the future. The relationship was nearly as strong in 2000 as in 1996. Gore and Bush virtually tied because the summary measure was modestly closer to splitting evenly between the two parties in 2000, compared to 1996, and because Gore did somewhat poorer among weak Democrats than Clinton had four years earlier.

We have seen that both party identification and retrospective evaluations have been consistently and strongly related to the vote, but these two measures are also strongly related to each other in every election. Do they both still contribute independently to the vote? The answer, as can be seen in Table 8-8, is yes. In this table, we have examined the combined impact of party identification and retrospective evaluations upon voting choices in the past seven presidential elections. To simplify the presentation, we have used the threefold grouping of the summary retrospective evaluations measure, and we have also regrouped party iden-

TABLE 8-7 Retrospective Evaluations among Partisan Groups, 1976–2000

Summary measure of retrospective evaluations[a]	Party identification							
	Strong Democrat	Weak Democrat	Independent, leans Democrat	Independent	Independent, leans Republican	Weak Republican	Strong Republican	Total
1976[b]								
Democratic	80%	53%	62%	39%	16%	19%	6%	42%
Neutral	11	23	24	28	28	25	23	23
Republican	10	24	15	33	56	57	71	35
Total	101%	100%	101%	100%	100%	101%	100%	100%
(N)	(314)	(535)	(249)	(293)	(238)	(314)	(206)	(2,149)
1980								
Democratic	45%	29%	18%	11%	8%	7%	4%	20%
Neutral	26	21	25	22	8	9	2	17
Republican	29	50	57	68	85	84	93	62
Total	100%	100%	100%	101%	101%	100%	99%	99%
(N)	(299)	(294)	(157)	(160)	(144)	(197)	(123)	(1,304)
1984								
Democratic	77%	54%	65%	27%	9%	9%	5%	37%
Neutral	12	17	13	22	15	18	5	14
Republican	12	29	21	52	76	73	90	49
Total	101%	100%	99%	101%	100%	100%	100%	100%
(N)	(303)	(356)	(197)	(181)	(241)	(270)	(239)	(1,787)
1988								
Democratic	79%	61%	64%	32%	20%	17%	6%	42%
Neutral	11	19	24	34	32	28	19	23
Republican	10	20	12	35	48	55	75	36
Total	100%	100%	100%	101%	100%	100%	100%	101%
(N)	(287)	(305)	(199)	(167)	(228)	(239)	(245)	(1,670)

(Table continues)

TABLE 8-7   (continued)

	Party identification							
Summary measure of retrospective evaluations[a]	Strong Democrat	Weak Democrat	Independent, leans Democrat	Independent	Independent, leans Republican	Weak Republican	Strong Republican	Total
1992[b]								
Democratic	90%	80%	85%	72%	39%	32%	12%	61%
Neutral	7	12	8	16	28	29	26	17
Republican	3	9	7	12	32	39	62	21
Total	100%	101%	100%	100%	99%	100%	100%	99%
(N)	(339)	(340)	(267)	(207)	(245)	(268)	(221)	(1,886)
1996[b]								
Democratic	77%	72%	59%	37%	25%	19%	3%	47%
Neutral	20	19	28	29	13	25	10	20
Republican	3	9	13	35	62	56	87	33
Total	100%	100%	100%	101%	100%	100%	100%	100%
(N)	(162)	(150)	(91)	(50)	(79)	(130)	(93)	(756)
2000[b]								
Democratic	82%	57%	56%	34%	23%	23%	11%	44%
Neutral	9	22	26	25	14	20	9	18
Republican	9	21	19	41	63	56	81	38
Total	100%	100%	101%	100%	100%	99%	101%	100%
(N)	(159)	(128)	(142)	(100)	(112)	(94)	(110)	(846)

[a] The neutral category is the same as that on the full scale, while the Democratic [Republican] category is the combination of all three Democratic [Republican] categories on the full scale.
[b] Numbers are weighted.

TABLE 8-8 Percentage of Major-Party Voters Who Voted for the Republican Candidate, by Party Identification and Summary Retrospective Measures, 1976–2000

| Party identification[a] | Summary retrospective[b] | | | | | | | |
| | Republican | | Neutral | | Democratic | | Total | |
	%	N	%	N	%	N	%	N
A. Voted for Ford, 1976[c]								
Republican	96	(269)[d]	90	(98)	35	(54)	87	(421)
Independent	85	(183)	73	(133)	16	(187)	56	(503)
Democratic	53	(111)	30	(96)	5	(404)	18	(611)
Total	84	(563)	65	(327)	11	(645)	49	(1,535)
B. Voted for Reagan, 1980								
Republican	100	(217)	75	(12)	33	(12)	95	(241)
Independent	82	(183)	36	(36)	24	(25)	69	(244)
Democratic	51	(135)	6	(78)	7	(140)	24	(353)
Total	81	(535)	21	(126)	11	(177)	58	(838)
C. Voted for Reagan, 1984								
Republican	99	(344)	86	(42)	39	(18)	95	(404)
Independent	91	(230)	77	(62)	10	(110)	67	(402)
Democratic	72	(97)	32	(62)	5	(333)	22	(492)
Total	93	(671)	63	(166)	8	(461)	59	(1,298)
D. Voted for G. Bush, 1988								
Republican	97	(277)	93	(84)	46	(37)	91	(398)
Independent	86	(124)	64	(94)	15	(131)	54	(349)
Democratic	67	(54)	27	(63)	5	(296)	16	(413)
Total	91	(455)	64	(241)	11	(464)	53	(1,160)

(Table continues)

TABLE 8-8 (continued)

Party identification[a]	Summary retrospective[b]							
	Republican		Neutral		Democratic		Total	
	%	N	%	N	%	N	%	N
E. Voted for G. Bush, 1992[c]								
Republican	99	(187)	89	(87)	57	(61)	89	(335)
Independent	86	(72)	83	(56)	15	(233)	40	(362)
Democratic	58	(24)	32	(41)	4	(422)	9	(487)
Total	92	(282)	75	(185)	12	(717)	41	(1184)
F. Voted for Dole, 1996[c]								
Republican	96	(121)	74	(27)	45	(20)	86	(168)
Independent	91	(47)	29	(28)	9	(47)	45	(122)
Democratic	50	(12)	0	(43)	2	(175)	4	(230)
Total	92	(180)	29	(98)	7	(242)	40	(520)
G. Voted for G. W. Bush, 2000[c]								
Republican	98	(103)	92	(18)	69	(20)	93	(141)
Independent	86	(71)	39	(39)	34	(75)	55	(185)
Democratic	41	(24)	20	(28)	2	(149)	8	(201)
Total	87	(198)	44	(85)	17	(244)	48	(527)

[a] Democratic [Republican] identifiers were those classified as strong and weak Democrats [Republicans]. Independents include those who lean toward either party and "pure" independents.

[b] The neutral category is the same as that on the full scale, while the Democratic [Republican] category is the combination of all three Democratic [Republican] categories on the full scale.

[c] Numbers are weighted.

[d] The numbers in parentheses are the totals on which percentages are based.

tification into the three groups of strong and weak Republicans, all three independent categories, and strong and weak Democrats.

Table 8-8 shows the percentage of major-party voters who voted Republican by both party identification and retrospective evaluations. Reading across the rows reveals that for all elections, retrospective evaluations are strongly related to the vote, regardless of the voter's party identification. Reading down each column shows that in all elections, party identification is related to the vote, regardless of the voter's retrospective evaluations. Moreover, party identification and retrospective evaluations have a combined impact on how people voted. For example, in 2000 among Republicans with pro-Republican evaluations, 98 percent voted for Bush; among Democrats with pro-Democratic evaluations, only 2 percent did. Note also the overall similarity, especially among the past five elections. The most important reason that the Republicans won a smaller victory in 1988 than 1984 appears to be the less positive retrospective evaluations, while Clinton's victory in 1992 appears to be due to the decidedly negative assessments of the Republican incumbent, and his victory in 1996 to be due to the positive assessments of him and his party. In 2000 George W. Bush did better than Clinton's opponents primarily by holding on better to the support of Republicans and independents, especially those for whom retrospective evaluations were neutral or pro-Democratic. Thus, partisanship is a key component for understanding the evaluations of the public and their votes, but the large changes in outcomes over time must be traced to retrospective and prospective evaluations, simply because partisanship does not change substantially over time.

In sum, partisanship appears to affect the way voters evaluate incumbents and their performance. Positions on issues have been a bit different. Although partisans in the 1970s and early 1980s were likely to be closer to their party's nominee on policy, the connection was less clear than between partisanship and retrospective evaluations. It is only recently that prospective evaluations have emerged as being nearly as important a set of influences on candidate choice as retrospective evaluations. It may well be that the strengthening of this relationship is a reflection of the increasingly sharp cleavages between the parties among candidates and officeholders.[19] Still, policy-related evaluations are influenced partly by history and political memory and partly by the candidates' campaign strategies. Partisan attachments, then, limit the ability of a candidate to control his or her fate in the electorate, but such attachments are not entirely rigid. Candidates have some flexibility in the support they receive from partisans, especially depending upon the candidates' or their predecessor's performance in office and upon the policy promises they make in the campaign.

CONCLUSION

Party loyalties affect how people vote, how they evaluate issues, and how they judge the performance of the incumbent president and his party. In recent years, research has suggested that party loyalties not only affect issue prefer-ences, perceptions, and evaluations, but also may affect partisanship. There is good reason to believe that the relationship between partisanship and these fac-tors is more complex than any model that assumes a one-way relationship would suggest. Doubtless, evaluations of the incumbent's performance may also affect party loyalties.[20]

As we saw in this chapter, there was a substantial shift toward Republican loy-alties over the 1980s; among whites, the clear advantage Democrats have enjoyed over the past four decades appears to be gone. To some extent, this shift in party loyalties must have reflected Reagan's appeal and his successful performance in office, as judged by the electorate. It also appears that he was able to shift some of that appeal in Bush's direction in 1988 directly, by the connection between performance judgments and the vote, and also indirectly, through shifts in party loyalties among white Americans. Bush lost much of the appeal he inherited, pri-marily because of negative assessments of his performance in office over the economy, and he was also not able to hold on to the high approval ratings he had attained in 1991 after the success in the Persian Gulf War. In 1996 Clinton demonstrated that a president could rebound from a weak early performance as judged by the electorate and benefit from a growing economy.

The 1996 election stood as one comparable to the reelection campaigns of other recent, successful incumbents. Clinton received marks as high as or higher than Nixon's in 1972 and Reagan's in 1984 for his overall performance and for his handling of the economy. With strong retrospective judgments, the electorate basically decided that one good term deserved another.

The political landscape was dramatically different after the 1996 election compared to the time just before the 1992 elections. While the proportion of Democrats to Republicans in the electorate had been quite close for over a decade, the general impression was that Republicans had a "lock" on the White House, while the Democrats' nearly forty year majority in the U.S. House was thought to be unbreakable. The 1992 election demonstrated that a party has a lock on the presidency only when the public believes that party's candidate will handle the office better than the opposition. The 1994 elections so reversed conventional thinking that some then considered Congress a stronghold for the Republican Party. Conventional wisdom, a lengthy history of such out-comes, and the apparent strength of the Republican delegation seemed to ensure that the GOP would gain seats in the 1998 congressional elections. But not only did Republicans fail to gain any congressional seats in 1998, they actu-ally lost five House seats. This loss so shocked politicians that Speaker Newt Gingrich of Georgia resigned his office and his seat. A Democratic resurgence seemed to be in the making. The Republicans' handling of the impeachment and Senate trial of Clinton seemed to further set the stage for Democratic gains. Perhaps the single most surprising fact leading into the 2000 presiden-tial race was the high approval ratings an impeached, but not convicted, Clinton held.

The question for the 2000 campaign was why Gore was unable to do better than essentially tie Bush in the election (whether counting by popular or electoral votes). We must remember, however, how closely balanced all other key indicators were. Partisanship among whites was essentially evenly split between the two parties, with a Republican advantage in turnout at least partially offsetting the Democratic partisanship of blacks. Prospective issues, as in most election years, only modestly favored one side or the other. Retrospective evaluations, however, provided Gore with a solid edge, as did approval ratings of Clinton on the economy.

The failure, then, was in Gore's inability to translate that edge in retrospective assessments into a more substantial edge in the voting booth. Retrospective evaluations were important factors in voters' choices, and it appears that such evaluations were almost as strongly related to the vote in 2000 as in other recent elections. But Gore failed to push that edge to turn a virtual tie into an outright win.

Our evidence indicates that he might well have gained more had he emphasized his role in the Clinton administration and the administration's (alleged) role in the economic boom that lasted through the 2000 election. Our evidence does not, however, speak to the contention made by Gore and others in support of his campaign decision that, by emphasizing his ties with Clinton, he would make relevant not just the good, such as economic performance, but also the bad, such as Clinton's personal and ethical lapses and those of his administration (including Gore's handling of campaign fund raising in 1996). Of course, all such "what if" questions are hypothetical, counterfactual, and not directly amenable to empirical investigation. Moreover, our analyses are not directed toward the ethical and personal evaluations of Clinton, only his professional side. Still, our results do show Clinton with high approval ratings, suggesting that voters might have been keeping a distinction between Gore and a successful president and the strong economy on the one hand, and Gore and the unfaithful president he served on the other. If voters appear to have done so with respect to Clinton himself, why not for his vice president?

PART 3

The 2000 and 2002 Congressional Elections

✦✦✦

So far we have discussed the 2000 presidential election—the main political event of that year and the major factor that shaped the 2002 midterm elections. But the president shares responsibility with Congress, which must enact a legislative program and approve major appointments. Having concluded our discussion of George W. Bush's election, we will turn now to the selection of the 107th and the 108th Congresses.

There were many elections in 2000. In addition to the presidential election, there were 11 gubernatorial elections, 34 elections for the U.S. Senate, and elections for all 435 members of the U.S. House of Representatives.[1] Unlike 1980, when the Republicans gained control of the U.S. Senate, or the 1994 midterm election in which the Republicans won control of the U.S. House of Representatives for the first time in four decades and regained control of the Senate, which they had lost in 1986, the 2000 election held no major surprises. Control of both the House and Senate was at stake in 2000, and the outcome was remarkably close. The Republicans retained control of the House for the fourth consecutive election, a winning streak they had not equaled for seventy-two years.[2] But the Republicans lost two House seats, winning 221 seats to the Democrats' 212, with two independents—the narrowest margin of control since the 1952 election.[3] In the Senate contests the Republicans won fifteen races, the Democrats nineteen, reducing the GOP total from fifty-four to fifty, thus breaking even with the Democrats. This was the first time since 1881 that the Democrats and Republicans each had an equal number of seats in the Senate.[4] Only Vice President Dick Cheney's power to cast a tie-breaking vote allowed the Republicans to maintain control. Then in June 2001, after James M. Jeffords of Vermont announced that he was quitting the Republican Party, the GOP lost control of the Senate.

The 2002 elections also contained no major surprises. Even though parties holding the White House have historically lost seats in midterm elections, few experts expected the GOP to lose control of the House, although some were surprised at the party's ability to *gain* seats. But the gain was modest, six seats, giving the GOP 229 spots to the Democrat's 205, with one seat held by an independent. The Republicans won twenty-two of the thirty-four Senate races, gaining two seats in the Senate and majority control. But only Republican representative Saxby Chambliss's defeat of incumbent Democrat Max Cleland in Georgia was seen as an upset. The GOP now held a fifty-one to forty-eight seat majority. The major consolation for the Democrats was in the nation's thirty-six gubernatorial contests; although the Democrats won only fourteen of these races, they took control in four large battleground states—Illinois, Michigan, Pennsylvania, and Wisconsin—and retained control of California.

By electing a Republican president and by retaining Republican control in the House and Senate, voters in 2000 briefly ended divided government. For the first time since the Eighty-third Congress ended in 1955, the Republicans held the presidency and both houses of Congress. All the same, there was very little change in Congress, at least until the Jeffords defection seven months after the election. The 2002 election once again ended divided government, the pattern that has prevailed in most of postwar American politics.

Even though Al Gore won more popular votes than George W. Bush, Bush fared much better than Bob Dole in 1996 and won a much larger share of the vote than his father had in 1992. Why, despite these gains at the presidential level, did the Republicans lose seats in both the House and Senate in 2000? On the other hand, given that the public strongly disapproved of the lame-duck 105th House impeachment of Bill Clinton in December 1998, why were the Democratic gains so small? The margin between the parties in both congressional chambers is slight: Who will gain power in these bodies in future elections? What are the prospects for the Republicans continuing their winning streak in House races? Do the Democrats have a chance of regaining control of the House and becoming the majority party in the Senate?

Chapter 9 attempts to answer these questions by examining election results. In 2000, 403 House incumbents sought reelection and 394 of them won. Only forty-one new members were elected to the House, and neither party was able to gain many of the seats held by the other party. As we will see, twenty-seven incumbent senators sought reelection, but only twenty-one were reelected. There were thirteen new senators: ten were Democrats, only three were Republicans.

We will examine the geographic basis of party support and show that there has been a major transformation paralleling—though not quite as dramatically—changes we observed in presidential elections. We will also see how these regional shifts have transformed the parties within Congress.

This chapter also explains why incumbents, and especially House incumbents, usually win. Incumbency is a major resource, and House challengers usually lack the experience and the money to launch an effective campaign. Incumbents have been winning by increasing margins, and we will discuss alternative explanations for this. However, this trend has recently been reversed and we will discuss the reasons for this reversal. Senate incumbents are more vulnerable than House incumbents. Why are they more likely to lose? We will also see how House leaders in 2000 often encouraged members of their party to run for a safe House seat rather than follow the more risky route of running for the Senate.

Although most incumbents are reelected, some face greater obstacles than others. We will examine the factors that make challengers competitive. We find that previous political experience and adequate funding are the most important assets for winning a new seat. Senate challengers are more likely to possess both, which is one reason they are more likely to win.

We examine the impact of the 2000 elections on Congress. Some have argued that the close partisan balance in both chambers gave additional power to House and Senate moderates. Yet even though both Democrats and Republicans have moderate members, the parties are sharply divided over many issues, and the room for compromise is limited. As we will see, Bush might find it difficult to deliver on his pledge to provide bipartisan leadership.

Chapter 9 ends by discussing the prospects for the 2002 election and for the early elections of the decade, as seen ten months before the 2002 elections were held. Expectations about the 2002 election were shaped by a basic historical fact: in the forty midterm elections between 1842 and 1998, the party holding the presidency had lost strength in the House in thirty-eight elections. One of these exceptions was 1934, during Franklin Delano Roosevelt's first term, but the other was 1998. So the tendency for the party holding the presidency to lose seats is not a natural law, but results from conditions that place the incumbent party at risk. We will review the extensive research on models of House elections, but we should bear in mind that political science modelers predicted that Gore would win the 2000 presidential election. In any event, as of early 2002, the facts necessary to model the election were not available. Even so, these models provide insight into the dynamics that affect congressional election outcomes. Predictions about 2002 were further complicated by the reapportionment and redistricting that followed the 2000 census. Most experts predicted that the reallocation of congressional seats and the redrawing of congressional boundaries would slightly benefit the Republican Party. We also examine the prospects for the 2002 Senate elections. The Republicans were defending twenty seats and the Democrats fourteen, although the Republicans appeared to have more safe seats. It seemed reasonable to predict that the battles for control of the Senate and the House would be fierce.

Chapter 10 examines how voters make decisions—one of the most exciting and rapidly growing areas of research since the National Election Studies (NES) surveys introduced new questions in the 1978 congressional election survey. Because only a third of the Senate seats are contested in each election, our analysis is focused mainly on the House. This chapter examines how social forces influence voters' choices and compares the relationship of these factors to presidential voting. The effects of party loyalty and incumbency on voters' choices are also assessed, and in some cases, such as the relationship of party identification and the vote, we can examine relationships in all congressional elections between

1952 and 2000. (The NES data for the 2002 election will not be available until after our book is published.) We examine the ways in which congressional voting can be seen as a referendum on the performance of a particular member of Congress, and we also show that voting can be viewed as a referendum on the president's performance. And we also attempt to discover whether Al Gore or George W. Bush had "coattails," that is, whether they drew votes for legislators of their party. We conclude that the way a person votes for president does affect the way he or she votes for Congress, but that the major factors influencing voting choices are party identification and incumbency. In past elections the Democrats were able to capitalize on their incumbency advantage to win votes. The Republicans have only a narrow incumbency edge, but they may be able to use this to retain congressional power.

Chapter 11 examines the 2002 elections, paralleling our analysis of candidates and outcomes in the 2000 contest. We first turn to the success of incumbents in gaining reelection, again showing that the vast majority of House incumbents who seek reelection are successful. Senate incumbents are usually reelected as well, but they are not as successful as their colleagues in the House. By examining each party's success in challenging incumbents and in open-seat contests, we will see that Republican gains in both chambers came from their wins in open-seat races.

Party representation from the nation's regions changed little between the 107th and the 108th Congresses. The major surprise is that none of the net gains for the GOP came from the South. Democratic losses were mainly in the Midwest, which had lost five seats as a result of reapportionment.

Discussing which party won the election must be done within the context of expectations. According to historical standards, the Republicans clearly won because their modest House gains ran counter to long-term historical patterns. Yet most experts and politicians expected relatively little change in either chamber, although the balance of power in the Senate was clearly at stake. Because Bush had high approval ratings throughout 2002, academic models predicted that the GOP also would do relatively well. Likewise, since the GOP had only a slim majority in the House, the Republicans were not "exposed" to large losses. The two factors working against the Republicans were the weak economy and corporate scandals. But Bush avoided damage from both these problems. Moreover, following the advice of his chief political advisor, Karl Rove, Bush actively campaigned in close contests and, we conclude, this strategy was successful. Moreover, the Republicans appear to have been more successful at stimulating turnout among their supporters than the Democrats were.

In chapter 9 we discuss the potential effects of reapportionment and redistricting, and in chapter 11 we assess their actual impact. Even though the Republicans did not have complete control of redistricting in many states, they were in control in some of the larger states that were gaining or losing seats. The GOP made good use of this control. The Democrats controlled more states, but their strategic situation was not as good. Although it is not easy to determine the effect of redistricting and reapportionment, the Republicans appear to have gained five seats as a result.

We then turn to candidate resources in 2002, although the spending data needed to complete our analysis are not yet official. Previous political experience was an important factor in predicting the success of House candidates in open-seat races. A preliminary discussion of spending in congressional races shows the increasing importance of the national parties in funding candidates and suggests that Democrats more than Republicans may be hurt by the new campaign finance bill that outlaws "soft" money.

We next discuss the impact of the 2002 election on Congress. Now that the Republicans control both chambers, President Bush will have greater opportunity to carry out his policies, and one of his near-term goals will be targeted tax cuts to stimulate the lagging economy. But the president does not have complete control of the policy agenda, and social conservatives within the GOP are expected to push for more limits on abortions, more support for religious groups, and funding for sexual abstinence programs. We also discuss organizational changes that followed the 2002 elections, as well as changes in leadership that resulted from the resignation of Richard A. Gephardt, D-Mo., as House minority leader and of Trent Lott, R-Miss., as the potential Senate majority leader.

Finally, we turn to prospects for the 2004 congressional election, as well as subsequent congressional elections during this decade. Very few House seats are competitive, so even though Democrats would need to win only twelve seats to gain control of the House in 2004, this will be a difficult task unless there are dramatic developments that hurt Bush and his party. In the Senate, Democrats will need to defend nineteen seats, whereas the Republicans need to defend only fifteen. But even though the Republicans seem likely to retain control of the House, they would still be a very long way from equaling the Democratic dominance of winning twenty straight elections between 1954 and 1992.

Chapter 9

Candidates and Outcomes in 2000

◆◆◆

The congressional elections of 2000 were shaped by the electoral earthquake of 1994. In that year the Republicans unexpectedly won control of both chambers of the Congress, the first time the GOP had won the House since the 1952 election. In the 1996 election they held the House for a consecutive election (something they had not done since the 1920s) and defended their majority again in 1998. However, the Democrats gained ground in the House in each of those elections. In the Senate, the Republicans added to their majority in 1996 and broke even in 1998. Thus, going into the elections of 2000, the GOP still had control of Congress, but that control was again on the line. As it turned out, the Republicans succeeded in maintaining a majority in the House, but not in the Senate. In the House, they ended up with a somewhat narrower margin, winning 221 seats to the Democrats' 212, with two independents.[1] This was a net loss of two seats for the GOP. In the Senate, on the other hand, the Republicans lost four seats, resulting in a 50–50 seat division of the chamber.

In this chapter, we shall examine the pattern of congressional outcomes for 2000 and how they compared with outcomes of previous years. We seek to explain why the 2000 results took the shape they did—what factors affected the success of incumbents seeking to return and what permitted some challengers to run better than others. We also discuss the likely impact of the election results on the politics of the 107th Congress. Finally, we consider the implications of the 2000 results for the 2002 midterm elections and for elections in the near future.

ELECTION OUTCOMES IN 2000

Patterns of Incumbency Success

Most races involve incumbents, and most incumbents are reelected. This generalization has been true for every set of congressional elections since the Second World War, although the degree to which it has held true has varied somewhat from one election to another. Table 9-1 presents information on election outcomes for House and Senate races involving incumbents between 1954 and 2000.[2] During this period, an average of 93 percent of the House incumbents and 83 percent of the Senate incumbents who sought reelection were successful.

In 2000 the proportion of representatives reelected (98 percent) was noticeably above the twenty-four-election average (and virtually identical to 1998), while the success rate for senators (78 percent) was substantially worse than that for the members of the House, and somewhat lower than the Senate average since 1954. The results for the House contrasted markedly with elections earlier in the decade. Incumbent success was depressed in 1992 by higher than usual defeat rates both in primaries and general elections. The large number of losses occurred in part because it was the election after a census (when redistricting changed many district lines and forced a number of representatives to face one another in the same district), and in part because of a major scandal involving many House incumbents.[3] In 1994 the lower rate of reelection was due almost entirely to the general election defeat of an unusually large number of Democrats, causing the turnover of partisan control of the House. By contrast 2000 had very few primary defeats (two Democrats and one Republican), and the proportion that lost in the general election was only a bit higher (1.5 percent). In the 2000 Senate races, on the other hand, the number of incumbents seeking reelection was higher than in recent elections, and incumbents fared worse than any year since 1986. (We will discuss this below.)

During the period covered by Table 9-1, House and Senate outcomes have sometimes been similar, and in other instances have exhibited different patterns. For example, in most years between 1968 and 1988, House incumbents were substantially more successful than their Senate counterparts. In the three elections between 1976 and 1980, House incumbents' success averaged over 93 percent, while senators averaged only 62 percent. By contrast, the success rates in the five elections before 2000 were fairly similar. Now we have seen a marked divergence. Indeed, in 2000 even though there were more than ten times as many incumbent House contests as incumbent Senate races, the same number of members were defeated in each body.

It appears that the variation in the comparative results between the two bodies results from at least two factors. The first is primarily statistical: House elections routinely involve around 400 incumbents, while Senate contests usually have fewer than 30. A comparatively small number of cases are more likely to produce volatile results over time. Thus the proportion of successful incumbents tends to vary more in the Senate than in the House. Second, Senate races during the earlier period were more likely than House races to be vigorously contested. In many years a substantial number of representatives had no opponent at all or had one who was inexperienced, underfunded, or both. Senators, on the other hand, often had strong, well-financed opponents. Thus representatives were advantaged relative to senators. In the early 1990s the competitiveness of House elections increased, reducing the relative advantage for representatives, although

TABLE 9-1   House and Senate Incumbents and Election Outcomes, 1954–2000

Year	Incumbents running (N)	Primary defeats (N)	Primary defeats (%)	General election defeats (N)	General election defeats (%)	Reelected (N)	Reelected (%)
House							
1954	(407)	(6)	1.5	(22)	5.4	(379)	93.1
1956	(410)	(6)	1.5	(15)	3.7	(389)	94.9
1958	(394)	(3)	0.8	(37)	9.4	(354)	89.8
1960	(405)	(5)	1.2	(25)	6.2	(375)	92.6
1962	(402)	(12)	3.0	(22)	5.5	(368)	91.5
1964	(397)	(8)	2.0	(45)	11.3	(344)	86.6
1966	(411)	(8)	1.9	(41)	10.0	(362)	88.1
1968	(409)	(4)	1.0	(9)	2.2	(396)	96.8
1970	(401)	(10)	2.5	(12)	3.0	(379)	94.5
1972	(392)	(13)	3.3	(13)	3.3	(366)	93.4
1974	(391)	(8)	2.0	(40)	10.2	(343)	87.7
1976	(383)	(3)	0.8	(12)	3.1	(368)	96.1
1978	(382)	(5)	1.3	(19)	5.0	(358)	93.7
1980	(398)	(6)	1.5	(31)	7.8	(361)	90.7
1982	(393)	(10)	2.5	(29)	7.4	(354)	90.1
1984	(411)	(3)	0.7	(16)	3.9	(392)	95.4
1986	(393)	(2)	0.5	(6)	1.5	(385)	98.0
1988	(409)	(1)	0.2	(6)	1.5	(402)	98.3
1990	(407)	(1)	0.2	(15)	3.7	(391)	96.1
1992	(368)	(20)	5.4	(23)	6.3	(325)	88.3
1994	(387)	(4)	1.0	(34)	8.8	(349)	90.2
1996	(384)	(2)	0.5	(21)	5.5	(361)	94.0
1998	(401)	(1)	0.2	(6)	1.5	(394)	98.3
2000	(403)	(3)	0.7	(6)	1.5	(394)	97.8
Senate							
1954	(27)	(0)	—	(4)	15	(23)	85
1956	(30)	(0)	—	(4)	13	(26)	87
1958	(26)	(0)	—	(9)	35	(17)	65
1960	(28)	(0)	—	(1)	4	(27)	96
1962	(30)	(0)	—	(3)	10	(27)	90
1964	(30)	(0)	—	(2)	7	(28)	93
1966	(29)	(2)	7	(1)	3	(26)	90
1968	(28)	(4)	14	(4)	14	(20)	71
1970	(28)	(1)	4	(3)	11	(24)	86
1972	(26)	(1)	4	(5)	19	(20)	77
1974	(26)	(1)	4	(2)	8	(23)	88
1976	(25)	(0)	—	(9)	36	(16)	64

TABLE 9-1 (continued)

Year	Incumbents running (*N*)	Primary defeats (*N*)	Primary defeats (%)	General election defeats (*N*)	General election defeats (%)	Reelected (*N*)	Reelected (%)
1978	(22)	(1)	5	(6)	27	(15)	68
1980	(29)	(4)	14	(9)	31	(16)	55
1982	(30)	(0)	—	(2)	7	(28)	93
1984	(29)	(0)	—	(3)	10	(26)	90
1986	(27)	(0)	—	(6)	22	(21)	78
1988	(26)	(0)	—	(3)	12	(23)	88
1990	(30)	(0)	—	(1)	3	(29)	97
1992	(27)	(1)	4	(3)	11	(23)	85
1994	(26)	(0)	—	(2)	8	(24)	92
1996	(20)	(0)	—	(1)	5	(19)	95
1998	(29)	(0)	—	(3)	10	(26)	90
2000	(27)	(0)	—	(6)	22	(21)	78

the past two cycles have seen competition confined to a narrower range of districts. We will consider this issue in more detail later in the chapter.

We next turn from the consideration of incumbency to party. Figure 9-1 portrays the proportion of seats in the House and Senate held by the Democrats after each election since 1952. It graphically demonstrates how large a departure from the past the elections of 1994 through 2000 were. In House elections before 1994, high rates of incumbent participation, coupled with high rates of incumbent success, led to fairly stable partisan control. Most important, the Democrats had won a majority in the House in every election since 1954 and had won twenty consecutive national elections. This was by far the longest period of dominance of the House by the same party.[4] This winning streak was terminated by the cataclysm of 1994, when the GOP made a net gain of fifty-two representatives, winning 53 percent of the total seats. They held their majority in each subsequent election, although, as noted above, there were successive small shifts back to the Democrats. In the Senate, the last period of Republican control was much more recent. They had taken the Senate in the Reagan victory of 1980, and then retained it in the next two elections. When the class of 1980 faced the voters again in 1986, however, the Democrats made significant gains and won back the majority. They held the Senate until 1994, when the GOP regained control. In 1996 the Republicans expanded their margin; in fact, the 55 percent of the seats they achieved that year (and repeated in 1998) was the highest Republican percentage in either chamber during this forty-eight-year period. Then in 2000 fortune turned against them, resulting in the 50-50 division of the Senate.

The combined effect of party and incumbency in the general election of 2000 is shown in Table 9-2. Overall, the Republicans won 51 percent of the

FIGURE 9-1 Democratic Share of Seats in the House and Senate, 1953–2001

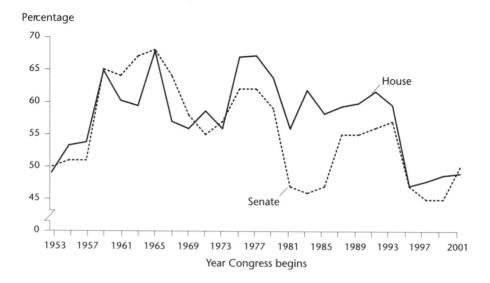

races for House seats, but only 44 percent of the Senate contests. Despite the sharp partisanship of both the presidential and congressional races, incumbents of both parties did very well in House races. Ninety-eight percent of House Republican incumbents in the general election won reelection, and 99 percent of House Democrats were successful. In Senate races, 90 percent of

TABLE 9-2 House and Senate General Election Outcomes, by Party and Incumbency, 2000 (in percentages)

| | Democratic incumbent | No incumbent | | Republican incumbent | Total |
		Democratic seat	Republican seat		
House					
Democrats	99	40	20	2	49
Republicans	1	60	80	98	51
Total	100	100	100	100	100
(*N*)	(202)	(10)	(25)	(198)	(435)
Senate					
Democrats	90	80	50	29	56
Republicans	10	20	50	71	44
Total	100	100	100	100	100
(*N*)	(10)	(5)	(2)	(17)	(34)

Democratic incumbents won, but only 71 percent of GOP incumbents survived. A significant cause of the Democrats' failure to retake the House was their poor success rate in open-seat contests. In those races the Democrats lost more than half of their own open seats, and they were only able to carry 20 percent of the larger number of Republican open seats. Indeed, the Democrats' 2000 performance in open seats was only slightly better than their success rate in the disastrous year of 1994.[5]

The important points from these Senate and House results are that in the 2000 House races, the GOP was able to fight the Democrats to an outcome that virtually maintained the status quo, that this was the third consecutive election in which they had successfully defended their majority, and that the Democrats picked up substantial ground in the Senate. We will explore below the implications of this election series for future Democratic prospects.

Regional Bases of Power

The geographic pattern of 2000 outcomes in the House and Senate can be seen in the partisan breakdowns by region in Table 9-3.[6] For comparison, we also present corresponding data for 1981 (after the Republicans took control of the Senate in Ronald Reagan's first election, and for 1953 (the last Congress before 1995 in which the Republicans controlled both chambers). In the House, comparing 2001 to 1981, we see that the GOP share was very similar in the East, Midwest, and West. The big shift compared to 1981 was the substantial Republican gains in the South and the border states. Overall, the Republicans won a majority of seats in all regions but the East and West in 2000. The pattern is similar in the Senate. Between 1981 and 2001 GOP gains were limited to two regions (the South and border), while they lost slightly in the West and noticeably in the Midwest and the East. In 2001 the Republicans had a majority only in the West and South.

The 2001 results are more interesting when viewed from the longer historical perspective. In 1953 there were sharp regional differences in party representation in both houses. In the intervening years, these differences have greatly diminished. The most obvious changes have occurred in the South. The percentage of southern seats held by the Democrats declined from 94 percent in 1953 to 42 percent in 2001. In 1953 the Democrats held all twenty-two southern Senate seats, but in 2001 they controlled only nine. The regional shift was less dramatic for congressional representation than for presidential elections (see chapter 3), but in both instances there was a move away from Democratic dominance.

This change in the partisan share of the South's seats in Congress has had an important impact on that region's influence within the two parties. The South used to be the backbone of Democratic congressional representation. This, and the tendency of southern members to build seniority, gave southerners disproportionate power within the Democratic Party in Congress. Because of declining

TABLE 9-3   Party Shares of Regional Delegations in the House and Senate, 1953, 1981, and 2001

	1953			1981			2001		
Region	Demo-crats (%)	Repub-licans (%)	(N)	Demo-crats (%)	Repub-licans (%)	(N)	Demo-crats (%)	Repub-licans (%)	(N)
House									
East	35	65	(116)	56	44	(105)	61	39	(89)
Midwest	23	76	(118)ᵃ	47	53	(111)	46	54	(96)
West	33	67	(57)	51	49	(76)	54	46	(93)
South	94	6	(106)	64	36	(108)	42	58	(125)
Border	68	32	(38)	69	31	(35)	38	62	(32)
Total	49	51	(435)	56	44	(435)	49	51	(435)
Senate									
East	25	75	(20)	50	50	(20)	60	40	(20)
Midwest	14	86	(22)	41	59	(22)	64	36	(22)
West	45	55	(22)	35	65	(26)	39	61	(26)
South	100	0	(22)	55	45	(22)	41	59	(22)
Border	70	30	(10)	70	30	(10)	50	50	(10)
Total	49	51	(96)	47	53	(100)	50	50	(100)

ᵃ Includes one independent.

Democratic electoral success in the region, the numerical strength of southern Democrats in Congress has waned. In 1953, with the Republicans in control of both chambers, southerners accounted for around 45 percent of Democratic seats in the House and Senate. By the 1970s southern strength had declined, stabilizing at between 25 and 30 percent of Democratic seats. In 2001 southerners accounted for 25 percent of Democratic House seats and only 18 percent of Democratic senators.

The South's share of Republican congressional representation presents the reverse picture. Minuscule at the end of World War II, it has grown steadily, reaching about 20 percent after the 1980 elections and 32 percent after 2000. As a consequence of these changes, southern influence has declined in the Democratic Party and grown in the GOP, to the point that southerners dominate the Republican leadership positions in both houses of Congress.[7] Because southerners of both parties tend to be more conservative than their colleagues from other regions, these shifts in regional strength have tended to make the Democratic Party in Congress more liberal and the Republican Party more conservative.[8]

Other regional changes since 1953, while not as striking as those in the South, are also significant. In the 1953 House, the Republicans controlled the East and West by two-to-one margins, and the Midwest by three-to-one; in 2001 they held only a narrow advantage in the Midwest, and the Democrats had a majority of eastern and western seats. The Senate also has exhibited substantial shifts away from Republican dominance of the East and Midwest. On balance, we might refer to these changing patterns of geographic representation as the "deregionalization" of congressional elections. Partisan representation is notably more regionally homogeneous in the Congress of 2001 than it was in the Congress of 1953.

National Forces in the Congressional Elections

The patterns of outcomes discussed above were shaped by a variety of influences. As with most congressional elections, the most important among these were the resources available to individual candidates and how those resources were distributed between the parties in particular races. We will discuss those matters shortly, but first we consider a number of potential and actual national-level influences that were particular to 2000.

The first question with regard to national forces is whether there was a pattern in public opinion that advantaged one party or the other. Such "national tides" can occur in both presidential election years and midterms, and they can have a profound impact on the outcomes of congressional elections. Often these tides flow from reaction to presidents or presidential candidates. For example, in 1964 the presidential landslide victory of Lyndon B. Johnson over Barry M. Goldwater carried over to major Democratic gains in both congressional chambers, and Ronald Reagan's 10-point margin over Jimmy Carter in 1980 helped Republicans achieve an unexpected majority in the Senate and major gains in the House. Similarly, negative public reactions to events in the first two years of Bill Clinton's presidency played a major part in the Republicans' congressional victories in 1994.

It is readily apparent that 2000 was not an election with a significant national tide. Indeed it is most striking for the remarkably even balance between the parties across all three national races—president, House, and Senate. The narrow popular-vote margin in favor of Gore shows that neither presidential candidate had a strong enough popular advantage to greatly influence the overall congressional vote. Nor did the electorate exhibit a desire for revenge against the incumbent's party. We will examine the direct link between presidential approval and the congressional vote in the next chapter, but we can note here that Clinton's job approval remained high throughout 2000 and stood at 57 percent in the national exit poll.[9] Furthermore, when asked whether their House vote was cast to support or oppose Clinton, fully 70 percent said Clinton was not a factor in their choice.

Another potential national influence is public reaction to the performance of Congress. In the 1996 presidential race, Clinton and the Democrats tried to focus public attention on what they claimed was the extremism and excesses of the new GOP congressional majority, albeit with only limited success.[10] In 2000 there was less opportunity for either side to benefit politically from such a strategy because, as Gary C. Jacobson has pointed out, the public's opinion of congressional performance was considerably more positive than it had been in elections in the 1990s.[11] Al Gore did try to arouse public opinion by echoing Harry S. Truman's campaign slogan of 1948 criticizing the "do-nothing Congress," but there is no indication that it benefited him or his party's congressional candidates.[12]

One factor that probably limited any national effect from judgments about Congress and its performance was divided partisan control of the government. When the public concluded in 1994 that it did not like the way Congress and the president were doing business, it was easy to hold the Democrats responsible because the party had unified control. Indeed, the Republicans in the Senate were able to take advantage of the situation and block passage of a range of bills, with the expectation that the Democrats would be blamed.[13] In 2000 the Republican Congress and Clinton approached the election in an impasse on a number of issues, including major appropriations bills, and they were unable to resolve these conflicts before Election Day. Final agreements were left to a post-election "lame-duck" session of Congress. However, whatever dissatisfaction the public felt about this situation was muted because Congress was in Republican hands while the president was a Democrat.

Efforts of National Parties and Their Allies

One specific national-level influence worth our attention is the efforts of congressional party leaders and their allies to influence the races and their outcomes. Until a couple of decades ago, the activities of national parties in congressional elections were very limited. Individual candidates were mostly self-starters who were largely on their own in raising money and planning strategy. More recently, this situation has changed substantially, and party leaders and organizations now play a substantial role in recruiting and funding their candidates.[14] As we will see below, the quality of candidates and their level of funding are two of the central determinants of election outcomes. Moreover, because party control of the House, and perhaps the Senate, was seen to be in serious doubt in 2000, both parties had particularly strong incentives to be active.

Because of the high stakes in 2000, both parties started recruiting candidates early. By the beginning of April 1999, the Republicans had already secured commitments from candidates in seventeen top open-seat and challenger races. Rep. Thomas M. Davis III, R-Va., the chairman of the National Republican Congressional Committee (NRCC), said, "We are not going to be out-recruited."[15] Democrats were also active early and had some successes, using poll data to try to persuade uncertain potential contenders that this would be a good year for them to run.[16] Even within a party, however, there are potential conflicts of interest regarding recruitment when control of both chambers is at stake. House members are among the best potential Senate candidates. Indeed, nearly half of current senators formerly served in the House. Senate recruiters would want to encourage attractive representatives to try to move up, but the open seats created by such candidates would be harder for the House party to hold. Thus House leaders would be distinctly less enthusiastic about those prospects. In particular, Democrats in 2000 felt this cross-pressure, and Senate party leaders tried to cooperate with House leaders by refraining from encouraging House Democrats to try to make the jump up. Meanwhile, House leaders emphasized the small number of seats Democrats needed to take majority control to persuade their tempted members to stay put. As a spokesman for the Democratic Congressional Campaign Committee (DCCC) said: "We all understand people's commitment to serve, . . . but we think there is an enormous opportunity in serving in the majority in the U.S. House of Representatives."[17] Similar efforts were made by Republican leaders in their efforts to defend their majority. For example, Davis of the NRCC said he was particularly aggressive in successfully persuading James E. Rogan of California not to run against Democratic senator Dianne Feinstein in 2000 because no other candidate could have held the seat for the GOP.[18] Unfortunately for Rogan and the Republicans, he lost his reelection bid.

Party leaders were particularly concerned about potential open seats in which the partisan balance was nearly equal. When representatives from such districts did decide to seek higher office, the leaders often sought the departing representative's help in recruiting a possible successor. For example, when Debbie Stabenow, the Democratic representative from the eighth district of Michigan, was deciding whether to challenge Senator Spencer Abraham in 2000, she first contacted state senator Dianne Byrum to make sure Byrum was interested in trying to succeed her in the House.[19] In the end Stabenow defeated Abraham, but Byrum lost the House seat to Mike Rogers by 111 votes, the closest race in the nation.

While national party involvement in candidate recruitment has been growing, until very recently party leaders had tended to refrain from involvement if there was serious competition for the nomination. Local partisans often resent what they regard as efforts from Washington to dictate the selection of nominees. Even that limit, however, has increasingly been ignored recently. There was a major conflict among Republicans in 1998 when Speaker Newt Gingrich sought to engineer the selection of a particular candidate in a special election in California, and his choice was rejected in the GOP primary. In 2000 both national parties tried to influence candidate selection in several races. In a New Jersey House district represented by a Democratic freshman, Republican Speaker Dennis J. Hastert and the NRCC supported a relatively moderate former member of the House for their party's nomination. Majority Leader Dick Armey and Majority Whip Tom DeLay, however, backed the more conservative candidate who had lost the seat in 1998.[20] Meanwhile, the DCCC endorsed candidates in competitive primaries in Arkansas, New Jersey, and Pennsylvania, engendering intraparty controversy in each instance.[21] The parties have had mixed success both in influencing the nominations in these races, and in eventually winning the seats. In the New Jersey race, for example, the NRCC got their moderate nominee, but he narrowly lost the general election; in Pennsylvania the Democratic leaders failed to prevail in the primary, and the Democratic nominee lost the open-seat race.

In addition to recruitment, party leaders have grown increasingly active in fund raising, pursuing many alternative strategies. For example, top party leaders solicit donations to the congressional campaign committees such as the NRCC and the DCCC, and they appear at fund-raisers for individual candidates in their districts. During the August 2000 congressional recess, Speaker Hastert went to seventeen districts, where he raised $690,000 for GOP candidates; Majority Leader Armey appeared in fourteen districts, and Minority Leader Richard A. Gephardt assisted nine Democrats.[22] Leaders also have found more innovative ways to raise funds. As part of their "Retain Our Majority Program," a group of senior Republican representatives led by Armey held a set of fund-raisers for threatened incumbents and promising challengers.[23] In June of 2000 the NRCC raised $3.2 million from other GOP members in safe districts for its "Battleground 2000" effort, with more coming in October, for an eventual total of $16 million.[24]

Meanwhile Democrats sought donations for the DCCC from senior members, initially asking for $50,000 and then $100,000, but they ran into resistance from some who worried about potential electoral threats in the future.[25] Moreover, party leader fund raising was not limited to the House. In February of 2000 Minority Leader Tom Daschle, D-S.D., had asked the nine members of his leadership team and the most senior Democrats on each Senate committee to donate at least $50,000 to the Democratic Senatorial Campaign Committee (DSCC), with other senators asked to give $20,000.[26]

Party leaders are able to do more to help candidates' reelection efforts than just raise money, at least for the House majority. Because the majority has greater influence over the content of bills, they can add or remove provisions that will enhance their members' reelection chances. When Democrats criticized congressional Republicans for failing to compensate workers at a Kentucky nuclear weapons plant who had been exposed to radiation, the Republican incumbent in the district got the leadership to agree to a plan to pay the workers a lump sum.[27] In other instances the assistance does not involve money for districts, but an opportunity to be seen working for constituents. For example, we mentioned the GOP efforts to defend the district of California representative James Rogan. His district contains the largest concentration of residents of Armenian descent in the country. Rogan had sponsored a resolution condemning as genocide the killing of hundreds of thousands of Armenians in Turkey between 1915 and 1923, but had been unable to get a House vote on it because the Clinton administration said it would damage relations with Turkey. However, GOP leaders agreed to let the resolution have a vote, and it was clear that electoral politics were the reason. As Tom Davis of the NRCC said: "The fact that this is of interest to Rogan's constituents is not lost on the leadership. . . . This resolution would be a very tangible debating point for him."[28]

CANDIDATES' RESOURCES AND ELECTION OUTCOMES

Seats in the House and Senate are highly valued posts for which candidates compete vigorously. In contests for these offices, candidates draw on whatever resources they have. To explain the results of congressional elections we must consider the comparative advantages and disadvantages of the various candidates. In this section we will discuss the most significant resources available to candidates and the impact of those resources on the outcomes of congressional elections.

Candidate Quality

One major resource that candidates can draw on is the set of personal abilities that foster electoral success. Few constituencies today offer a certain victory for one of the two major parties, so election outcomes usually depend heavily on candidate quality. A strong, capable candidate is a significant asset for a party; a weak, inept one is a liability that is difficult to overcome. In his study of the activities of House members in their districts, Richard F. Fenno Jr. described how members try to build support within their constituencies, establishing bonds of trust between constituents and their representative.[29] Members attempt to convey to their constituents a sense that they are qualified for their job, a sense that they identify with their constituents, and a sense of empathy with constituents and their problems. Challengers of incumbents and candidates for open seats must engage in similar activities to win support. The winner of a contested congressional election will usually be the candidate who is better able to establish these bonds of support with constituents and to convince them that he or she is the person for the job.

One indicator of candidate quality is previous success at winning elective office. The more important the office a candidate has held, the more likely it is that he or she had to overcome significant competition to obtain the office. Moreover, the visibility and reputation for performance that usually accompany public office can also be significant electoral assets. For example, a state legislator who is running for a House seat can appeal to the electorate on the basis of preparation for congressional service obtained in the previous office because of the similarities in tasks facing a legislator. A state legislator also would have built a successful electoral organization that could be useful in conducting a congressional campaign. Finally, previous success in an electoral arena suggests that experienced candidates are more likely to be able to run strong campaigns than candidates without previous success or experience. Less adept candidates are likely to have been screened out at lower levels of office competition. For these and other reasons, an experienced candidate tends to have an electoral advantage over a candidate who has not held elected office.[30] Moreover, the higher the office previously held, the stronger the candidate will tend to be in the congressional contest.

In Table 9-4 we present data showing which candidates were successful in 2000, controlling for office background, party, and incumbency.[31] The vast majority of candidates who challenged incumbents lost regardless of the challengers' office background or party, but clearly House challengers with office experience had greater success than those who had none. Indeed, in this election cycle only current or former state legislators defeated House incumbents. In Senate races the results were similar. Every challenger who defeated an incumbent was in one of the top two categories of experience (representative and statewide office holder). The impact of candidate quality is also visible in races without incumbents, although the relationship is not quite so strong. Among candidates for the House, experienced Democrats were noticeably more successful than those who were not. Among Republicans, however, candidates without elective office won almost as often as those who had served in the state legislature. In Senate open-seat races, four of the seven winners had top-office experience, but two had no experience. We will discuss the latter cases below.

Given the importance of candidate quality, it is worth noting that during the 1980s there had been a decline in the proportion of House incumbents facing challengers who had previously won elective office, and this decline was reversed in 1992 and to some degree in 1996. In 1980, 17.6 percent of incumbents faced such challenges; in 1984, 14.7 percent did; in 1988, only 10.5 percent did. In 1992, due in large measure to perceptions of incumbent vulnerability because of redistricting and scandal, the proportion rose to 23.5 percent. In 1996 it was back down to 16.5 percent, and it remained at that level in 2000.[32] It is also important to note that in races against incumbents, Republicans were only slightly more likely than Democrats to field candidates with elective-office experience (17.8 percent versus 15.2 percent). In open-seat races, the Democrats ran experienced candidates in 57 percent of the contests, while 66 percent of these races included Republicans who had held elective office previously.[33] We will return to this partisan contrast in candidate quality later in the chapter.

Whether experienced politicians actually run for the House or the Senate is not an accident. These are significant strategic decisions made by politicians, and they have much to lose if they make the wrong choice. The choices will be governed by a host of factors that relate to the perceived chance of success, the potential value of the new office relative to what will be lost if the candidate fails, and the costs of running.[34] The chances of success of the two major parties vary from election to election, both locally and nationally. Therefore each election offers a different mix of experienced and inexperienced candidates from the two parties for the House and the Senate.

The most influential factor in the choice of a potential candidate is whether there is an incumbent in the race. High reelection rates tend to discourage potentially strong challengers from running, which in turn makes it more likely that the incumbents will win. In addition to the general difficulty of challenging incumbents, factors related to specific election years (both nationally and in a particular district) will affect decisions to run. For example, the Republican Party

TABLE 9-4   Success in House and Senate Elections, Controlling for Office
Background, Party, and Incumbency, 2000

Candidate's last office	Candidate is opponent of				No incumbent in district			
	Democratic incumbent		Republican incumbent		Democratic candidate		Republican candidate	
	(%)	(N)	(%)	(N)	(%)	(N)	(%)	(N)
House								
State legislature or U.S. House	10	(20)	24	(17)	36	(11)	83	(18)
Other elective office	0	(16)	0	(13)	33	(9)	60	(5)
No elective office	0	(124)	0	(129)	13	(15)	73	(11)
Senate								
U.S. House	0	(2)	67	(3)	0	(1)	25	(4)
Statewide elective office	100	(1)	43	(7)	100	(3)	0	(2)
Other elective office	0	(2)	—	(0)	—	(0)	100	(1)
No elective office	0	(5)	0	(6)	67	(3)	—	(0)

Note: Percentages show proportion of candidates in each category who won; numbers in parentheses are the totals on which percentages are based. The Arizona Senate race is not listed because Republican incumbent Jon Kyl ran uncontested.

had particular difficulty recruiting strong candidates in 1986 because of fears about a potential backlash from the Iran-contra scandals. On the other hand, recent research indicates that potential House candidates are most strongly influenced in their decisions by their perceived chances of winning their party's nomination.[35] Moreover, the actions of incumbents may influence the choices of potential challengers. For example, building up a large reserve of campaign funds between elections may dissuade some possible opponents, although analysis of Senate contests (which usually involve experienced challengers) indicates that this factor does not have a systematic impact in those races.[36]

As we have seen, most congressional races do not involve challengers who have previous office experience. Given their slight chance of winning, why do challengers without experience run at all? As Jeffrey S. Banks and D. Roderick Kiewiet pointed out, although the chances of success against incumbents may be small for such candidates, such a race may be their best chance of ever winning a seat in Congress.[37] If inexperienced challengers put off their candidacies until a time when there is no incumbent, their opposition is likely to include multiple experienced candidates from both parties. Moreover, as David Canon demonstrated, previous office experience is only an imperfect indicator of candidate quality, because some candidates without such experience can still have significant political assets and be formidable challengers.[38] For example, four former television journalists who had never previously held office won House seats in 1992, three of them by defeating incumbents. They were able to build on their substantial name recognition among voters to win nomination and election.[39] For more recent examples, consider two 2000 contests, one from each chamber. The Republican candidate for the House in Nebraska's third district was Tom Osborne, the extremely popular former head coach of the University of Nebraska's football team. Osborne was elected to an open seat with a phenomenal 82 percent of the vote. In the New York Senate race, the very visible (and ultimately successful) Democratic candidate was the former first lady Hillary Rodham Clinton.

Incumbency

One reason most incumbents win is that incumbency itself is a significant resource. Actually, incumbency is not a single resource, but rather a status that usually gives a candidate a variety of benefits. In some respects, incumbency works to a candidate's advantage automatically. For example, incumbents tend to be more visible to voters than their challengers.[40] Less automatic, but very important, is the public's tendency to view incumbents more favorably than challengers. Moreover, at least a plurality of the electorate in most districts will identify with the incumbent's political party. Incumbents can also use their status to gain advantages. Incumbents usually raise and spend more campaign funds than challengers, and they usually have a better-developed and more-experienced campaign organization. They also have assets, provided at public expense, that help them to both perform their jobs and provide electoral benefits.

Increasing Electoral Margins From the mid-1960s through the late 1980s, the margins by which incumbents were reelected increased (the pattern was less clear and more erratic in Senate elections than in House elections).[41] Analysts have been interested in these changing patterns for their own sake and from a belief that the disappearance of marginal incumbents would mean less congressional turnover and a locking in of current members.

An early explanation for the increased incumbent margins was offered by Edward R. Tufte, who argued that redistricting had protected incumbents of both parties.[42] This argument seemed plausible, because the increase in margins occurred about the same time as the massive redistrictings required by Supreme Court decisions of the mid-1960s. But other analysts showed that incumbents had won by larger margins both in states that had redistricted and in those that had not, as well as in Senate contests.[43] Thus redistricting could not be the major reason for the change.

Another explanation for the increase in incumbents' margins was the growth in the perquisites of members and the greater complexity of government. Morris P. Fiorina noted that in the post–New Deal period the level of federal services and the bureaucracy that administers them have grown tremendously.[44] More complex government means that many people will encounter problems in receiving services, and people who have problems frequently contact their representative to complain and seek help. Fiorina contended that in the mid-1960s new members of Congress placed greater emphasis on such constituency problem solving than had their predecessors. This expanded constituency service developed into a reservoir of electoral support. Although analyses of the impact of constituency services have produced mixed conclusions, it is likely that the growth of these services offers a partial explanation for changing incumbent vote margins and for the incumbency advantage generally.[45]

The declining impact of party loyalties offered a third explanation for the growth in incumbent vote margins, either alone or in interaction with other factors. Until the mid-1960s there was a very strong linkage between party identification and congressional voting behavior: most people identified with a political party; many people identified strongly; and most voters supported the candidate of their chosen party. Subsequently, however, the impact of party identification decreased, as we will see in chapter 10. John A. Ferejohn, drawing on data from the National Election Studies (NES), showed that the strength of party ties generally weakened and that within any given category of party identification the propensity to support the candidate of one's party declined.[46] An analysis by Albert D. Cover showed that between 1958 and 1974 voters who did not identify with the party of a congressional incumbent were increasingly more likely to defect from their party and support the incumbent, while there had been no increase in defections from party identification by voters of the incumbent's party.[47] Thus weakened party ties produced a substantial net benefit for incumbents.[48]

The Trend Reversed Whatever the relative importance of these factors, and the others we will discuss, in explaining the increase in incumbents' victory margins, the increase continued through the 1980s, as the data in Table 9-5 show. The average share of the vote for all incumbents was 61.7 percent in 1974; in 1980 it was 65.5. The share then continued to grow, peaking at 68.2 percent in 1986 and 1988.[49] These data are only for races in which both parties ran candidates. Thus they exclude contests where an incumbent ran unopposed. Such races were also increasing in number over this period; therefore the data actually understate the growth in incumbents' margins.

Then, in 1990, something changed. The average share of the vote for incumbents declined by nearly 5 percentage points. The decline was, moreover, not a result of a shift of voters toward one party, as with the decline from 1980 to 1982; both parties' incumbents suffered. Rather, the shift in incumbents' electoral fortunes was apparently the result of what was called the anti-incumbent mood among the voters. Early in 1990 pollsters and commentators began to perceive stronger anti-Congress sentiments within the electorate.[50] For the first time, analysts began to question whether incumbency remained the asset it used to be.

TABLE 9-5   Average Vote Percentages of House Incumbents, Selected Years, 1974–2000

Year	Democrats	Republicans	All incumbents
1974	68.5	55.2	61.7
1980	64.0	67.9	65.5
1982	67.9	59.9	64.1
1984	64.2	68.2	65.9
1986	70.2	65.6	68.2
1988	68.8	67.5	68.2
1990	65.8	59.8	63.5
1992	63.3	62.9	63.1
1994	60.0	67.6	62.8
1996	66.6	60.7	63.3
1998	65.0	61.6	63.3
2000	67.2	62.9	65.1

Note: These figures only include races where both major parties ran candidates.

There was, of course, nothing new about Congress being unpopular; Congress had long suffered ups and downs in approval, just as the president had. Indeed, Fenno had noted long before that candidates for Congress often sought election by running against Congress. They sought to convince voters that while most members of Congress were untrustworthy, they were different and deserved the voters' support.[51] What changed in 1990 was that Congress's unpopularity appeared to be undermining the approval of individual members by their own constituents. Yet as the data presented in Table 9-1 showed, even though there was a drop in the average percentage of the vote received by incumbents in 1990, the rate of reelection still reached 96 percent. The decline in vote margins was not great enough to produce a rash of defeats. Many observers wondered, however, whether 1990 was the beginning of a new trend: Would incumbents' electoral drawing power continue to decline?

In 1992 there were a number of scandals swirling around a large number of representatives of both parties, and public evaluation of Congress was very low. The incumbents' opponents emphasized that they were "outsiders" and not "professional politicians" (even when they had substantial political experience). The results from 1992 show that incumbents' share of the vote dropped a bit more. Republicans rebounded a little from their bad 1990 showing, while Democrats fell more than 2 percentage points. Yet again, however, the casualty rate among incumbents who ran in the general election was lower than many expected; 93 percent were reelected. (It is important to note, however, that a substantial number of incumbents had already been defeated in the primaries.) Then in 1994, although there was only a slight additional drop in incumbents' share of the vote overall, the drop was concentrated among Democrats, and their casualty rate was high. The result was the loss of their majority. Next, in 1996, there was a small rebound in incumbents' vote share, with Democrats increasing sharply while the GOP fell. That vote shift translated into eighteen Republican incumbents defeated, but only three Democrats. Finally, the results from 1998 and 2000—with the continuing Democratic effort to whittle away at the GOP majority—were little different from 1996.[52]

This discussion illustrates that incumbents' vote margins and incumbents' reelection success are related but distinct phenomena. When—as was true in the 1980s—the average share of the vote received by incumbents is very high, they can lose a lot of ground before a large number of defeats occur. What appears to have happened in 1990 is that many incumbents were subjected to vigorous contests for the first time in several years. Such challenges were then often repeated or extended to additional incumbents in 1992–1996. Potential candidates apparently looked at the political situation and concluded that incumbents who had previously looked unbeatable might now be defeated, and the number of candidates for Congress increased substantially. These vigorous contests by challengers who were stronger than usual resulted in a decrease in the share of the vote received by many incumbents. In most cases in 1990 the decrease was not large enough to bring the challenger victory; in later years, however, the increased competition caught up with a greater number of incumbents.

Campaign Spending

A third resource that has an important impact on congressional elections is campaign spending. The effects of campaign spending have received a great deal of attention in the past three decades because researchers gained access to more dependable data than had previously been available.[53] The data on spending have consistently shown that incumbents generally outspend their challengers, often by large margins, and that through the early 1990s the disparity had increased.[54] In 1990 incumbent spending averaged about $401,000, while challengers spent approximately $116,000—a ratio of 3.45-to-1. In 1992 challenger spending increased to an average of $160,000, but the stronger challenges of that year also stimulated the incumbents to keep pace, and their spending rose to $560,000. This was a ratio of 3.50-to-1, which left challengers and incumbents in about the same relative position as they had been in two years earlier.[55]

Disparities in campaign spending are linked to the increase in incumbents' election margins. Beginning in the 1960s, congressional campaigns relied more heavily on campaign techniques that cost money—for example, media time, campaign consulting, and direct mailing—and these items have become more and more expensive. At the same time, candidates were progressively less likely to have available pools of campaign workers from established party organizations or from interest groups, which have made using expensive media and direct mail strategies relatively more important. Most challengers are unable to raise significant campaign funds. Neither individuals nor the groups who are interested in the outcomes of congressional elections like to throw money away; before making contributions they usually need to be convinced that the candidate has a chance. Yet we have seen that few incumbents have been beaten. Thus it is often difficult to convince potential contributors that their money will produce results, and contributions are often not forthcoming. Most challengers are thus at a strategic disadvantage, and they are unable to raise sufficient funds to wage a competitive campaign.[56]

It is the ability to compete, rather than the simple question of relative amounts of spending, that is at the core of the issue. We have noted that an incumbent has many inherent advantages that the challenger must overcome if he or she hopes to win. But often the money is not there to overcome them. In 1990, for example, over 47 percent of challengers spent $25,000 or less. With so little money available, challengers are unable to make themselves visible to the electorate or to convey a convincing message. In such circumstances, most voters—being unaware of the positions, or perhaps even the existence, of the challenger—vote for the incumbent.

Data from 2000 on campaign spending and election outcomes seem consistent with this argument, but they also show changes in the political landscape.[57] The increased competitiveness during the 1990s that was shown by the data on incumbents' vote share is reflected in the spending figures. Challenger spending was up sharply compared to the 1990–1992 figures presented above, with an average of about $310,000. Incumbent spending was up also (averaging $890,000), but that reduced the incumbent-to-challenger ratio to 2.87-to-1.[58] On the other hand, this ratio is up a bit from 1996's 2.61, when there was a substantial effort by organized labor, which targeted thirty-two Republican incumbents, providing direct contributions to challengers as well as independent anti-incumbent advertising.[59] Linking spending to outcomes, Table 9-6 shows the relationship between the incumbent's share of the vote in the 2000 House elections and the amount of money spent by the challenger. It is clear that there is a strong negative relationship between how much challengers spend and how well incumbents do. In races where challengers spent less than $26,000, 98 percent of the incumbents received 60 percent or more of the vote. At the other end of the spectrum, in races where challengers spent $400,000 or more, 79 percent of the incumbents received less than 60 percent of the vote, and over half got less than 55 percent. These results are consistent with those in earlier House elections for which comparable data are available.[60]

These findings are reinforced by other research showing that challenger spending has a much greater influence on election outcomes than does incumbent spending.[61] This generalization has been questioned on methodological grounds,[62] but further research by Jacobson reinforced his earlier findings. Using both aggregate and survey data, he found that "the amount spent by the challenger is far more important in accounting for voters' decisions than is the amount of spending by the incumbent."[63] Analysis of Senate elections has also resulted in conflicting conclusions.[64]

TABLE 9-6   Incumbents' Share of the Vote in the 2000 House Elections, by Challenger Campaign Spending (in percentages)

| Challenger spending[a] | Incumbent's share of the two-party vote | | | | Total | (N) |
	70% or more	60–69%	55–59%	Less than 55%		
0–25	53.0	45.5	1.5	0.0	100.0	(134)
26–75	19.0	79.3	0.0	1.7	100.0	(58)
76–199	8.6	57.1	31.4	2.9	100.0	(35)
200–399	7.5	45.0	42.5	5.0	100.0	(40)
400 or more	1.4	19.7	26.8	52.1	100.0	(71)
All	26.3	47.0	14.5	12.1	100.0	(338)

Note: Challenger campaign spending that was unavailable was coded in the 0–25 row.

[a] In thousands of dollars.

It is true, of course, that challengers who appear to have good prospects will find it easier to raise money than those whose chances seem slim. Thus one might wonder whether these data are simply a reflection of the fulfillment of expectations, in which money flows to challengers who would have done well regardless of spending. Other research, however, indicates that this is probably not the case. In an analysis of the 1972 and 1974 congressional elections, Jacobson concluded, "Our evidence is that campaign spending helps candidates, particularly non-incumbents, by bringing them to the attention of the voters; it is not the case that well-known candidates simply attract more money; rather money buys attention."[65] From this perspective, having adequate funding is a necessary but not sufficient condition for a closely fought election contest, a perspective consistent with the data in Table 9-6. Heavily outspending one's opponent is not a guarantee of victory; the evidence does not support the conclusion that elections can be bought. If an incumbent outspends the challenger, the incumbent can still lose if the challenger is adequately funded and runs a campaign that persuades the voters. The 1996 elections (the last year with more than six House general election incumbent defeats) offer clear evidence of this. In eleven of the twenty-one races in which incumbents lost, the loser outspent the winner. In these contests, incumbents outspent challengers by 60 percent to 40 percent on average, and in three instances the loser spent more than twice as much. Most important, however, no victorious challenger spent less than $600,000. That may be a rough estimate of the amount needed to have a chance of winning against an incumbent.

On the other hand, a spending advantage is not any kind of guarantee for a challenger. In an extreme example from 2000, Republican challenger Phil Sudan spent $3.247 million against incumbent Ken Bentsen of Texas, who spent $1.354 million. Despite being outspent by more than two-to-one, Bentsen won over 60 percent of the vote. Based on this analysis, our view can be summarized as follows: if a challenger is to attain visibility and get his or her message across to the voters—neutralizing the incumbent's advantages in name recognition and perquisites of office—the challenger needs to be adequately funded. If both sides in a race are adequately funded, the outcome will tend to turn on factors other than money, and the relative spending of the two candidates will not control the outcome.

This argument carries us full circle to our earlier discussion and leads us to bring together the three kinds of resources that we have been considering—candidate experience, incumbency, and campaign spending. Table 9-7 presents data about these three factors in the 2000 House elections. We have categorized challenger experience as strong or weak depending on previous elective-office experience; challenger spending was classified as low or high depending on whether it was below or above $200,000.[66] The data show that each of the elements exerts some independent effect, but that the impact of spending seems to have been more consequential in 2000 than in the past, perhaps reflecting the growing attractiveness of "outsider" candidates. When challengers had weak experience and low spending (almost 60 percent of the races), all incumbents won, and 95 percent won with more than 60 percent of the vote. In the opposite situation, where the challenger had both strong experience and substantial spending, over 75 percent of the races were relatively close. The combined results for the two intermediate categories fall between the extremes. In addition, five of the six incumbent defeats occur in situations where the challenger is experienced and has strong spending. Yet note how few such races there were in 2000. Table 9-7 also reveals that it is very rare for a challenger with strong experience not to be able to raise substantial funds.

This combination of factors also helps to explain the greater volatility of outcomes in Senate races. Previous analysis has shown that data on campaign spending in Senate contests are consistent with what we have found true for House races: if challenger spending is above some threshold, the election is likely to be quite close; if it is below that level, the incumbent is likely to win by a large margin.[67] In Senate races, however, the mix of well-funded and poorly funded challengers is different. Senate challengers are more likely than their House counterparts to be able to raise significant amounts of money. Indeed in recent elections a number of challengers (and open-seat candidates) have been wealthy individuals who could provide a large share of their funding from their own resources. The most extreme example comes from 2000, when Jon Corzine, the Democratic candidate for the open New Jersey Senate seat, spent more than $60 million of his own money to defeat his opponent by 50-to-47 percent. Corzine spent a total of $63 million; the Republican spent $6.4 million.[68]

Senate challengers, moreover, are also more likely to possess significant office experience. Thus in Senate contests incumbents often will face well-funded and experienced challengers, and the stage is then set for the incumbents' defeat if other circumstances work against them. The lesson from the evidence presented in this section appears to be captured by the statement made by David Johnson,

TABLE 9-7   Incumbents' Share of the Vote in the 2000 House Elections, by Challenger Campaign Spending and Office Background (in percentages)

Challenger experience/ spending	70% or more	60–69%	55–59%	Less than 55%	Total	(N)	% of incumbents defeated
Weak/low	40.9	54.6	4.0	0.5	100.0	(198)	0.0
Strong/low	13.8	65.5	17.2	3.5	100.0	(29)	0.0
Weak/high	5.3	32.0	33.3	29.3	100.0	(75)	1.3
Strong/high	0.0	22.2	30.6	47.2	100.0	(36)	13.9

Note: Percentages read across. Strong challengers have held a significant elective office (see note 66). High-spending challengers spent more than $200,000.

the director of the Democratic Senatorial Campaign Committee, to Rep. Richard C. Shelby of Alabama, who was challenging Republican senator Jeremiah Denton in 1986. Shelby, who eventually won, was concerned that he did not have enough campaign funds, since Denton was outspending him two-to-one. Johnson responded: "You don't have as much money, but you're going to have enough—and enough is all it takes to win."[69]

THE 2000 ELECTIONS: THE IMPACT ON CONGRESS

Because the electoral politics of recent years have revolved around efforts to reinforce or reverse the gigantic shift to the Republicans in 1994, subsequent elections have naturally been viewed in relation to the consequences of that cataclysm. By that standard the elections of 2000 had modest immediate effects, although they set the stage for more important consequences a bit later. In terms of membership change, 2000 (like 1998) yielded considerably smaller shifts than elections earlier in the 1990s. The "class of 2000" included forty-one new representatives (9 percent of that body) and eleven new senators (11 percent). Moreover, 1992 through 1996 saw three consecutive elections with significant membership change, so the cumulative effect was profound. After 1996 nearly two-thirds of the Republicans in the House and almost half of the Democrats had come to that body in the previous three elections. In the Senate twenty-seven of the fifty-five GOP members and thirteen of the forty-five Democrats had less than six years service. With the high House reelection rates in 1998 and 2000, the membership has become a little less "bottom-heavy," with 32 percent of Republicans and 37 percent of Democrats arriving with the 1996 election or later. Because of the Democratic success in 2000, the impact on Senate membership was different between the two parties, the GOP proportion of junior members going down (sixteen of fifty with less than six years service), and the Democratic proportion going up (twenty of fifty).

The relatively small membership change yielded the narrowest of majorities in the House and a dead-even division of the Senate. This situation enhanced the importance of moderate members of both bodies. This occurred in the context of a long-term decline of such members in the Congress, and an increase in the number of conservative Republicans and liberal Democrats. Twenty-five or thirty years ago, there was considerable ideological overlap between the parties. The Democrats had a substantial conservative contingent, mostly from the South, one as conservative as the right wing of the Republican Party. Similarly, the GOP had a contingent (primarily northeasterners) as liberal as northern Democrats. In addition, each party had members who held the positions between the two ends of the political spectrum. During the intervening years, however, because of changes in the electorate and in the Congress, this overlap between the parties began to disappear.[70] By the mid-1980s both parties in both houses of Congress had become more politically homogeneous, and in each chamber there was little departure from a complete ideological separation of the two parties. Thus in the 107th Congress, elected in 2000, substantial majorities of each party had sharply different policy preferences from those in the other party, with the balance of power being held by a small group of members in the middle. This created a difficult situation for leaders in both parties in both chambers.

The House: Coping With a Razor-Thin Margin

In 1995 the new Republican majorities instituted major institutional changes, especially in the House.[71] By comparison, the changes in House organization for the 107th Congress were comparatively modest, although still important. The biggest formal rules change involved a decision by Speaker Hastert to remove jurisdiction over securities and insurance from the powerful Commerce Committee (renamed Energy and Commerce), transferring those matters to a new committee on Financial Services (to replace the old Banking and Financial Services Committee). The jurisdictional shift angered Commerce members in both parties, but they did not have the numbers to challenge it.

This alteration, however, took place in the context of, and was related to, major personnel changes that were the legacy of the election of 1994. One of the new rules the House GOP adopted when they won their new majority was a term limit of six years on committee and subcommittee chairs. That limit was reached with the 2000 elections, and while not every committee chair had to be replaced, thirteen of them had run out of time. Some members, including a number of the term-limited chairs, did not see the merit of this process of replacement, and they sought to eliminate the rule. This effort was soundly defeated by a vote in the Republican Conference (the caucus of all House Republicans).[72] Rather than simply use the old seniority norm and let the longest serving Republican on each committee rise to the chairmanship, Hastert decided to let members compete for the leadership posts. More than two dozen Republicans sought the positions, and in many instances the party's Steering Committee passed over the more senior members. In one particularly striking example, Marge Roukema, a moderate from New Jersey, was in line by seniority to be the chair of the Banking Committee and its successor, Financial Services. She would have been the first woman to chair a major house committee, but she lost out to Michael G. Oxley of Ohio, who had not even been a member of the Banking Committee in the previous Congress.

Beyond the question of who would chair committees, both Republican and Democratic leaders had to deal with factional divisions within their parties and other personal interests of individual members. A major issue involved committee assignments. Among Republicans, competition centered on whether any freshmen would get assigned to the four most powerful committees: Appropriations, Energy and Commerce, Rules, and Ways and Means. Before 1994 such appointments were virtually nonexistent, but there were nineteen after that election and more after each subsequent election. In December 2000, however, Hastert sent a letter to incoming freshmen warning them not to expect any top appointments, and in January 2001 the actual assignments bore out the warning when no new member received any of the twelve vacant slots. The freshmen were disappointed but apparently not angered by their lack of success.[73]

For Democrats, the central committee-assignment issue was how many slots they would be allocated. Because they had narrowed the partisan division in the House, they demanded a larger share of the committee seats than they had in the previous Congress. Democratic leaders were under a lot of pressure from members who wanted seats on the most desirable committees. They tried to exert pressure by letting Democratic moderates take the lead in the effort, asking them to communicate to their GOP counterparts that Republican legislative priorities could be affected by the results. The Republican leaders, however, being worried about their ability to control the committees, resisted. They contended that the party ratio had not changed significantly so there was no reason to shift the balance, while Democrats countered that the previous Congress's allocations had been unfair to begin with. The GOP did allot a few additional committee seats to the Democrats, but in each instance they also added an extra seat for themselves. Thus the balance between the parties was not altered.

Because of the close division of the chamber, moderates in both parties recognized their importance and sought more influence over the agenda and policy outcomes. Among Democrats there were two groups that had existed for some years, and after 2000 they both had more members than in previous congresses. First there was the most conservative set of Democrats, known as the "Blue Dogs." They had thirty-two members, a majority of whom were from the South and border states. The other group was the House New Democratic Coalition (NDC), with seventy-two members. They were a bit to the left of the Blue Dogs ideologically (although about two-thirds of that group also belonged to the coalition).[74] The NDC and Blue Dogs wanted their party to focus on issues such as "jobs, education, and health care" and to present a more moderate image, while the Democratic leadership was looking for ways to work with both groups and to elect more moderate members in the search for a House majority.[75]

The moderate Democrats also sought to work with their GOP counterparts, and in December of 2000 ten centrists from both parties formed a new bipartisan group that, in the words of one member, was "driven by a desire to get things done."[76] They asserted that the only way to get things done was the bipartisan way. GOP conservatives did not welcome the group, however; one senior staffer claimed that the group's Republicans were "undercutting [the] teamwork within the Conference."[77]

The Senate: A Major Transition—and Then Another

The four-seat net gain for the Senate Democrats had a much more profound institutional effect than the shift in the House because it deprived the GOP of the clear majority control they had enjoyed since their victory in 1994. Once Vice

President Dick Cheney was sworn in on January 20 the Republicans would be able to win straight party-line conflicts with his tie-breaking vote, but the Democrats could—if sufficiently provoked—use extended debate to tie up the Senate and prevent action on organization or other matters. Negotiations proceeded throughout December. GOP members appeared willing to accept equality between the parties in committee funding, staffing, and space, but a number of prospective Republican chairs spoke out against some Democrats' demands for equal membership and at least some "cochairmen."

Finally, at the beginning of January, Republican leader Trent Lott of Mississippi and Democratic leader Daschle reached an agreement that Lott sold to his reluctant party colleagues. Lott would continue to be majority leader (and Daschle to be minority leader), but party representation on committees would be evenly divided, as would staff, funds, and space. All committee chairs, however, would still be Republicans. In addition, either party's leader could bring a bill to the floor if a committee's vote were tied. (Previously such bills would stay stuck in committee.) The GOP sought this guarantee to prevent the Democrats from bottling up President George W. Bush's legislative priorities. Lott said, "This resolution may haunt me, but it's fair and it allows us to get on with the people's business."[78]

During the first few months of the "power-sharing" agreement, there were some problems, but things went fairly smoothly (partly because the legislative agenda was still not very heavy). Some committees worked out arrangements quickly, while others took months, but eventually all got moving. One important issue, however, had not been addressed by the agreement: How would the Senate members of conference committees (which work out differences on individual pieces of legislation between the chambers) be appointed? In normal times the majority would get more members than the minority, but now if Democrats got equal representation they could block agreement on legislation favored by the Bush administration and the GOP. This became a pressing concern as more major legislation passed both houses, but with no way to bring the two sides to final agreement, the problem could not be resolved. By May it looked as though this issue could lead to complete legislative chaos, but then an event occurred that largely rendered it moot. In the biggest political bombshell to hit Washington since the Supreme Court resolved the presidential election, Sen. James M. Jeffords, R-Vt., announced that he was leaving the Republican Party and would vote with the Democrats to organize the Senate, making them the majority.

Before considering the causes and consequences of the Jeffords decision, we will discuss a few more effects of the election on the Senate, and then the early interactions between the Congress and the new president—topics that were intimately related to the decision. As we noted, the top Senate leaders in both parties remained the same. The only leadership contest involved a challenge by Pete V. Domenici, R-N.M., for the chairmanship of the party's Policy Committee held by Larry E. Craig of Idaho. The challenge was apparently an effort to get the GOP leadership to adopt a less conservative strategy in the wake of the loss of five incumbents in 2000.[79] Craig survived Domenici's effort by a narrow 26–24 margin.

Senate moderates recognized that with the 50–50 division, they would be even more important than their counterparts in the House. Moderate Senate Democrats had had an organized group for a few years, and the elections left them with twenty members among the fifty Democrats. GOP moderates launched their own organization at the beginning of 2001, recruiting John McCain, R-Ariz., among others.[80] In addition, as in the House, the moderates began to organize across party lines, forming the Senate centrist coalition. Almost one-third of the Senate's membership showed up for the first meeting, and Lott and Daschle attended to give their blessings to the effort.[81]

Congress and (the Brief Period of) One-Party Control of Government

As we noted in chapter 2, during the campaign Bush criticized the Democrats for undermining bipartisanship in Washington. And, on the night his victory was confirmed by the Supreme Court, he appeared in Austin with the Democratic Speaker of the Texas legislature to symbolize his commitment to work across party lines. This stated commitment struck a positive chord with the electorate, and on the eve of his inauguration polls indicated that the public believed he could deliver. Seventy-four percent said that they believed he could work effectively with Congress to get things done.[82]

After taking office, the new president sought to show his symbolic commitment to working with legislators in the other party by showing up at retreats organized for Democrats in both chambers. When he arrived at the House Democrats' meeting in Pennsylvania, he was greeted with a thirty-second standing ovation. He answered questions and heard a variety of complaints, including comments about the GOP leadership's treatment of the Democrats on the question of committee ratios.[83] In addition, Bush met frequently with congressional Democrats individually and in small groups, including five White House visits by Sen. Edward M. "Ted" Kennedy, D-Mass., during the first month of his term.[84]

While symbolic acts of bipartisanship were relatively easy to engineer, actual bipartisan actions on legislation were more difficult to deliver. The kind of partisan divisions on policy we discussed above are rooted in the different constituencies of the two parties and in real differences over policy among members of Congress. Thus disagreements spring only partly from a desire by politicians to achieve electoral advantage, and compromise is rarely easy to engineer between committed legislators on opposite sides. Clearly Bush made some efforts to work with Democrats on legislation in the early months. One obvious example was on his education plan, where Bush agreed to compromises with Democrats in both the House and Senate in order to build support for a bill.[85] On the other hand, the House GOP leadership engineered a victory in their chamber in March on the president's proposed tax cut without any pretense of consulting with Democrats. Sen. John B. Breaux, D-La., a leading moderate who could have had a cabinet appointment in the administration, warned that such tactics "were creating a legacy of bitterness. . . . [They] represent the same old culture of 'win, no matter what' that I thought Bush was trying to get away from."[86]

The president and members of both parties in Congress have policy and political interests at stake, and bipartisan action is hard to achieve if it jeopardizes those interests. Bush and congressional Republicans and Democrats want to be reelected, and each party wants majority control. Thus neither side wants to be seen as a roadblock to passage of the public's priorities lest voters take out their wrath at the polls. Yet there are also the policy activists who seek to tug each party in opposite directions. Moderates such as Breaux and Jeffords argue for compromise in the middle. On the other hand, conservatives such as House leaders Armey and DeLay want the kinds of policy results they have been trying to achieve for years. After Bush's election, DeLay said, "We have the House, we have the Senate, we have the White House, which means we have the agenda." Moreover, he said, in the House the GOP would "act exactly the same way we have been. . . . We'll write conservative bills and ask the Democrats to participate."[87]

The pressure for conservative policy results was visible in the House action on the tax cut mentioned above. It was also apparent when the matter was taken up by the Senate during the consideration of the budget resolution. Reducing taxes has been one of the main issues motivating Republican conservatives, and it was a centerpiece of the Bush campaign. Most Democrats, however, and a few moderate Republicans worried that if cuts were too large, there would not be enough money for other priorities. Thus when the Senate voted, only one Democrat (Zell Miller of Georgia, who cosponsored the president's plan) joined with the GOP in support of the proposed $1.6 trillion cut, and three Republicans went the other way and backed a reduction to $1.25 trillion. The defectors were Arlen Specter of Pennsylvania, Lincoln Chafee of Rhode Island, and Jeffords of Vermont.

GOP conservatives and administration officials were angry over the moderates' actions, and retaliation was considered. There was talk of leaving Chafee off of the conference committee for a brownfields bill that he had sponsored. Lott contended publicly that the reason was Chafee's low seniority, but others noted different reasons. A senior Republican staffer said: "This is a reminder to Chafee that he has got to play ball."[88] As for Jeffords, the Bush administration considered backing a proposal to end a program that set dairy prices in New England and was politically important to the Vermont senator.[89] He was also left off the guest list when an award was presented to a Vermont teacher at the White House, and White House staffers gave interviews to Vermont reporters to pressure him to support the president. Then a bombshell dropped. Word leaked that Jeffords was going to leave the GOP and become an independent.

The Jeffords Switch and Its Aftermath

It was later revealed that the Senate Democratic leader had initially approached Jeffords about switching parties during the tax debate in April 2001.[90] The talks included the possible offer of the chairmanship of the Environment and Public Works Committee, even though he was not currently a member. Republicans were unaware of a possible change until the Vermont senator informed Lott on May 21. The Republican leadership made a last ditch effort to keep him, scheduling separate meetings with Bush and Cheney, and with a group of GOP moderates. The latter approached Lott with a possible deal that would have given Jeffords an appointive leadership post. (They also sought to counteract the potential switch by getting Zell Miller of Georgia to leave the Democrats, but he refused.)

In the end the efforts were for naught. Jeffords went to Vermont and announced that he would become an independent and vote with the Democrats on organizing the Senate. He contended that the slights and pressures had nothing to do with his decision. Rather, he said, he could "see more and more instances where I'll disagree with the president on very fundamental issues—the issues of choice, the direction of the judiciary, tax and spending decisions, missile defense, energy and the environment."[91]

The effects of the Jeffords decision were substantial, and they demonstrate some of the consequences of party control. For the membership of the Senate did not change, and the same 100 people were voting on the floor. But the Democrats became the majority, and Daschle the majority leader. Daschle pledged to honor the "spirit of bipartisanship" and contended that "polarized positions are an indulgence . . . that the Senate cannot afford and our nation will not tolerate."[92] These sentiments, however, did not eliminate the real interparty differences on policy and legislative priorities. For example, as majority leader Lott had blocked the Senate-passed campaign finance bill from being sent to the House for action, and he had joined with the Bush administration in the decision to prevent the "patients' bill of rights" from coming to the Senate floor. Shortly after the Democrats became the majority, the Senate reversed both of these decisions and passed the Democrat-supported version of the patients' bill of rights.

Now Democrats became chairs of all of the Senate committees and brought new priorities to their posts. For example, Carl Levin, D-Mich., immediately announced plans to investigate high gasoline prices, with the possibility of holding hearings. Chairmanships could also bolster potentially vulnerable Democrats up for reelection in 2002, such as Tom Harkin of Iowa (Agriculture) and Max Baucus of Montana (Finance). Other Democrats were bolstered by new committee assignments that came because their party received one additional seat on each Senate committee, reflecting their new majority status. That status would also mean that the Democrats would have a majority of the Senate contingent on every conference committee, giving them considerable leverage over final agreements between the chambers on legislation. Majority control also gave the Democrats potential influence over sensitive decisions on judicial and other nominees by President Bush. In negotiating the transition, GOP senators tried to hold out for a promise that Supreme Court nominees would be guaranteed floor votes, but the Democrats resisted. In the end, both parties agreed to language that they would follow past "practices and precedents of the committee and the Senate" when dealing with nominees.[93]

In the wake of the Senate change, the administration contended that it would stick with the same agenda, with Bush using "the bully pulpit" of the presidency to pressure Senate Democrats to accede to his priorities. They also criticized Jeffords's actions and questioned his motives.[94] But the White House had to begin to adjust because they no longer had the benefits of unified party control of government. And while the Democrats' new position came with new risks, including the chance that they could be blamed if the legislative process deadlocked and did not produce results, they were surely happier with the new circumstances than with the old.

THE 2002 ELECTIONS AND BEYOND

The Elections of 2002

Expectations about midterm elections are usually shaped by a strong historical pattern: the party of the president lost strength in the House in twenty-three of the twenty-five midterm elections in the twentieth century. The first column in Table 9-8 shows the magnitude of these losses in midterms since World War II. They average 25.2 seats for the president's party. There was, however, considerable variation in the outcomes, from the 55-seat loss by the Democrats in 1946 to the 5-seat Democratic gain in 1998. Another consideration related to the president, however, clarifies the context for judgment. During the first midterm election of his presidency, the president may be able to make a plausible appeal that he has not had enough time to bring about substantial change or to solidify many achievements. Moreover, even if things are not going very well, voters may not be inclined to blame a president who has served for such a short time. But four years later (if the president is fortunate enough to face a second midterm), appeals of too little time are unlikely to be persuasive. After six years, if the economy or foreign policy are not going well, voters may seek a policy change by reducing the number of the president's partisans in Congress.

The second and third columns in Table 9-8 indicate that this is what has usually happened in the past. Losses by the president's party in the first midterm election of a presidency have tended to be much smaller than losses in subsequent midterms.[95] Indeed, with the exception of the results in 1986, 1994, and 1998, the two categories yield two fairly homogeneous sets of outcomes that are sharply different from one another. In the six midterm elections besides 1994

TABLE 9-8   House Seat Losses by the President's Party in Midterm Elections, 1946–1998

All elections			First term of administration			Later term of administration		
1946:	55	Democrats	1954:	18	Republicans	1946:	55	Democrats
1950:	29	Democrats	1962:	4	Democrats	1950:	29	Democrats
1954:	18	Republicans	1970:	12	Republicans	1958:	47	Republicans
1958:	47	Republicans	1978:	11	Democrats	1966:	47	Democrats
1962:	4	Democrats	1982:	26	Republicans	1974:	43	Republicans
1966:	47	Democrats	1990:	9	Republicans	1986:	5	Republicans
1970:	12	Republicans	1994:	52	Democrats	1998:	(+5)	Democrats
1974:	43	Republicans						
1978:	11	Democrats		Average: 18.9			Average: 31.6	
1982:	26	Republicans						
1986:	5	Republicans						
1990:	9	Republicans						
1994:	52	Democrats						
1998:	(+5)	Democrats						

Average: 25.2

that took place during a first term, the president's party lost between four and twenty-six seats, with an average loss of thirteen. In the five elections after the first term (excluding 1986 and 1998), the range of losses was between twenty-nine and fifty-five seats, with an average loss of forty-four. (We will discuss the atypical results later.)

Models of House Elections In the past two decades, a number of scholars have constructed and tested models of congressional election outcomes, focusing especially on midterms, seeking to isolate the factors that most strongly influence the results. The first models, constructed by Tufte and by Jacobson and Samuel Kernell, focused on two variables: presidential approval and a measure of the state of the economy.[96] Tufte hypothesized a direct influence by these forces on voter choice and election outcomes. The theory was that an unpopular president or a poor economic situation would cause the president's party to lose votes and, therefore, seats in the House. In essence, the midterm elections were viewed as a referendum on the performance of the president and his party. Jacobson and Kernell, on the other hand, saw more indirect effects of presidential approval and the economy. They argued that these forces affected election results by influencing the decisions of potential congressional candidates. If the president is unpopular and the economy is in bad shape, potential candidates will expect the president's party to perform poorly. As a consequence, strong potential candidates of the president's party will be more inclined to forego running until a better year, and strong candidates from the opposition party will be more inclined to run because they foresee good prospects for success. According to Jacobson and Kernell, this mix of weak candidates from the president's party and strong opposition candidates will lead to a poor election performance by the party occupying the White House. To measure this predicted relationship, their model relates the partisan division of the vote to presidential approval and the economic situation early in the election year. This, they argued, is when decisions to run for office are being made, not at the time of the election, so it is not appropriate to focus on approval and the economy at that time. This view has come to be called the "strategic politicians hypothesis."[97]

More recent research has built from this base. One model, developed by Alan I. Abramowitz, Albert D. Cover, and Helmut Norpoth, considered a new variable: short-term party evaluations.[98] They argued that voters' attitudes about the economic competence of the political parties affect the impact of presidential approval and economic conditions on voting decisions. If the electorate judges that the party holding the presidency is better able to deal with the problems voters regard as most serious, the negative impact of an unpopular president or a weak economy will be reduced. The authors concluded from their analysis of both aggregate votes and responses to surveys in midterm elections that there is evidence for their "party competence" hypothesis.

All of these models used the division of the popular vote as the variable to be predicted, and they focused only on midterm elections. More recent work has merged midterm results with those of presidential years, contending that there should be no conceptual distinction between them. These efforts have sought to predict changes in seats without reference to the division of the vote. For example, a study by Bruce I. Oppenheimer, James A. Stimson, and Richard W. Waterman argued that the missing piece in the congressional election puzzle is the degree of "exposure," or "the excess or deficit number of seats a party holds measured against its long-term norm."[99] If a party wins more House seats than normal, those extra seats will be vulnerable in the next election, and the party is likely to suffer losses. Thus the party that wins a presidential election does not automatically benefit in House elections. But if the president's party does well in the House races, it will be more vulnerable in the subsequent midterm elections. Indeed, the May 1986 article by Oppenheimer and his colleagues predicted only small Republican losses for 1986 because Reagan's large 1984 victory was not accompanied by substantial congressional gains for his party. The actual result in 1986 was consistent with this prediction, for the GOP lost only five seats.

Another model of House elections was constructed by Robin F. Marra and Charles W. Ostrom Jr.[100] They developed a "comprehensive referendum voting model" of both presidential year and midterm elections, and included factors such as foreign policy crises, scandals, unresolved policy disputes, party identification, and the change in the level of presidential approval. The model also incorporated measures reflecting hypothesized relationships in the models we discussed earlier: the level of presidential approval, the state of the economy, the strategic politicians hypothesis, exposure, and party competence. The model was tested on data from all congressional elections from 1950 through 1986.

The Marra-Ostrom analysis showed significant support for most of the predicted relationships. The results indicated that the most powerful influences affecting congressional seat changes were presidential approval (directly and through various events) and exposure. The model was striking in its statistical accuracy: the average error in the predicted change was only four seats. The average error varied little whether presidential or midterm years were predicted, and the analysis demonstrated that the usually greater losses for the president's party in second midterm years resulted from negative shifts in presidential approval, exposure, and scandals.

Drawing on the insights of these various models, we can see how these factors may influence outcomes in the 2002 House elections. How well the economy is doing and what proportion of the voters approve of Bush's performance early in the year may encourage or discourage high-quality potential challengers. The same variables close to election time may lead voters to support or oppose a Republican candidate based on their judgments of the job the Bush administration is doing. In the summer of 2001 Bush's approval was above the 50 percent mark, and the economy continued to lag compared to the sustained growth of the Clinton years. Then after the September 11 terrorist attacks on the World Trade Center and the Pentagon, Bush's approval rating soared to 90 percent even though the economy continued to worsen. If Bush remains popular and the economy recovers, the Republican chances will be much better than we would normally expect. The usual midterm losses happen for reasons; they are not part of the laws of nature. Therefore if the usual reasons for such losses (such as a recession or an unpopular president) are not present in 2002, we should not expect the consequent losses to occur.[101] Furthermore, Republican exposure is not high due to the loss of the most marginal districts in the 1996, 1998, and 2000 elections. Thus there are few vulnerable GOP seats for the Democrats to target. Finally, the impact of events such as the crises and scandals in the Marra-Ostrom model reminds us that there are many unforeseeable events that may influence the 2002 congressional election results.

The Effects of Reapportionment and Redistricting

One thing that is likely to affect the elections of 2002 is the reapportionment and redistricting that follows from the census of 2000. Reapportionment is the redistribution of House seats among the states after every census due to the population shifts it reveals. The recent census results yielded a transfer of twelve total seats among eighteen states (eight gainers and ten losers).[102] This is quite a bit fewer than the nineteen seats that shifted after the 1990 census. Once the states have the census results they begin the process of redistricting—redrawing the boundaries of their House districts. (Actually only forty-three states must do this, because seven states have only one representative.)[103]

By federal law, all states with more than one House seat must establish districts, one for each seat. According to the Supreme Court's "one-person, one-vote" rulings, the population of all of the districts within a state must be as equal in population as possible. The first battle of the redistricting process for 2002 involved the question of which census figures would be used. During the Clinton administration, the Democrats had sought to adjust the actual census count through statistical sampling in order to compensate for the undercount (particularly of minorities) that occurs in every census. The Republicans resisted this adjustment for the same reasons that the Democrats sought it: because the Republicans believed the adjusted figures would benefit the Democrats in both reapportionment and redistricting. The GOP took the matter to court, and in early 1999 the Supreme Court ruled that sampling could not be employed to adjust the numbers used for the apportionment of House seats. But the Court left open the question of whether sampling could be used for other purposes, such as districting and the allocation of federal funds. This issue was settled, however, by the outcome of the presidential election, for the Bush administration ruled against the use of adjusted figures for redistricting.

With this matter out of the way, the process of district line drawing began state by state. There is, not surprisingly, great variation in how this is done. In most instances districts are created through the regular legislative process of a state law signed by the governor, although five states (Arizona, Hawaii, Idaho, New Jersey, and Washington) have removed districting from direct political control by the creation of independent districting commissions.[104] The Republican Party is in a much better position regarding districting than it was a decade ago because of major gains in governorships and state legislative seats in 1994, which have been augmented in some instances since. As a result of the 2000 elections, the GOP has complete control of the process in a number of large states, such as Florida, Michigan, Ohio, and Pennsylvania. In most of these states the Republicans are making a determined effort to cut down the number of Democratic representatives. In Michigan, for instance, the legislature adopted a plan that put six Democratic incumbents in pairs in three districts while creating two open seats tilted in favor of the Republicans. In other states, such as Virginia (where the Republicans have eight seats, counting the one held by independent ally Virgil H. Goode Jr.), the party's plan merely seeks to strengthen the GOP's hold on its current districts.

Democrats, on the other hand, control the legislature and the governorship in a number of states (including the big prize of California, with its 53 seats), where they in turn will try to exploit their advantage. They do not, however, appear to be in as strong a strategic position to produce gains in those states as the Republicans are in the ones they control. For example, in California the Democrats gained four seats in 2000, so there are few opportunities to create more advantageous districts. Apparently most of their effort will go into strengthening their hold on the newly won seats, although they will try to create a new Hispanic-majority district with the additional seat the state gained. In some states, the Democrats will have effective control where it may not appear so on the surface. In Arkansas and Tennessee, for instance, the Democrats control both houses of the legislature, and the Republicans have the governorship. In both states, however, the legislature can override the governor's veto of a districting bill by a simple majority vote, rendering him an ineffective check on Democratic plans.

Finally, in many states control of redistricting is divided between the two parties. In some of these states a compromise that provides some benefit for both sides will be reached. Legislators in Nevada (which went from two to three seats) crafted a plan in a one-day session. The plan protected the two incumbents and created a competitive third district. In other states in this situation there is likely to be deadlock. If no compromise is reached in those cases, the decision on drawing lines will pass to the courts. (Court challenges are also possible in other states. The Democrats have already launched one against the Michigan plan discussed above.) All in all, there are seventeen states (with 152 seats) that have split authority over districting, thirteen (with 144 seats) where the Democrats have complete control, and eight (with 98 seats) where the Republicans dominate. The remaining states (with 41 seats) have commissions or a single district.

An important uncertainty in the districting process this round involves the interpretation of the Voting Rights Act, which was originally passed in 1965 to protect minorities' right to vote. When the act was renewed in 1982, amendments were included to foster the creation of legislative districts that had black or Latino majorities. (Such districts are termed "majority-minority" districts.) As interpreted by the federal Justice Department, the law required that where it was possible to create or retain a majority-minority district, that had to be done. These rules applied to the South and to a few other states with large Latino populations. In those states, the Justice Department had to approve new districting plans before they could take effect. The requirement to create majority-minority districts was supported by most leaders of minority groups, who wanted more members of Congress from their racial or ethnic group. It was also supported by the Republican Party, which believed that by concentrating minority voters who usually supported Democrats within a few districts, many Democratic incumbents whom those voters had supported in the past would be undermined. Because of the pressures from the Justice Department, the districting process resulted in a number of districts with very convoluted lines.[105]

The creation of majority-minority districts also led to a number of lawsuits by conservatives on the grounds that such plans were discriminatory on the basis of race and so violated the federal Constitution. In 1993, in the case of *Shaw v. Reno*, the Supreme Court expressed concern about "bizarrely shaped" districts that had been drawn for racial purposes and indicated that such districting plans could violate the equal protection clause. In 1995 the Court went much further. By a five–four vote in *Miller v. Johnson*, the justices declared Georgia's districting plan unconstitutional because it had responded to the Justice Department's pressure to create three majority-minority districts without constitutional justification.[106] Indeed, the majority said that any plan in which race was "the predominant factor" was seriously suspect. The Court reinforced its position by declaring majority-minority districts invalid in other states, but in the 2001 case of *Hunt v. Cromartie* it pulled back a bit. In that case the justices ruled that the use of race in drawing boundaries is not automatically unconstitutional if the primary motivation was political rather than racial.[107]

The key issue for the current round of redistricting is whether legislatures will be permitted under the Voting Rights Act to reduce the minority composition of districts below a majority in order to create a larger number of districts in which minorities could have a major influence. The New Jersey redistricting commission did just that in redrawing the state legislature's boundaries, and the new plan was upheld by a federal district court.[108] The ruling will be appealed by the Republicans, and the resolution of this question could have a major impact on the shape of districts for this decade and beyond.

Both parties want to put the best face possible on the districting situation in order to influence the decisions of potential candidates and donors. NRCC chair Davis contended that the Republicans' position was so good that redistricting would yield the party a net gain of ten seats because the biggest population gains were in sunbelt states, where the GOP is politically advantaged.[109] Martin D. Frost of Texas (chair of the Democratic Caucus), on the other hand, argued that the Republican claims were overblown because much of the population growth in a number of states was due to increases among Hispanics, who tilt toward his party. He did say, however, that the Democrats would be happy to break even on redistricting.[110] The views of most neutral analysts fall in between these positions. As we have said, the GOP does have a significant advantage in some big states. The Democrats, however, appear partly to counterbalance that by advantages in some smaller states. Moreover, it is important to note that these expectations may be completely overwhelmed by political forces specific to the 2002 election. Many open seats will be created by redistricting and retirements, and if there is a substantial national tide favoring one party, the effects of the line drawing could be muted or neutralized.

Some Additional Considerations

A few further points related to the previous discussion are necessary to complete our analysis of the prospects for 2002 House races. The vulnerability of individual members varies across parties and across other attributes, and we should not expect those distributions to be similar from election to election. For example, in one year a party may have a relatively high percentage of freshmen or of members who won by narrow margins in the preceding election, while in another year the party's proportion of such potentially vulnerable members may be low. As Table 9-9 shows, both parties have a similar (and relatively small) number of members who won with less than 55 percent of the vote. Thirty-one

TABLE 9-9   Percentage of the Vote Received by Winning House Candidates, by Party and Type of Race, 2000

Percentage of the vote	Democrats			Republicans		
	Reelected incumbent	Successful challenger	Open seat	Reelected incumbent	Successful challenger	Open seat
55 or less	19	4	5	17	2	12
55.1–60.0	20	0	1	30	0	6
60.1–70.0	65	0	1	92	0	5
70–100	96	0	2	55	0	3
Total	200	4	9	194	2	26

Republicans and twenty-eight Democrats fell into this category. This is an almost identical number of marginal seats for each party as resulted from the 1998 elections, but it is substantially fewer than the total of ninety-five after 1996. It is in this type of district that potentially strong challengers are most likely to come forward and where the challengers who do run are most able to raise adequate campaign funds.

As our earlier analysis indicates, the parties' respective successes in recruiting strong candidates for open seats and in opposing the other party's incumbents can be expected to play a significant role in shaping outcomes for 2002. Both Democratic and Republican campaign organizations were actively pursuing recruits during 2001. Of particular note here is the potential impact of term limits in the states. Although the term limits movement failed to impose restrictions on members of Congress, it succeeded in getting limits adopted in twenty states on state legislators, and those limits are beginning to take effect. One potential outlet for a state legislator who cannot run for reelection is to seek a congressional seat.

Also related to the questions of candidate recruitment and district vulnerability is the potential number of open seats. We have seen that open seats are more likely to switch parties than are those with incumbents, and that both parties are more likely to field strong candidates for open seats. Moreover, we saw that the Democrats' lack of success in open-seat races in 2000 was the principal reason for their failure to take control of the House. As of the summer of 2001, it appears that there may be many more retirements from the House and representatives seeking other offices than in other recent elections. Rep. Davis of the NRCC estimated that there could be between sixty and eighty voluntary departures.[111] Thus while the number of potentially vulnerable incumbents may be fewer than in recent years, the number of competitive House races could be substantial.

A final factor is adequate campaign funding. How successful challengers for 2002 are at raising campaign money will play a large role in the results in competitive districts. Campaign committees of both parties are already extremely active in raising money, reflecting the fact that control of both chambers is on the line, and their activities have been very successful. The Republicans raised $111.8 million between January and June of 2001, a record for the first six months of a two-year election cycle. This was nearly twice the Democrats' total of $61.2 million. Moreover, 63 percent of the GOP amount was "hard money"—donations that are limited in amount by law and which can be used for payment of various campaign activities. (The rest is "soft money," which is raised by parties in unlimited amounts and is supposed to be put to noncampaign uses, such as increasing turnout.) On the other hand, a majority of Democrats' funds was raised in the less desirable soft money.[112] Thus Democrats could be at a significant disadvantage in terms of party funding. It is important to remember, however, that the lion's share of campaign funds is still raised by individual candidates.

Senate Races in 2002

Because there are few Senate races and because they are relatively independent of one another, we have focused our discussion of 2002 on the House to this point. We will now close with a few comments about the upper body's contests. Because of the six-year Senate terms, a different set of seats are up for election every two years, and their partisan composition varies as well. Even though the full Senate is almost evenly divided, the Republican seats up this time outnumber the Democrats' by 20-to-14. The GOP, however, also has more apparently safe seats, so the party situations are actually relatively even. The number of open seats will be one factor that will affect party fortunes since, as we have seen, they are more likely to switch party control. At this point there are three sure vacancies due to the retirements of Republicans Strom Thurmond of South Carolina, Jesse Helms of North Carolina, and Phil Gramm of Texas. Among incumbents, the Democrats have the larger number of clearly vulnerable members, and in almost every instance the GOP has one or more strong potential candidates. Of particular concern are two freshmen from southern states that Bush carried handily in 2000: Mary L. Landrieu of Louisiana and Max Cleland of Georgia. Democrats also have a number of attractive targets with strong potential challengers. Especially interesting is the seat of Sen. Robert C. Smith of New Hampshire. Smith is an ideological conservative who sought the Republican presidential nomination in 2000, and when he lost he quit the party. He returned a few months later to assume a Senate committee chair, but his support among Republicans was undermined. Because of that, and because he is likely to draw a strong Democratic opponent (three-term governor Jeanne Shaheen), and Republican representative John E. Sununu decided to challenge Smith in the primary. How all these potential and actual candidacies play out will largely determine which party will benefit from the 2002 Senate races.

To summarize, then, it appears that House races in 2002 may see a blunting of the usual shift against the party that holds the White House. This situation is similar in many respects to that of 1998, and we saw that the Democrats actually gained seats that year. The potentially large number of open seats does create the possibility for a substantial shift, but this seems likely only if there is a national tide for one of the parties. Given, however, that the size of the GOP majority is so small, the struggle for control of the House may still be in doubt. The same is true in the Senate, where the party split may again be extremely close.

Beyond 2002: Continued Uncertainty of Congressional Control?

Just as every election has implications for those that follow, the elections of 2002 will have an impact on subsequent contests. We do not know those results, so we cannot yet describe the effects. Beyond that, there are a few general considerations worth mentioning that are likely to have an impact on future congressional contests.

We have seen that the demographic shifts over the past decade revealed by the census have political implications, and the American population will continue to change with further consequences. One of the most important developments over the past ten years was the remarkable growth of the Latino share of the electorate, which increased from 3 to 7 percent between 1988 and 2000.[113] This rapid growth is likely to continue, and that is offering both opportunities and concerns to the two parties. Voter News Service (VNS) exit poll data show that Gore beat Bush among Hispanics by 67-to-31 percent even though the Republican had run well among that ethnic group in Texas in both the gubernatorial and presidential races. The same poll indicated that in the vote for the House, the Democrats took 64 percent and the Republicans 35 percent. GOP analysts hope that as Latinos make economic gains, they will shift more to the Republican Party, but they worry about the consequences if this shift does not happen. Alex Castellanos, a Republican media consultant, said: "The left side of the spectrum is growing. Our side is shrinking. . . . The Reagan coalition is not enough to win any more." And Matthew Dowd, who did polling for the Bush campaign, said that if every ethnic group votes exactly the same in 2004 as it did in 2000, the GOP will lose both the popular and electoral votes.[114] This, of course, also has important implications for House and Senate races.

It is clear that both parties are making strong efforts to attract Latino voters. Bush frequently appears before Hispanic audiences and speaks to them in Spanish. He is also making prominent Latino appointments and highlights his meetings with Vicente Fox, the president of Mexico. Further, the administration mentioned the possibility of another amnesty for Mexicans living illegally in the United States, and when the Democrats argued that such a program should be open to immigrants from all sources, Bush indicated a willingness to entertain the possibility. How this tug-of-war for Latino political support comes out will have significant consequences throughout this decade and beyond.

It is also important to note that the consequences of the new set of House district lines will not necessarily all be revealed in the elections of 2002 but will continue to play out over the decade. After the 1990 census the Republicans had a significant role in the ensuing redistricting and were able to shift district patterns in their direction. For various reasons this new political advantage was not reflected very much in the results in 1992, but it was a substantial asset in the party's landslide victory in 1994.

Finally, the issue of campaign finance reform remains unsettled, and how it is resolved could have a great impact on congressional elections. As of this writing, a bill that bans soft-money donations to national-party committees and restricts independent expenditures close to an election has passed the Senate (the roadblock in earlier years) but has not received a floor vote in the House. Opponents of reform have long argued that regulations of this type were unconstitutional (and they hoped that if a bill passed the courts would rescue them from its provisions), but a couple of major judicial rulings in the past two years have cast doubt on that position. In 2000 the Supreme Court ruled that states have the right to regulate donations to state political campaigns without violating the First Amendment, and in 2001 the Court upheld federal restrictions on how much a political party can spend in coordination with its congressional candidates.[115] No one can be certain about the effects if such a bill were to become law, but clearly a lot of risk-averse politicians are worried that the consequences would be significant. Without soft money the recently expanded role of national parties in congressional races would likely be pared back. Like the other issues discussed above, we will watch with interest to see what comes to pass.

Chapter 10

The Congressional Electorate in 2000

In the preceding chapter we viewed congressional elections at the district and state level and saw how those outcomes came together to form a national result. In this chapter we consider congressional elections from the point of view of the individual voter, using the same National Election Studies (NES) surveys we employed to study presidential voting. We discuss how social forces, issues, partisan loyalties, incumbency, and evaluations of congressional and presidential performance influence the decisions of voters in congressional elections. We also try to determine the existence and extent of presidential coattails.

SOCIAL FORCES AND THE CONGRESSIONAL VOTE

In general, social forces relate to the congressional vote the same way they do to the presidential vote (Table 10-1).[1] This has been true in our previous analyses of national elections, but the relationship is even tighter in 2000. The vote for Democratic House candidates and the vote for Al Gore are very similar, both in the aggregate and in virtually all the categories we used in the presidential vote analysis (see Table 5-1).[2] This is true even though the presidential race did not involve an incumbent, while a substantial majority of House races did. This may reflect the closer relationship between party identification and the vote in recent elections for both the president and Congress demonstrated in analyses by Larry M. Bartels.[3]

Consider, for example, the relationship between voting and gender. In the total electorate Al Gore received 51 percent of the vote and House Democrats got 52 percent. Among white female voters, Democrats ran three points better for the House than the presidency, and they did two points better among white males. (Except for the discussion of voting and race, the analysis here, as in chapter 5, is limited to white voters.) The gender results are interesting when compared to the past. In 1988 there was a small gender gap in the presidential vote (about three

TABLE 10-1   How Social Groups Voted for Congress, 2000 (in percentages)

Social group	Democratic	Republican	Total	(N)
Total electorate	52	48	100	(836)
Electorate, by race				
African American	92	8	100	(77)
White	47	53	100	(702)
Hispanic (of any race)	70	30	100	(30)
Whites, by gender				
Female	51	49	100	(383)
Male	41	59	100	(319)
Whites, by region				
New England and Mid-Atlantic	52	48	100	(162)
North Central	50	50	100	(228)
South	32	68	100	(148)
Border	33	67	100	(46)
Mountain and Pacific	57	43	100	(117)
Whites, by birth cohort				
Before 1924	59	41	100	(46)
1924–1939	44	56	100	(145)
1940–1954	48	52	100	(213)
1955–1962	40	60	100	(128)
1963–1970	44	56	100	(94)
1971–1978	57	43	100	(44)
1979–1982	52	48	100	(23)
Whites, by social class				
Working class	43	57	100	(173)
Middle class	47	53	100	(460)
Farmers	(4)	(3)	—	(7)
Whites, by occupation of head of household				
Unskilled manual	41	59	100	(71)
Skilled, semiskilled manual	45	55	100	(102)
Clerical, sales, other white collar	48	52	100	(185)
Managerial	38	62	100	(124)
Professional and Semiprofessional	55	45	100	(150)

(Table continues)

TABLE 10-1   (continued)

Social group	Democratic	Republican	Total	(N)
Whites, by level of education				
Eight grades or less	56	44	100	(16)
Some high school	50	50	100	(36)
High school graduate	46	54	100	(200)
Some college	44	56	100	(211)
College graduate	45	55	100	(155)
Advanced degree	54	46	100	(82)
Whites, by annual family income				
Less than $15,000	50	50	100	(10)
$15,000 to $24,999	60	40	100	(40)
$25,000 to $34,999	59	41	100	(59)
$35,000 to $49,999	47	53	100	(64)
$50,000 to $64,999	43	57	100	(84)
$65,000 to $84,999	44	56	100	(119)
$85,000 to $104,999	41	59	100	(56)
$105,000 to $144,999	42	58	100	(45)
$145,000 and over	26	74	100	(34)
Whites, by union membership[a]				
Member	62	38	100	(114)
Nonmember	44	56	100	(584)
Whites, by religion				
Jewish	87	13	100	(23)
Catholic	50	50	100	(227)
Protestant	39	61	100	(370)
None, no preference	60	40	100	(75)
White Protestants, by whether born again				
Not born again	51	49	100	(180)
Born again	29	71	100	(185)
White Protestants, by religious commitment				
Medium or low	47	53	100	(163)
High	41	59	100	(130)
Very high	16	84	100	(67)
White Protestants, by religious tradition				
Mainline	45	55	100	(154)
Evangelical	33	67	100	(150)

TABLE 10-1   (continued)

Social group	Democratic	Republican	Total	(N)
Whites, by social class and religion				
Working-class Catholics	45	55	100	(64)
Middle-class Catholics	50	50	100	(135)
Working-class Protestants	45	55	100	(87)
Middle-class Protestants	38	62	100	(246)

Note: Numbers are weighted. The thirty-six respondents for whom direction of vote was not ascertained and the thirty-seven voters who voted for other candidates have been excluded from the analysis.

[a] Whether respondent or family member in union.

points), with women more likely to vote Democratic than men, but there was no gap in the House vote. By 1996, however, the gender gap was more pronounced in the vote for both the president and representatives; the major-party share of the vote was 12 points more Democratic for women in the former case and 7 points more Democratic in the latter. In 2000 the aggregate vote for the House was up to 10 points more Democratic among women, 1 point *greater* than in the presidential vote.

The presidential and congressional voting patterns are similar within many other social categories, including race, social class, education, income, and religion. For both the presidential and the congressional vote, African Americans were substantially more likely to vote Democratic. Among major-party voters, the difference was 47 points for the presidential race and 45 points in House contests. Working-class voters were 4 points *less* Democratic than middle-class voters, and 4 points less Democratic for president (a reversal in both races compared to 1996). Catholics were 11 points more likely than Protestants to vote Democratic for representative, and among Protestants, those who did not claim to be "born again" were 22 points more Democratic than those who did claim that status. This latter gap was 11 points greater than in 1996. Religious commitment was also related to congressional voting preferences, though the relationship was not quite as strong as that between religious commitment and presidential voting choices. Forty-seven percent of the white Protestants who had medium or low levels of religious commitment voted Democratic, while Protestants who scored very high gave the Democrats only 16 percent.

There are some differences in the ways the presidential and congressional vote relate to income categories, but it is likely that these differences reflect the smaller number of cases in those categories. The overall patterns are similar and consistent: the propensity to vote Democratic is greater in lower categories of income.

There are, however, a few differences worth noting in the way social forces relate to the two types of votes. One is with respect to region: in the West, the Democrats ran 5 points better for the House than for the presidency. This advantage is probably reflected in the House gains the party made in California.

Among union voters the Democrats ran 18 points better for the House than among nonunion voters, but this gap was only 12 points for the presidency. Finally, with respect to education, the Democrats' support among those with advanced degrees was noticeably better for representative than for president. It should be noted, however, that all of these differences involve categories with relatively small numbers of respondents, so the results may simply be due to sampling variation. The bottom line is that presidential and congressional voting among social groups were strikingly similar in 2000.

ISSUES AND THE CONGRESSIONAL VOTE

In chapter 6 we analyzed the impact of issues on the presidential vote in 2000. Any attempt to conduct a parallel analysis for congressional elections is hampered by limited data. One interesting perspective on issues in the congressional vote is gained by asking whether voters are affected by their perceptions of where candidates stand on the issues. Previous analysis has demonstrated a relationship between a voter's perception of House candidates' positions on a liberal-conservative issue scale and the voter's choice.[4] Unfortunately, the 2000 NES survey does not contain similar questions on the perceived position of House candidates on issues. We can, however, draw on other research to shed further light on this question. In two articles, Alan I. Abramowitz used NES surveys to demonstrate a relationship between candidate ideology and voter choice in both House and Senate elections.[5] For the 1978 Senate election, Abramowitz classified the contests according to the clarity of the ideological choice the two major-party candidates offered to voters. He found that the higher the ideological clarity of the race, the more likely voters were to perceive some difference between the candidates on a liberalism-conservatism scale, and the stronger the relationship was between voters' positions on that scale and their votes. Indeed, in races with a very clear choice, ideology had approximately the same impact on the vote as party identification. In an analysis of House races in 1980 and 1982, Abramowitz found that the more liberal the voter was, the more likely he or she was to vote Democratic; but the relationship was statistically significant only in 1982.

Another perspective was offered in an analysis by Robert S. Erikson and Gerald C. Wright.[6] They examined the positions of 1982 House candidates on a variety of issues (expressed in response to a CBS News/*New York Times* poll) and found that, on most issues, most of the districts were presented with a liberal Democrat and a conservative Republican. They also found that moderate candidates did better in attracting votes than more extreme candidates. In a more recent study, involving the 1994 House elections, Erikson and Wright show that both the issue stands of incumbents (measured by positions on roll call votes) and the district's ideology (measured by the district's propensity to vote for Michael S. Dukakis in the 1988 presidential election) are strongly related to the congressional vote.[7] The same authors, in a study of the 1998 elections, employ a measure of candidate ideology that was derived from candidates' responses to questions about issues rather than from roll calls. That analysis confirms that incumbent ideology has a substantial effect on vote share, with moderates gaining more votes relative to more extreme members. The ideology of the challengers does not have a consistent effect, reflecting the lesser visibility of their positions to the electorate.[8]

We examined the relationships between issues and congressional voting choices in 2000, analyzing the issues we studied in chapter 6. For the most part, the relationships between issue preferences and congressional vote choices were weak and inconsistent, and these relationships were even weaker when we controlled for the tendency of Democratic Party identifiers to have liberal positions on these issues and of Republicans to have conservative issue preferences. However, partisan loyalties clearly affect congressional voting, even when we take issue preferences into account. Therefore, before considering the effects of other factors, we will provide more information about the effects of party identification on House voting.

PARTY IDENTIFICATION AND THE CONGRESSIONAL VOTE

As our previous discussion demonstrates, party identification has a significant effect on voters' decisions. Table 10-2 (corresponding to Table 8-4 on the presidential vote) reports the percentage of whites voting Democratic for the House, across all categories of partisanship, from 1952 through 2000. The data reveal that the proportion of voters who cast ballots in accordance with their party identification declined substantially from 1952 through the 1980s. During the 1990s, however, there was some resurgence of party voting for the House, especially among Republican identifiers.

Consider first the strong identifier categories. In every election from 1952 through 1964, at least nine strong party identifiers out of ten supported the candidate of their party. After that, the percentage dropped, falling to four out of five in 1980, then fluctuating through 1992. But in the past four elections, strong identifiers showed levels of loyalty more similar to those in the late 1960s. The relationship between party and voting among weak party identifiers shows a more erratic pattern, although in most years before 1994 defection rates tend to be higher since the 1970s than earlier. (Because we present the percentage of major-party voters who voted Democratic, the defection rate for Democrats is the reported percentage subtracted from 100 percent.) Note that the tendency to defect was stronger among Republicans, which reflected the Democrats' greater number of incumbents, as discussed in chapter 9. Probably reflecting the effects of the Republicans' majority status and the corresponding increase in the number of their incumbents, since 1994 the tendency of Democrats to defect rose, whereas among Republicans it fell. We consider this further in the next section.

TABLE 10-2   Percentage of White Major-Party Voters Who Voted Democratic for the House, by Party Identification, 1952–2000

Party identification	1952	1954	1956	1958	1960	1962	1964	1966	1968	1970	1972
Strong Democrat	90	97	94	96	92	96	92	92	88	91	91
Weak Democrat	76	77	86	88	85	83	84	81	72	76	79
Independent, leans Democrat	63	70	82	75	86	74	78	54	60	74	78
Independent, no partisan leanings	25	41	35	46	52	61	70	49	48	48	54
Independent, leans Republican	18	6	17	26	26	28	28	31	18	35	27
Weak Republican	10	6	11	22	14	14	34	22	21	17	24
Strong Republican	5	5	5	6	8	6	8	12	8	4	15

Note: To approximate the numbers on which these percentages are based, see Table 8-2. Actual *N*s will be smaller than those that can be derived from Table 8-2 because respondents who did not vote (or who voted for a minor party) have been excluded from these calculations. Numbers also will be lower for the presidential election years because the voting report is provided in the postelection interviews that usually

Despite this increase in defections from party identification since the mid-1960s, strong party identifiers continue to be notably more likely to vote in accord with their party than weak identifiers. In most years, weak Republicans were more likely to vote Republican than independents who leaned toward the Republican Party, although in 1996 and 1998 these groups were about equally likely to vote Republican. Weak Democrats were more likely to vote Democratic than independents who leaned Democratic in most of the elections from 1952 through 1978, but in a number of elections since then this pattern has been reversed, and in 2000 the two groups were equally likely to vote Democratic. In general, then, the relationship between party identification and the vote was strongest in the 1950s and early 1960s, grew less strong thereafter, and recently has shown some rebound.

If party identifiers were defecting more frequently in House elections after the early 1960s, to whom were they defecting? As one might expect from the preceding chapter, the answer is to incumbents.

INCUMBENCY AND THE CONGRESSIONAL VOTE

In chapter 9 we mentioned Albert D. Cover's analysis of congressional voting behavior from 1958 through 1974.[9] Cover compared the rates of defection from party identification among voters who were of the same party as the incumbent and those who were of the same party as the challenger. The analysis showed no systematic increase over time in defection among voters who shared identification with incumbents, the proportions defecting ranging between 5 percent and 14 percent. Among voters who identified with the same party as challengers,

1974	1976	1978	1980	1982	1984	1986	1988	1990	1992	1994	1996	1998	2000
89	86	83	82	90	87	91	86	91	87	87	87	88	88
81	76	79	66	73	66	71	80	80	81	73	70	60	69
87	76	60	69	84	76	71	86	79	73	65	70	62	71
54	55	56	57	31	59	59	66	60	53	55	42	45	50
38	32	36	32	36	39	37	37	33	36	26	19	23	27
31	28	34	26	20	33	34	29	39	35	21	19	25	15
14	15	19	22	12	15	20	23	17	16	6	2	8	11

contain about 10 percent fewer respondents than the preelection interviews in which party identification was measured. The 1954 survey measured voting intention shortly before the election. Except for 1954, the off-year election surveys are based on a postelection interview.

however, the rate of defection—that is, the proportion voting for the incumbent instead of the candidate of their own party—increased steadily from 16 percent in 1958 to 56 percent in 1972, then dropped to 49 percent in 1974. Thus the decline in the strength of the relationship between party identification and House voting appeared to be due in large measure to increased support for incumbents. Because there were more Democratic incumbents, this tendency was consistent with the higher defection rates among Republican identifiers, as seen in Table 10-2.

Controlling for party identification and incumbency, we present in Table 10-3 data on the percentage of respondents who voted Democratic for the House and the Senate in 2000 that confirm this view. In both House and Senate voting we find the same relationship as Cover did. As we present the percentage of major-party voters who voted Democratic, the defection rate for Democrats is the reported percentage subtracted from 100 percent. Among Republicans, the percentage reported in the table is the defection rate. (By definition, independents cannot defect.) For the House, the proportion of voters defecting from their party identification is low when that identification is shared by the incumbent: 3 percent among both Democrats and Republicans.[10] When, however, the incumbent belongs to the other party, the rates are much higher: 29 percent among Democrats and 32 percent among Republicans. Note also that the support of the independents is skewed sharply in favor of the incumbent. When there was an incumbent Democrat running, 73 percent of the independents voted Democratic; when there was an incumbent Republican, 69 percent of the independents voted Republican.

The analogous pattern is somewhat weaker in the data on Senate voting (although it is stronger than in some of our previous analyses of Senate data). When given the opportunity to support a Republican House incumbent,

TABLE 10-3 Percentage of Respondents Who Voted Democratic for the House and Senate, by Party Identification and Incumbency, 2000

| | Party identification | | | | | |
| | Democrat | | Independent | | Republican | |
Incumbency	(%)	(N)	(%)	(N)	(%)	(N)
House						
Democrat	97	(135)	73	(78)	32	(74)
None	76	(121)	46	(22)	8	(25)
Republican	71	(116)	31	(80)	3	(125)
Senate						
Democrat	98	(102)	75	(73)	32	(69)
None	86	(58)	59	(34)	14	(37)
Republican	83	(96)	47	(60)	4	(99)

Note: Numbers in parentheses are totals on which percentages are based. Numbers are weighted. In this table and in subsequent tables in this chapter, we combine strong and weak Democrats and strong and weak Republicans. Independents include those who lean toward either party and "pure" independents.

29 percent of the Democratic identifiers defected. Faced with the opportunity to support an incumbent Republican senator, only 17 percent defected. Because the proportion of the electorate that has the chance to vote for Democratic and Republican senatorial candidates will vary greatly from election to election, it is difficult to make generalizations about the overall effects of incumbency in Senate contests from this type of data. In the remainder of this chapter we continue to explore this relationship among party identification, incumbency, and congressional voting.

THE CONGRESSIONAL VOTE AS A REFERENDUM

In chapter 7 we analyzed the effect of perceptions of presidential performance on the vote for president in 2000, more or less viewing that election as a referendum on Bill Clinton's job performance, especially about the most salient concern among voters: the economy. A similar conception can be applied here, employing different perspectives. On the one hand, a congressional election can be considered as a referendum on the performance of a particular member of Congress in office; on the other hand, it can be viewed as a referendum on the performance of the president. We will consider both possibilities here.

As we noted in chapter 9, for some time public opinion surveys have shown that the approval ratings of congressional incumbents are very high, even when judgments on the performance of Congress as an institution are not. While traveling with House incumbents in their districts, Richard F. Fenno Jr. noted that the people he met overwhelmingly approved of the performance of their own

TABLE 10-4   Percentage of Voters Who Supported Incumbents' in House Voting, by Party and Evaluations of Incumbent's Performance, 2000

| | Voters' evaluation of incumbent's job performance | | | |
| | Approve | | Disapprove | |
	(%)	(N)	(%)	(N)
Incumbent is of same party as voter	98	(214)	78	(9)
Incumbent is of opposite party	53	(108)	2	(48)

Note: Numbers in parentheses are totals on which percentages are based. Numbers are weighted. The total number of cases is markedly lower than for previous tables because we have excluded respondents who did not evaluate the performance of the incumbent and those who live in a district that had no incumbent running.

representative, although at the time the public generally disapproved of the job the institution was doing.[11] Data in the 2000 NES survey again indicate widespread approval of House incumbents: among respondents who had an opinion, 83 percent endorsed their member's job performance. Approval was widespread, regardless of the party identification of the voter or the party of the incumbent. Indeed, an examination of all combinations of these two variables shows that the lowest approval rate for incumbents is the 68 percent level achieved by Republican members among Democratic Party identifiers.

Further evidence indicates, moreover, that the level of approval has electoral consequences. Table 10-4 shows the level of pro-incumbent voting among voters who share the incumbent's party and among those who are of the opposite party, controlling for whether they approve or disapprove of the incumbent's job performance. If voters approve of the member's performance and share his or her party identification, support is overwhelming. At the opposite pole, among voters from the opposite party who disapprove, support is negligible. In the mixed categories, the incumbents receive intermediate levels of support. Because approval rates are very high even among voters of the opposite party, most incumbents are reelected by large margins even in a difficult year such as 1994.

In chapter 9 we pointed out that midterm congressional elections were influenced by public evaluations of the president's job performance. Voters who think the president is doing a good job are more likely to support the congressional candidate of the president's party. Less scholarly attention has been given to this phenomenon in presidential election years, but the 2000 NES survey provides us with the data needed to explore the question.

On the surface at least, there would appear to be a strong relationship. Among voters who approved of Clinton's job performance, 68 percent voted Democratic for the House; among those who disapproved of the president's performance, only 24 percent supported Democrats. In 1980 there was a similar relationship between the two variables, but when controls were introduced for party identification and incumbency, the relationship all but disappeared.[12] Approval of

TABLE 10-5   Percentage of Respondents Who Voted Democratic for the House, by Evaluation of Clinton's Performance, Party Identification, and Incumbency, 2000

	Evaluation of Clinton's job							
	Incumbent is Republican				Incumbent is Democrat			
Party	Approve		Disapprove		Approve		Disapprove	
identification	(%)	(N)	(%)	(N)	(%)	(N)	(%)	(N)
Democrat	71	(103)	70	(10)	97	(127)	100	(8)
Independent	35	(49)	26	(31)	82	(55)	58	(19)
Republican	9	(32)	1	(85)	41	(27)	27	(44)

Note: Numbers in parentheses are totals on which percentages are based. Numbers are weighted.

Jimmy Carter increased the Democratic House vote by a small amount among Democrats but had virtually no effect among independents and Republicans. In 2000, however, the results were very different. Table 10-5 presents the relevant data on House voting, controlling for party identification, incumbency, and evaluation of Clinton's job performance. We discovered that even with these controls, evaluations of the president's job had some impact on House voting by Republicans and independents, although the effect was smaller than what we found in 1996. (The lack of any relationship among Democrats may be due to the very small numbers of respondents from the party who disapproved of Clinton's job performance.) To be sure, Republicans were still more likely both to disapprove of Clinton and to vote Republican than were Democrats. Yet even after controlling for the pull of incumbency, within the Republican and independent party identification categories those who approved of Clinton's job performance were more likely to vote Democratic for the House than were those who disapproved, and the difference in all four categories was larger than the corresponding difference in 1980.

PRESIDENTIAL COATTAILS AND THE CONGRESSIONAL VOTE

Another perspective on the congressional vote, somewhat related to the presidential referendum concept we just considered, is the impact of the voter's presidential vote decision, or the length of a presidential candidate's coattails. That is, does a voter's decision to support a presidential candidate make him or her more likely to support a congressional candidate of the same party, so that the congressional candidate, as the saying goes, rides into office on the president's coattails?

Expectations about presidential coattails have been shaped in substantial measure by the period of the New Deal realignment. Franklin D. Roosevelt won by landslide margins in 1932 and 1936 and swept enormous congressional majorities into office with him. Research has indicated, however, that such strong pulling power by presidential candidates has declined since World War II.[13] In an analysis of the coattail effect since 1868, Randall L. Calvert and John A. Ferejohn pointed out that the effect is a combination of two factors: how many voters a presidential candidate can pull to congressional candidates of his party and how many congressional seats can be shifted between the parties by the addition of that number of voters.[14] (The second aspect is called the seats/votes relationship, or the swing ratio.)

Ferejohn and Calvert discovered that the relationship between presidential voting and congressional voting from 1932 through 1948 was virtually the same as it was from 1896 through 1928 and that the impact of coattails was strengthened by an increase in the swing ratio. In other words, the same proportion of votes pulled in by a presidential candidate produced more congressional seats in the New Deal era than before it. After 1948, they argued, the coattail effect declined because the relationship between presidential and congressional voting decreased. Analyzing data from presidential elections from 1956 through 1980, Calvert and Ferejohn reached similar conclusions about the length of presidential coattails.[15] They found that although every election during the period exhibited significant coattail voting, over time the extent of such voting probably declined. More recently, James E. Campbell and Joe A. Sumners concluded from an analysis of Senate elections that presidential coattails exert a modest but significant influence on the Senate vote.[16]

Data on the percentage of respondents who voted Democratic for the House and Senate in 2000, controlling for their presidential vote and their party identification, are presented in Table 10-6. For both houses, a strong relationship is apparent. Within each party identification category, the proportion of Bush voters who supported Democratic congressional candidates is substantially lower than the proportion of Gore voters who supported Democratic candidates. There are too few Nader voters to draw any conclusions about his effect.

Because we know that this apparent relationship could be just an accidental consequence of the distribution of different types of voters among Democratic and Republican districts, in Table 10-7 we present the same data on House voting in 2000, but this time controlling for the party of the House incumbent. When we made this comparison in 1996, we found that despite this additional control, the relationship held up very well. Within every category for which comparisons were possible, Dole voters supported Democratic candidates at substantially lower rates than did Clinton voters. In 2000, however, there are so few defectors within the two major parties that the comparisons are largely limited to independents, where the effect remains substantial. These limited data are consistent with the interpretation that the presidential vote exerted some influence on the congressional vote, although not as strong an influence as partisanship and congressional incumbency. Where comparisons are possible, the results in both Table 10-6 and Table 10-7 are similar to the corresponding data for 1980 through 1996. Within the various categories of party identification and

TABLE 10-6   Percentage of Respondents Who Voted Democratic for the House and Senate, by Party Identification and Presidential Vote, 2000

Presidential	Party identification					
	Democrat		Independent		Republican	
Vote	(%)	(N)	(%)	(N)	(%)	(N)
House						
Bush	28	(18)	29	(84)	12	(204)
Gore	87	(289)	73	(100)	29	(14)
Nader	—	(1)	57	(14)	—	(1)
Senate						
Bush	31	(16)	26	(69)	12	(192)
Gore	93	(243)	86	(83)	47	(17)
Nader	—	(1)	86	(14)	—	(3)

Note: Numbers in parentheses are totals on which percentages are based. Numbers are weighted. No percentage is reported where the total *N* is less than 10.

TABLE 10-7   Percentage of Respondents Who Voted Democratic for the House, by Presidential Vote, Party Identification, and Incumbency, 2000

Party identification	Voted for Bush		Voted for Gore		Voted for Nader	
	(%)	(N)	(%)	(N)	(%)	(N)
	Incumbent is Democrat					
Democrat	—	(4)	98	(127)	—	(1)
Independent	46	(22)	95	(41)	58	(12)
Republican	30	(66)	—	(7)	—	(1)
	Incumbent is Republican					
Democrat	18	(11)	76	(105)	—	(0)
Independent	14	(36)	48	(40)	—	(4)
Republican	3	(118)	—	(7)	—	(0)

Note: Numbers in parentheses are totals on which percentages are based. Numbers are weighted. No percentage is reported where the total *N* is less than 10.

congressional incumbency, the relationship between presidential voting and congressional voting seems to be roughly the same in these six elections.[17]

CONCLUSION

In this chapter we have considered a variety of possible influences on voters' decisions in congressional elections. We found that social forces have some impact on that choice. There is evidence from the work of other researchers that issues also have an effect. Incumbency has a major and consistent impact on voters' choices. It solidifies the support of the incumbent's partisans, attracts independents, and leads to defections by voters who identify with the challenger's party. Incumbent support is linked to a positive evaluation of the representative's job by the voters. The tendency to favor incumbents currently appears to benefit the Republican Party in House races. Within the context of this incumbency effect, voters' choices also seem to be affected by their evaluations of the job the president is doing and by their vote for president. Partisanship has some direct impact on the vote, even after controlling for incumbency. The total effect of partisanship is, however, larger, because most incumbents represent districts that have more partisans of their party than of the opposition. Thus the long-term advantage of Democrats in congressional elections was built on a three-part base: there were more Democrats than Republicans in the electorate; most incumbents of both parties achieved high levels of approval in their constituencies; and the incumbents had resources that made it possible for them to create direct contacts with voters. With the GOP now in the majority in Congress, the Republicans may continue to benefit from the last two factors while they try to reduce their weakness on the first.

Chapter 11

The 2002 Congressional Elections

✦✦✦

In chapter 9 we focused on the Republicans' efforts to retain their House majority since the election of 1994, which ended the Democrats' unparalleled dominance there. We also considered the Democrats' efforts to overturn the GOP
House majority and their success (with the help of James M. Jeffords of Vermont)
in regaining control of the Senate. In this chapter we will discuss the pattern of
outcomes in the 2002 congressional races to determine whether there is any collective message in the individual results and to assess the implications of these
outcomes for future elections.

The magnitude of the shift in electoral results from 2000 was small, but those
results were also significant and historic. The Republicans won twenty-two of the
thirty-four Senate contests, for a total of fifty-one seats in the 108th Congress.
This was a net gain of two seats and yielded a shift of majority control back to the
GOP. In the House the GOP won 229 seats to the Democrats' 205, with one seat
taken by an independent.[1] The Republicans gained six seats, leaving the
Democrats twelve seats short of the majority control they sought. Despite the
shift of only eight seats net to the Republicans in both chambers combined, many
observers were surprised by the GOP's ability to buck the historical patterns we
discussed in chapter 9, and the Democrats too were mightily disappointed. Our
attempt to discover the patterns underlying these results begins with a closer
examination of the congressional outcomes.

THE PATTERN OF OUTCOMES

The data on incumbency and electoral success in Table 11-1 provide an update of
the information found in Table 9-1. The data show that incumbents continued to
be very successful. Only sixteen House incumbents lost, and eight of those were
in either primary or general election races with two incumbents pitted against
each other, and where incumbent defeats had to occur. Moreover, the number of

TABLE 11-1   House and Senate Incumbents and Election Outcomes, 2002

Chamber	Incumbents running (N)	Primary defeats (%)	(N)	General election defeats (%)	(N)	Reelected (%)	(N)
House	398	2.0	(8)	2.0	(8)	96.0	(382)
Senate	26	4	(1)	8	(2)	88	(23)

Note: Senator Jean Carnahan (Mo.) is not treated as an incumbent. In the House, Bob Barr (Ga.), Cynthia McKinney (Ga.), Gary Condit (Calif.), Lynn Rivers (Mich.), Brian Kerns (Ind.), Frank Mascara (Pa.), Tom Sawyer (Ohio), and Earl Hilliard (Ala.) were defeated in their party's primaries. In the Senate, John Sununu defeated incumbent Bob Smith in the New Hampshire Senate primary.

incumbents seeking reelection (398) was also high, especially for a post-reapportionment election. (By contrast, the last such election in 1992 saw only 368 incumbents running.) The combination of these factors—many incumbents with a high success rate—resulted in a relatively small freshman class of only fifty-two members. In the Senate contests, incumbents' success was somewhat lower than that in the House, but still quite high at 88 percent, with one primary defeat and only two losses in the general election.[2] Fewer than half of the elections since 1954 posted higher rates of incumbent success in the Senate.

Table 11-2 shows the combined effects of party and incumbency in 2002. Given the overall results, the pattern for both parties basically reflects what we have just seen for the two houses. In both House and Senate contests involving incumbents, Democrats and Republicans performed about the same in the aggregate. In open seats, however, the GOP did better than the Democrats in both chambers. In both House and Senate contests, the Republicans held on to a higher proportion of their larger number of open seats. Moreover, the GOP won two-thirds of the twelve new districts that resulted from reapportionment.[3] More than anything else, it was the Republicans' success in open seats that permitted them to win control of both Houses and restore the unified Republican government that resulted briefly from the 2000 elections.

Not surprisingly, the small partisan shifts translated into small changes in the party shares of regional delegations. However, the changes displayed in Table 11-3 are instructive. Despite the importance of the South in the Republicans' seizing of the congressional majority in 1994, and their retention of it through the 2000 elections, none of the GOP net gain in 2002 came from this region. In the House, the two parties each gained three more seats net of the six added to the South by reapportionment, and in the Senate two incumbent losses cancelled each other. Moreover, in the border states in the House, the Democrats were actually better off after 2002, mainly because of the gain of two seats in Maryland (although their share of Senate seats in the region did decline by one). And in the East and West both parties' shares of seats were almost identical in both houses. Rather, it was in the Midwest that the damage to the Democrats accrued. With the loss of five seats to the region because of reapportionment, the Democrats ended the

TABLE 11-2   House and Senate General Election Outcomes, by Party and
Incumbency, 2002 (in percentages)

| | Democratic incumbent | No incumbent | | | Republican incumbent | Total |
		Democratic seat	New seat	Republican seat		
House						
Democrats	99	67	33	18	1	48
Republicans	1	33	67	82	99	52
Total	100	100	100	100	100	100
(*N*)	(189)[1]	(15)	(12)	(22)	(197)[2]	(435)
Senate						
Democrats	91	33	—	0	7	35
Republicans	9	67	—	100	93	65
Total	100	100	—	100	100	100
(*N*)	(11)	(3)	—	(5)	(15)	(34)

[1] Excludes three Democratic incumbents who were defeated by Republican incumbents.

[2] Excludes one Republican incumbent who was defeated by a Democratic incumbent.

contest with nine fewer seats than before, while the GOP gained four. We will
return to this subject in our discussion of reapportionment and redistricting.

ASSESSING VICTORY AND EXPLAINING THE RESULTS

After every election, one question that is always of interest is: Which party won
and which party lost? This question is vital to politicians and citizens because the
public interpretation of election outcomes can affect the calculations of politicians and their ability to advance their policy agendas, and it can also affect their
relationships with each other. Politicians use their interpretations of the results,
and those of other observers, to infer (rightly or wrongly) the political desires of
the voters. For example, in 1980 Ronald Reagan's convincing electoral vote victory over President Jimmy Carter and the substantial gains made by the
Republicans in the congressional elections were interpreted as a wholesale
endorsement of the Republican agenda of tax cuts, reductions of social spending, and increases in defense expenditures. As a consequence, all of these policies
were enacted into law in the subsequent Congress.

To evaluate a party's success we must apply some standard—a "yardstick"—
to measure victory. The standard provides us with a set of expectations against
which the actual results can be compared. In addition, as we saw in chapter 9,
expectations or hypotheses about election outcomes can be combined in models of the electoral process that can provide explanations as well as predictions.
We will, in turn, consider the historical pattern, the expectations of participants

TABLE 11-3   Party Shares of Regional Delegations in the House and Senate, before and after 2002 Elections

	Before			After		
Region	Democrats (%)	Republicans (%)	(N)	Democrats (%)	Republicans (%)	(N)
House						
East	61	39	(89)	60	40	(84)
Midwest	46	54	(96)	38	62	(91)
West	54	46	(93)	53	47	(98)
South	42	58	(125)	42	58	(131)
Border	38	62	(32)	45	55	(31)
Total	49	51	(435)	47	53	(435)
Senate						
East	60	35	(20)[1]	60	35	(20)[1]
Midwest	64	36	(22)	59	41	(22)
West	39	61	(26)	39	61	(26)
South	41	59	(22)	41	59	(22)
Border	50	50	(10)	40	60	(10)
Total	50	49	(100)[1]	48	51	(100)[1]

[1]Includes James M. Jeffords of Vermont, who is an independent.

and observers, and the insights from academic models as yardsticks by which to measure the relative success of each party.

Historical Trends

In chapter 9 we presented data on seat changes in midterm House elections (see Table 9-8). Recall that the party that held the White House lost strength in all but two midterms in the twentieth century. Thus, based on this trend alone, many observers would probably have expected Republican losses in 2002. The question was how great those losses would be. The historical results also showed that a party's losses were larger in the second or later midterm of an administration than in the first midterm. In fact, we can see an even clearer picture of the historical trends by introducing an additional variable: Whether the president's party held a majority in the House before the election. Remember that the "exposure" hypothesis discussed in chapter 9 argued that the more seats a party held (relative to the recent historical pattern), the more vulnerable it would be to losses. Similarly, we might expect that a majority party would be more vulnerable than a minority. Table 11-4 reconfigures the data from Table 9-8 and shows that this expectation is correct. On average, before 2002 minority parties lost fewer seats than majority parties in postwar midterm elections, both overall and

TABLE 11-4   Average Seat Losses by the President's Party in Midterm
Elections, 1946–1998

President's party in the House	First term of administration	Later term of administration	Total
Majority	21.3 ($N = 4$)[1]	43.7 ($N = 3$)[2]	30.9 ($N = 7$)
Minority	15.7 ($N = 3$)[3]	22.5 ($N = 4$)[4]	19.6 ($N = 7$)
Total	18.9 ($N = 7$)	31.6 ($N = 7$)	25.2 ($N = 14$)

[1] 1954, 1962, 1978, and 1994.

[2] 1946, 1950, and 1966.

[3] 1970, 1982, and 1990.

[4] 1958, 1974, 1986, and 1998.

when we control for first or later midterms of an administration. Note, however, that the impact of first versus later midterms also continues to hold.

In light of these historical patterns, the actual showing of the Republicans in the House races was impressive. The only gains by the president's party in a midterm in the twentieth century were by the Democrats in 1934 in Franklin D. Roosevelt's first term (when the GOP was still suffering from the public's negative reaction to the Great Depression), and in Clinton's second term in 1998. While we did not previously discuss in detail similar data for the Senate, we can draw similar conclusions. In general, in the postwar period the party that controlled the White House did better in first midterms (averaging a net loss of only one seat per election) than in later midterms (when they have lost an average of seven seats).[4] So in the Senate contests the GOP did a little better than the previous pattern. Thus in both chambers the Republicans improved on this yardstick for midterm elections.

Observers' Expectations

The preelection expectations of politicians and media analysts provide another standard for judging election outcomes. Even if a party loses ground, it may try to claim victory (at least a "moral victory") if it performs notably better than was anticipated. These publicly stated expectations are shaped in part by the historical standards we just discussed, but they are also influenced by polls and by recent political events.

Of course, the anticipations voiced by politicians during election campaigns are a mixture of predictions, hopes, and public-relations statements. They cannot be taken entirely at face value. In the year leading up to the 2002 elections, however, estimates of the likely outcome were probably less variable than usual, especially from more neutral observers. This may have reflected the lessons of 1998, which demonstrated that—for the reasons we discussed in chapter 9— midterm losses for the president's party were not part of the laws of nature.

Much of the speculation about the House revolved around the anticipated impact of redistricting. We will discuss that subject in more detail later, but we should note here that the consequences of redistricting constrained general expectations about the election results. We noted previously (p. 230) that after 2000 there were few vulnerable Republican districts for the Democrats to target, and redistricting made that number even smaller. As a consequence, even early in the election year analysts concluded that there would be a relatively small number of contested districts, and so the chances of major gains for either party were slim. For example, in late April of 2002 Charles Cook (one of the most prominent journalists covering congressional elections) estimated that there would be only forty-seven competitive races.[5] At about the same time, another well-known analyst (Stuart Rothenberg) put the number at fifty-three.[6] In Senate races, as one would expect from the discussion in chapter 9, there was a larger proportion of potentially competitive races. Even there, however, the number was not large, and it was distributed about evenly between the parties. (Rothenberg, for example, listed six Republican and five Democratic seats as toss-ups or as having a narrow advantage for the incumbent party in late February.)[7]

Early in the year Republicans received information that gave them reason to be hopeful about their chances to improve on the historical pattern. At an early February retreat, Rep. Thomas M. Davis III, R-Va., the Chairman of the National Republican Congressional Committee (NRCC), "told his colleagues that House Republicans have 'a tremendous opportunity' to pick up seats. . ." But he also warned them that a lot could change before the elections. Poll data showed great support for President Bush in the wake of the terrorist attacks on September 11, 2001, and approval for GOP positions on issues like homeland defense and economic security.[8] The same week Democrats received warnings at their retreat about their correspondingly unattractive prospects. Poll results from twenty-two key house districts indicated that the party's candidates faced significant deficits among "persuadable" voters on a range of issues.[9]

As a consequence of this and other information, public expectations of politicians generally stayed within narrow bounds with few exceptions. In July, when public anger over corporate accounting scandals was peaking, House Minority Leader Richard A. Gephardt, D-Mo., grandiosely spoke of a possible Democratic gain of forty seats, but reality set in soon after when Republican maneuvers prevented public blame from settling on them.[10] GOP estimates were more realistic. Speaker Dennis J. Hastert, R-Ill., for example, said in late September that he anticipated a gain of "two or three" seats for his party.[11]

The reality was that strategists of neither party could detect a strong national trend in their direction.[12] The implication, given the strategic context, was that either party could make gains and that any gains were likely to be small. Confirming this, on the Sunday before the election the *Washington Post* ran its biennial set of predictions from twelve pundits, consultants, and journalists. Half predicted no change or Republican gains, and only one (Ralph Nader) expected a Democratic majority. Similarly, no one predicted a Senate gain of more than two seats either way, although ten did expect the Democrats to retain their majority.[13] Thus, while the House and Senate results may have departed from historical patterns, they were fairly close to the expectations of observers in the months leading up to election day.

Academic Insights

In looking forward to the election of 2002 in chapter 9, we discussed a number of academic models of House elections. In the next section we discuss a number of the variables that were employed in these models. At this point we want to consider only the collective picture they offered regarding Republican prospects. Most of these models include variables that measure the performance of the economy and the level of approval for the president. In 2002 the economy was not doing well in objective terms (although, as we will see, Bush and the GOP were not necessarily held responsible for this situation), but Bush's approval ratings were extraordinarily high at 62 percent.[14] Regarding "exposure," or the number of seats held by the president's party relative to a historical trend, the Republicans had only a bare majority in the House, and the number of seats they held was below the average of the previous four elections.

Thus the variables that had been judged to be important in predicting the level of partisan success in congressional elections indicated a mixed message about Republican prospects in 2002, but they certainly did not offer a strong expectation of GOP losses. There were, moreover, additional factors that were arguably important in 2002 that previous models did not take account of, especially the war on terrorism and domestic security.

NATIONAL AND LOCAL INFLUENCES IN CONGRESSIONAL ELECTIONS

Thomas P. "Tip" O'Neill, the former Democratic Speaker of the House, was well known for asserting "all politics is local." Yet, as our previous discussion indicates, this characterization is not entirely correct with regard to congressional elections. National-level factors, such as the state of the economy, can also influence the results. Thus, every election is affected by both local and national forces, although the relative impact of each will vary from one election to the next. We now turn to a consideration of some factors that were relevant to the 2002 congressional elections.

President Bush in 2002: The Economy, Job Approval, and War

Two factors that have an important impact on election outcomes are the economy and evaluations of the president. Indeed, as we showed in chapter 7, the two tend to be closely related, because the president is usually held accountable when the economy is doing poorly. The performance of the U.S. economy in 2002 was not very good by objective standards, with unemployment higher than in the Clinton years, and a stock market that was headed for its third consecutive year of losses. More important than these objective facts is the public's perceptions of the economy, and those were not good either. A *New York Times*/CBS News poll just before Election Day indicated that 53 percent of respondents believed that the condition of the economy was bad or very bad. Moreover, 34 percent thought the economy was getting worse, whereas only 17 percent thought it was getting better. (The remainder said it was staying the same, or had no opinion.)[15]

Of course the Bush White House recognized from the outset the importance of the economy, both for 2002 and for the president's reelection. Recalling that many observers thought Bush's father had seemed insufficiently concerned about the economic plight of ordinary people (and that the perception may have cost him reelection), the president made a point of demonstrating his interest in the issue. In January 2002 he took a two-day trip down the Mississippi River, saying he was there "to understand how our economy works." He contended that the best course was to expand foreign trade to create jobs. The administration also argued for sticking with the large tax cuts it had engineered the year before.[16]

The Democrats thought they had a chance to get some leverage on the economic issue when the revelation of a wave of corporate accounting scandals was followed by further declines in the stock market. Republicans, however, avoided much damage by being critical of corporate practices and pushing for laws containing new regulations. The White House was also responsive. Karl Rove, Bush's top political advisor, pressured corporate executives to support a bill imposing corporate accounting reforms that had been drafted by Democrat Paul S. Sarbanes of Maryland. Rove then organized an "economic summit" in Waco, Texas, which gave the president the chance to demonstrate concern about the economy. Then the "Justice Department, urged on by GOP political consultants, made several high-profile arrests of corporate chiefs, complete with handcuffs." [17]

These strategies insulated Bush and the Republicans from serious political damage. In early July, after the scandals broke, 63 percent of respondents to a national poll thought that "big business" had too much influence over decisions in the Bush administration. Yet by 53–41 percent, they said that Bush had more interest in protecting the interests of ordinary Americans than those of large corporations.[18] Approval of Bush's economic performance waned as November approached, but even on the eve of the election public approval exceeded disapproval by 46–43 percent.[19]

The ability to mitigate, if not neutralize, the negative impact of the economy played a significant part in the success of the Republicans' larger strategy for 2002. Their planning for this effort began early in 2001, under Rove's leadership. Rather than try to keep the president distanced from the campaign (and from blame for losses), Rove concluded that Bush "would have to bear the brunt if we lost, whatever he did or didn't do. . . . We decided that he ought to be engaged. At least that way he'd have a better chance to beat the history." [20] The president's performance since September 11 yielded him widespread popular approval—over 60 percent in the months before the election. (Perhaps even more importantly, his approval among Republicans was around 90 percent, giving him substantial leverage in activating his party's base.) That performance and approval also gave the campaign a theme: security.

Rove made the plan clear in January 2002, when he told the Republican National Committee that "We can go to the country on this issue because they trust the Republican Party to do a better job of protecting and strengthening America's military might and thereby protecting America." [21] The White House decision to seek congressional approval for military action against Iraq, followed by efforts to rally United Nations support, kept the issue front and center throughout the campaign. The GOP effort was also advantaged by the Democrats' decision, under pressure from union supporters, to resist giving the president extensive new controls over personnel in the proposed Department of Homeland Security. A number of Republican candidates attacked their opponents on this stand for being "soft" on security. This included Democratic senator Max Cleland of Georgia, even though he was a decorated Vietnam veteran who lost an arm and both legs in the war. (Cleland was the sole Democrat incumbent senator to lose.)

The focus on security not only cost Democrats support, it also made it difficult to get out their message on other issues. They sought to blame the Republicans for the low volume of major bills passed by Congress. A number of Democratic candidates tried to use the votes of some Republicans for free trade against them. The Democratic leadership also tried to soft pedal some of the party's previously problematic issues like gun control, and some of their candidates sought to neutralize the security issue by emphasizing their previous military service.[22] None of these efforts was able, however, to neutralize the effects of the White House plan.

First, the president had spent a great deal of time all year (along with Vice President Dick Cheney) raising funds for Republican candidates, helping the party to raise $527 million compared to $343 million accumulated by the Democrats. Bush and his advisors were also intimately involved in recruiting candidates and planning to stimulate voting by the party's supporters (both of which we will discuss below). Most visible of all were the president's personal campaign efforts. He traveled extensively throughout the fall, including visits to fifteen states in the last five days, urging activists to turn out the vote.[23] Perhaps most damaging to the Democrats, Bush's efforts may have given a focus to the campaign that the other side lacked. In a preelection poll, respondents said that Republicans had a clear plan for the country by 46–39 percent, while the response for the Democrats was 31–52 percent. Moreover, 43 percent of those who voted said their vote was a vote for Bush, while only 17 percent said they were voting against him.[24]

Turnout in 2002

In chapter 4 we talked about the long-term decline in voter turnout and the possible reasons for it.[25] Worries among political strategists about a continuation of that trend figured prominently in the parties' strategies for 2002. Democrats and their allies among unions and in the black community have worked intensely in recent years to stimulate turnout for their candidates, and analysts in both parties recognized success for these efforts in 1998 and 2000.[26] For example, the Republican National Committee studied the results from previous elections and concluded that, "In both 1998 and 2000, the Democrats did a better job of motivating and turning out their voters. . . . We underperformed in the final stages of the last two elections." [27]

GOP leaders wanted to avoid a repeat of this pattern, and they were particularly concerned about voter participation in 2002 because turnout had been so sparse in the primaries that year (about 17 percent of people of voting age in the thirty-seven states with statewide contests for both parties).[28] To that end they organized a number of get-out-the-vote efforts. One was the "72-Hour Task Force" that passed up the previous practice of using phone banks to stimulate turnout to focus instead on personal calls and face-to-face contacts on doorsteps. This was linked to STOMP (Strategic Task Force to Organize and Mobilize People), organized by Rep. Tom DeLay, R-Texas, House majority whip. This effort sought to raise money and to organize safe Republican representatives to recruit volunteers to go to competitive districts to work on persuasion and turnout.[29] As late as six weeks before the election, DeLay sought an additional $600,000 in soft money for the effort, and during the final 72 hours he rented 73 buses and 245 vans to move 8,000 volunteers to targeted districts.[30]

The Democrats and their allies had a get-out-the-vote effort of their own, as in previous years. Indeed, with fifteen days to go before the election, the AFL-CIO had completely halted television ads on behalf of candidates in order to focus all of their efforts on turnout activities. They planned to have thousands of union activists going door-to-door in key states and districts with a special focus on targeting union members, as well as distributing twelve million leaflets.[31]

The usual means of evaluating the impact of efforts like these on the composition of the electorate is the exit poll, which asks questions of voters as they leave the polls. Unfortunately, due to technical difficulties on election night, the national exit poll data were not released. We do know that overall turnout was 39.3 percent of all voting-age citizens, which was up from 37.6 percent in the 1998 midterm elections.[32] We cannot, however, measure whether this increase is disproportionately made up of additional Republican voters. Preliminary evidence from individual states yields a mixed picture, but on balance it appears to support the view that the GOP's efforts were at least partly successful. For example, in Florida—where the president's brother was reelected governor—overall turnout was up by four percentage points from four years earlier. Yet in two of the Democrats' strongest counties (Palm Beach and Broward), it was down.

Similarly, in Maryland, turnout was down noticeably in the three populous counties carried by the losing Democratic candidate for governor, while in the home county of the Republican winner it was up nearly five points.[33] Another case is Georgia, where the Democrats suffered major defeats in the loss of the incumbent senator and governor. In 1998 an estimated 29 percent of the voters were black, while in 2002 only 18 or 19 percent were.[34] Moreover, the overall level of turnout was up from the 47 percent in 1998 to 54 percent in 2002.[35] Thus there is some reason to believe that the Republicans' ability to defy history in 2002 was due to greater success in activating their base and getting their supporters to the polls.

Reapportionment and Redistricting

In chapter 9 we discussed the potential impact of reapportionment and redistricting on the 2002 House elections. As we indicated, the redistribution of House seats among the states, coupled with the requirement that most states redraw their district lines, sets the stage for a possible shift in party fortunes. The consequences of the process rest in large measure on who draws the lines and what they are trying to accomplish. The results from 2002 illustrate that fact.

Even though the Republicans did not have complete control of redistricting in many states, they were in an advantageous position because most of the states they controlled were large, and many were gaining or losing seats. This gave GOP state legislators many options in drawing district lines, and they made the most of them. Pennsylvania, for example, lost two House seats, and the redistricting plan put three pairs of Democratic incumbents together in new districts.[36] This led two Democratic incumbents to retire, and in November the delegation's partisan balance switched from ten Democrats and eleven Republicans to seven and twelve, respectively. Similarly, Michigan lost one seat and the Republican districting plan matched three pairs of Democratic incumbents while creating two new districts tilted to the GOP. Two Democrats ran for other offices (including David E. Bonior, the House minority whip, who unsuccessfully sought the nomination for governor), and one other lost in the primary for a House seat. The final outcome was six Democrats and nine Republicans, compared to nine and seven before the elections.

The Democrats completely controlled more states and more total districts, but their strategic situation was not as good. They did, however, try to make the most of their opportunities. In Maryland, for example, the party's plan targeted a Republican incumbent (Constance A. Morella) and the district of another GOP member who was running for governor.[37] Democrats won both seats. The situation in Georgia, however, demonstrates that one-party control of redistricting is no guarantee of success. The state gained two seats, and the Democrats paired up two sets of Republican incumbents. (One—Saxby Chambliss—ran for the Senate and defeated Max Cleland.) The result was four open seats, and the Democrats had hoped to win all of them. However, due to some weak candidates and to the GOP surge in the state, the new seats split two and two. Also, as we noted in chapter 9, the Democrats had done so well in California in 2000 that despite their control of districting they could not exploit much advantage. Instead they sought to shore up their weaker incumbents, and had to settle for only gaining the single additional district that came to the state through reapportionment.

The largest number of districts were in states that had split party control, and those situations generally led either to compromise or to deadlock and a fight in the courts. In New York, for example, the Republican governor and state senate compromised with the Democratic state assembly to produce a plan that matched one pair of incumbents in each party. Then one of each pair retired from the House. If it had not been for the upset of a Republican incumbent in a different district, each party would have lost one seat as anticipated. In Texas, on the other hand, legislative stalemate led to a court suit. Initially a state judge proposed a plan that damaged the prospects of five Democratic incumbents. A week later, after a number of state politicians appealed for the judge to revise his plan, he did so, submitting a set of districts that basically protected all incumbents. A few days later, a three-judge federal court stepped in and imposed a different plan that also largely protected incumbents. The Supreme Court upheld the plan, and in the elections the Republicans gained only the two seats that were added by reapportionment.[38]

The Supreme Court also had to step in to settle the last lingering dispute over reapportionment. Recall that in chapter 9 we discussed the fight over the use of statistical sampling to adjust census figures, and noted that the Court had ruled that this could not be used to determine the distribution of House seats among the states. Utah officials claimed that a method used by the Census Bureau to impute information about households where they were unable to make direct contact with the residents was equivalent to sampling adjustments and violated the Constitution's requirement of "an actual enumeration" of the population. They further claimed that the practice cost the state the last House seat allocated, which went to North Carolina instead. A federal court ruled against Utah, and the state appealed to the Supreme Court. In June 2002 the court ruled against Utah, confirming the one-seat gain for North Carolina.[39]

Finally, we want to try to assess the net effects of redistricting and reapportionment. This is not a simple matter, because it is difficult to detect district line changes that prevented a party from gaining a seat it would otherwise have won. For example, in Michigan, the district of Republican freshman Mike Rogers (who had won the closest House race in 2000) was changed to add more GOP voters. In 2002 he won 68 percent against a weak opponent. We have no way of knowing whether he would have won reelection without the assistance of redistricting. The best we can do is to calculate the net changes in states that redrew their lines and sum the results across all states. In the eight states that added districts, the net gain for the Republicans was eight seats and for the Democrats four.[40] In the ten states that lost districts, on the other hand, the GOP broke even and the Democrats lost twelve seats. The combination of these two results is a net gain of eight seats for the Republicans. Finally there were four states (Louisiana, Maryland, Minnesota, and Tennessee) in which there was no change in the number of districts, but which did experience a change in party balance. In those state the Democrats made a net gain of three seats. Thus, using these figures, the combined national impact of redistricting and reapportionment is a net loss of five seats for the Democrats. This is about halfway between the anticipated effects by the two parties cited in chapter 9. However the main effect of the process is the creation of even more safe districts for both parties, and the corresponding decrease in partisan competition for the House.[41]

Candidate Resources

In chapter 9 we focused on candidates' resources in each district—specifically incumbency, candidate quality, and campaign spending—to explain outcomes in House elections. We will conclude our analysis of 2002 by returning to these factors, paying particular attention to the increased role of the national parties in marshaling them.[42]

Incumbency We have already discussed incumbency in this chapter, noting particularly that incumbents have an extremely high success rate. But incumbent success is not an immutable fact of nature. Reelection rates for incumbents vary over time, as we have seen, and they vary between the parties. In the Republican landslide of 1994, for example, 15 percent of Democrats were beaten in House races, whereas not a single GOP incumbent lost. This was a very one-sided election in which the voters punished the incumbents of a single party.[43] In the 1992 House races, on the other hand, defeats of incumbents were less one-sided. The elections occurred in the context of a financial scandal in the House and of national redistricting after the 1990 census. Sixteen Democrats and eight Republicans lost their seats to the opposition party in the general election, while an additional fourteen Democrats and five Republicans had lost in the primaries.[44]

Incumbent success was higher in 2002 than in 1992 or 1994 simply because the underlying political conditions were more favorable to incumbents. As we have noted previously, the Republicans avoided much blame for the weakness in the economy. In addition, while the approval rating of Congress did not match the president's, it was considerably higher than it had been in the early 1990s. Perhaps most important for incumbent success was the positive evaluation by voters of their own incumbent, which we discussed in the last chapter. In October 2002, 58 percent of respondents to a national survey by the Pew Research Center said that their own representative should be reelected. And while only 39 percent said that most members of the House should be reelected, the comparable figure in an early 1994 poll had been 28 percent.[45]

This very positive environment for incumbents was reflected in the election, not only in their high reelection rates but also in increased margins of victory.

TABLE 11-5   Success in House and Senate Elections, Controlling for Office Background, Party, and Incumbency, 2002

Candidate's last office	Candidate is opponent of				No incumbent in district			
	Dem. incumbent		Rep. incumbent		Dem. candidate		Rep. candidate	
	(%)	(N)	(%)	(N)	(%)	(N)	(%)	(N)
House								
State leg. or U.S. House	6	(16)	20	(5)	53	(17)	85	(20)
Other elect. office	0	(14)	0	(12)	38	(13)	63	(8)
No elect. office	1	(123)	1	(133)	22	(18)	47	(19)
Senate								
U.S. House	33	(3)	—	(0)	0	(1)	100	(3)
Statewide elect. office	0	(5)	17	(6)	20	(5)	100	(2)
Other elect. office	—	(0)	0	(2)	0	(1)	50	(2)
No elect. office	0	(2)	0	(4)	0	(1)	100	(1)

Note: Percentages show proportion of candidates in each category who won; numbers in parentheses are the totals on which percentages are based. The Kansas, Massachusetts, Mississippi, and Virginia Senate races are not listed, because Pat Roberts, John Kerry, Thad Cochran, and John W. Warner (respectively) did not face a major party opponent. See also notes 1 and 2 of Table 11-2.

In 2002 the average share of the vote for all incumbents in races contested by both parties was 66.3 percent; for Republican incumbents the figure was 66.1 percent, while for Democrats it was 66.4 percent.[46] This is the highest average figure since 1988 (see Table 9-5), and it is even more impressive when we remember that it includes only races contested by a majority-party opponent. Another indicator of the strong position of incumbents is that the number of safe seats in which one major party chose not to field a candidate was very high: seventy-nine incumbents (forty-four Republicans and thirty-five Democrats) were unopposed. Had these seats been contested, and thus the vote results included in our calculations, the average incumbents' share of the vote would surely have been higher.

Candidate Quality Table 11-5 shows data on the success of candidates in 2002, controlling for office background, party, and incumbency.[47] This corresponds to the 2000 evidence listed in Table 9-4. We see that in all categories of House races, there is at least some link between previous office experience and candidate success. With only four incumbent losses there is little variation to explain there. In open seats, however, candidates in both parties with office experience were more likely to win than those with none, and candidates with the highest level of experience had the greatest success. In the Senate races there are few cases, and the general success of Republicans in open seats overshadows office experience.

As we discussed in chapter 9, decisions by politicians on whether to run for office are important strategic choices. In particular, we discussed the argument offered by Gary C. Jacobson and Samuel Kernell that these decisions would be shaped by potential candidates' evaluations of the national electoral context. In 2002 the historical pattern of out-party gains in midterms might have offered Democrats some incentives, but the high level of Bush's popularity might have been an even greater deterrent.

We do not have systematic data for this election or for 2000 on which candidates considered running and which chose not to. To be sure, there are various examples of the two parties trying to recruit candidates in 2002, succeeding in some instances and failing in others. One might be tempted to presume that the data in the previous section showing the number of uncontested seats are evidence of candidate reluctance, but the vast majority of these were safe seats where the opposition would have very little chance.

A rough but better indicator of party success at recruitment is the number of experienced candidates who chose to run against incumbents. The data in Table 11-5 show that there were forty-seven candidates with office experience who opposed incumbents in House races in 2002, seventeen of them running against Republicans and thirty of them running against Democrats. This number falls short of the eighty experienced candidates (fifty-three of them Republicans) who ran in 1992, which as we noted could have been expected to be a good year for the GOP due to redistricting and the House financial scandal.[48] It was also fewer than the sixty-three who ran in 1996, forty-two of them Democrats, when there were a large number of freshmen Republicans who had won in 1994 by narrow margins and the Democrats thought they had a good chance to retake control of the House. On the other hand, the number of experienced candidates in 2002 was more than the thirty-nine who ran in 1990 or the forty-three who sought House seats in 1988, both of which were years in which incumbents were expected to do well, and was very close to the fifty-two who ran in 1994. Like 1994, however, the number of experienced Democratic candidates was lower than the number for Republicans. Indeed, the seventeen experienced Democrats is the lowest number since 1990, when sixteen ran.

The national parties' roles in candidate recruitment have been expanding in recent years. These parties each want to win majority control of the House, and thus have strong incentives to want the strongest possible candidates to run. They now have, moreover, considerable resources at their disposal that can provide incentives for potential candidates. First, as we shall see in the next section, the national party organizations play a significant and increasing role in fund raising. In addition, they can provide expertise, advice, and political contacts that can be very useful in campaigns. In the past, however, they would normally not have become involved if there was possible competition for the party's nomination.[49]

Increasingly, though, national officials have sought to influence the choice in potentially competitive situations. Certainly the most prominent examples of this in the 2002 campaigns involved the Bush White House and Sen. Bill Frist, R.-Tenn., the chair of the National Republican Senatorial Campaign Committee. In the spring of 2001, Frist initiated secret polling on possible GOP Senate candidates in ten states. The results indicated that the party would have a good chance of success if the right candidates ran, and Frist presented this information to Karl Rove.[50] Subsequently Frist, Rove, Vice President Dick Cheney, President Bush, and even the president's father became involved in recruiting candidates. President Bush himself persuaded South Dakota Republican representative John Thune to give up his candidacy for governor and switch to a Senate race against Democratic incumbent Tim Johnson. Cheney persuaded a potential primary opponent of their chosen candidate Norm Coleman, the mayor of St. Paul, Minnesota, to drop out, while Frist urged former cabinet member Elizabeth Dole to enter the race in North Carolina. When she did, the White House made it clear that she was their choice, undermining the candidacies of potential Republican opponents.[51]

Republican House leaders also were heavily involved in candidate recruitment. Former Rep. James Dickey of Arkansas was persuaded to run again for the House by promises from Speaker Hastert to restore his appointment to the Appropriations Committee and his seniority if he won.[52] NRCC chair Davis successfully urged former state GOP chair Bob Beauprez of Colorado to seek a House seat because Davis feared that the state's Republican lieutenant governor would be a weak candidate.[53]

Democrats were also involved in candidate selection and recruitment. Party leaders endorsed the primary opponent of Rep. Gary Condit, D-Cal., who had become embroiled in a scandal involving Chandra Levy, a female intern who had disappeared.[54] The Democrats were not, however, as successful as the Republicans in recruiting top Senate contenders. On the other hand, they did successfully recruit candidates in two extremely unusual situations. In the New Jersey race, incumbent Democrat Robert Torricelli was embroiled in an ethics scandal, and his voter support was dropping. Just five weeks before the election, Torricelli decided to withdraw from the race and give his party the chance to offer a stronger candidate. Democratic leaders successfully sought former senator Frank Lautenberg (who had retired two years earlier). Republicans tried to block the Democratic move in court, but the New Jersey Supreme Court approved the substitution unanimously. Then in Minnesota, ten days before the voting, Democratic senator Paul Wellstone was killed in a plane crash while campaigning for reelection. Former vice president and senator Walter F. Mondale was quickly recruited as a replacement for Wellstone. The Democrats had fifty percent success with these last-minute efforts; Lautenberg won, but Mondale lost. It seems likely that this nationalization of candidate recruitment will continue to intensify.

Campaign Spending In chapter 9 we argued that a principal reason for both the frequency of incumbents being reelected and the growth in their margins of reelection through the 1980s was that challengers found it increasingly difficult to raise the money necessary to compete. Our evidence, and that of other analysts such as Jacobson, showed that when challengers could raise an adequate amount of money, much of the incumbency advantage could be neutralized and competitive elections would usually result. Thus how much candidates raise and spend is an important determinant of outcomes.

Data compiled by the Federal Election Commission for the 2002 election show that aggregate spending was down 10 percent from the record levels in the 2000 elections. These results are misleading, however, because they are due entirely to a drop in spending by challengers against incumbents in both parties. Median spending by incumbents was up for both Democrats (+18 percent) and Republicans (+17 percent), and spending increased for open-seat candidates as well.[55] Moreover, other evidence indicates that spending continues to escalate. For example, by the middle of October reports showed that spending on television advertising for the 2002 campaigns neared $1 billion. This was a massive increase from the $672 million spent in the presidential election year of 2000.[56] Individual candidates certainly spent a great deal of money. Incomplete data show that in House races 189 candidates spent more than $1 million, 41 of whom spent more than $2 million. The largest amount spent by a candidate was $8 million, by Democratic challenger James Humphreys of West Virginia, and he lost! In Senate contests, seventy-four candidates spent more than $1 million, twenty-five of whom exceeded $5 million. The two highest-spending candidates were the two parties' nominees in North Carolina, Elizabeth Dole (Republican) and Erskine Bowles (Democrat), who spent $13.5 million and $13.2 million respectively.[57]

Moreover, as we noted earlier, the Republican Party substantially outraised the Democrats, and the disparity in the amount of money available increased as the elections neared. For example, through the end of September the NRCC had raised $130 million for House races compared to the $73 million accrued by the Democratic Congressional Campaign Committee (DCCC). In terms of money on hand on September 30, the GOP ratio was greater at $20 million–$10 million.[58] Republican Party spending often compensated for shortfalls in candidates' own fund raising. For example, the party boosted Ginny Brown-Waite's ultimately successful challenge to Democratic incumbent Karen L. Thurman in Florida. "Without party backing, Brown-Waite would have been outspent 2 to 1, $1.3 million to $694,519. As it was, she could match Thurman almost dollar for dollar." [59] The 2002 numbers also suggest that the financial disparity between the two parties may grow further. Of the $343.7 million the Democrats raised, 63 percent came in the form of "soft" money, which will be outlawed under the new campaign finance reform bill. For the Republicans, only 45 percent of their $527.4 million was in soft money.[60]

THE 2002 ELECTIONS: THE IMPACT ON CONGRESS

Like the aftermath of the 2000 elections, the changes produced by the elections of 2002 were modest compared to 1994. In the Senate the Republicans are again in control by a small margin (one seat more than after 2000), and they continue to have narrow control in the House. Thus, like 2000, the recent elections restored unified Republican control of government. That restoration and its consequences are the most important legacies of 2002. Also like two years earlier, there were important surprises in store in the wake of the elections.

The Bush Agenda and Return of One-Party Government

We have talked about how politicians often seek to interpret election results in a way that benefits their interests; 2002 was no exception. The day after the voting, White House spokespersons were claiming new impetus for the president's agenda. Press Secretary Ari Fleischer said, "It's a big victory. . . . There's a lot of work that the American people want Democrats and Republicans to team up on that's not getting done. . . . Those days may be over." [61] Yet the view that Bush's hand was strengthened was not limited to Republican partisans. Like the aftermath of Reagan's victory in 1980, even some Democrats concluded that the electorate had endorsed the president's views. For example, Tony Coelho, Al Gore's campaign manager in 2002, said, "The White House took a huge gamble; they rolled the dice, and it worked. . . . They won the 2000 election legitimately last night. He got his mandate, he got his victory and now he can govern for two years." [62]

The election outcomes had a legislative impact even before the new 108th Congress convened at the beginning of January 2003, because the 107th Congress had not finished its business and had to meet in a postelection "lame-duck" session. The president made his influence felt immediately. He got Republican Senate leaders to accept a budget ceiling that would require cutting $10 billion from the current year's spending bills, although they left the actual details of those bills to the new session.[63] Bush also finally secured passage of a bill to create a Department of Homeland Security, and its provisions were largely what he had wanted. There were some last minute problems in securing Senate passage, however, because the House had included some unrelated special-interest provisions in their final version of the bill. These included a provision that would block lawsuits against some drug companies over vaccine additives suspected of causing autism in children. Three GOP moderates secured commitments from party leaders in both chambers that these offending provisions would be revisited in the new Congress before they would give their support to the bill permitting passage.[64]

Among other Bush victories were passage of a terrorism insurance bill (which would have the government provide a backstop in the case of future terrorist attacks that would protect private insurance companies against massive losses), and confirmation of one of his stalled Appeals Court nominees.[65] There was not, however, clear sailing on everything. The House took up the conference report on a bill designed to make it harder for consumers to wipe out debt by declaring bankruptcy (which was strongly supported by the business community). Republican social conservatives blocked passage because of a provision that would have prevented antiabortion protesters from using bankruptcy law to avoid fines.[66] This illustrates the continuing effort of conservative ideologues to pull their party to the right, which could cause difficulties for Bush and legislative leaders in the 108th Congress.

With the reinstatement of unified party government, the Bush administration can expect Congress to be more responsive to the president's agenda than it was in the past two years. Of course the administration generally had its way on security issues, and that will surely continue as preparations for a possible war with Iraq go forward. On the domestic front, tax cuts remain an important issue for the Republican base, and the president will seek to push a number of proposals. One effort will seek to make permanent the $1.35 trillion-dollar tax cut passed in 2001. (The cut is due to expire in 2010.) Most observers, however, believe that effort will be largely symbolic because of the return of budget deficits. Bush has also proposed a set of targeted tax cuts designed to stimulate the lagging economy, including a proposed abolition to the tax on dividends for individuals. While some stimulus package is likely, the dividend proposal will be controversial, even for some Republicans concerned about the deficit. Also a high priority for the administration is filling the large number of judicial vacancies, where Senate Democrats blocked Bush appointments. Here too there will be conflict, especially over the nomination of Charles Pickering of Mississippi, who had previously been rejected by the Senate Judiciary Committee because of alleged racial insensitivity. On the other hand, the president's chief of staff, Andrew Card, indicated that it was unlikely that another proposal to permit people to invest part of their Social Security contributions in the stock market would be acted on before the 2004 election.[67]

It is important to note, however, that despite the boost provided by the 2002 results, the president does not have complete control of the policy agenda. Others have political power and legislative desires. For example, GOP social conservatives have been frustrated by their inability to move their agenda, and they now expect more success. They hope to push new limits on abortions, as well as more support for religious groups and funds for sexual abstinence programs.[68] In addition, business groups have their own priorities, like a new energy bill to permit expanded oil and gas exploration in the Rocky Mountains.[69]

Organizational Changes in the 108th Congress

The 108th Congress began with an unusual amount of leadership change in the House during the week after the November elections. Gephardt stepped down as House minority leader, and Nancy Pelosi, D-Calif., became the first woman to lead a political party in Congress. All of the other top Democratic leaders in the House were also new, including Steny Hoyer, D-Md., who succeeded Pelosi as minority whip. Among House Republicans, Hastert was renewed as Speaker, but six other top leaders were new. This included the succession of Majority Whip DeLay to majority leader and the selection of Roy Blunt, R-Mo., only in his fourth House term, as whip. In the Senate there was little change (at least in November), with the only switch in a top job being the election of Mitch McConnell, R-Ky., as the new Senate majority whip.

Organizationally, the majority Republicans continued small steps to further strengthen their party leadership in the House. The party conference voted to require that subcommittee chairs on the prestigious Appropriations Committee had to be approved by the party Steering Committee (which is strongly influenced by the top party leaders).[70] Previously the subcommittee chairs were selected by the Appropriations Committee chair and had a lot of independence. It is significant to note that the proposal for the new rule came from Speaker Hastert himself and is part of the ongoing effort to exert more leadership control over the top committees.[71] On another front, GOP leaders tried to forestall a contest for the vacant chairmanship of the Agriculture Committee by indicating to members that their preferred choice was Rep. Robert W. Goodlatte of Virginia.[72] The GOP also removed the term limit on the Speaker. House Democrats, on the other hand, did not adopt significant rules changes. The new minority leader did, however, assert her independence by indicating that she would not be bound by oral promises for choice committee assignments made by her predecessor.[73]

The more informal Senate adopted few formal rules changes. The most important one was actually done by the Republicans long before the election. In June they voted to keep six-year term limits on committee chairs, although they also adopted a separate six-year limit as ranking member.[74] This was a crucial move for senators who were completing six years at the top of a committee but had lost the chair in the wake of the Jeffords switch. In addition, the party altered its committee assignment procedure. Previously all assignments were made by members choosing assignments in seniority order until all vacancies were filled. Now there will be two rounds of each Republican senator selecting seats on the dozen most prestigious committees. Then the remaining seats on those committees, plus *all* seats on the other eight Senate committees, will be assigned by the party leader.[75]

More Leadership Change: The Fall of Trent Lott

One of the landmark events of the end of the 107th Congress was the retirement from the Senate of Strom Thurmond of South Carolina. Former governor of his state and a senator since 1954 (first as a Democrat, then as a Republican), Thurmond had also been a candidate for president on the prosegregation States Rights ticket in 1948. At a combined 100th birthday party and retirement celebration for Thurmond on December 5, 2002, Sen. Trent Lott said, "I want to say this about my state: When Strom Thurmond ran for president, we voted for him. We're proud of it. And if the rest of the country had followed our lead, we wouldn't have had all these problems over all these years, either." [76] This was just a few weeks after GOP senators selected Lott as the new majority leader.

Initially only a little notice was taken of the remarks, but within a week a furor began to build. Lott contended that his remarks were off the cuff, intended to make an old colleague feel good. Journalists, however, scrutinized Lott's past votes and remarks on racial matters, discovering that he had made essentially the same statement in 1980 while campaigning for Ronald Reagan in Mississippi.[77] They also highlighted other events from his career, like his opposition as a representative to the extension of the Voting Rights Act in 1981 (one of only twenty-four members to vote against) and his 1983 opposition to making Martin Luther King's birthday a national holiday.[78] Despite his repeated efforts to apologize, negative reactions to Lott's remarks came from all across the political spectrum. Conservative editors and columnists criticized Lott, and even his hometown newspaper, *Mississippi Press,* said he shouldn't be majority leader.[79]

By far the most important critical voice was that of the president. One week after the Thurmond party, he spoke about Lott's statement in a speech in Philadelphia. He said those remarks "do not reflect the spirit of our country," and that "any suggestion that the segregated past was acceptable or positive is offensive and it is wrong." [80] Bush then ordered his staff not to speak about the matter, and also refrained from further comment himself. To many observers, these actions signaled the White House's desire for Lott to be replaced while seeking to avoid any perception of meddling in the internal business of the Senate Republicans. The president did authorize a statement from his press secretary that he didn't think Lott should resign, but he did not offer any public support himself. On Sunday, December 15, Sen. Don Nickles, R-Okla., said his colleagues should consider replacing Lott, and in the next couple of days many anonymous Republicans were saying Lott had no chance to stay on and that the White House wanted him out. On Wednesday Secretary of State Colin Powell said he "deplored" Lott's words, and the president's brother, Governor Jeb Bush of Florida, said, "something's going to have to change." The last straw came on Thursday, when Senator Frist of Tennessee announced that he was a candidate for majority leader. The next day Lott resigned the post, and within a week Frist was elected to replace him.

It was clear that Republicans were worried that the reactions to what Lott said would endanger Bush's legislative agenda and his reelection, as well as the party's efforts to achieve solid majority status nationally. Having secured the support of white conservatives in the South, the Republicans wanted to get the votes of moderates and to reach out to conservatives among African Americans and other minorities. The selection of Bill Frist as leader certainly presents a different face to the country compared to Lott. He lacks Lott's lifelong involvement in politics and the baggage that goes with it. Frist did not even vote until he was thirty-four (in 1989) and didn't seek office until 1994 when he won his Senate seat.[81] He is a heart-transplant surgeon and is connected to his family's business—the nation's largest for-profit hospital chain. His greatest asset in rising to his party's leadership was his performance as head of the Senatorial Campaign Committee in 2002. He is also close personally to the president and has presented a moderate style by supporting additional international spending to fight AIDS.

Whether the swap of Frist for Lott will make a difference in the public's perception of the GOP or in the success of the party's legislative program remains to be seen. The Senate and the House both remain deeply divided along party and ideological lines. Because the party balance remains close, the small number of moderate members of both parties will remain important to determining outcomes. There will still, however, be strong pressures on those moderates to side with their copartisans during policy conflicts. Frist will have to balance the responsibilities of being party leader and the point man in the Senate for the Bush agenda. As we have noted, Republican conservatives have a long wish list. Even though much legislation is vulnerable to being blocked by the Senate's tradition of unlimited debate, there are legislative devices (like budget reconciliation bills) that can be used to pass some controversial proposals and cannot be filibustered. So the public's perceptions of the Democratic and Republican parties, and thus those parties' political fortunes, will depend not only on the styles of their leaders, but also on the policies these leaders promote.

THE 2004 ELECTIONS AND BEYOND

We will conclude this chapter with a look forward to the congressional elections of 2004 and later and a discussion of the factors likely to influence them.

General Considerations for 2004

In chapter 9 we emphasized that—looking ahead to 2002—approval of the president and the performance of the economy would be important in shaping the outcomes of the upcoming elections. The same is true for 2004. As we showed above, Bush and his party benefited from the saliency of national security issues and by the public's high opinion of the president's performance in that area. It was also clear, however, that public endorsement was not as great on domestic policy matters. Thus prospects in the 2004 congressional elections rest partly on the perceived importance of various issues, and partly on the voters' perceptions of the parties' performance on those issues. Postelection polling makes clear that the public does not share the president's views on all of the major proposals on his agenda. For example, respondents disapproved by 55 to 39 percent of the administration's plan to authorize oil drilling in the Arctic National Wildlife Refuge in Alaska. Moreover, by a two-to-one margin they said that protecting the environment was more important than producing energy, while by seven to one they believed Bush had the opposite view.[82] In addition, public views are decidedly mixed on the desirability of unified party control at the national level. Forty-three percent thought it was good for the country, whereas 42 percent said it was bad. In particular, among independents the evaluation was negative by 29–38 percent.[83]

Thus the prospects are not certain for either party. Each has potential advantages and disadvantages. We will address those that are specific to the House and Senate in the next two sections. Here we want to note some general considerations that can influence the outcomes in 2004. First there is the fate and impact of the new campaign finance reform law. In March 2002 the Congress passed, and the president reluctantly signed, a bill that bars political parties from raising and spending soft money. (Independent groups and political action committees [PACs], however, will still be permitted to accept soft money donations.) In December 2002 a panel of three federal judges heard arguments about the constitutionality of that law. Opponents of the law contend that its restrictions are a violation of the free speech guarantees of the First Amendment. Supporters, on the other hand, argue that the law is necessary to remove the appearance of corruption in the national government, and so it is constitutional under previous Supreme Court rulings. It was clear during the arguments that at least two of the judges had serious concerns about the free-speech implications of the law, but the real test for the new restrictions will come if the case goes to the Supreme Court, as seems almost inevitable.[84]

If the campaign finance law survives constitutional challenge, it will change the way campaigns are funded, but the beneficiaries of the changes are not certain. As we noted earlier, soft money accounted for a much larger proportion of Democrats' spending in 2002 than it did for Republicans. Thus the initial expectation may be that the GOP will benefit. This is reinforced by another provision of the new law (which is unlikely to be struck down), which doubles the amount that individual donors can give to a candidate. Republicans have benefited more from these direct donations in the past. On the other hand, new restrictions always induce new behavior, and the parties and their allies are searching for new alternative mechanisms to secure access to the money that will be lost. For example, so-called "527" nonprofit PACs (named because of the section of the law that regulates them) will be able to raise and spend soft money so long as they don't coordinate their activities with a national committee.[85] The parties have also set up state organizations that will be allowed to solicit soft-money contributions.[86]

Beyond the new law, patterns of fund raising are likely to change in response to the Republicans' unified majority status. The majority party can have more influence on policy, and thus it is likely to be more attractive to donors. Data on contributions show that over the past decade money from business groups has shifted from a balance between the parties to a strongly pro-Republican tilt.[87] Thus in the important area of campaign funding, there are new uncertainties but the probability of a greater Republican advantage.

In addition to possible fund-raising disadvantages, the Democrats have to solve the problem of turning out their supporters. As we saw above, they apparently didn't do as well in 2002 as the Republicans did or as well as they had done in the past. Both Democratic partisans and neutral commentators debated what the Democrats' problem was—whether it was just Bush's popularity or a lack of a Democratic message or something else. Whatever the answer, the Democrats must find a way to motivate their base vote to turn out in 2004 and beyond. To some observers the 2002 Louisiana Senate race offers some possible lessons. Democrat Mary L. Landrieu was seeking election to a second term. Louisiana's peculiar election system requires candidates of all parties to run together in a first round in November. If the top candidate does not win a majority, the top two vote-getters face each other in a runoff in December. Landrieu ran a campaign that stressed her support for many of President Bush's policies (a campaign similar to Max Cleland's failed effort in Georgia). She finished first against three Republicans and another Democrat, but she received only 46 percent of the vote.

In the runoff the Republicans went all out to defeat Landrieu, with the GOP Senate Campaign Committee spending more than $250,000 on behalf of her opponent, Susan Terrell, the Louisiana Elections Commissioner. Bush appeared for Terrell multiple times.[88] However, in the runoff Landrieu changed her strategy; she emphasized differences with the president, and claimed she would be an "independent voice" for Louisiana. She also secured endorsements and campaign support from prominent African American politicians who had been lukewarm about her candidacy. Black turnout increased in the second election, and Landrieu won a narrow victory. Thus some Democrats believe that pointing out differences with the GOP is a way to turn out their vote, while others argue that "moving to the left" will turn off moderate voters and lead to defeat. It is likely that this debate will continue.

House Races in 2004

In addition to the general context of the election, we contended in chapter 9 that one important thing to focus on is the potential vulnerability of individual incumbents. Table 11-6 shows the distribution of winning percentages in 2002 across the parties and types of races. We previously noted that the number of close races (outcome 55 percent or less) was down sharply in 1998 and 2000 (fifty-nine) compared to the ninety-five in 1996. In 2002, reflecting the effects of redistricting, the number of close races fell even further, to fifty-three. These

TABLE 11-6   Percentage of the Vote Received by Winning House Candidates, by Party and Type of Race, 2002

Percentage of the vote	Republicans			Democrats		
	Reelected incumbent	Successful challenger	Open seat	Reelected incumbent	Successful challenger	Open seat
55 or less	13	2	10	15	2	11
55.1–60.0	20	0	9	19	0	2
60.1–70.0	72	0	8	63	0	3
70–100	92	0	3	88	0	3
Total	197	2	30	185	2	19

potentially vulnerable members are relatively evenly distributed across the parties: twenty-five Republicans and twenty-eight Democrats. These previously close contests are likely to dominate the efforts of the respective parties in 2004.

Another source of strong contests is open seats. Unless there is an unexpectedly large number of retirements, it is not likely that the number of open seats in the next election will be as large as the forty-nine in 2002, since some of these openings resulted from redistricting. There may be, however, a number of Republican representatives who will be tempted to run for Democratic Senate seats. Also important for 2004, as we emphasized earlier, is candidate quality. Both parties are already at work trying to recruit candidates for that year's House races, and the effort will continue for the next year or more.

A final consideration for 2004 House contests is redistricting. We have already talked about the impact of line redrawing for 2002, but it is possible that the process may not be over. In two states where the Democrats benefited by the resolution of redistricting in 2002, the GOP may seek to redraw the lines. In Georgia the Republicans gained the governorship and control of the state senate and may seek to shore up their new members who won narrowly, or to undermine Jim Marshall, a freshman Democrat who won only 51 percent of the vote.[89] The Democrats, however, still control the state house, and will likely resist efforts to draw new lines. In Texas the Republican position is stronger, because they have unified control of the government after gaining a majority of the state house. The federal court that imposed the 2000 plan made it temporary. Texas, however, faces serious fiscal problems and has a legislature that meets only one hundred days every two years. If the GOP tries to redistrict, Democrats will probably charge them with wasting time on political matters instead of dealing with real problems.[90]

Democrats may also have some chances to redistrict again. In Oklahoma and New Mexico courts imposed plans after partisan deadlocks due to divided government. The Democrats won unified control in both states in 2002 and so may consider reopening the court plans. In addition, there are some court suits in progress. In Pennsylvania the Democrats have sued to overturn the Republican plan on the grounds that it violates the equal protection clause of the

Constitution. In addition there is an ongoing case in which a three-judge federal court had voided the GOP plan because it had too large a population deviation between the largest and smallest districts. The judges allowed the plan to be used for 2002, however, in order to avoid delaying the state's primaries. But they said they would hear further arguments to determine if changes needed to be made for 2004.[91] Finally, the Supreme Court heard a Democratic appeal of the outcome of the redistricting process in Mississippi. The state government had deadlocked, and both federal and state courts drew up redistricting plans. The federal plan became law because the Justice Department failed to give its approval to the state court's plan within the sixty-day approval period required under the Voting Rights Act. The Democrats regard the federal plan to be tilted toward the Republicans and want the Supreme Court to rule that the federal court improperly blocked the state plan. Though it is likely that any result will affect only Mississippi, it is possible that the Supreme Court could address broader issues and cause redistricting to be reopened in other states.[92]

Senate Races in 2004

Unlike the House, where all seats are up for election every two years, Senate contests offer quite a different set of races each time. In contrast to the last two election cycles, the thirty-four seats up in 2004 will have more Democratic seats at risk than Republican ones (nineteen versus fifteen). Moreover, seven of the Democrats (but only three of the Republicans) won with less than 55 percent of the vote. And twenty-two of the Senate races will be in states that Bush carried in 2000, whereas only twelve of the contests are in states Gore won. Because of this context, Republicans argue that the Democrats will have little chance to take back the Senate in the next election. This conclusion is reinforced when one considers individual incumbents. The GOP may have the single most vulnerable incumbent (Peter G. Fitzgerald of Illinois), who won narrowly in 1998 against a weak incumbent, and who is likely to face a strong challenger. There are, however, few other vulnerable GOP senators. On the other hand, a number of Democrats face potentially difficult races. John Edwards of North Carolina is running for president. He can seek his Senate seat at the same time, but would likely have difficulty satisfying the two different constituencies simultaneously. Harry Reid of Nevada won by only 428 votes in 1998, and will have a strong challenger. Senators Byron Dorgan of North Dakota and Russ Feingold of Wisconsin could also be vulnerable if a particular opponent runs, and Barbara Boxer of California will also likely have a strong challenge.[93]

As we have shown, even more than in House races, the outcomes of Senate races will depend on who chooses to seek office and what seats are open. At this point only one incumbent (Democrat Zell Miller of Georgia) has announced his retirement, but there are other possibilities in both parties, especially Democrat Ernest F. "Fritz" Hollings of South Carolina, who will be eighty-two by election day. On the Republican side, at least one seat will have an appointed incumbent. Republican senator Frank H. Murkowski of Alaska sought and won the governorship in 2002. He resigned from the Senate and then appointed his daughter, Lisa, to succeed him. While Alaska is tilted politically toward the Republican Party, Democrats may be encouraged to find a strong challenger because of the circumstances of her appointment. As with the House, candidate recruitment is underway for both parties, and the White House is playing an active role. Rep. Richard M. Burr of North Carolina has already been contacted by Bush officials about a possible candidacy for the Senate seat currently held by John Edwards.[94]

Beyond 2004: The Ongoing Battle for Partisan Dominance

We have emphasized the uncertainty of predicting which party will control the two houses of Congress. The preceding discussion of the House and Senate prospects for 2004, however, indicate that the Republicans are favorites to continue being the majority party in both chambers, and that advantage may persist in 2006. As we have emphasized, the redistricting process in 2002 resulted in a reduction of the number of potentially competitive seats (although demographic changes by 2006 and later may alter the situation somewhat). Thus for Democrats to have a chance to win the House, they will probably need a strong national tide against the Republicans due to problems in the economy, scandals, failed international involvement (like a war with Iraq), or the public perception that the party has become too extreme on domestic policy. In the Senate the Democrats will again be defending more seats than the GOP in 2006, and their incumbents will include a disproportionate number of freshmen who are likely to be more vulnerable to challenges. Moreover, until the Democrats can find a way to gain some ground in the South and the mountain West, they will be at a competitive disadvantage.

More generally, although we pointed out that the Republican gains in congressional races in 2002 were very limited in number, other results from the election offer more grounds for concern for the Democrats. In state legislative races the Republicans gained about 200 seats in the aggregate. This is truly historic, because the president's party has averaged a loss of 350 seats in every midterm since 1938.[95] It is likely that this result was influenced in part by the larger than usual number of open seats created by term limits in twenty-two states, but it does show that the shift toward the GOP reached beyond the limited congressional gains. On the other hand, the Democrats were not without their bright spots for the future. In particular, the Democratic dominance of California continued to grow despite the unpopularity of the party's incumbent governor who was seeking reelection. The Democrats captured all eight statewide races for the first time since 1882 and retained majorities in both houses of the legislature.[96] In addition, Democrats gained control of the governorship in four large battleground states: Illinois, Michigan, Pennsylvania, and Wisconsin. These developments, coupled with the unfolding pattern of demographic changes we have discussed and the indeterminate consequences of campaign finance reform, offer continued uncertainty about the two parties' future prospects. It will be interesting to see what happens.

PART 4

The 2000 and 2002 Elections in Perspective

◆◆◆

A careful analysis of voting patterns provides evidence for speculating about future elections. But winning in politics is partly a matter of luck, as Nicolò Machiavelli reminded us more than four centuries ago. "Fortune," he wrote, "is arbiter of half our actions, but she . . . leaves the other half, or close to it, for us to govern."[1] Anyone who wins a presidential election by carrying Florida, the nation's fourth most populous state, by 537 votes out of nearly 6 million cast was obviously lucky. Indeed, even if George W. Bush was aided by astute Republican officials in retaining his lead over Al Gore, he was also aided by a poorly constructed ballot designed by a Democratic election official in Palm Beach county, which led some voters who intended to vote for Gore to vote for Pat Buchanan or to cast invalid "overvotes."

The Monica Lewinsky scandal also helped Bush. The presidential sex scandal may have prevented Gore from emphasizing his ties to Bill Clinton and thus to the successes of the Clinton-Gore administration. The public approved of Clinton's performance as president, but Gore did not capitalize on these positive feelings to the extent that George Bush did when he ran as Ronald Reagan's vice president in 1988. The Lewinsky scandal demonstrates the role that chance events play in politics. There have often been sex-related scandals in U.S. politics. Thomas Jefferson, Andrew Jackson, and Grover Cleveland were all accused of immorality.[2] But Clinton left DNA evidence to support Monica Lewinsky's allegations, whereas no such tests were possible to substantiate charges against Jefferson and Cleveland.[3]

Even control of the U.S. Senate in the 107th Congress may have hinged upon a chance event. In Missouri the Democratic candidate, incumbent governor Mel Carnahan, was in a closely contested race with the first-term Republican senator, John Ashcroft. Three weeks before the election, Carnahan, his son, and an aide were killed in a plane crash, and under Missouri law it was impossible to put a new Democratic candidate on the ballot. But the Democratic lieutenant governor announced that he would name Carnahan's widow, Jean Carnahan, to the

Senate seat if the now-deceased Mel Carnahan defeated Ashcroft. Carnahan won by a margin of 50.5 percent to 48.4 percent, probably aided by a sympathy vote. In Washington state, the Democratic challenger, Maria Cantwell, won by an even narrower margin, defeating Republican incumbent Slade Gorton by 2,229 votes out of nearly 2.5 million cast. These two narrow Democratic victories helped to set the stage for the Democrats' gaining control of the Senate when James M. Jeffords of Vermont unexpectedly abandoned the Republican Party to become an independent and to caucus with the Democrats.

The 2002 midterm contest again demonstrated the importance of chance events. In Minnesota the incumbent Democratic senator, Paul Wellstone, was in a close race against Republican Norm Coleman, the mayor of St. Paul. Polls were showing Wellstone drawing ahead and holding a small lead. But ten days before the election Wellstone, his wife and daughter, and three aides were killed in a plane crash. The Democrats hoped that Wellstone's death would generate a sympathy vote, and they decided to nominate former vice president Walter F. Mondale to replace him. But a memorial service held a week before the election turned into a political rally, which hurt Mondale's candidacy. Coleman wound up defeating Mondale 50 percent to 47 percent. Meanwhile, Jean Carnahan of Missouri was unable to hold onto the Senate seat to which she had been appointed, losing by a single percentage point to Republican James M. Talent, a former four-term congressman who had narrowly lost a gubernatorial election two years earlier.

Of course, the close balance between the Democrats and Republicans may be part of a long-term pattern that has eroded the Democratic majority without making the Republicans the majority party. But that scarcely means that the closeness of the 2000 presidential election was inevitable. Even a 2 percent across-the-board shift in Bush's advantage would have led to Bush winning five additional states (Iowa, Minnesota, New Mexico, Oregon, and Wisconsin) and forty additional electoral votes. A 2 percent across-the-board shift to Gore would have gained him six additional states (Florida, Missouri, Nevada, New Hampshire, Ohio, and Tennessee) for an additional seventy-six electoral votes. Such hypothetical versions of the 2000 election would still be close by historical standards, but they would not be among the closest elections in U.S. history. Likewise, the overall balance of control in the Senate remained remarkably close after the 2002 midterm.

The U.S. government has constitutional features that make it more predictable than most other democracies. Writing in 1984, Arend Lijphart classified the United States as the only established democracy with a presidential political system.[4] Unlike parliamentary democracies, in which no one can predict when elections will be held, congressional and presidential elections are held at fixed intervals. Indeed, even if the president must be replaced, no election is held to replace him.[5] Thus we know that all 435 House seats will be filled in 2004, and a third of the Senate seats will be. Moreover, we know that Bush's first term will end on January 20, 2005. Although election dates are not constitutionally fixed, we can be confident that presidential and congressional elections will be held on November 2, 2004, and that midterm elections will be held on November 7, 2006.

What will occur in the next presidential election and thereafter? What are the prospects for the Democrats becoming the majority party again? The Democrats will need to choose a standard-bearer for 2004, and we will examine the way that rules changes, in particular the movement to even greater front-loading in the delegate selection process, will affect the Democratic nomination contest. Secondly, we explore Republican prospects, noting that internal divisions within the party may complicate its efforts to hold political power. We next discuss the chances of a new political party, and by examining the demise of the Reform Party point to problems that new political parties face in the American political system. Lastly, we consider the likelihood of continued electoral volatility, the pattern that has prevailed in postwar American politics.

Chapter 12

The 2000 and 2002 Elections
and the Future of American Politics

✦✦✦

In his classic study of political parties, Maurice Duverger argued that in some democracies there is a clearly dominant political party. Despite competitive elections, a single party is consistently at the center of political power. A party, Duverger wrote, "is dominant when it holds the majority over a long period of political development." Although a dominant party may occasionally lose an election, it remains dominant because "it is identified with an epoch" and because "its doctrines, ideas, methods, its style, so to speak, coincide with those of the epoch." One reason a party dominates is because it is believed to be dominant. "Even the enemies of the dominant party, even citizens who refuse to give it their vote," Duverger wrote, "acknowledge its superior status and its influence; they deplore it but admit it." [1]

Duverger's concept of the dominant party provides insights about the decline of the Democratic Party after 1964. Scholars of comparative politics provide at least four clear examples of dominant parties: Mapai in Israel (now the Labor Party), the Christian Democrats (DC) in Italy, the Social Democratic Party in Sweden, and the Liberal Democratic Party (LDP) in Japan. [2] Duverger argued that if a country had free elections, a dominant party was always in peril. "The dominant party wears itself out in office, it loses its vigour, its arteries harden." And, he concluded, "Every domination bears within itself the seeds of its own destruction." [3]

Duverger appears to have been prophetic. [4] Mapai was the dominant party even before Israel attained statehood in 1948. Asher Arian writes:

> In the years immediately following independence, Mapai epitomized the dominant party. The largest vote getter, the key ingredient of any government coalition, the standard-bearer of society's goals, and the articulator of its aspirations, Mapai also had the tremendous political advantages of a

united and integrated leadership; a broad-based, well-functioning, and flexible political organization; no serious political opposition; and control over the major economic and human resources flowing into the country.[5]

Mapai remained dominant until 1977, when an electoral "upheaval" drove the Alignment (the successor to Mapai) from office, and it did not become the leading party in a coalition again until 1992. Although the Alignment was the largest party in the Knesset after the 1996 election, the Israeli electorate also voted directly for prime minister, and Labor again lost power. Labor, running under an electoral list named "One Israel," was the largest party in the 1999 Knesset election, and its leader, Ehud Barak, was elected prime minister. But One Israel won only 26 of the 120 Knesset seats. Moreover, two years later it again lost power when Ariel Sharon, the leader of the opposition Likud, won a landslide election for prime minister.[6] And in the Knesset election held in January 2003, Labor won only nineteen seats.

In Italy the Christian Democrats, with American support, won nearly half the vote in 1948. They lost power more gradually than did Israel's Mapai, but they suffered a major loss in the 1983 election, which brought to power Italy's first socialist prime minister. By 1994, with revelations of widespread corruption, the DC lost two-thirds of its remaining support, and a new coalition of parties, led by media magnate Silvio Berlusconi, came to power.[7] In the 1996 election the remnants of the DC lost even more support, and a coalition of new political parties, known as the Olive Tree coalition, came to power, only to be replaced by a more leftist coalition in 1998. In the 2001 election the remnants of the DC, running as part of the Casa delle Libertà (House of Freedom), won only 3 percent of the vote. The main party in the coalition, Forza Italia (Forward Italy), was Berlusconi's party, and he once again became prime minister.

The Swedish Social Democratic Party came to power in 1932, and although it was forced into opposition in 1976 and 1979, it returned to power in 1982. But in 1991 the nonsocialist parties won an absolute majority of the vote. The Social Democratic Party regained power in 1994, and despite winning only 36 percent of the vote, it narrowly held power in 1998. Although four parties made a concerted effort to defeat the Social Democrats in 2002, the party gained ground, winning 40 percent of the vote. Clearly it remains an important political force, but it is not the markedly dominant party that it was before 1976.

Since its formation in 1955 the Japanese Liberal Democratic Party has consistently been the largest party in the country's House of Representatives, but in 1993, in the face of mounting scandals, the LDP split and the prime minister dissolved the House of Representatives and called new elections. Although it was still the largest party, the LDP was excluded from the coalition formed after the election. The LDP won nearly half the seats in the House of Representatives in 1996, and it formed a government supported by several smaller parties. The LDP suffered major losses in the Upper House elections in 1998, forcing the resignation of prime minister Ryutaro Hashimoto. In the 2000 election for the House of

Representatives, the Liberal Democrats did not win enough seats to reestablish themselves as the dominant party, although they continued to rule in coalition with smaller parties. The LDP was initially expected to do poorly in the summer 2001 Upper House elections, but it selected a dynamic new leader, Junichiro Koizumi, and surpassed expectations, providing its coalition with a majority of the seats. Still, it seems unlikely that the LDP will once again become a dominant party. Its chances, however, will improve if Koizumi succeeds in implementing the reforms necessary to revitalize the long-flagging Japanese economy.

Writing in 1958, Duverger argued that the Democrats were the dominant party in the United States, even though Dwight D. Eisenhower, running as a Republican, had been elected president in both 1952 and 1956. Duverger viewed Eisenhower's election as a personal victory that did not change the balance of partisan power.[8] Scholars writing in 1964 might have seen the Democrats as even more dominant. The Democrats had won the White House under Franklin D. Roosevelt in 1932 and then won six of the next eight elections. In 1964, under Lyndon B. Johnson, the Democrats had won by a landslide over Republican Barry M. Goldwater and gained thirty-eight seats in the House. The only Republican victories between 1932 and 1964 had come under a former general, Eisenhower, who had been courted by both the Democratic and the Republican Parties. The Republicans, much like the Whigs, who ran William Henry Harrison in 1840 and Zachary Taylor in 1848, defeated the Democrats by choosing a war hero as their standard-bearer. Both generals elected by the Whigs died shortly after taking office, whereas Eisenhower served two full terms. Between the Seventy-third Congress, elected in 1932, and the Eighty-ninth Congress, elected in 1964, the Republicans had held a majority for only four years (the Eightieth Congress, elected in 1946, and the Eighty-third Congress, elected in 1952).

In retrospect, it is easy to see that Democratic dominance had within it "the seeds of its own destruction," seeds found in the composition of the coalition that supported it. The Democratic Party drew support from northern blacks and from southern whites. This coalition was sustainable only as long as discrimination against African Americans in the South was not a major political issue. After the civil rights movement began in the mid-1950s, ignoring racial injustice in the South became untenable. By backing the Civil Rights Act of 1964 and the Voting Rights Act of 1965, Johnson chose a position that was morally correct, and he may have had strategic goals in mind as well. However, his decision to aggressively seek African American voters helped end Democratic dominance in presidential elections. In hindsight, the seeds of future Democratic defeats can be seen in Johnson's landslide victory over Goldwater, for in addition to winning his home state of Arizona, Goldwater carried Alabama, Georgia, Louisiana, Mississippi, and South Carolina. By the end of the 1960s, African Americans in these states could vote and, as Johnson expected, they voted heavily Democratic. Even so, in most subsequent presidential elections, these states, as well as the remaining southern states, have voted Republican. Virginia has voted Republican in all nine presidential elections held since 1964.

From 1968 to 1988 the Republicans won five of six presidential elections, and the only victory for the Democrats came in 1976 when Jimmy Carter narrowly defeated Gerald R. Ford, the president who had pardoned Richard M. Nixon after he was forced out of office because of the Watergate scandal. Several political scientists, writing in 1988, argued that the Republicans had become the dominant party in presidential elections.[9]

Yet after the 1988 election, it appeared that the coalition that had supported Ronald Reagan and his successor, George Bush, also had within it the seeds of its own destruction. Reagan had created a coalition of both social conservatives, for whom the battle against abortion and the right to hold prayers in public schools were important issues, and economic conservatives, who believed that reducing the power of the government was the key to economic growth. Although both Reagan and Bush mainly paid lip service to conservative social values, they provided tangible benefits to social conservatives by a series of court appointments, especially to the Supreme Court, that put *Roe v. Wade* in jeopardy. In 1992, when Republican economic policies no longer appeared to provide economic growth, many economic conservatives, and some social conservatives, deserted Bush, although many turned to H. Ross Perot instead of to Bill Clinton. In 1994 two-thirds of the Perot voters who went to the polls voted Republican, contributing to the party's legislative landslide.

Despite Clinton's reelection in 1996, the Democrats did not return to electoral dominance, for they failed to gain control of Congress. Between 1828 and 1996, the Democrats had won the presidency twenty times in forty-three elections, but 1996 was the first time the Democrats won the White House without winning control of the U.S. House of Representatives. Although the Democrats unexpectedly gained five seats in the House in 1998, the Republicans retained control of both chambers. In 2000 the Democrats gained another two seats in the House, but they were still short of control. Moreover, despite their popular vote victory, they lost the presidency as well.

When George W. Bush became president in January 2001, the Republicans held the presidency, the House, and the Senate for the first time since the Eighty-third Congress ended in January 1955. Divided government, the prevalent pattern in postwar American politics, had ended. But Republicans had won the presidency with a minority of the popular vote, capturing 271 electoral votes, only one more than the 270-vote majority required. They held only a 221-to-212 edge in the House and controlled the Senate only because Vice President Dick Cheney could cast the tie-breaking vote in a chamber divided between fifty Republicans and fifty Democrats. And after James M. Jeffords of Vermont left the Republican Party to become an independent in May 2001, the Democrats regained the Senate and divided government returned.

As we saw, the Republicans gained six House seats in the 2002 midterm elections, and they gained two seats in the Senate, reclaiming majority control. These results, like those in 1998, run contrary to historical patterns. There have been forty-one midterm elections between 1842 and 2002, and the party controlling the White House has lost strength in the House in all but three of these contests.[10]

After the 2000 elections, it was evident that there was no majority party in American politics, and despite exuberance among many Republicans after the 2002 midterms, we would still argue that there is no clear majority party. It would be unwise to make specific predictions about American party politics, but we can rely on what we have already learned to evaluate alternative possibilities. First, we discuss the likelihood of a resurgent Democratic Party. Second, we examine Republican prospects for the future. Third, we explore prospects for a new political party, paying particular attention to the reasons why the Reform Party failed to effectively challenge the two major parties. Finally, we discuss the likelihood of continued electoral volatility.

PROSPECTS FOR THE DEMOCRATS

When Clinton assumed the presidency in January 1993, the Democratic Party had a majority in the House and the Senate, and twelve years of divided government came to an end. Although Clinton had won only 43 percent of the popular vote, he had, at least in principle, the opportunity to create a policy agenda that would transform the Democrats into the majority party for decades to come. Despite some early policy successes, the second year of his presidency was marked by major policy failures. The ambitious health care reforms that Clinton proposed received little legislative support, and he abandoned his own reforms to back a proposal by Senate majority leader George J. Mitchell. Ultimately, no health care bill was passed in either the House or the Senate. Clinton also failed to achieve significant welfare reform, another important policy goal.

Whatever prospects the Democrats had to seize the policy agenda ended with the Republican midterm victory of 1994. After the Democrats' defeat, Clinton moved to the political center. In 1996 he signed legislation substantially changing the welfare system, transferring authority to the states, thus ending "welfare as we know it." Even though he moved to the political center, he did not entirely abandon liberal Democratic goals. Indeed, the electorate saw substantial differences between Clinton and the Republican presidential nominee, Bob Dole, on policy issues. However, the main reasons for Clinton's decisive reelection were the good condition of the economy and the favorable retrospective evaluations of Clinton and the Democratic Party.

In 2000 Al Gore, responding to the need to minimize defections to the Green Party candidate, Ralph Nader, made some populist appeals. Even so, although the electorate saw clear policy differences between Al Gore and George W. Bush, voters had seen sharper differences between Clinton and Dole four years earlier. On balance, as we saw in chapter 6, the issue preferences of the electorate did not clearly favor either candidate. However, as we noted in chapter 7, the electorate had positive retrospective evaluations toward the incumbent party that should have worked more to Gore's advantage.

Because the Republicans control the White House, the Democratic Party does not have the ability to control the policy agenda. Even after the dramatic Republican capture of Congress in 1994, Republican representatives eventually lost much of the initiative to Clinton. With Bush's election in 2000, and with the Republicans holding on to the House and regaining control of the Senate in 2002, the Democrats will find it difficult to regain the initiative for the next two years.

Because the balance between the parties is so close, it would take only a small shift to bring the Democrats back into power. As we saw in chapter 3, the electoral vote balance between the political parties is close to even. So although Bush won every southern state, only a minute shift would have given Gore Florida's twenty-five electoral votes, and a small shift would have enabled him to hold his home state of Tennessee. Moreover, the Democrats can win the presidency even without southern support. In both 1992 and 1996 Clinton won some southern electoral votes, but in both elections he could have won with no southern support. As long as the Democrats continue to do well in the Northeast, the Pacific Coast, and the Midwest, they can win.

Writing after the 1996 election, James W. Ceaser and Andrew W. Busch maintained, "the striking similarity of the 1992 and 1996 presidential elections provides a clear warning that the Democrats may be in the process of constructing a new and durable presidential majority." But they also wrote that "the balance today between the parties remains quite close," with both parties having a "reasonable prospect" of building a winning coalition.[11] And they refer to the 2000 elections as "The Politics of the Perfect Tie." [12]

The Democrats still retain their lead in party loyalties among the electorate (see chapter 8), although that lead may have narrowed slightly since 2000. According to the 2000 General Social Survey, 57 percent of all party identifiers were Democrats; in a survey of about twenty-eight hundred Americans conducted in early 2002, 55 percent were.[13] However, as we saw in chapter 4, Democratic Party identifiers are somewhat less likely to vote than are Republican identifiers. Democrats can argue about whether they should focus on increasing turnout or on winning back the widespread defections among the working class, union members, and Roman Catholics that have undermined the New Deal coalition, but these strategies are not mutually exclusive. The Democrats need to understand the reasons why they do so poorly among white men, a social group that makes up two-fifths of the electorate, and among whom Gore won less than two-fifths of the vote. Without increased support from white men, the Democrats will find it difficult once again to become the majority party.

Despite their losses in 2002, one can still write an optimistic scenario for the Democrats. John B. Judis and Ruy Teixeira foresee favorable prospects for the Democrats in their widely discussed book *The Emerging Democratic Majority.*[14] They argue that demographic groups that tend to support the Democrats are becoming a growing percentage of the active electorate, especially African Americans, Hispanics, and Asian Americans. Women also tend to support the Democratic Party. Moreover, professionals, who used to support the Republican Party, are increasingly supporting the Democrats. Democratic strength, they argue, will be based in urban areas that specialize in the production of ideas, which Judis and Teixeira call "ideopolises." But they are not claiming that a Democratic majority is a certainty. "This survey is not intended to show that a Democratic majority is inevitable," they write. "What it shows is that over the next decade, the Democrats will enter elections at an advantage over the Republicans in securing a majority. Whether Democrats actually succeed will depend, in any given race, on the quality of the candidates they nominate and on the ability of candidates and their strategists to weld what is merely a potential majority into a real one." [15]

Before either party can win the 2004 presidential election, it will need to nominate presidential and vice presidential candidates. Although it seems likely that Bush will begin his 2004 reelection campaign with a substantial lead, there is also a good chance that his prospects may change dramatically. As we have seen, peace and prosperity are the two most important forces in presidential elections. The aftermath of the September 11, 2001, attacks and the war on terrorism have been important sources of Bush's high approval ratings, and in January 2003, 58 percent approved of the job he was doing as president. The war continues, however, and can therefore be the source of even higher approval, or it could lead, if events turn negative, to a substantial decline. The economy has emerged from a brief recession but remains in the doldrums. It, too, is therefore poised to be a source of heightened or depressed approval for the incumbent. This uncertainty about the future of both peace and prosperity means that there is unusual uncertainty about Bush's reelection prospects. Moreover, Democrats are well aware that Bush's father had close to 90 percent approval levels after the Persian Gulf War ended in February 1991, only to be easily defeated less than two years later.

Democrats who seek to challenge Bush in 2004 will need to take into account the rules under which the nomination process will be conducted. As in every year since the nomination system of 1972 began, specific aspects of the rules have changed. Most importantly, the front-loading that we saw to be so vital to Bush's nomination success in 2000 (see chapter 1) remains. The Democratic Party has a "window" during which delegates may be chosen, and that window will begin a month earlier than it did in 2000. For 2004, states other than Iowa and New Hampshire must choose their delegates between February 3 and June 8, whereas in 2000 that window began March 7 and ended June 6. As usual, Iowa's caucuses and the New Hampshire primary will be held before other events, and they will be held five days earlier than they were in 2000. The Iowa caucuses are scheduled to be held January 19, whereas in 2000 they were held January 24; the New Hampshire primary is scheduled for January 27, whereas in 2000 it occurred February 1. Most other states have not yet chosen the dates for their primaries or caucuses, although by early 2003 South Carolina and Missouri had scheduled their primaries for February 3, the first date that the selection window will be open.[16] Most states will probably choose early dates, perhaps making February 3, February 10, or February 17 the "Super Tuesday" of 2004— that is, the date on which the largest number of delegates are selected. The result is that the forces that made the pre-campaign season so important in 2000 will be at least as strong in 2004. The campaign before the campaign (sometimes called the "invisible primary") will likely be critical to the Democratic candidates' hopes. Although we believe that, because of the president's commanding approval ratings and the politics that underlie them, the nature of the 2004 campaign is much more likely to be shaped by him than by changes in the rules, the extreme level of front-loading in 2004 could lead to several scenarios.

One possibility is that a leading contender will drive most of the opposition from the race. As we saw in chapter 1, Al Gore's front-runner status convinced most potential Democratic contenders to forego a race for the Democratic nomination. In many respects the 2000 Republican contest provides a more relevant example because it did not begin with such a clear front-runner. Yet, as we saw, Bush's ability to raise funds and support in 1999 all but drove Elizabeth Dole from the race. Indeed, as we note in chapter 1, half the Republicans who considered running for the 2000 presidential nomination had dropped out before the election year began. But with Gore announcing on December 15, 2002, that he would not run for president, there is no clear Democratic front-runner. Of course, not all of the Democrats being talked about as presidential possibilities will decide to enter the contest, but we expect a large number to be competing when 2004 begins.

Without a clear front-runner in the field, it is possible that no one will be able to dominate in the pre-campaign period and that several Democrats might divide the votes in the primaries and caucuses. Since the Democrats do not allow winner-take-all rules in allocating delegates but instead use proportional representation, delegate strength would also be allocated among several candidates. In earlier years candidates who achieved early success would gain momentum, and the field would be winnowed down to a small number of contenders, with most of the delegates left to be selected. The candidate that gained early momentum would have time to capture a majority of the delegates. But with the overwhelming majority of delegates chosen early, a momentum-based strategy may not lead to outright victory but to a deadlock in which the convention might actually choose the presidential nominee. This scenario is possible because the momentum-based strategy—one that translates an upset primary victory into new opportunities to raise money and then, in turn, uses those resources to increase chances of winning later primaries—takes time. Candidates have incentives to work around such problems. Sen. John McCain and, to a lesser extent, former senator Bill Bradley deployed the Internet to solicit and receive funds, using secure credit card technology. After McCain's victory in the New Hampshire primary, Internet technology enabled him to raise newly generated momentum-based funds instantaneously. We can expect even greater emphasis on such strategies in 2004.

But even if the Internet allows a candidate to raise money more quickly, it still takes time to use those resources to change voters' preferences and voting choices. As a result, unless more than two candidates share most of the vote, it seems likely that a winner will emerge before the convention. The last time a

Democratic national convention took more than a single ballot to choose its presidential candidate was 1952, when the convention took three ballots to nominate Adlai E. Stevenson.[17] But that was in an era when political leaders had much greater influence over the delegates, so a contested convention in 2004 would be unprecedented.

Who will run for the Democratic nomination? The possible field is large, and new names are "floated" frequently. The potential candidate most affected by Gore's announcement was Sen. Joseph I. Lieberman of Connecticut, Gore's running mate in 2000. Lieberman said that he definitely would not run if Gore ran but that he might run if Gore did not. In mid-January 2003 he announced his candidacy. Several candidates announced before Lieberman. Gov. Howard Dean of Vermont had formally declared his candidacy by the end of 2002, and Sen. John Kerry of Massachusetts also announced that he was running. In early January freshman senator John Edwards of North Carolina announced his candidacy, followed by the former minority leader of the House, Richard A. Gephardt of Missouri. The week after Lieberman's announcement, civil rights activist Al Sharpton of New York declared his intention to enter the fray. The Gore decision also highlighted other prominent Democrats, such as Sen. Bob Graham of Florida, the highest-ranking elected Democrat from the state that ultimately decided the 2000 election outcome.

This cast of characters reflects many of the regularities typical of serious presidential contenders that we pointed to in chapter 1. The large number of actual or exploratory candidacies is typical for the party out of power. Thus the Democratic race for 2004 shapes up like all of the other contested Democratic nomination contests held since 1972. Although the high degree of front-loading may lead to unusual outcomes, it still seems likely that a winner will emerge before the convention.

PROSPECTS FOR THE REPUBLICANS

Given their unexpected triumph in the 1994 midterm elections, the Republicans' failure to win the presidency was a major disappointment. But losing seats in the 1998 midterm elections was seen as a major disaster. A few days after these unexpected losses, Newt Gingrich announced that he would not serve as Speaker of the House and that he would resign his seat in the House. The Republican Party has deep divisions between economic and social conservatives, and recriminations that followed the election highlighted these divisions. Even after their losses in the 1998 midterm, the Republicans may have suffered other self-inflicted wounds. Many observers viewed those elections as a clear sign that the public did not want Clinton to be impeached, but in December 1998 the lame-duck 105th Congress voted, largely along party lines, to pass two articles of impeachment. That Senate trial itself led to dissatisfaction among some social conservatives, since even some Republicans voted to acquit Clinton.

Despite these conflicts, most Republican leaders rallied behind Bush's nomination campaign. At times Bush specifically sought conservative support. During the South Carolina primary campaign, for example, he visited Bob Jones University, which at the time prohibited interracial dating. After his nomination, however, Bush downplayed his appeals to social conservatives. Rather, he portrayed himself as a moderate, "compassionate conservative." For example, as Wilson Carey McWilliams wrote, "Bush's position on abortion was calibrated to be relaxed just enough to attract Independents—increasingly reticent about abortion, but still committed to some 'choice'—without offending conservatives." [18] Although Pat Buchanan offered social conservatives a chance to make a statement, the Buchanan campaign was flagging, and a vote for Buchanan would be a "wasted" vote in what would clearly be a close election. McWilliams argued, "the religious right's willingness to accept Bush as a candidate despite his leaning toward the moral center was partly a pragmatic adjustment. Having learned the hard lesson of its marginality during the Clinton years, the right was prepared to trust Bush's personal journey of faith and the fact that he could 'talk the talk.' " [19]

The difficulty of satisfying social conservatives was exemplified in the controversy over whether to allow federal funding for embryonic-stem-cell research. In his first nationally televised address in August 2001, Bush announced that he would approve federal funding but only for studies of the sixty stem-cell lines that he said already existed. Gov. William J. Janklow, R-S.D., compared Bush's decision with Solomon's decision to divide the baby (1 Kings 3:25). Although some "pro-life" advocates saw Bush's announcement as too much of a compromise, most appeared satisfied. The Reverend Jerry Falwell praised Bush, saying, "I've never been prouder of George W. Bush." On the other hand, some groups that supported embryonic-stem-cell research argued that the decision was too restrictive, since there may not be sixty viable stem-cell lines and that, even if there were, they may not be genetically diverse enough to allow adequate research.[20]

Given the complexity of the scientific controversy over embryonic-stem-cell research, it probably will not emerge as an issue with electoral consequences. But Bush may need to appoint justices to the Supreme Court, and they will need to be confirmed by a closely divided Senate.

Bush's positions on the environment may also be unpopular with the electorate. Although it seemed unlikely that the Senate would ratify the Kyoto accords on the environment, Bush's announcement that the United States would not support the treaty isolated the country diplomatically. His decision to back away from his campaign promise to reduce carbon dioxide emissions may also prove unpopular. Moreover, Bush's early success in reducing taxes may place a strain on introducing new programs, including reforms of the military that Bush argued were necessary during the campaign.

All the same, Bush may be in a strong position to win reelection in 2004 if the economy improves. However, because the Republicans control both the House and the Senate, it will be difficult to blame policy failures on the Democrats. In addition, the Democrats seem well positioned to challenge the Republicans on many issues. As we saw, the electorate appears to favor pro-choice policies on abortion and protection of the environment, and it opposes reducing restrictions on handguns. On the other hand, if the Republicans can maintain their dominance among white males, and especially among southern whites, they may be in a position to become a majority party.

But in our view they are not the majority party, in part because the Democrats still hold a lead in the partisan loyalties among the electorate. According to Donald Green and Eric Schickler, the Republicans made gains in 2002 because the public approved of their positions on a strong military and national security. But, they point out, the Republican triumphs in 2002 "are not the result of some noteworthy shift in partisan allegiances." [21] As they note, the Democrats retain about a five-percentage-point lead in party identification, a lead that is the same as it was ten years ago.

In 2004, however, the Republicans will likely enjoy the luxury of choosing their candidate without a contested, and potentially divisive, nomination contest. Barring the truly unforeseen, Bush will be in a strong position and will face no meaningful challenge for his party's nomination. Indeed, after the controversy surrounding his 2000 victory, it would have been difficult to imagine his strength two years later. Whether he maintains his current strength through January 2004 (when the race for the Republican nomination formally begins) and into September of that year (when the general election campaign is in full force) depends on the status of peace and prosperity. The president has some control over future peace and prosperity, but both can change due to events entirely beyond his control.

Although we cannot foresee what will happen, we can anticipate the kinds of circumstances that might lead to significant changes in Bush's evaluations by the public. The war on terrorism could lead to a significant decline in support for the president in at least two imaginable cases. First, support would decrease if there were a major terrorist attack that affected American lives and fortunes, especially if it were seen as an attack that the government could and should have been able to prevent. However, if the attack were viewed as entirely unavoidable, it might lead to a new "rally 'round the flag" surge in presidential support. The second possible cause of declining support is a major expansion of the war, including launching a war against Iraq or even North Korea. Such conflicts could lead to greatly enhanced or depressed approval. Substantial American casualties, especially if they were accompanied by a perception that no clear victory had been attained, could lead to an erosion in presidential support, just as the protracted conflict in Vietnam led to a decline in support for Lyndon B. Johnson's presidency. Quick success, on the other hand, could lead to just the reverse.

In many respects, prosperity is similar to peace. The direction of the economy will likely translate into the direction of presidential approval. Peace and prosperity, however, may well interact. One interpretation of the prosperity factor over the last year is that a relatively mild recession was simply overshadowed by the highly charged issue of terrorism. Continued economic weakness, however, could be seen as related to—even due to the expense of—an ongoing and seemingly intractable struggle in the war on terrorism or to a protracted struggle in Iraq. If so, the president's standing could be affected dramatically.

The importance of peace and prosperity reflects our view that, at least for now, the president's standing is the most important factor shaping the 2004 campaign. High levels of approval make it highly unlikely that Bush will face any meaningful opposition for renomination, and these strong approval ratings will probably affect the strategies of Democratic contestants. In other words, the 2004 presidential election should be Bush's election to win or to lose, but Bush does not completely control his own standing. In many ways, too, he does not control events, although barring unmitigated triumph or tragedy, Bush and his administration have some impact on his standing among the public through their *reaction* to events that may be beyond his control.

A good illustration of this point is his reaction to the circumstances surrounding Sen. Trent Lott of Mississippi, who as the Republican leader in the Senate was poised to be the majority leader in the 108th Congress. As we saw in chapter 11, during the one hundredth birthday party for retiring senator Strom Thurmond, R-S.C., Lott said he was proud that Mississippi had voted for Thurmond during his 1948 presidential bid and that the country would have been better off had Thurmond been elected. Because Thurmond's States' Rights Democrats (Dixiecrats) candidacy was based on an appeal to preserve racial segregation, Lott's comments led to a firestorm of controversy that threatened to undermine Bush's efforts to recruit minorities to the Republican Party. Bush's response, rebuking Lott and distancing himself from the senator, appears to have spared the president, if not his party, from such a reaction. And with Sen. Bill Frist, R-Tenn., replacing Lott as the new majority leader in the Senate, Bush has a close friend and ally at the Senate's helm. At the same time, the controversy over Lott's remarks may complicate Republican efforts to cut into the Democratic dominance among minority voters.

PROSPECTS FOR A NEW POLITICAL PARTY

For the past 150 years the Democrats and the Republicans have held a duopoly in American politics. Ever since the election of Franklin Pierce in 1852, either a Democrat or a Republican has won the presidency. And of the thirty-five presidential elections from 1864 (when Abraham Lincoln ran for reelection) through 2000, there have been only six contests in which a third-party or independent candidate won the electoral vote of even a single state. Moreover, the Republicans and the Democrats have dominated Congress. The last Congress in which more than one out of ten members was from a third party was the Fifty-fifth (1897–1899). From the Seventy-sixth Congress (1939-1941) to the present, there has never been a single House in which more than two members did not affiliate with one of the major parties. In his comparative study of twenty-seven democracies, Arend Lijphart classifies the United States as having the lowest number of "effective electoral parties" and the second lowest number of "effective parliamentary parties." [22]

Clearly, third parties in the United States face many obstacles, the most formidable of which are the rules by which candidates win office. With the exceptions of Maine and Nebraska, all states and the District of Columbia have winner-take-all rules for allocating their presidential electors. To win the electoral votes of these states, a presidential candidate (or, to be more precise, a slate of electors pledged to a presidential candidate) must win a plurality of the votes within the states. Perot did not win a single electoral vote in 1992 or 1996. The only third parties to win electoral votes were the States' Rights Democrats in 1948 and the American Independent Party in 1968, and all of their votes came from the states of the old Confederacy. Despite some regional variation in Perot's vote in 1992, he had no regional base, and there was very little regional variation in Perot's support in 1996.

Third parties have a difficult time getting on the ballot, although recent court decisions have made access to the ballot easier than it was before George C. Wallace's 1968 candidacy. Independent or third-party candidates also have financial problems, and federal election laws place a limit on their ability to raise money. Democratic and Republican candidates are guaranteed federal funding, whereas third-party candidates receive funding only if they win 5 percent of the vote and only after the election. In 1992 Perot spent $65 million of his own money. In 1996 he accepted $29 million in federal funding (based on what he was entitled to as a result of his 1992 popular vote total). Based on Perot's 1996 vote, the Reform Party was entitled to $12.6 million in federal funding in 2000, one of the reasons the party's nomination was attractive.

In 1992 Perot ran as an independent, but in 1995 he announced that he would help fund efforts to create a new political party, the Reform Party. One of his basic claims was that Americans wanted a new political party. This new party, Perot predicted, would be "the largest party in the country" and would replace either the Republican or the Democratic Party.[23] But Perot's share of the popular vote fell from 18.9 percent to 8.4 percent. By the summer of 2000 the Reform Party was badly split. Perot was no longer providing financial support, and Jesse Ventura, the Reform Party governor of Minnesota, elected in 1998, had resigned, declaring that the national party was "dysfunctional." Two conventions were held, one nominating Pat Buchanan, the other selecting John Hagelin, who had run as the Natural Law Party candidate in 1992 and 1996. The Federal Election Commission was forced to decide who the party nominee was because it had the authority to provide federal funding. It ruled in favor of Buchanan. But Buchanan won only 0.43 percent of the vote. The Green Party was much more successful, drawing 2.7 percent of the vote, but it fell short of its goal of winning five percentage points and will not qualify for federal funding in 2004.

One may ask whether either the Reform Party or the Green Party is, or ever was, a political party. In effect, the Reform Party was never much more than a vehicle for Ross Perot's presidential candidacy, and it fell into disarray by 2000. The Green Party was willing to nominate Nader, even though Nader is not a member of the party, because it needed someone to give it visibility and credibility. But it, too, seems ill positioned to pose a serious challenge to the major parties. Environmentalist parties usually win only a small percentage of the vote and are heavily disadvantaged by the plurality-vote-win rules used in American elections.[24]

As Joseph A. Schlesinger reminds us, a political party in a democracy is an organized attempt to gain political office by winning elections.[25] When the Republican Party emerged in 1854, it ran candidates for office at every level in the nonslave states. Politically ambitious Whigs, as well as members of the Free Soil and Know Nothing Parties, could become Republicans and seek office for state legislatures, Congress, and governorships. In the Thirty-fourth Congress, the first elected after the Republican Party was founded, 108 of the 234 House members were Republicans. The Republican Party provided the collective good of limiting slavery, but it also provided selective incentives for individuals seeking political office. Politically ambitious citizens today may want selective incentives, such as office for themselves, as well as collective goods, such as the election of Perot or the protection of the environment.[26]

Third parties face another fundamental problem: they find it difficult to recruit attractive presidential candidates. The very openness of the major-party nomination process encourages strong candidates to seek either the Republican or the Democratic presidential nomination. There are no restraints on entering the primaries, and a major-party nomination will probably continue to attract far more votes than it repels. Strong candidates who actually have a chance of winning the presidency are likely to seek one of the major-party nominations.[27]

PROSPECTS FOR CONTINUED ELECTORAL VOLATILITY

For the moment *dealignment* seems to be an accurate term to describe the American party system. The old party system is in disarray, but nothing has replaced it. Admittedly, the Democrats could be positioned to regain their majority status if the war on terrorism is viewed as a failure and especially if the economy falters. But if the Republicans can hold the presidency in 2004 and retain control of the House and the Senate, they may be situated to establish electoral dominance.

There are many reasons, however, for predicting continued electoral volatility. The most obvious is the appeal of Perot. More than nineteen million Americans voted for Perot in 1992, even though he had a negligible chance of winning and even though Clinton's margin in the polls was not large enough for voters to be confident that he would be elected. Even in 1996, Perot won eight million votes, and a total of 10 percent of the vote was cast for Perot and other minor-party candidates. The 1992 and 1996 elections mark the first instances since the Civil

War that the two major parties failed to win 90 percent of the vote in two consecutive elections.

Part of Perot's success in both 1992 and 1996 derived from the weak party loyalties of the American electorate. Although the strength of party identification is somewhat greater than its postwar low in 1978, it is considerably weaker than it was between 1952 and 1964, the years Philip E. Converse labeled the "steady-state" period in American party loyalties.[28] During that period, 22 percent of the electorate were classified as independents. In the 2000 National Election Study (NES) survey, 40 percent were. Moreover, in the 2000 General Social Survey, 42 percent were classified as independents, although that number had dropped to 37 percent in the 2002 General Social Survey.[29] Although some self-professed independents may be "hidden partisans," the claim of independence does in fact reveal a lack of strong commitment to a party.[30] Furthermore, even though the percentage of strong partisans is higher than its postwar low in 1978, it remains below what it was during the steady-state period. Between 1952 and 1964, 36 percent of the electorate claimed to be strong party identifiers. In the 2000 NES survey, 31 percent were, compared with only 25 percent in the 2000 General Social Survey. Party loyalties were slightly higher in the General Social Survey conducted in early 2002, but only 27 percent were strong party identifiers. Weak partisans and self-professed independents are more volatile in their voting choices than are voters with strong party ties.

As we saw in chapters 5 and 10, with the exception of race, social forces have a relatively weak influence on voting behavior, which may also contribute to electoral volatility. Today few voters feel bound to a political party by social class, religion, or ethnicity. This absence of affiliation increases the proportion of the electorate that is likely to switch its vote from one election to the next.

Finally, the low turnout in 2000 may be seen as another indicator of dealignment, and even though turnout increased slightly in 2002 compared with electoral participation in 1998, it was still low by historical standards. As we saw in chapter 4, past realignments have been characterized by increases in electoral participation and the mobilization of new groups into the electorate. Of course, there is no necessary reason why a new realignment, should one occur, must bear all of the hallmarks of previous realignments. It would be difficult to consider any alignment as stable when nearly half the politically eligible population does not vote.

In the early 2000s the American party system seems to be in a state of deadlock, with either party capable of winning future elections. It seems unlikely, however, that either the Democrats or the Republicans can establish electoral dominance. Even so, they seem likely to retain their duopoly. The U.S. electoral system, like that in Britain, provides considerable protection for the two major parties. Ultimately, however, the people can displace a major party, although this has not happened in the United States since the 1850s or in Britain since the 1920s. But the ability of the Democrats and the Republicans to retain their duopoly ultimately depends on the ability of their leaders to solve the nation's problems.

Notes

◆◆◆

INTRODUCTION TO PART 1

1. See, for example, Benjamin Ginsberg and Martin Shefter, *Politics by Other Means: The Declining Importance of Elections in America* (New York: Basic Books, 1990).

2. E. J. Dionne Jr., "The Clinton Enigma: Seeking Consensus, Breeding Discord," in *The Election of 2000: Reports and Interpretations,* ed. Gerald M. Pomper et al. (New York: Chatham House, 2001), 4–5.

3. For an excellent summary of the differences between Gore and Bush, see William Crotty, "The Election of 2000: Close, Chaotic, and Unforgettable," in *America's Choice 2000,* ed. William Crotty (Boulder, Colo.: Westview, 2001), 16–22.

4. James W. Ceaser and Andrew E. Busch, *The Perfect Tie: The True Story of the 2000 Presidential Election* (Lanham, Md.: Rowman and Littlefield, 2001), 1.

5. Ibid., 20.

6. John H. Aldrich and Thomas Weko, "The Presidency and the Election Process: Campaign Strategy, Voting, and Governance," in *The Presidency and the Political System,* 2d ed., ed. Michael Nelson (Washington, D.C.: CQ Press, 1988), 251–267.

7. Bush's approval rating reached a record 90 percent in a CNN/*USA Today* Gallup poll conducted September 21–22, 2001. However, high approval ratings after a crisis tend to decline. See The Gallup Organization, "Bush's High Approval Ratings among Most Sustained for Presidents," *Poll Analysis,* November 2, 2001 (www.gallup.com/poll/releases/pr011102.asp).

8. Phil Gailey, "Republicans Start to Worry about Signs of Slippage," *New York Times,* August 25, 1985, E5.

9. For an excellent discussion, see Richard G. Niemi and Herbert F. Weisberg, "Is the Party System Changing?" in *Controversies in Voting Behavior,* 4th ed., ed. Richard G. Niemi and Herbert F. Weisberg (Washington, D.C.: CQ Press, 2001), 371–385.

10. V. O. Key Jr., "A Theory of Critical Elections," *Journal of Politics* 17 (February 1955): 4.

11. V. O. Key Jr., "Secular Realignment and the Party System," *Journal of Politics* 21 (May 1959): 198.

12. These two states were, and still are, the most heavily Catholic states. Both of these states voted Republican in seventeen of the eighteen presidential elections from 1856 through 1924, voting Democratic only when the Republican Party was split in 1912.

13. V. O. Key Jr., *Parties, Politics, and Pressure Groups*, 5th ed. (New York: Thomas Y. Crowell, 1964), 186.

14. James L. Sundquist, *Dynamics of the Party System: Alignment and Realignment of Political Parties in the United States*, rev. ed. (Washington, D.C.: Brookings Institution, 1983), 4.

15. Lawrence G. McMichael and Richard J. Trilling, "The Structure and Meaning of Critical Realignment: The Case of Pennsylvania," in *Realignment in American Politics: Toward a Theory*, eds. Bruce A. Campbell and Richard J. Trilling (Austin: University of Texas Press, 1980), 25.

16. In addition to the eleven states that formed the Confederacy (Alabama, Arkansas, Florida, Georgia, Louisiana, Mississippi, North Carolina, South Carolina, Tennessee, Texas, and Virginia), Delaware, Kentucky, Maryland, and Missouri were slave states. The fifteen free states in 1848 were Connecticut, Illinois, Indiana, Iowa, Maine, Massachusetts, Michigan, New Hampshire, New Jersey, New York, Ohio, Pennsylvania, Rhode Island, Vermont, and Wisconsin. By 1860 three additional free states (California, Minnesota, and Oregon) had been admitted into the Union.

17. Michael Nelson, "Constitutional Aspects of the Elections," in *The Elections of 1988*, ed. Michael Nelson (Washington, D.C.: CQ Press, 1989), 198.

18. Byron E. Shafer, "The Election of 1988 and the Structure of American Politics: Thoughts on Interpreting an Electoral Order," *Electoral Studies* 8 (April 1989): 11.

19. Ronald Inglehart and Avram Hochstein, "Alignment and Dealignment of the Electorate in France and the United States," *Comparative Political Studies* 5 (October 1972): 343–372.

20. Russell J. Dalton, Paul Allen Beck, and Scott C. Flanagan, "Electoral Change in Advanced Industrialized Democracies," in *Electoral Change in Advanced Industrialized Democracies: Realignment or Dealignment?* eds. Russell J. Dalton, Scott C. Flanagan, and Paul Allen Beck (Princeton: Princeton University Press, 1984), 14.

21. Russell J. Dalton and Martin P. Wattenberg, "The Not So Simple Act of Voting," in *Political Science: The State of the Discipline II*, ed. Ada W. Finifter (Washington, D.C.: American Political Science Association, 1993), 202.

22. Bo Särlvik and Ivor Crewe, *Decade of Dealignment: The Conservative Victory of 1979 and Electoral Trends in the 1970s* (Cambridge: Cambridge University Press, 1983).

23. Harold D. Clarke et al., *Absent Mandate: Canadian Electoral Politics in an Era of Restructuring* (Toronto: Gage Educational Publishing, 1996), 183.

24. The Republicans won control of the House in eight consecutive elections between 1884 and 1908, far short of the twenty consecutive Democratic victories from 1954 through 1992.

25. Brian Nutting and H. Amy Stern, eds., *CQ's Politics in America, 2000: The 107th Congress* (Washington, D.C.: CQ Press, 2001), iv.

26. All of the other SRC surveys we employ are based mainly upon in-person interviews. The move toward telephone interviews was necessitated by the increased costs of in-person interviews as well as reduced funding for the 2000 surveys by the National Science Foundation.

27. The size of the voting-age population is based upon an estimate provided by Walter Dean Burnham. He estimates the politically eligible population to be 195,500,000 (personal communication, June 4, 2001). Because we usually analyze responses to key questions measured only in the postelection interview (e.g., how people said they voted for president or Congress), we often restrict our analysis to the 1,555 respondents in the 2000 postelection survey.

28. For a brief nontechnical introduction to polling, see Herbert Asher, *Polling and the Public: What Every Citizen Should Know,* 5th ed. (Washington, D.C.: CQ Press, 2001).

29. For a brief description of the procedures used by the SRC to carry out its sampling for in-person interviews, see Paul R. Abramson, *Political Attitudes in America: Formation and Change* (San Francisco: W. H. Freeman, 1983), 18–23. For a more detailed description, see Survey Research Center, *Interviewer's Manual,* rev. ed. (Ann Arbor, Mich.: Institute for Social Research, 1976).

30. The magnitude of sampling error is greater for proportions near 50 percent and diminishes somewhat for proportions above 70 percent or below 30 percent. The magnitude of error diminishes markedly for proportions above 90 percent or below 10 percent. For the sake of simplicity, we report confidence levels for percentages near 50 percent.

31. For an excellent table that allows us to evaluate differences between two groups, see Leslie Kish, *Survey Sampling* (New York: Wiley, 1965), 580. Kish defines the difference between two groups to be significant if the results are more than two standard errors apart.

32. In 2000, as well as in 1958, 1960, 1974, 1976, 1992, 1994, 1996, and 1998, a weighting procedure is necessary to obtain a representative result, and we report the "weighted" number of cases. For the 2000 NES we weight by V000002 when we are presenting results for analyses that do not include the postelection interview. (For example, we use this weight when we report the distribution of party identification among whites and among blacks.) Whenever we present results that include postelection interview results (for example, whether respondents said they voted, how they voted for president, or how they voted for Congress) we weight by V000002a.

1. THE NOMINATION STRUGGLE

1. Reagan's approval ratings in 1988 were not as elevated as Clinton's in 2000 but were nonetheless unusually high. Chapter 7 (see especially Table 7-6) provides the relevant data and discussion.

2. For more on these nomination contests, see Paul R. Abramson, John H. Aldrich, and David W. Rohde, *Change and Continuity in the 1988 Elections,* rev. ed. (Washington, DC: CQ Press, 1991), esp. chap. 1; and Gerald Pomper et al., *The Election of 2000: Reports and Interpretations* (New York: Chatham House, 2001), esp. chap. 2, "The Presidential Nominations," by William G. Mayer, 12–45.

3. See Paul R. Abramson, John H. Aldrich, and David W. Rohde, *Change and Continuity in the 1992 Elections,* rev. ed. (Washington, D.C.: CQ Press, 1995), 26–30.

4. See Paul R. Abramson, John H. Aldrich, and David W. Rohde, *Change and Continuity in the 1996 and 1998 Elections,* (Washington, D.C.: CQ Press, 1999), chap. 1.

5. See Joseph A. Schlesinger, *Ambition and Politics: Political Careers in the United States* (Chicago: Rand McNally, 1966); and Schlesinger *Political Parties and the Winning of Office* (Ann Arbor: University of Michigan Press, 1991).

6. The Republican Party has always used simple majority rule to select its nominees. The Democratic Party required that the nominee be selected by a two-thirds majority in every convention from its founding (except 1840) until 1936, when the requirement changed to a simple majority.

7. Since some states object to this feature or object to registration with a party at all, any Democratic delegates so selected would not be recognized as properly selected, and therefore such state parties use other procedures for choosing their delegates.

8. Since the 1980 campaign, the Democratic Party has required that all its state parties select their delegates within a three-month "window," beginning in March. Designed to reduce the length of the primary, the requirement excepted Iowa and New Hampshire anyway, to respect their "traditions." The Republicans had no such rules until 2000, but many (although not all) states followed the Democratic example. Because primary elections are run by state governments and to reduce the considerable expense involved, both party primaries were held at the same time and thus within the confines of the Democratic window.

9. The importance of "momentum" and related dynamics is developed in John H. Aldrich, *Before the Convention: Strategies and Choices in Presidential Nomination Campaigns* (Chicago: University of Chicago Press, 1980). See also, Larry M. Bartels, *Presidential Primaries and the Dynamics of Public Choice* (Princeton: Princeton University Press, 1988).

10. He was aided in part by virtue of the one-third of the delegates who had been selected in 1967, before Johnson's renomination was opposed.

11. The Republican Party does not require that its delegates be bound. Many states (especially those that hold primaries and write their laws following Democratic Party rules) do bind Republican delegates.

12. See esp., Andrew E. Busch, "New Features of the 2000 Presidential Nominating Process," in *In Pursuit of the White House: How We Choose Our Presidential Nominees,* ed. William G. Mayer (New York: Chatham House Publishers, 2000), 57–86.

13. Abramson, Aldrich, and Rohde, *Change and Continuity in the 1996 and 1998 Elections,* chap. 1.

14. The most important adaptation politicians have made to campaign finance requirements is the acquisition and use of "soft money," that is, money that can be raised and spent without limit for party building and turnout efforts. Soft money became controversial in 1996 over the increasingly vast sums raised, the sources of contributions, and the alleged misuse of soft money for promoting election of candidates. Soft money is not, however, a major factor in intra-party competition, including presidential nomination campaigns.

15. This account of the importance of preprimary campaigning is developed in Phil Paolino, "Candidate Name Recognition and the Dynamics of the Pre-Primary Period of the Presidential Nomination Process," (Ph.D. diss., Duke University, 1995).

16. This point is developed in an editorial column by political scientist Theodore J. Lowi, "The Governors Voted, and Bush Got His Win," *Raleigh News and Observer,* August 27, 2000, 27A.

2. THE GENERAL ELECTION CAMPAIGN

1. For a discussion of electoral-vote strategies from 1988–1996, see Daron R. Shaw, "The Methods behind the Madness: Presidential Electoral-College Strategies, 1988–1996," *Journal of Politics* 61 (November 1999): 893–913.

2. These preelection surveys are based on telephone polls. Given that nearly half of the adult population does not vote, polling agencies use a variety of procedures to identify likely voters. This introduces an additional element of uncertainty to all preelection polls.

3. Quoted in the *Washington Post,* August 20, 2000, A8.

4. Quoted in Katharine Q. Seelye, "Still Riding Wave, a Confident Gore Heads to Florida for Fall Push," on the *New York Times* Web site (www.nytimes.com), September 4, 2000.

5. *Washington Post,* September 5, 2000, A1.

6. See Ibid., September 16, 2000, A8.

7. *New York Times,* October 7, 2000, A11.

8. *Washington Post,* August 20, 2000, A8.

9. *New York Times,* September 2, 2000, A1, A10.

10. *Washington Post,* September 10, 2000, A10.

11. *Newsweek,* November 20, 2000, 88.

12. Ibid., 93.

13. *Washington Post,* September 24, 2000, A1.

14. Ibid., September 24, 2000, A18.

15. *Washington Post,* October 8, 2000, A12.

16. *Newsweek,* November 20, 2000, 89.

17. Quoted in Allison Mitchell, "Bush Derides Gore for Rejecting Debate Plan," on the *New York Times* Web site (www.nytimes.com), September 5, 2000.

18. *Newsweek,* November 20, 2000, 98.

19. *New York Times,* October 3, 2000, A19.

20. Quoted in Richard L. Berke, "Bush and Gore Stake Out Differences in First Debate," on the *New York Times* Web site (www.nytimes.com), October 4, 2000.

21. Television debates between presidential candidates were first held in the Kennedy-Nixon contest of 1960, but were not resumed until the 1976 Carter-Ford contest. The worst audience ever was in the first debate in 1976. See Jim Rutenberg, "TV Audience for Debate Is Smaller than Expected," on the *New York Times* Web site (www.nytimes.com), October 5, 2000.

22. *Newsweek,* November 20, 2000, 104.

23. *Washington Post,* October 17, 2000, A1.

24. *Newsweek,* November 20, 2000, 109.

25. *New York Times,* October 27, 2000, A27.

26. Ibid., October 23, 2000, A1.

27. *New York Times,* October 27, 2000, A13.

28. *New York Times,* October 28, 2000, A1; *Newsweek,* November 20, 2000, 119–120.

29. *Newsweek,* November 20, 2000, 124.

30. *Washington Post,* October 27, 2000, A12.

31. Ibid., October 29, 2000, A23.

32. Ibid., October 26, 2000, A1.

33. *Newsweek,* November 20, 2000, 120B.

34. *New York Times,* October 25, 2000, A1, A20.

35. *Washington Post,* November 7, 2000, A17.

36. Ibid., October 26, 2000, A24.

37. Ibid., November 2, 2000, A20.

38. *New York Times,* November 6, 2000, A24.

39. *New Republic,* November 13, 2000, 14.

40. For an excellent discussion of efforts to increase turnout in the 2000 election, see M. Margaret Conway, "Political Participation in America: Who Decides What?" in *America's Choice 2000,* ed. William Crotty (Boulder, Colo.: Westview, 2001), 79–94.

41. *Washington Post,* August 7, 2000, A1.

42. Ibid., August 21, 2000, A4.

43. *USA Today,* October 19, 2000, 1A.

44. *Newsweek,* November 20, 2000, 111.

45. *USA Today,* October 10, 2000, 14A.

46. *Newsweek,* November 20, 2000, 117.

47. *New York Times,* November 2, 2000, A21.

48. *Washington Post,* October 21, 2000, A1.

49. *New York Times,* November 7, 2000, A1, A23.

50. Ibid., November 7, 2000, A22.

51. *Newsweek,* November 20, 2000, 126.

52. There has been a lot of interesting research in recent years on the impact of presidential campaigns on outcomes. See, for example, Thomas H. Holbrook, *Do Campaigns Matter?* (Thousand Oaks, Calif.: Sage Publications, 1996); James E. Campbell, *The American Campaign* (College Station: Texas A&M University Press, 2000); and Darron R. Shaw, "A Study of Presidential Campaign Effects from 1956 to 1992," *Journal of Politics* 61 (May 1999): 387–422.

53. For a discussion of the concept of party identification, see chapter 8. For the questions used to measure party identification, see chapter 4, note 53. The question used to measure the point at which the respondent decided how to vote was asked in the postelection interview and read as follows: "How long before the election did you decide that you were going to vote the way you did?"

54. For a discussion of the performance of these models in light of the actual results, see the set of articles in *PS: Political Science and Politics* 34 (March 2001).

55. The exit polls were done by the Voter News Service, and the results were downloaded from the CNN/All Politics Web site on December 12, 2000 (www.cnn.com/ELECTION/2000/epolls/US/P000.html).

3. THE ELECTION RESULTS

1. This chronology is drawn from *Deadlock: The Inside Story of America's Closest Election,* written by the political staff of the *Washington Post* (New York: Public Affairs, 2001), vii–xv. Another detailed account of the postelection contest in Florida is provided by *New York Times* correspondents. See *36 Days: The Complete Chronicle of the 2000 Presidential Election Crisis* (New York: Times Books, 2001).

2. "Florida Voter Errors Cost Gore the Election," *USA Today,* May 11–13, 2000, 1, 4.

3. Katherine Q. Seelye, "Divided Civil Rights Panel Approves Election Report," *New York Times,* June 9, 2001, 8. See also Ford Fessenden, "Ballots Cast by Blacks and Older Voters Were Tossed in Far Greater Numbers," *New York Times,* November 12, 2001, A17.

4. See David Barstow and Don Van Natta Jr., "How Bush Took Florida: Mining the Overseas Absentee Vote," *New York Times,* July 17, 2001, 1, 16–19.

5. Ford Fessenden and John M. Broder, "Study of Disputed Florida Ballots Finds Justices Did Not Cast the Deciding Votes," *New York Times,* November 12, 2001, A1, A16.

6. Adam Nagourney and David Barstow, "Inside the Campaign: G.O.P.'s Depth Outdid Gore's Team in Florida," in *36 Days*, 339.

7. For the presidential election results, by state, from 1824, see *Presidential Elections: 1789–1996* (Washington, D.C.: Congressional Quarterly, 1997), 87–127.

8. One elector from the District of Columbia abstained to protest the District's lack of representation in Congress. She made it clear, however, that she would have voted for Gore if her vote were necessary to defeat George W. Bush.

9. In 1988 a Democratic elector from West Virginia cast her vote for president for Lloyd Bentson, the Democratic vice presidential candidate.

10. In the disputed election of 1876, records suggest that Samuel J. Tilden, the Democrat, won 51.0 percent of the popular vote and that Rutherfold B. Hayes, the Republican, won 48.0 percent. In 1888 Grover Cleveland, the incumbent Democratic president, won 48.6 percent of the vote, and Benjamin Harrison, the Republican, won 47.8 percent.

11. The fourteen winners were James K. Polk (Democrat) in 1844 with 49.5 percent; Zachary Taylor (Whig) in 1848 with 47.3 percent; James Buchanan (Democrat) in 1856 with 45.3 percent; Abraham Lincoln (Republican) in 1860 with 39.9 percent; James A. Garfield (Republican) in 1880 with 48.3 percent; Grover Cleveland (Democrat) in 1884 with 48.5 percent; Cleveland in 1892 with 46.1 percent; Woodrow Wilson (Democrat) in 1912 with 41.8 percent; Wilson in 1916 with 49.2 percent; Harry S. Truman (Democrat) in 1948 with 49.6 percent; John F. Kennedy (Democrat) in 1960 with 49.7 percent; Richard M. Nixon (Republican) in 1968 with 43.4 percent; Bill Clinton (Democrat) in 1992 with 43.0 percent; and Clinton in 1996 with 49.2 percent. The results for Kennedy can be questioned, however, mainly because voters in Alabama voted for individual electors, and one can argue that Richard M. Nixon won more popular votes than Kennedy.

12. Britain provides an excellent example of the effects of plurality-vote win systems on third parties. In Britain, like the United States, candidates for the national legislature run for single-member districts, and in all British parliamentary districts the plurality-vote winner is elected. Since the 1935 general election, the Liberal Party (and more recently the Alliance and the Liberal Democratic Party) has received a smaller share of the seats in the House of Commons than it won in the popular vote. For example, in the June 2001 election the Liberal Democratic Party won 18 percent of the nationwide popular vote but won only 8 percent of the seats in the House of Commons.

13. The New England states include Connecticut, Maine, Massachusetts, New Hampshire, Rhode Island, and Vermont. Although the U.S. Bureau of the Census classifies several border states and the District of Columbia as southern, we use an explicitly political definition: the eleven states that made up the old Confederacy, which are Alabama, Arkansas, Florida, Georgia, Louisiana, Mississippi, North Carolina, South Carolina, Tennessee, Texas, and Virginia.

14. Third-party candidates are not always underrepresented in the electoral college. In 1948 J. Strom Thurmond, the States-Rights Democrat, won only 2.4

percent of the popular vote, but he won 7.3 percent of the electoral vote. Thurmond won 55 percent of his total popular vote in the four states that he carried (Alabama, Louisiana, Mississippi, and South Carolina), all of which had very low turnout. He received no popular votes at all in thirty-one of the forty-eight states.

15. Maurice Duverger, *Political Parties: Their Organization and Activity in the Modern State,* trans. Barbara North and Robert North (New York: Wiley, 1963), 217. In the original, Duverger's formulation is, "le scrutin majoritaire à un seul tour tend au dualisme des partis." Duverger, *Les Partis Politiques,* 3d ed. (Paris: Armand Colin, 1958), 247. For a discussion of Duverger's law, see Willliam H. Riker, "The Two-Party System and Duverger's Law: An Essay on the History of Political Science," *American Political Science Review* 76 (December 1982): 753–766. For a more recent statement of Duverger's views, see Duverger, "Duverger's Law Forty Years Later" in *Electoral Laws and Their Political Consequences,* ed. Bernard Grofman and Arend Lijphart (New York: Agathan Press, 1986, 69–84). For extensive discussions of the effects of electoral laws, see Rein Taagepera and Matthew Soberg Shugart, *Seats and Votes: The Effects and Determinants of Electoral Systems* (New Haven: Yale University Press, 1989); and Gary W. Cox, *Making Votes Count: Strategic Coordination in the World's Electoral Systems* (New York: Cambridge University Press, 1997).

16. Duverger, *Political Parties,* 218.

17. William H. Riker, *The Art of Political Manipulation* (New Haven: Yale University Press, 1986), 79.

18. Gerald M. Pomper, "The Presidential Election," in *The Election of 2000: Reports and Interpretations,* ed. Gerald M. Pomper et al. (New York: Chatham House, 2001), 149.

19. For a comparison of the U.S. and French systems for electing presidents, see Paul R. Abramson et al., "Third-Party and Independent Presidential Candidates in American Politics: Wallace, Anderson, and Perot," *Political Science Quarterly* 110 (fall 1995): 349–397. For an argument against runoff elections, see Mark P. Jones, *Electoral Laws and the Survival of Presidential Democracy* (Notre Dame: Notre Dame University Press, 1995).

20. The Marquis de Condorcet (1743–1794) was a French philosopher best known for his theories of human progress. For a discussion of his principles of social choice, see Duncan Black, *The Theory of Committees and Elections* (Cambridge: Cambridge University Press, 1958).

21. The only other elections in which incumbent presidents were defeated in two straight elections were in 1888, when Grover Cleveland was defeated by Benjamin Harrison and 1892 when Harrison was defeated by Cleveland.

22. For a discussion of agenda setting during this period, see William H. Riker, *Liberalism Against Populism: A Confrontation Between the Theory of Democracy and the Theory of Social Choice* (San Francisco: W. H. Freeman, 1982), 213–232; and John H. Aldrich, *Why Parties? The Origin and Transformation of Political Parties in America* (Chicago: University of Chicago Press, 1995), 126–156.

23. Michael Nelson, "The Presidential Election," in *The Elections of 1988,* ed. Michael Nelson (Washington, D.C.: CQ Press, 1989), 195–196.

24. As a result of the Twenty-third Amendment (ratified in 1961), the District of Columbia has had three electoral votes since the 1964 presidential election.

25. Alex Keyssar, "This Election's Lesson: Win the Small States," in *36 Days,* 321–322.

26. Michael Nelson, "The Presidential Election," in *The Elections of 2000,* ed. Michael Nelson (Washington, D.C.: CQ Press, 2001), 81.

27. According to the U.S. Bureau of the Census, the West includes thirteen states: Alaska, Arizona, California, Colorado, Hawaii, Idaho, Montana, Nevada, New Mexico, Oregon, Utah, Washington, and Wyoming. But as Walter Dean Burnham has pointed out, for presidential elections the 96th meridian of longitude provides a dividing line. See Walter Dean Burnham, "The 1980 Earthquake," in *The Hidden Election: Politics and Economics in the 1980 Presidential Campaign,* ed. Thomas Ferguson and Joel Rogers (New York: Pantheon, 1981), 111. For this chapter, we therefore will consider Kansas, Nebraska, North Dakota, Oklahoma, and South Dakota to be western. Even though Texas lies mainly to the west of this meridian, we have classified it as southern, since it was a former Confederate state.

28. U.S. Department of Commerce, U.S. Bureau of the Census, *Statistical Abstract of the United States,* 101st ed. (Washington, D.C.: U.S. Government Printing Office, 1980).

29. See Paul R. Abramson, John H. Aldrich, and David W. Rohde, *Change and Continuity in the 1992 Elections,* rev. ed. (Washington, D.C.: CQ Press, 1995), 82–85; Abramson, Aldrich, and Rohde, *Change and Continuity in the 1996 and 1998 Elections* (Washington, D.C.: CQ Press, 1999), 53.

30. The eight mountain states are Arizona, Colorado, Idaho, Montana, Nevada, New Mexico, Utah, and Wyoming.

31. See Joseph A. Schlesinger, *Political Parties and the Winning of Office* (Ann Arbor: University of Michigan Press, 1991), Figure 5-1, 112. Schlesinger does not report the exact values, but he has provided them to us in a personal communication. Including the District of Columbia, which has voted since 1964, increases the standard deviation, since it always votes more Democratic than the most Democratic state. We have reported Schlesinger's results for the states, not the alternative results that include the District of Columbia.

32. V. O. Key Jr., *Southern Politics in State and Nation* (New York: Alfred A. Knopf, 1949), 5.

33. There have been many excellent studies of the postwar South. For one that presents state-by-state results, see Alexander P. Lamis, *The Two-Party South,* 2d exp. ed. (New York: Oxford University Press, 1990). For two others, see Earle Black and Merle Black, *Politics and Society in the Postwar South* (Cambridge: Harvard University Press, 1987); and Black and Black, *The Vital South: How Presidents Are Elected* (Cambridge: Harvard University Press, 1991).

34. Alabama, Georgia, Louisiana, Mississippi, and South Carolina are generally considered the five Deep South states. These are also the five states with the largest percentage of African Americans.

35. Southern politicians also suffered additional setbacks at the 1948 Democratic presidential nominating convention. Their attempts to weaken the civil rights plank of the platform were defeated. In addition, Hubert H. Humphrey, then mayor of Minneapolis, argued that the proposed civil rights platform was too weak and offered an amendment for a stronger statement. Humphrey's amendment was passed by a $651\frac{1}{2}$ to $582\frac{1}{2}$ margin.

36. Kennedy made a symbolic gesture that may have helped him with African Americans. Three weeks before the election, Martin Luther King Jr. was arrested in Atlanta for taking part in a sit-in demonstration. Although all the other demonstrators were released, King was held on a technicality and sent to the Georgia State Penitentiary. Kennedy telephoned King's wife to express his concern, and his brother Robert F. Kennedy made a direct appeal to a Georgia judge that led to King's release on bail. This incident received little notice in the press but had a great effect in the African American community. See Theodore H. White, *The Making of the President, 1960* (New York: Antheneum, 1961), 361–363.

37. See Abramson, Aldrich, and Rohde, *Change and Continuity in the 1992 Elections*, Figure 2-1, 47.

38. Marjorie Randon Hershey, "The Campaign and the Media," in *The Election of 1988: Reports and Interpretations*, ed. Gerald M. Pomper, et al. (Chatham, N.J.: Chatham House), 74.

39. Michael Nelson, "Constitutional Aspects of the Elections," in *The Elections of 1988*, 193–195; James C. Garand and Wayne T. Parent, "Representation, Swing, and Bias in U.S. Presidential Elections," *American Journal of Political Science* 35 (November 1992), 1001–1031.

40. Abramson, Aldrich, and Rohde, *Change and Continuity in the 1992 Elections*, 89.

41. Abramson, Aldrich, and Rohde, *Change and Continuity in the 1996 and 1998 Elections*, 57–58.

42. For an interesting, if alarmist, discussion of this possibility, see David W. Abbott and James P. Levine, *Wrong Winner: The Coming Debacle in the Electoral College* (New York: Praeger, 1991).

INTRODUCTION TO PART 2

1. For an excellent collection of articles dealing with some of the major controversies, see Richard G. Niemi and Herbert F. Weisberg, eds., *Controversies in Voting Behavior*, 4th ed. (Washington, D.C.: CQ Press, 2001). For another excellent summary of the research, see Russell J. Dalton and Martin P. Wattenberg, "The Not So Simple Act of Voting," in *Political Science: The State of the Discipline*

II, ed. Ada W. Finifter (Washington, D.C.: American Political Science Association, 1993), 193–218.

2. For an excellent summary of alternative theoretical perspectives to the study of political behavior, see Edward G. Carmines and Robert Huckfeldt, "Political Behavior: An Overview," in *A New Handbook of Political Science*, ed. Robert E. Goodin and Hans-Dieter Klingemann (New York: Oxford University Press, 1996), 223–254.

3. Paul F. Lazarsfeld, Bernard Berelson, and Hazel Gaudet, *The People's Choice: How the Voter Makes Up His Mind in a Presidential Campaign*, 2d ed. (New York: Columbia University Press, 1948), 27. See also Bernard R. Berelson, Paul F. Lazarsfeld, and William N. McPhee, *Voting: A Study of Opinion Formation in a Presidential Campaign* (Chicago: University of Chicago Press, 1954).

4. See Robert R. Alford, *Party and Society: The Anglo-American Democracies* (Chicago: Rand McNally, 1963); Richard F. Hamilton, *Class and Politics in the United States* (New York: Wiley, 1972); and Seymour Martin Lipset, *Political Man: The Social Bases of Politics*, exp. ed. (Baltimore: Johns Hopkins University Press, 1981). For a more recent book that uses this perspective, see Jeff Manza and Clem Brooks, *Social Cleavages and Political Change: Voter Alignments and U.S. Party Coalitions* (Oxford: Oxford University Press, 1999).

5. Angus Campbell et al., *The American Voter* (New York: Wiley, 1960).

6. For the single best summary of Converse's views on voting behavior, see Philip E. Converse, "Public Opinion and Voting Behavior," in *Nongovernmental Politics*, ed. Fred I. Greenstein and Nelson W. Polsby, vol. 4 of *Handbook of Political Science* (Reading, Mass.: Addison-Wesley, 1975), 75–169. For an excellent summary of public opinion research from a social-psychological perspective, see Donald R. Kinder and David O. Sears, "Public Opinion and Political Action," in *Special Fields and Applications*, ed. Gardner Lindzey and Elliot Aronson, vol. 2 of *Handbook of Social Psychology* (New York: Random House, 1985), 659–741. For an alternative approach to the study of political psychology, see Paul M. Sniderman, Richard A. Brody, and Philip E. Tetlock, with others, *Reasoning and Choice: Explorations in Political Psychology* (Cambridge: Cambridge University Press, 1991). See also, Sniderman, "The New Look in Public Opinion Research," in *Political Science: The State of the Discipline II*, 219–245. For another perspective, see John R. Zaller, *The Nature and Origins of Mass Opinion* (Cambridge: Cambridge University Press, 1992).

7. Warren E. Miller and J. Merrill Shanks, *The New American Voter* (Cambridge: Harvard University Press, 1996). Although reemphasizing the importance of party identification, this book also demonstrates a shift away from the social-psychological tradition employed by Miller and his colleagues in *The American Voter.*

8. Anthony Downs, *An Economic Theory of Democracy* (New York: Harper and Row, 1957); William H. Riker, *A Theory of Political Coalitions* (New Haven: Yale University Press, 1962).

9. See, for example, William H. Riker and Peter C. Ordeshook, "A Theory of the Calculus of Voting," *American Political Science Review* 62 (March 1962): 25–32; John A. Ferejohn and Morris P. Fiorina, "The Paradox of Not Voting: A Decision Theoretic Analysis," *American Political Science Review* 68 (June 1974): 525–536; and Morris P. Fiorina, *Retrospective Voting in American National Elections* (New Haven: Yale University Press, 1981). For summaries of much of this research, see Melvin J. Hinich and Michael Munger, *Analytical Politics* (Cambridge: Cambridge University Press, 1977); and Kenneth A. Shepsle and Mark S. Bonchek, *Analyzing Politics: Rationality, Behavior, and Institutions* (New York: Norton, 1997). For an interesting perspective that combines rational choice and psychological approaches, see Samuel L. Popkin, *The Reasoning Voter: Communication and Persuasion in Presidential Campaigns* (Chicago: University of Chicago Press, 1991).

10. The most important exception, at least in the study of elections, is Fiorina's *Retrospective Voting,* to which we refer extensively. For an interesting critique of the rational choice perspective, see Donald P. Green and Ian Shapiro, *Pathologies of Rational Choice Theory: A Critique of Applications in Political Science* (New Haven: Yale University Press, 1994). For critiques of Green and Shapiro's work, see Jeffrey Friedman, ed., *The Rational Choice Controversy: Economic Models of Politics Reconsidered* (New Haven: Yale University Press, 1996).

4. WHO VOTED?

1. The estimate of 90 million nonvoters is based upon Walter Dean Burnham's estimate that the potential electorate was 195,000,000. (Personal communication, June 5, 2001.)

2. This chapter focuses on only one form of political participation, voting. For an excellent study of other forms of political participation in the United States, as well as a different perpective on electoral participation, see M. Margaret Conway, *Political Participation in the United States,* 3d ed. (Washington, D.C.: CQ Press, 2000). For a major study of many forms of political participation, see Sidney Verba, Kay Lehman Schlozman, and Henry E. Brady, *Voice and Equality: Civic Voluntarism in American Politics* (Cambridge: Harvard University Press, 1995).

3. It is difficult to calculate the total number of voters, but in most elections more people vote for president than for any other office. As the 2000 election made clear, however, not all of these votes are counted.

4. In 1916 women had full voting rights only in Arizona, California, Colorado, Idaho, Kansas, Montana, Nevada, Oregon, Utah, Washington, and Wyoming. Only 10 percent of the U.S. population lived in these states. For a provocative discussion of the struggle for women's suffrage, see Alan P. Grimes, *The Puritan Ethic and Women's Suffrage* (New York: Oxford University Press, 1967). For another

interesting discussion, see Holly J. McCammon et al., "How Movements Win: Gendered Opportunity Structures and the U.S. Women's Suffrage Movements, 1866–1919," *American Sociological Review* 66 (February 2001): 49–70.

5. See Martin J. Kousser, *The Shaping of Southern Politics: Suffrage Restrictions and the Establishment of the One-Party South, 1880–1910* (New Haven: Yale University Press, 1974). For a more general discussion of the decline of turnout in the late nineteenth century, see Paul Klepppner, *Who Voted? The Dynamics of Electoral Turnout, 1870–1980* (New York: Praeger, 1982), 55–82.

6. There has been a great deal of disagreement about the reasons for and the consequences of registration requirements. For some of the more interesting arguments, see Walter Dean Burnham, "The Changing Shape of the American Political Universe," *American Political Science Review* 59 (March 1965): 7–28; Philip E. Converse, "Change in the American Electorate," in *The Human Meaning of Social Change*, ed. Angus Campbell and Philip E. Converse (New York: Russell Sage, 1972), 266–301; and Walter Dean Burnham, "Theory and Voting Research: Some Reflections on Converse's 'Change in the American Electorate,' " *American Political Science Review* 68 (September 1974): 1002–1023. For another interesting perspective, see Frances Fox Piven and Richard A. Cloward, *Why Americans Don't Vote* (New York: Pantheon, 1988), 26–95.

7. For a rich source of information about the introduction of the Australian ballot and its effects, see Jerrold G. Rusk, "The Effect of the Australian Ballot on Split-Ticket Voting: 1876–1908," *American Political Science Review* 64 (December 1970): 1220–1238.

8. For example, see Burnham's estimates of turnout among the politically eligible voting-age population, which include results through 1984. Burnham, "The Turnout Problem," in *Elections American Style*, ed. A. James Reichley (Washington, D.C.: Brookings Institution, 1987), 113–114. Because Burnham's turnout denominator is smaller than ours, his estimates of turnout are somewhat larger. Although there are advantages to Burnham's calculations, we use the voting-age population as our base for two reasons. First, it is difficult to estimate the size of the noncitizen population, and official estimates of turnout by the U.S. Bureau of the Census use the voting-age population as the turnout denominator. Second, even though only citizens can vote in present U.S. elections, citizenship is not a constitutional requirement of voting. National legislation determines how long it takes to become a citizen, and state law imposes citizenship as a condition of voting. According to Burnham's estimates, turnout among the politically eligible population was 52.7 percent in 1988, 56.9 percent in 1992, 50.8 percent in 1996, and 53.9 percent in 2000. (Based on personal communications, June 21, 1993; July 1, 1997; and June 4, 2001.)

9. The estimate of turnout among the politically eligible population is based upon Burnham, "Turnout Problem."

10. See Glenn Firebaugh and Kevin Chen, "Vote Turnout among Nineteenth Amendment Women: The Enduring Effects of Disfranchisement," *American Journal of Sociology* 100 (January 1995): 972–996.

11. Robert Toner, "Parties Pressing to Raise Turnout as Election Nears," *New York Times,* October 20, 1996, Y1, Y4. For estimates of the effects of this reform on turnout, see Raymond E. Wolfinger and Jonathan Hoffman, "Registering and Voting with Motor Voter," *PS* 34 (March 2001): 85–92.

12. For our analysis of the reasons for the increase in turnout in 1992, see Paul R. Abramson, John H. Aldrich, and David W. Rohde, *Change and Continuity in the 1992 Elections,* rev. ed., (Washington, D.C.: CQ Press, 1995), 120–123. As we point out, it is difficult to demonstrate empirically that Perot's candidacy made an important contribution to the increase in turnout. For additional analyses, see Stephen M. Nichols and Paul Allen Beck, "Reversing the Decline: Voter Turnout in 1992," in *Democracy's Feast: Elections in America,* ed. Herbert F. Weisberg (Chatham, N.J.: Chatham House, 1995), 62–65; and Steven J. Rosenstone, Roy L. Behr, and Edward H. Lazarus, *Third Parties in America: Citizen Response to Major Party Failure,* 2d ed. (Princeton: Princeton University Press, 1996), 254–257.

13. In our analysis of the 1980, 1984, 1988, and 1992 elections, we also made extensive use of published reports using the Current Population Surveys. In our analysis of the 1996 election, only a preliminary report was available, but we used it where we could to compare these findings with those of the NES survey. However, as of the time this chapter went to press even the preliminary results of the 2000 Current Population Survey had not been published.

14. We classified five respondents who said they voted, but who said that they did not vote for president, as nonvoters.

15. Respondents were asked the following question: "In talking to people about the elections, we often find that a lot of people were not able to vote because they weren't registered, they were sick, or that they just didn't have time. Which of the following statements best describes you: One, I did not vote (in the election this November); Two, I thought about voting this time, but didn't; Three, I usually vote, but didn't this time; or Four, I am sure that I voted." Providing these four options was an innovation designed to provide more accurate reports, although we have no information about its success in attaining this goal. The 18-point discrepancy between reported turnout in the 2000 survey and actual turnout among the politically eligible population is close to the average discrepancy between reported turnout and actual turnout among the politically eligible population.

16. Vote validation studies were conducted after the 1964, 1976, 1980, 1984, and 1988 presidential elections and after the 1978, 1986, and 1990 midterm elections. Mainly for reasons of cost they were discontinued after 1990. Fortunately, even though validation studies were not conducted in the most recent elections, these past studies provide considerable information about the sources of bias in overreporting.

Most analyses that compare results of reported turnout with those of turnout as measured by the validation studies suggest that *relative* measures of turnout among most social groups can be compared using reported turnout. However, these studies suggest that blacks are more likely to overreport voting than whites.

As a result, turnout differences between the races are always greater when turnout is measured by the vote validation studies. For results between 1964 and 1988, see Paul R. Abramson and William Claggett, "Racial Differences in Self-Reported and Validated Turnout in the 1988 Presidential Election," *Journal of Politics* 53 (February 1991): 186–187. For results for 1990, see Abramson, Aldrich, and Rohde, *Change and Continuity in the 1992 Elections*, 382.

For an extensive discussion of the factors that contribute to false reports of turnout, see Brian D. Silver, Barbara A. Anderson, and Paul R. Abramson, "Who Overreports Voting?" *American Political Science Review* 80 (June 1986): 613–624. For a more recent study arguing that biases in reported turnout are more severe, see Robert Bernstein, Anita Chada, and Robert Montjoy, "Overreporting Voting: Why It Happens and Why It Matters," *Public Opinion Quarterly* 65 (spring 2001): 22–44.

17. See Michael W. Traugott and John P. Katosh, "Response Validity in Surveys of Voting Behavior," *Public Opinion Quarterly* 43 (fall 1979): 359–377; and Barbara A. Anderson, Brian D. Silver, and Paul R. Abramson, "The Effects of Race of the Interviewer on Measures of Electoral Participation by Blacks in SRC National Election Surveys," *Public Opinion Quarterly* 52 (spring 1988): 53–83.

18. As we note in the introduction to part 1, half the respondents were interviewed by telephone. For respondents interviewed by telephone we relied upon each respondent's own report to the following question, "What racial or ethnic group or groups best describes you?" For respondents who were interviewed in-person, we relied upon the interviewer's classification of each respondent's race, as long as the interviewer was confident of his or her classification. If the interviewer reported not being confident, we relied upon the respondent's own ethnic classification.

19. The vote validation studies are not free from error, for some true voters may be classified as validated nonvoters if no record can be found of their registration or if the records inaccurately fail to show that they voted. The voting records where African Americans tend to live are not as well maintained as the records where whites are likely to live. Still, it seems unlikely that the finding that blacks are more likely to falsely report voting results from the poorer quality of black voting records. See Paul R. Abramson and William Claggett, "The Quality of Record-Keeping and Racial Differences in Validated Turnout," *Journal of Politics* 54 (August 1992): 871–880.

20. See Katherine Tate, "Black Political Participation in the 1984 and 1988 Presidential Election," *American Political Science Review* 85 (December 1991): 1159–1176. For a more extensive discussion, see Tate, *From Protest to Politics: The New Black Voters in American Elections*, enl. ed. (Cambridge: Harvard University Press, 1994).

21. As we explain in chapter 3, we consider the South to include the eleven states of the old Confederacy. In our analyses of the NES surveys, however, we do not consider residents of Tennessee to be southern because the University of Michigan Survey Research Center conducts samples in Tennessee to represent

the border states. In this analysis, as well as analyses of regional differences using NES surveys later in this book, we classify the following ten states as southern: Alabama, Arkansas, Florida, Georgia, Louisiana, Mississippi, North Carolina, South Carolina, Texas, and Virginia.

22. We report the results for all Hispanics, regardless of race. The U.S. Bureau of the Census notes that Hispanics may be of any race and classifies most Hispanics as white.

23. See Raymond E. Wolfinger and Steven J. Rosenstone, *Who Votes?* (New Haven: Yale University Press, 1980), 93–94.

24. Ibid., 46–50.

25. See Benjamin Highton and Raymond E. Wolfinger, "The First Seven Years of the Political Life Cycle," *American Journal of Political Science* 45 (January 2001): 202–209.

26. We use this distinction because it allows us to make comparisons over time and is especially useful for studying change over the entire postwar period, as we do in chapter 5. However, there are problems in measuring social class in the 2000 election survey since the spouse's occupation was not measured. In fact, for all years through 1984, we used the head of household's occupation to measure social class. In 1988, 1992, and 1996, the head of household was not specified, and for married women we used the husband's occupation to measure social class. A reanalysis of the 1984 NES survey suggested that we were able to come close to reproducing the head of household's occupation through this procedure.

We turned to the 1996 NES to examine differences between using the head of household's occupation and using the respondent's occupation. The relationships were very close regardless of which measure was used, but the overall size of the middle class was larger when the respondent's occupation was used. For example, among respondents who could be classified as either middle or working class ($N = 1,540$), 62 percent were middle class based upon their own occupations; among respondents who could be classified based upon either their own or spouse's occupations ($N = 1,483$), 56 percent were middle class.

27. Our measure of family income is based upon the respondent's estimate of his or her family's income in 1999 before taxes. For in-person interviews, we relied upon the interviewer's assessment of family income where the respondent refused to reveal his or her family income or when the interviewer thought the respondent was answering dishonestly. Comparable information was not available for respondents interviewed by telephone.

28. See Wolfinger and Rosenstone, *Who Voted?* 13–36.

29. Respondents who said they were Christians were asked, "Would you call yourself a born-again Christian, that is, have you personally had a conversion experience related to Jesus Christ?"

30. David C. Leege and Lyman A Kellstedt and others, *Rediscovering the Religious Factor in American Politics* (Armonk, N.Y.: Sharpe, 1993). We are grateful to Leege for providing us with the detailed information used to construct this

variable. We constructed the measure as follows: respondents who prayed several times a day received 2 points, those who prayed less often received 1 point, and those who never prayed received 0 points; those who attended religious services at least once a week received 2 points, those who attended less frequently received 1 point, and those who never attended received 0 points; those who said that religion provided "a great deal" of guidance in their lives received 2 points, those who said it provided "quite a bit" received 1 point, and those who said it provided "some" or no guidance received 0 points; respondents who said the Bible was literally true or "the word of God" received 2 points, those who said it "was written by men and is not the word of God" received 0 points. Respondents received a score of 1 for each ambiguous, don't know, or not ascertained response; respondents with more than two such responses were excluded from the analysis. Scores ranged from 0 to 8. In regrouping this variable into three categories, we classified respondents with 8 points as "very high," those with 6 or 7 points as "high," and those with a score below 6 as "low or medium" in religious commitment.

31. Kenneth D. Wald, *Religion and Politics in the United States*, 3d ed. (Washington, D.C.: CQ Press, 1997), 173.

32. R. Stephen Warner, *New Wine in Old Wineskins: Evangelicals and Liberals in a Small-Town Church* (Berkeley: University of California Press, 1988), 33, 34.

33. We are grateful to David Leege for providing us with the specific NES codes used to classify Protestants according to their religious tradition. These codes are based upon the religious denomination variable in the codebook provided by the Inter-university Consortium for Political and Social Research. Categories 50, 60, 70, 100–109, 120–149, 160–219, 221–223, 231–233, 240, 250–269, 271–275, 280, 282, 289, 292, and 293 were classified as evangelicals; categories 80, 90, 110, 150–159, 220, 229, 230, 249, 270, 276, 279, 281, and 290–291 were classified as mainline.

34. Wolfinger and Rosenstone, *Who Votes?* 13–36.

35. Silver, Anderson, and Abramson's analysis of the 1964, 1968, and 1980 vote validation studies shows that respondents with higher levels of formal education do have very high turnout. However, their analysis also shows that persons with high levels of formal education who do not vote are more likely to falsely claim to have voted than those with lower levels of formal education. (See Silver, Anderson, and Abramson, "Who Overreports Voting?") Our analysis shows a similar pattern with the 1978, 1984, 1986, 1988, and 1990 vote validation studies. We do not know if a similar pattern would be found in 2000, but if it were, the results in Table 4-3 may somewhat exaggerate the relationship between formal education and turnout.

36. Richard A. Brody, "The Puzzle of Political Participation in America," in *The New American Political System*, ed. Anthony King (Washington, D.C.: American Enterprise Institute, 1978), 287–234.

37. Bear in mind the options for answering the voting participation were different in 2000 than in previous NES surveys (see note 15). As we point out, how-

ever, the degree to which the 2000 NES overestimated turnout compared with actual turnout was about the same as in previous NES surveys.

38. Walter Dean Burnham, "The 1976 Election: Has the Crisis Been Adjourned?" in *American Politics and Public Policy,* ed. Walter Dean Burnham and Martha Wagner Weinberg (Cambridge: MIT Press, 1978), 24; Thomas E. Cavanagh, "Changes in American Voter Turnout, 1964–1976," *Political Science Quarterly* 96 (spring 1981): 53–65.

39. Ruy A. Teixeira, *The Disappearing American Voter* (Washington, D.C.: American Enterprise Institute, 1992), 66–67. Teixeira is skeptical about the findings from NES surveys that show turnout did not decline among college graduates.

40. Jan E. Leighley and Jonathan Nagler, "Socioeconomic Class Bias in Turnout, 1964–1988: The Voters Remain the Same," *American Political Science Review* 86 (September 1992): 725–736. For an analysis of congressional elections that supports Leighley and Nagler's conclusions, see Todd G. Shields and Robert K. Goidel, "Participation Rates, Socioeconomic Class Biases, and Congressional Elections: A Crossvalidation," *American Journal of Political Science* 41 (April 1997): 683–691.

41. For estimates of the impact of generational replacement between 1960 and 1980, see Paul R. Abramson, *Political Attitudes in America: Formation and Change* (San Francisco: W. H. Freeman, 1983), 56–61.

42. This procedure assumes that educational levels were the same in 2000 as they were in 1960, but that reported levels of turnout were the same as those observed in the 2000 NES survey.

43. Teixeira, *Disappearing American Voter,* 47.

44. Steven J. Rosenstone and John Mark Hansen, *Mobilization, Participation, and Democracy in America* (New York: Macmillan, 1993), 214–215.

45. Teixeira, *Disappearing American Voter,* 47.

46. Rosenstone and Hansen, *Mobilization, Participation, and Democracy,* 215.

47. Warren E. Miller, "The Puzzle Transformed: Explaining Declining Turnout," *Political Behavior* 14, no. 1 (1992): 1–43. See also, Warren E. Miller and J. Merrill Shanks, *The New American Voter* (Cambridge: Harvard University Press, 1996), 95–114.

48. Robert D. Putnam, *Bowling Alone: The Collapse and Revival of American Community* (New York: Simon and Schuster, 2000), 265.

49. George I. Balch, "Multiple Indicators in Survey Research: The Concept 'Sense of Political Efficacy,' " *Political Methodology* 1 (spring 1974): 1–43. For an extensive discussion of feelings of political efficacy, see Abramson, *Political Attitudes in America,* 135–189.

50. Ruy A. Teixeira, *Why Americans Don't Vote: Turnout Decline in the United States, 1960–1984* (New York: Greenwood Press, 1987). In his more recent study, *Disappearing American Voter,* Teixeira develops a measure of party-related characteristics that includes strength of party identification, concern about the electoral outcome, perceived differences between the parties, and knowledge of the parties and candidates (40–42).

51. Paul R. Abramson, John H. Aldrich, and David W. Rohde, *Change and Continuity in the 1980 Elections,* rev. ed. (Washington, D.C.: CQ Press, 1983, 85–87). For a more detailed analysis using probability procedures to estimate the impact of these attitudinal changes, see Abramson and Aldrich, "The Decline of Electoral Participation in America," *American Political Science Review* 76 (September 1982): 502–521.

52. Paul R. Abramson, John H. Aldrich, and David W. Rohde, *Change and Continuity in the 1984 Elections,* rev. ed. (Washington, D.C.: CQ Press, 1987), 115–118; Abramson, Aldrich, and Rohde, *Change and Continuity in the 1988 Elections,* rev. ed. (Washington, D.C.: CQ Press, 1991); 103–106; Abramson, Aldrich, and Rohde, *Change and Continuity in the 1992 Elections,* 117–120; Abramson, Aldrich, and Rohde, *Change and Continuity in the 1996 and 1998 Elections,* (Washington, D.C.: CQ Press, 1999), 81–84.

53. In 2000, respondents were asked: "Generally speaking, do you think of yourself as a Republican, a Democrat, an Independent, or what?" Persons who called themselves Republicans or Democrats were asked, "Would you call yourself a strong Republican (Democrat) or a not very strong Republican (Democrat)?" Those who called themselves Independents, answered "no preference," or named another party were asked: "Do you think of yourself as closer to the Republican party or to the Democratic party?" Respondents with no partisan preference are usually classified as Independents. They are classified as "apoliticals" only if they have low levels of political interest and involvement.

In previous NES surveys, respondents were asked, "Generally speaking, do you usually think of yourself as a Republican, a Democrat, an Independent, or what?" The word *usually* was not included in 2000.

54. Angus Campbell et al., *The American Voter* (New York: Wiley, 1960), 120–167.

55. This expectation follows from the rational-choice perspective. For the most extensive discussion of party identification from this view, see Morris P. Fiorina, *Retrospective Voting in American National Elections* (New Haven: Yale University Press, 1981), 84–105. For a more recent discussion, see John H. Aldrich, "Rational Choice and Turnout," *American Journal of Political Science* 37 (February 1993): 246–278. For a comment on Aldrich's essay, see Robert W. Jackman, "Rationality and Political Participation," *American Journal of Political Science* 37 (February 1993): 279–290. For an extensive critique of the rational-choice approach to the study of electoral participation, see Donald P. Green and Ian Shapiro, *Pathologies of Rational Choice: A Critique of Applications in Political Science* (New Haven: Yale University Press, 1994), 47–71.

56. Respondents who disagreed with both of these statements were scored as high in their feelings of political effectiveness, those who agreed with one statement and disagreed with the other were scored as medium, and those who agreed with both statements were scored as low. Respondents who scored "don't know" or "not ascertained" to one statement were scored either high or low depending upon their answer to the remaining statement, but those with "don't know" or "not ascertained" responses to both statements were excluded from the

analysis. In 1988, 1992, 1996, and 2000 respondents were asked whether they "strongly agreed," "agreed," "neither agreed nor disagreed," "disagreed," or "strongly disagreed" to each statement. For all four years, we classified respondents who "neither agreed nor disagreed" with both statements as medium on this measure. This scoring decision has little effect on the results since only 3 percent of the respondents in 1988, 2 percent in 1992, 3 percent in 1996, and 4 percent in 2000 answered "neither agreed nor disagreed" to both statements.

57. This is consistent with the findings of Bruce E. Keith and his colleagues that independents who feel closer to one of the parties are as politically involved as weak partisans. See Bruce E. Keith et al., *The Myth of the Independent Voter* (Berkeley: University of California Press, 1992), 38–59.

58. This calculation is based upon the assumption that each partisan strength and sense of political efficacy category was the same size as we observed in 1960, but that reported turnout for each category was the same as that observed in 2000. For a full explanation of this technique, see Abramson, *Political Attitudes in America,* 296.

59. Our estimates are based upon an algebraic standardization procedure. To simplify our analysis, we combined whites with an eighth grade education or less with whites who had not graduated from high school, and we combined weak partisans and independents who leaned toward a party.

60. For a discussion of political trust, see Abramson, *Political Attitudes in America,* 193–238.

61. Respondents were asked, "How much of the time do you think you can trust the government in Washington to do what is right—just about always, most of the time, or only some of the time?"

62. Respondents were asked, "Would you say the government is pretty much run for a few big interests looking out for themselves, or that it is run for the benefit of all the people?"

63. Respondents were asked, "The political parties try to talk to as many people as they can to get them to vote for their candidate. Did anyone from the political parties call you up or come around to talk with you about the campaign this year?"

64. As Paul R. Abramson and William Claggett show, the effects of elite recruitment on increasing turnout persist even when one takes into account that political elites are more likely to recruit people who have participated in the past. See Paul R. Abramson and William Claggett, "Recruitment and Political Participation," *Political Research Quarterly* 54 (December 2001): 905–916.

65. Respondents were asked who they thought would be elected president. Those who named a candidate were asked, "Do you think the election will be close or do you think that [the candidate named] will win by quite a bit?" Those who said they did not know who would win were asked, "Do you think the Presidential race will be close or will one candidate win by quite a bit?"

66. See John H. Aldrich, "Some Problems in Testing Two Rational Models of Participation," *American Journal of Political Participation* 20 (November 1976): 713–733.

67. Orley Ashenfelter and Stanley Kelly Jr., "Determinants of Participation in Presidential Elections," *Journal of Law and Economics* 18 (December 1975): 721.

68. James DeNardo, "Turnout and the Vote: The Joke's on the Democrats," *American Political Science Review* 74 (June 1980): 406–420.

69. Abramson, Aldrich, and Rohde, *Change and Continuity in the 1980 Elections,* 88–92; Abramson, Aldrich, and Rohde, *Change and Continuity in the 1984 Elections,* 119–124; Abramson, Aldrich, and Rohde, *Change and Continuity in the 1988 Elections,* 108–113.

70. Abramson, Aldrich, and Rohde, *Change and Continuity in the 1992 Elections,* 124–128.

71. The results for 1980, 1984, and 1988 are based upon the responses of people whose voting was verified through checking of the voting and registration records. However, the Republican turnout advantage was also found when we studied reported electoral participation.

72. Abramson, Aldrich, and Rohde, *Change and Continuity in the 1996 and 1998 Elections,* 86–89.

73. The full seven-point issue scales upon which this measure is based were asked of only the respondents interviewed in-person. This accounts for the relatively small number of cases in this part of Table 4-5.

74. In 2000 only a random half sample was asked the two questions about the most important problem, which accounts for the relatively small number of cases in this part of Table 4.5.

75. Gerald M. Pomper, "The Presidential Election," in *The Election of 2000: Reports and Interpretations,* ed. Gerald M. Pomper et al. (New York: Chatham House, 2001), 143.

76. See Wolfinger and Rosenstone, *Who Votes?* 108–114.

77. Piven and Cloward, *Why Americans Don't Vote,* 21. For similar arguments, see Walter Dean Burnham, "Shifting Patterns of Congressional Voting Participation," in *The Current Crisis in American Politics* (New York: Oxford University Press, 1981), 166–203.

78. See Seymour Martin Lipset, *Political Man: The Social Bases of Politics,* enl. ed. (Baltimore: Johns Hopkins University Press, 1981), 226–229. Lipset emphasizes the dangers of sudden increases in political participation.

79. Gerald M. Pomper, "The Presidential Election," in *The Election of 1980: Reports and Interpretations,* ed. Gerald M. Pomper et al. (Chatham, N.J.: Chatham House, 1981), 86.

5. SOCIAL FORCES AND THE VOTE

1. The social characteristics used in this chapter are the same as those used in chapter 4. The variables are described in notes to that chapter. For similar tables showing the results for the 1980, 1984, 1988, 1992, and 1996 elections, see Paul R. Abramson, John H. Aldrich, and David W. Rohde, *Change and*

Continuity in the 1980 Elections, rev. ed. (Washington, D.C.: CQ Press, 1983), 98–99; Abramson, Aldrich, and Rohde, *Change and Continuity in the 1984 Elections,* rev. ed. (Washington, D.C.: CQ Press, 1987), 136–137; Abramson, Aldrich, and Rohde, *Change and Continuity in the 1988 Elections,* rev. ed. (Washington, D.C.: CQ Press, 1991), 124–125; Abramson, Aldrich, and Rohde, *Change and Continuity in the 1992 Elections,* rev. ed. (Washington, D.C.: CQ Press, 1995), 133–135; and Abramson, Aldrich, and Rohde, *Change and Continuity in the 1996 and 1998 Elections* (Washington, D.C.: CQ Press, 1999), 93–95.

2. Unless otherwise indicated our report from this exit poll is based upon "Who Voted: A Portrait of American Politics, 1976–2000," *New York Times,* November 12, 2000, sec. 4, 4. Exit polls have three main advantages. First, they are less expensive to conduct than the multistage probability samples conducted by the Survey Research Center of the University of Michigan. Second, partly because of the exit polls' lower cost, a large number of people can be sampled. Third, because persons are selected to be interviewed as they leave the polling stations, the vast majority have actually voted for president. But these surveys have four disadvantages. First, exit polls do not sample the growing number of voters who are using absentee ballots. Second, the questionnaires themselves must be relatively brief. Third, it is difficult to supervise the fieldwork to be sure that the interviewers are using proper procedures to select the respondents. Last, these studies are of little use in studying turnout, since persons who do not go to the polls are not sampled. For a discussion of the procedures used to conduct exit polls, as well as some of their limitations, see Albert H. Cantril, *The Opinion Connection: Polling, Politics, and the Press* (Washington, D.C.: CQ Press, 1991).

3. This brief discussion cannot do justice to the complexities of black electoral behavior. For an important study based upon the Black National Election Study survey conducted by the Survey Research Center and the Center for Political Studies of the University of Michigan, see Patricia Gurin, Shirley Hatchett, and James S. Jackson, *Hope and Independence: Blacks' Response to Electoral and Party Politics* (New York: Russell Sage Foundation, 1989). For two important studies that use the 1984 black national election study and the 1988 follow-up study, see Michael C. Dawson, *Behind the Mule: Race and Class in African American Politics* (Princeton: Princeton University Press, 1994); and Katherine Tate, *From Politics to Protest: The New Black Voter in American Elections,* enl. ed. (Cambridge: Harvard University Press, 1994).

4. According to our estimates using the NES surveys, 21 percent of Gore's votes came from black voters; according to our calculations using the VNS exit poll, 19 percent of Gore's votes came from blacks.

5. Although we have examined the results for blacks for all of the categories in Table 5-1, we do not present them. Given the relatively small number of blacks sampled, the number of blacks in these categories is too small to present meaningful results, and our discussion of blacks is based upon the VNS exit poll.

6. For a review of research on Hispanics, as well as on African Americans, see Paula D. McClain and John D. Garcia, "Expanding Disciplinary Boundaries: Black, Latino, and Racial Minority Groups in Political Science," in *Political Science: The State of the Discipline II*, ed. Ada W. Finifter (Washington, D.C.: American Political Science Association, 1993), 247–279. For analyses of Hispanic voting behavior in the 1996 elections, see Rudolfo O. de la Garza and Louis DeSipio, eds., *Awash in the Mainstream: Latino Politics in the 1996 Election* (Boulder, Colo.: Westview Press, 1999).

7. For an extensive review of the research literature on women and politics, see Susan J. Carroll and Linda M. G. Zerilli, "Feminist Challenges to Political Science," in *Political Science: The State of the Discipline II*, 55–76. For a global comparison, see Barbara J. Nelson and Najma Chowdhury, eds., *Women and Politics Worldwide* (New Haven: Yale University Press, 1994).

8. See Abramson, Aldrich, and Rohde, *Change and Continuity in the 1980 Elections*, 290.

9. Unlike our analyses of previous NES surveys, we did not find a higher gender gap among respondents with high family incomes.

10. The NES survey reports six types of marital status: married and living with spouse, never married, divorced, separated, widowed, and partners who are not married. In this paragraph we compare the first two of these groups.

11. Based upon a Web site provided by the Cable News Network: www.cnn.com/ELECTION/2000/epolls/US/P000.html. The results were downloaded on December 14, 2000.

12. The report on the VNS poll did not present separate results for the border states.

13. Robert S. Erikson, "The 2000 Presidential Election in Historical Perspective," *Political Studies Quarterly* 116 (spring 2001): 46. Jeffrey M. Stonecash, using NES surveys from 1952 through 1996, argues that income differences in voting have increased. See Jeffrey M. Stonecash, *Class and Party in American Politics* (Boulder, Colo.: Westview Press, 2000). These differences, however, were weak and inconsistent in the 2000 elections.

14. See Walter Dean Burnham, *Critical Elections and the Mainsprings of American Politics* (New York: Norton, 1970); Everett Carll Ladd Jr., with Charles D. Hadley, *Transformations of the American Party System: Political Coalitions from the New Deal to the 1970s*, 2d ed. (New York: Norton, 1978).

15. This information comes from the CNN Web site cited in note 11.

16. For the best summary of religious differences in American political life, see Kenneth D. Wald, *Religion and Politics in America*, 3d ed. (Washington, D.C.: CQ Press, 1997).

17. David C. Keege and Lyman A. Kellstedt, with others, *Rediscovering the Religious Factor in American Politics* (Armonk, N.Y.: Sharpe, 1993).

18. Robert Axelrod, "Where the Votes Come From: An Analysis of Electoral Coalitions, 1952–1968," *American Political Science Review* 66 (March 1972): 11–20. Axelrod continued to update his results through the 1984 elections. For

his most recent update, which includes the cumulative results from 1952 through 1980, see Axelrod, "Presidential Election Coalitions in 1984," *American Political Science Review* 80 (March 1986): 281–284.

19. John R. Petrocik, *Party Coalitions: Realignment and the Decline of the New Deal Party System* (Chicago: University of Chicago Press, 1981).

20. Harold W. Stanley, William T. Bianco, and Richard G. Niemi, "Partisanship and Group Support over Time: A Multivariate Analysis," *American Political Science Review* 80 (September 1986): 969–976. Stanley and his colleagues assess the independent contribution that group memberships make toward Democratic Party loyalties after controls are introduced for membership in other pro-Democratic groups. For an update and extension through 1996, see Stanley and Niemi, "Party Coalitions in Transition: Partisanship and Group Support, 1952–1996," in *Reelection 1996: How America Voted*, ed. Herbert F. Weisberg and Janet M. Box-Steffensmeier (New York: Chatham House, 1999): 162–180. For an alternative approach, see Robert S. Erikson, Thomas D. Lancaster, and David W. Romero, "Group Components of the Presidential Vote, 1952–1984," *Journal of Politics* 51 (May 1989): 337–346.

21. For a discussion of the importance of the working class to the Democratic presidential coalition, see Paul R. Abramson, *Generational Change in American Politics* (Lexington, Mass.: D.C. Heath, 1975).

22. See Axelrod, "Where the Votes Come From."

23. The NORC survey, based upon 2,564 civilians, uses a quota sample that does not follow the probability procedures used by the University of Michigan Survey Research Center. Following the procedures common at the time, southern blacks were not sampled. Because the NORC survey overrepresented upper-income groups and the middle and upper classes, it cannot be used to estimate the contribution of social groups to the Democratic and Republican presidential coalitions.

24. Abramson, *Generational Change*, 65–68.

25. As Figure 5-1 shows, Clinton did win a majority of the major-party white vote in 1992 and 1996.

26. Racial voting, as well as our other measures of social cleavage, are affected by including Wallace voters with Nixon voters in 1968, Anderson voters with Reagan voters in 1980, Perot voters with Bush voters in 1992, and Perot voters with Dole voters in 1996. For reports on the effects of including these independent or third-party candidates, see Abramson, Aldrich, and Rohde, *Change and Continuity in the 1996 and 1998 Elections*, 102, 104–106, 108, and 111. There are so few Nader voters that including them with Gore voters has only a negligible effect on these measures.

27. As we explain in chapter 3, we consider the South to include the eleven states of the old Confederacy. Because we cannot use this definition with either the 1944 NORC survey or the 1948 University of Michigan Survey Research Center survey, we have not included these years in our analysis of regional differences among the white electorate.

28. According to our analysis of the NES survey, 43 percent of Gore's southern vote came from African American voters. However, our analysis of the VNS poll suggests that 35 percent of his southern vote came from blacks.

29. The VNS data, however, show relatively little variation in the share of the union vote for Democratic presidential candidates between 1984 and 2000.

30. See Robert R. Alford, *Party and Society: The Anglo-American Democracies* (Chicago: Rand McNally, 1963); Seymour Martin Lipset, *Political Man: The Social Bases of Politics*, exp. ed. (Baltimore: Johns Hopkins University Press, 1981); Ronald Inglehart, *Modernization and Post-Modernization: Cultural, Economic, and Political Change in 43 Societies* (Princeton: Princeton University Press, 1997).

31. The variation in class voting is smaller if one focuses on class differences in the congressional vote, but the data clearly show a decline in class vote between 1952 and 2000. See Russell J. Dalton, *Citizen Politics: Public Opinion and Political Parties in Advanced Industrial Democracies*, 3d ed. (New York: Chatham House, 2002), 152.

32. As Table 5-2 shows, in 1996 class voting among whites was 6 percentage points. We redid this analysis defining social class according to the respondent's own occupation and class voting among whites was 7 points. As the table shows, in 1996 class voting for the entire electorate was 9 percentage points. When we redid this analysis defining social class according to the respondent's own occupation, class voting was 10 points.

33. As we saw in chapter 4, when we define social class according to the respondent's own occupation, the overall size of the working class falls and the overall size of the middle class grows. As the relatively small size of the working class in 2000 results largely from a redefinition in the way our measure of class is constructed, in these estimates we will assume that the sizes of the white working class and the white middle class were the same as in the 1996 NES.

34. See Mark N. Franklin, "The Decline of Cleavage Politics," in *Electoral Change: Responses to Evolving Social and Attitudinal Structures in Western Countries*, ed. Mark N. Franklin, Thomas T. Mackie, and Henry Valen, with others (Cambridge: Cambridge University Press, 1992), 383–405. See also Ronald Inglehart, *Modernization and Postmodernization*, 237–266.

35. Jeff Manza and Clem Brooks, *Social Cleavages and Political Change: Voter Alignments and U.S. Party Coalitions* (Oxford: Oxford University Press, 1999).

36. U.S. Department of Commerce, U.S. Bureau of the Census, *Statistical Abstract of the United States*, 120th ed. (Washington, D.C.: U.S. Government Printing Office, 2000), 62 (downloaded July 5, 2001, from the U.S. Census Bureau Web site: www.census.gov/prod/www.statistical-abstract-us.html). We list these states in the descending order of the estimated number of Jews. The estimates of the number of Jews in each state are based mainly upon estimates provided by local Jewish organizations.

37. Robert Huckfeldt and Carol Weitzel Kohfeld, *Race and the Decline of Class in American Politics* (Urbana: University of Illinois Press, 1989).

38. For evidence on this point, see Paul R. Abramson, *Political Attitudes in America: Formation and Change* (San Francisco: W. H. Freeman, 1983), 65–68.

39. Edward G. Carmines and James A. Stimson, *Issue Evolution: Race and the Transformation of American Politics* (Princeton: Princeton University Press, 1989). For a critique of their thesis, see Alan I. Abramowitz, "Issue Evolution Reconsidered: Racial Attitudes and Partisanship among the U.S. Electorate," *American Journal of Political Science* 38 (February 1994): 1–24.

40. James W. Ceaser and Andrew E. Busch, *Upside Down and Inside Out: The 1992 Elections and American Politics* (Lanham, Md.: Rowman and Littlefield, 1993), 168–171.

6. CANDIDATES, ISSUES, AND THE VOTE

1. This set of attitudes was first formulated and tested extensively in Angus Campbell et al., *The American Voter* (New York: Wiley, 1960), using data from what are now called the National Election Studies (NES) surveys. The authors based their conclusions primarily on data from a survey of the 1956 presidential election, a rematch between the Democrat Adlai E. Stevenson and the Republican (and this time incumbent) Dwight D. Eisenhower.

2. See, for example, Wendy M. Rahn et al., "A Social-Cognitive Model of Candidate Appraisal," *Information and Democratic Processes,* ed. John A. Ferejohn and James H. Kuklinski (Urbana: University of Illinois Press, 1990), 136–159, and sources cited therein. Ronald Reagan was generally perceived to be especially attractive on personal grounds, while Bill Clinton was the extreme version of the exact opposite. These considerations about Clinton helped shape Gore's campaign strategy, downplaying administration successes for fear of making Clinton's personal scandals more prominent as well.

3. In fact, there were more than three candidates running in 2000. In its pre-election interview, the National Election Studies (NES) survey also measured evaluations of the Reform Party candidate, Pat Buchanan. Because so few people rated Buchanan as their first choice, we exclude him from our analyses.

4. For the most extensive explication of the theory and tests in various electoral settings, see Gary W. Cox, *Making Votes Count: Strategic Coordination in the World's Electoral Systems* (New York: Cambridge University Press, 1997).

5. These elections are discussed in Paul R. Abramson, John H. Aldrich, and David W. Rohde, *Change and Continuity in the 1980 Elections,* rev. ed. (Washington, DC: CQ Press, 1983); Abramson, Aldrich, and Rohde, *Change and Continuity in the 1992 Elections,* rev. ed. (Washington, DC: CQ Press, 1995); and Abramson, Aldrich, and Rohde, *Change and Continuity in the 1996 and 1998 Elections* (Washington, DC: CQ Press, 1999).

6. Jerome H. Black, "The Multicandidate Calculus of Voting: Application to Canadian Federal Elections," *American Journal of Political Science* 22 (August

1978): 609–638; Bruce Cain, "Strategic Voting in Britain," *American Journal of Political Science* 22 (August 1978): 639–655.

7. See Paul R. Abramson et al., "'Sophisticated' Voting in the 1988 Presidential Primaries," *American Political Science Review* 86 (March 1992): 55–69. As Cox points out, strategic voting occurs in other electoral systems as well *(Making Votes Count)*. For recent evidence that voters may employ strategic considerations in runoff elections, see Paul R. Abramson and John H. Aldrich, "Were Voters Strategic?" in *The Elections in Israel—1999*, ed. Asher Arian and Michal Shamir (Albany, N.Y.: SUNY Press, 2002), 33–44.

8. William H. Riker, *Liberalism Against Populism: A Confrontation Between the Theory of Democracy and the Theory of Social Choice* (San Francisco: W. H. Freeman, 1982): 85–88.

9. Bear in mind, however, that there is a slight pro-Gore bias in the 2000 NES survey (see chapter 5).

10. See Duncan Black, *The Theory of Committees and Elections* (Cambridge: Cambridge University Press, 1958), for a summary of Condorcet's writings on the subject. See also Riker, *Liberalism Against Populism*.

11. See Paul R. Abramson et al., "Third-Party and Independent Candidates in American Politics: Wallace, Anderson, and Perot," *Political Science Quarterly* 110 (fall 1995): 349–367; Abramson, Aldrich, and Rohde, *Change and Continuity in the 1996 and 1998 Elections*, 120–121.

12. According to the Voter News Service (VNS) exit poll, 47 percent of the Nader voters said they would have voted for Gore in a Gore-Bush race, 21 percent said they would have voted for Bush, and 32 percent said they would not have voted. See Gerald M. Pomper, "The Presidential Elections," *The Elections of 2000*, ed. Gerald M. Pomper et al. (New York: Chatham House, 2001), 152.

13. For an analysis of how the candidates' campaign strategies in 1986 shaped the voters' decisions, see John H. Aldrich and Thomas Weko, "The Presidency and the Election Campaign: Framing the Choice in 1996," *The Presidency and the Political System*, 6th ed., ed. Michael Nelson (Washington, D.C.: CQ Press, 2000).

14. These measures were first used in the NES survey of the 1968 election. They were used extensively in presidential election surveys beginning in 1972. The issue measures used in chapter 7 were also used extensively beginning in the 1970s. Therefore, in this and the following two chapters, we restrict our attention to the past eight elections.

15. The median is based on the assumption that respondents can be ranked from most conservative to most liberal. The number of respondents who are more liberal than the median (or who see a candidate as more liberal than the median) is equal to the number who are more conservative (or see the candidate as more conservative) than the median. Because there are only 7 points on these scales, and because many respondents will choose any given point, the median is computed using a procedure that derives a median for grouped data.

16. The NES uses printed survey instruments when conducting in-person interviews, giving cards to the respondents as illustrated in Figure 6-2. Phone

surveys require a different type of issue question, and to avoid problems of comparison, we do not analyze issues voting for those surveyed by telephone. As a result, we consider the random half of the respondents who were interviewed in person.

In the NES survey "1" is the most conservative response on the government services and spending scale, but it is the most liberal response on the other scales. To increase comparability, we have "reversed" the government services and spending scale, so that "1" in the text, tables, and figures corresponds to the response, "Other people feel that it is important for the government to provide many more services even if it means an increase in spending," while "7" corresponds to the other endpoint.

17. Campbell et al., *American Voter*, 168–187.

18. Before 1996, the NES interviewers did not ask those who failed to place themselves on an issue scale where they thought the candidates stood. In 1996 and 2000 they asked respondents who did not place themselves on an issue where the candidates stood. Therefore, before 1996 those who failed to meet the first criterion were not able to meet any of the remaining ones. Although some people who express no preference on an issue might know the positions of one or both candidates, it is difficult to see how they could vote based on those perceptions if they had no opinion of their own.

19. In order to maintain comparability with previous election surveys, for 1996 and 2000 we have excluded respondents who did not place themselves on an issue scale from columns II, III, and IV, of Table 6-4. As we do not know the preferences of these respondents on the issue, we have no way to measure the way their issue preferences may have affected their vote.

20. For details, see Abramson, Aldrich, and Rohde, *Change and Continuity in the 1980 Elections*, Table 6-3, 130; Abramson, Aldrich, and Rohde, *Change and Continuity in the 1984 Elections*, rev. ed., (Washington, D.C.: CQ Press, 1987), Table 6-2, 174; and Abramson, Aldrich, and Rohde, *Change and Continuity in the 1988 Elections*, rev. ed. (Washington, D.C.: CQ Press, 1991), Table 6-2, 165; Abramson, Aldrich, and Rohde, *Change and Continuity in the 1992 Elections*, Table 6-6, 186; and Abramson, Aldrich, and Rohde, *Change and Continuity in the 1996 and 1998 Elections*, Table 6-6, 135.

21. Although this is evidence that most people claim to have issue preferences, it does not demonstrate that they do. For example, evidence indicates that some use the midpoint of the scale (point 4) as a means of answering the question even if they have ill-formed preferences. See John H. Aldrich et al., "The Measurement of Public Opinion about Public Policy: A Report on Some New Issue Question Formats," *American Journal of Political Science* 26 (May 1982): 391–414.

22. Morris P. Fiorina, *Retrospective Voting in American National Elections* (New Haven: Yale University Press, 1981).

23. We use "apparent issue voting" to emphasize several points. First, voting involves too many factors to infer that closeness to a candidate on any one issue was the cause of the voter's choice. The issue similarity may have been purely

coincidental, or it may have been only one of many reasons the voter supported that candidate. Second, we use the median perception of the candidates' positions rather than the voter's own perception. Third, the relationship between issues and the vote may be caused by rationalization. Voters may have decided to support a candidate for other reasons and also may have altered their own issue preferences or misperceived the positions of the candidates to align themselves more closely with their already favored candidate. See Richard A. Brody and Benjamin I. Page, "Comment: The Assessment of Policy Voting," *American Political Science Review* 66 (June 1972): 450–458.

24. Many individuals, of course, placed the candidates at different positions than the public did on average. Using average perceptions, however, reduces the effect of individuals rationalizing their perceptions of candidates to be consistent with their own vote, rather than voting for the candidate whose views are actually closer to their own.

25. This procedure counts every issue as equal in importance. It also assumes that what matters is that the voter is closer to the candidate on an issue; it does not consider how much closer the voter is to one candidate or the other.

26. Scores of +5, +6, and +7 were called strongly Republican, while similarly negative scores were called strongly Democratic. Scores of +3 and +4 were called moderately Republican, −3 and −4 were called moderately Democratic. Scores of +1 and +2 were called slightly Republican, with −1 and −2 being called slightly Democratic. A score of 0 was called neutral.

27. See Abramson, Aldrich, and Rohde, *Change and Continuity in the 1992 Elections*, 191; Abramson, Aldrich, and Rohde, *Change and Continuity in the 1996 and 1998 Elections*, 140.

7. PRESIDENTIAL PERFORMANCE AND CANDIDATE CHOICE

1. See Paul R. Abramson, John H. Aldrich, and David W. Rohde, *Change and Continuity in the 1992 Elections*, rev. ed. (Washington, DC: CQ Press, 1995), 203–208.

2. V. O. Key Jr., *Politics, Parties, and Pressure Groups*, 5th ed. (New York: Crowell, 1964), 568. Key's theory of retrospective voting is most fully developed in *The Responsible Electorate: Rationality in Presidential Voting, 1936–1960* (Cambridge: Harvard University Press, 1966).

3. Anthony Downs, *An Economic Theory of Democracy* (New York: Harper and Row, 1957).

4. Morris P. Fiorina, *Retrospective Voting in American National Elections* (New Haven: Yale University Press, 1981), 83.

5. See Benjamin I. Page, *Choices and Echoes in Presidential Elections: Rational Man and Electoral Democracy* (Chicago: University of Chicago Press, 1978). He argues that "party cleavages" distinguish the party at the candidate and mass levels.

6. Arthur H. Miller and Martin P. Wattenberg, "Throwing the Rascals Out: Policy and Performance Evaluations of Presidential Candidates, 1952–1980," *American Political Science Review* 79 (June 1985): 359–372. In this chapter, we do not examine retrospective evaluations of foreign policy, due both to the low concern over it in the public and (as a consequence) to the relative paucity of data about them.

7. Each respondent assesses governmental performance on the problem he or she considers the most important. In the seven most recent surveys, respondents were asked, "How good a job is the government doing in dealing with this problem—a good job, only fair, or a poor job?"

8. Negative evaluations are not surprising. After all, if you thought the government had been doing a good job with the problem, then it probably would not be your major concern. This reasoning seems to underlie the very low proportion of respondents in every survey who thought the government was doing a good job with their most important concern. Because the 1972 NES survey provided different responses, it cannot be compared directly with the other surveys. But even in 1972, relatively few respondents thought the government was being "very helpful."

9. See Gerald H. Kramer, "Short-Term Fluctuations in U.S. Voting Behavior, 1896–1964," *American Political Science Review* 65 (March 1971): 131–143; Fiorina, *Retrospective Voting;* M. Stephen Weatherford, "Economic Conditions and Electoral Outcomes: Class Differences in the Political Response to Recession," *American Journal of Political Science* 22 (November 1978): 917–938; D. Roderick Kiewiet and Douglas Rivers, "A Retrospective on Retrospective Voting," *Political Behavior* 6, no. 4 (1984): 369–393; D. Roderick Kiewiet, *Macroeconomics and Micropolitics: The Electoral Effects of Economic Issues* (Chicago: University of Chicago Press, 1983); Michael S. Lewis-Beck, *Economics and Elections: The Major Western Democracies* (Ann Arbor: University of Michigan Press, 1988); and Michael B. MacKuen, Robert S. Erikson, and James A. Stimson, "Peasants or Bankers? The American Electorate and the U.S. Economy," *American Political Science Review* 86 (September 1992): 597–611.

10. John E. Mueller, *War, Presidents, and Public Opinion* (New York: Wiley, 1973); Edward R. Tufte, *Political Control of the Economy* (Princeton: Princeton University Press, 1978). For a perceptive critique of the business cycle formulation, see James E. Alt and K. Alec Chrystal, *Political Economics* (Berkeley: University of California Press, 1983).

11. Fiorina, *Retrospective Voting.*

12. In the 1984 and 1988 surveys, this question was asked in both the preelection and the postelection waves of the survey. Since attitudes held by the public before the election are what count in influencing their choices, we use the first question. In both surveys, approval of Reagan's performance was more positive in the postelection interview: 66 percent approved of his performance in 1984, and 68 percent approved in 1988.

13. To construct this measure, we awarded respondents 2 points if they approved of the president's performance, 1 if they had no opinion, and 0 if they disapproved. Second, respondents received 2 points if they thought the government was doing a good job in handling the most important problem facing the country, 1 if they thought the government was doing only a fair job, and 0 if they thought it was doing a poor job. Finally, respondents received 2 points if they thought the incumbent president's party would do a better job at handling the most important problem, 1 point if they thought there was no difference between the parties, and 0 if they thought the challenger's party would do a better job. For all three questions, "don't know" and "not ascertained" responses were scored as 1, but respondents with more than one such response were excluded from the analysis. Scores on our measure were the sum of the individual values for the three questions, and thus ranged from a low of 0 (strongly against the incumbent's party) to 6 (strongly for the incumbent's party). Thus, the measure has seven possible values, corresponding to the seven categories in Figure 7-1.

14. See Paul R. Abramson, John H. Aldrich, and David W. Rohde, *Change and Continuity in the 1996 and 1998 Elections* (Washington, D.C.: CQ Press, 1999), 158–159.

15. For data from the 1976 and 1980 elections, see Paul R. Abramson, John H. Aldrich, and David W. Rohde, *Change and Continuity in the 1980 Elections*, rev. ed. (Washington, D.C.: CQ Press, 1983), 155–157, Table 7-8; for data from the 1984 elections, see Abramson, Aldrich, and Rohde, *Change and Continuity in the 1984 Elections*, rev. ed. (Washington, D.C.: CQ Press, 1987), 203–204, Table 7-8; for data from the 1988 elections, see Abramson, Aldrich, and Rohde, *Change and Continuity in the 1988 Elections*, rev. ed. (Washington, DC: CQ Press, 1991), 195–198, Table 7-7; and for data for the 1996 election, see Abramson, Aldrich, and Rohde, *Change and Continuity in the 1996 and 1998 Elections*, 159–161. The small number of 7-point issue scales included in the NES survey precluded performing this analysis with 1992 data.

8. PARTY LOYALTIES, POLICY PREFERENCES, AND THE VOTE

1. Angus Campbell et al., *The American Voter* (New York: Wiley, 1960). For a recent statement of the "standard" view of party identification, see Warren E. Miller, "Party Identification, Realignment, and Party Voting: Back to the Basics," *American Political Science Review* 85 (June 1991): 557–568; and Warren E. Miller and J. Merrill Shanks, *The New American Voter* (Cambridge: Harvard University Press, 1996), 117–183.

2. Campbell, *The American Voter*, 121. See also Morris P. Fiorina, *Retrospective Voting in American National Elections* (New Haven: Yale University Press, 1981), 85–86.

3. For the full wording of the party identification questions, see chapter 4, note 53.

4. Most "apoliticals" in this period were African Americans living in the South. As they were disenfranchised, questions about their party loyalties were essentially meaningless to them. For the most detailed discussion of how the NES creates its summary measure of party identification, see Arthur H. Miller and Martin P. Wattenberg, "Measuring Party Identification: Independent or No Partisan Preference?" *American Journal of Political Science* 27 (February 1983): 106–121.

5. For evidence of the relatively high level of partisan stability among individuals over time, see M. Kent Jennings and Gregory B. Markus, "Partisan Orientations over the Long Haul: Results from the Three-Wave Political Socialization Panel Study," *American Political Science Review* 78 (December 1984): 1000–1018.

6. V. O. Key Jr., *The Responsible Electorate: Rationality in Presidential Voting, 1936–1960* (Cambridge: Harvard University Press, 1966).

7. Morris P. Fiorina, "An Outline for a Model of Party Choice," *American Journal of Political Science* 21 (August 1977): 601–625; Fiorina, *Retrospective Voting.*

8. Benjamin I. Page provides evidence of this. See Page, *Choices and Echoes in Presidential Elections: Rational Man and Electoral Democracy* (Chicago: University of Chicago Press, 1978). Anthony Downs, in *An Economic Theory of Democracy* (New York: Harper and Row, 1957), develops a theoretical logic for such consistency in party stances on issues and ideology over time. For more recent theoretical and empirical development, see John H. Aldrich, *Why Parties? The Origin and Transformation of Political Parties in America* (Chicago: University of Chicago Press, 1995).

9. There is some controversy over how to classify these independent leaners. Some argue that they are mainly "hidden" partisans who should be considered identifiers. For the strongest statement of this position, see Bruce E. Keith et al., *The Myth of the Independent Voter* (Berkeley: University of California Press, 1992). In our view, however, the evidence on the proper classification of independent leaners is mixed. On balance, the evidence suggests that they are more partisan than independents with no partisan leanings, but less partisan than weak partisans. See Paul R. Abramson, *Political Attitudes in America: Formation and Change* (San Francisco: W. H. Freeman, 1983), 80–81, 95–96. For an excellent discussion of this question, see Herbert B. Asher, "Voting Behavior Research in the 1980s: An Examination of Some Old and New Problem Areas," in *Political Science: The State of the Discipline,* ed. Ada W. Finifter (Washington, D.C.: American Political Science Association, 1983), 357–360.

10. See, for example, Martin P. Wattenberg, *The Decline of American Political Parties, 1952–1996* (Cambridge: Harvard University Press, 1998).

11. These surveys were conducted annually, except for 1979, 1981, 1992, 1995, 1997, and 1999.

12. For the relationship between party identification among white voters to the three leading candidates in 1968, 1980, 1992, and 2000, see Paul R. Abramson,

John H. Aldrich, and David W. Rohde, *Change and Continuity in the 1996 and 1998 Elections* (Washington, D.C.: CQ Press, 1999), Table 8-9, 186–187.

13. See Larry M. Bartels, "Partisanship and Voting Behavior, 1952–1996," *American Journal of Political Science* 44 (January, 2000): 35–50.

14. Bernard R. Berelson, Paul F. Lazarsfeld, and William N. McPhee, *Voting: A Study of Opinion Formation in a Presidential Campaign* (Chicago: University of Chicago Press, 1954).

15. See Richard A. Brody and Benjamin I. Page, "Comment: The Assessment of Policy Voting," *American Political Science Review* 66 (June 1972): 450–458; Page and Brody, "Policy Voting and the Electoral Process: The Vietnam War Issue," *American Political Science Review* 66 (September 1972): 979–995; and Fiorina, " Outline for a Model of Party Choice."

16. The question measuring approval of the president's handling of economic policy was not asked in NES surveys before 1984. In our study of these earlier elections, an alternative measure of economic retrospective evaluations was created and shown to be nearly as strongly related to party identification. See Paul R. Abramson, John H. Aldrich, and David W. Rohde, *Change and Continuity in the 1984 Elections,* rev. ed. (Washington, D.C.: CQ Press, 1987), Table 8-6, 221. We also found nearly as strong a relationship between partisanship and perceptions of which party would better handle the economy in the data from 1972, 1976, and 1980 as from later surveys reported here. See Abramson, Aldrich, and Rohde, *Change and Continuity in the 1980 Elections,* rev. ed. (Washington, D.C.: CQ Press, 1983), 170, Table 8-6, 173.

17. For a description of this measure, see chapter 6. Since this measure uses the median placement of the candidates on the issue scales in the full sample, much of the projection effect is eliminated. For the relationship between party identification and the balance of issues measure in 1972, see Abramson, Aldrich, and Rohde, *Change and Continuity in the 1980 Elections,* Table 8-5, 171.

18. Recall that the summary measure of retrospective evaluations includes the presidential approval measure, the job the government is doing in handling the most important problem the respondent sees facing the country, and which party would do better at handling that problem. This measure could not be created from the 1972 election data. The presidential approval measure was asked of a different half of the sample than the most important problem questions in that survey.

19. See, for example, Aldrich, *Why Parties?*

20. Two important articles assess some of these relationships: Gregory B. Markus and Philip E. Converse, "A Dynamic Simultaneous Equation Model of Electoral Choice," *American Political Science Review* 73 (December 1979): 1055–1070; and Benjamin I. Page and Calvin C. Jones, "Reciprocal Effects of Policy Preferences, Party Loyalties and the Vote," *American Political Science Review* 73 (December 1979): 1071–1089. For a brief discussion of these articles, see Richard G. Niemi and Herbert F. Weisberg, *Controversies in Voting Behavior,* 2d ed. (Washington, D.C.: CQ Press, 1984), 89–95. For an excellent discussion of complex models of voting behavior and the role of party identification in these

models, see Asher, "Voting Behavior Research in the 1980s," 341–354. For another excellent introduction to some of these issues, see Richard G. Niemi and Herbert F. Weisberg, "Is Party Identification Stable?" in *Controversies in Voting Behavior*, 3d ed., ed. Richard G. Niemi and Herbert F. Weisberg (Washington, D.C.: CQ Press, 1993), 268–283.

INTRODUCTION TO PART 3

1. Between 1952 and 1988 seventeen states rescheduled their gubernatorial elections from presidential election years to nonpresidential years. Steven J. Rosenstone and John Mark Hansen estimate that in 1952 nearly half of the electorate lived in states in which there was a competitive gubernate election. In the 1988 election, according to their estimates, only 12 percent of the electorate lived in states with a competitive gubernatorial election. See Rosenstone and Hansen, *Mobilization, Participation, and Democracy in America* (New York: Macmillan, 1993), 183. In all eleven gubernatorial elections in 2000, both major parties ran candidates. According to our estimates, 12 percent of the voting-age population lived in these states. Rosenstone and Hansen argue that this change in the scheduling of elections is a major factor contributing to the decline of electoral participation.

2. The Republicans won a majority over the Democrats in 1918 after the United States, under Democrat Woodrow Wilson, entered World War I in April 1917. Republicans retained control through 1928, thereby winning six elections in a row. They lost control in 1930 after the 1929 Wall Street crash, which occurred under Republican Herbert C. Hoover.

3. After the 1952 election the Republicans held a 221 to 213 vote majority with one representative classified as miscellaneous.

4. At the beginning of the Forty-seventh Congress in 1881, the Republicans and Democrats each had thirty-seven senators; two senators were classified as miscellaneous.

9. CANDIDATES AND OUTCOMES IN 2000

1. The independents were Bernard Sanders of Vermont, who was first elected to the House in 1990, and Virgil H. Goode Jr. of Virginia, serving since 1996. Sanders had previously been elected mayor of Burlington, Vermont, running as a Socialist. For convenience in presenting results, we will treat him as a Democrat throughout this chapter. This seems reasonable because he has received his committee assignments from the Democratic Party, and the Democrats did not field a candidate against him in 1994 or 1998. In 2000 a maverick Democrat ran without party support, receiving only 5 percent of the vote, while Sanders won reelection with 69 percent to 18 percent for his Republican opponent.

Goode was initially elected as a Democrat but left the party in early 2000. We will count him as a Republican in this chapter because he receives his committee assignments from that party, and the GOP did not run a candidate against him in 2000.

2. *Incumbents* here is used only for elected incumbents. This includes all members of the House because the only way to become a representative is by election. In the case of the Senate, however, vacancies may be filled by appointment. We do not count appointed senators as incumbents. Special mention also needs to be made of the Louisiana House races. Louisiana has an unusual open primary system in which candidates from all parties run against one another in a single primary. If no candidate receives a majority, the top two vote getters, regardless of party, face each other in a runoff in November. In Louisiana contests we count the last round in each district as the controlling race. If that round involved only candidates of a single party, the race is counted as a primary and the winner as unopposed in the general election. If candidates of both parties were involved in the final round, it is treated as a general election.

3. The scandal involved the House Bank, in which many members deposited their paychecks. The Bank had a policy to honor the checks of members, even if they didn't have sufficient funds in their accounts to cover the checks. During 1991 the public learned about this practice and that there were hundreds of members who together had written thousands of these "overdrafts." Many of the members who had written the most overdrafts retired or were defeated in the primary or the general election. For more details, see Gary C. Jacobson, *The Politics of Congressional Elections,* 5th ed. (New York: Addison-Wesley Longman, 2001), 176–179.

4. The Republicans had won control of the House in eight consecutive elections from 1894 through 1908, far short of the Democratic series of successes.

5. In 1994 Democrats won 19 percent of Republican House seats and no GOP Senate seats. In their own open seats, they retained only 31 percent in the House and 0 percent in the Senate. See Paul R. Abramson, John H. Aldrich, and David W. Rohde, *Change and Continuity in the 1992 Elections,* rev. ed. (Washington, D.C.: CQ Press, 1995), 319. For a recent detailed analysis of open-seat house contests, see Ronald Keith Gaddie and Charles S. Bullock III, *Elections to Open Seats in the U.S. House* (Lanham, Md.: Rowman and Littlefield, 2000).

6. The regional breakdowns used in this chapter are as follows: *East*—Connecticut, Delaware, Maine, Massachusetts, New Hampshire, New Jersey, New York, Pennsylvania, Rhode Island, and Vermont; *Midwest*—Illinois, Indiana, Iowa, Kansas, Michigan, Minnesota, Nebraska, North Dakota, Ohio, South Dakota, and Wisconsin; *West*—Alaska, Arizona, California, Colorado, Hawaii, Idaho, Montana, Nevada, New Mexico, Oregon, Utah, Washington, and Wyoming; *South*—Alabama, Arkansas, Florida, Georgia, Louisiana, Mississippi, North Carolina, South Carolina, Tennessee, Texas, and Virginia; *Border*—Kentucky, Maryland, Missouri, Oklahoma, and West Virginia. This classification

differs somewhat from the one used in earlier chapters (and in chapter 10), but it is commonly used for congressional analysis.

7. In the Senate the minority leader is Trent Lott of Mississippi, and the assistant minority leader is Don Nickles of Oklahoma. In the House the majority leader is Dick Armey, and the majority whip is Tom DeLay. Both are from Texas.

8. Over the years changes in the southern electorate have also made southern Democratic constituencies more like northern Democratic constituencies and less like Republican constituencies, North or South. These changes also appear to have enhanced the homogeneity of preferences within the partisan delegations in Congress. See David W. Rohde, "Electoral Forces, Political Agendas, and Partisanship in the House and Senate," in *The Postreform Congress,* ed. Roger H. Davidson (New York: St. Martin's, 1992), 27–47.

9. The exit polls were done by the Voters News Service, and the results were downloaded from the CNN/All Politics Web site (www.cnn.com/ALLPOLITICS/). It should be noted, however, that when asked about their reaction to Clinton as a person, only 36 percent of the respondents were favorable and 60 percent were unfavorable. As we show in chapter 7, in the 2000 NES survey, 67 percent approved of Clinton's performance as president.

10. See Abramson, Aldrich, and Rohde, *Change and Continuity in the 1996 and 1998 Elections* (Washington, D.C.: CQ Press, 1999), 207–212.

11. Gary C. Jacobson, "A House and Senate Divided: The Clinton Legacy and the Congressional Elections of 2000," *Political Science Quarterly* 116 (spring 2001): 7–8.

12. *Washington Post,* July 9, 2000, A6.

13. See Abramson, Aldrich, and Rohde, *Change and Continuity in the 1992 Elections,* 329.

14. For a discussion of the increased role of national party organizations in congressional elections over the past two decades, see Paul S. Herrnson, *Congressional Elections,* 2d. ed. (Washington, D.C.: CQ Press, 1998), chap. 4.

15. *Roll Call,* April 7, 1999, 11.

16. Ibid., March 25, 1999, 13.

17. Ibid., February 25, 1999, 18.

18. *New York Times,* September 22, 1999, 20.

19. *The Hill,* April 21, 1999, 15.

20. *Washington Post,* May 8, 2000, A3.

21. See *Roll Call,* June 12, 2000, 15; ibid., March 13, 2000, 11; and *The Hill,* May 17, 2000, 1.

22. *The Hill,* September 6, 2000, 3.

23. *Roll Call,* February 7, 2000, 24.

24. Ibid., July 24, 2000, 1; and *The Hill,* October 4, 2000, 3.

25. Ibid., September 18, 2000, 10.

26. Ibid., June 26, 2000, 24.

27. *Washington Post,* October 8, 2000, A12.

28. *New York Times,* October 7, 2000, A11.

29. Richard F. Fenno Jr., *Home Style: House Members in Their Districts* (Boston: Little, Brown, 1978). For a discussion of how relationships between representatives and constituents have changed over time, see Fenno, *Congress at the Grassroots* (Chapel Hill: University of North Carolina Press, 2000).

30. For example, analysis of Senate races in 1988 indicated that both the political quality of the previous office held and the challenger's political skills had an independent effect on the outcome of the race. See Peverill Squire, "Challenger Quality and Voting Behavior in U.S. Senate Elections," *Legislative Studies Quarterly* 27 (May 1992): 247–263. For systematic evidence on the impact of candidate quality in House races, see Gary C. Jacobson, *The Electoral Origins of Divided Government: Competition in U.S. House Elections, 1946–1988* (Boulder, Colo.: Westview, 1990), chap. 4.

31. Data on office backgrounds were taken from various issues of *Congressional Quarterly Weekly Report.*

32. Data on earlier years are taken from our studies of previous national elections.

33. Note that the figures in this paragraph include races in which only one of the parties fielded a candidate, as well as contests where both did.

34. See Jacobson, *Electoral Origins of Divided Government;* Jon R. Bond, Cary Covington, and Richard Fleischer, "Explaining Challenger Quality in Congressional Elections," *Journal of Politics* 47 (May 1985): 510–529; and David W. Rohde, "Risk-Bearing and Progressive Ambition: The Case of Members of the U.S. House of Representatives," *American Journal of Political Science* 23 (February 1979): 1–26.

35. L. Sandy Maisel and Walter J. Stone, "Determinants of Candidate Emergence in U.S. House Elections: An Exploratory Study," *Legislative Studies Quarterly* 22 (February 1997): 70–96.

36. See Peverill Squire, "Preemptive Fund-raising and Challenger Profile in Senate Elections," *Journal of Politics* 53 (November 1991): 1150–1164.

37. Jeffrey S. Banks and D. Roderick Kiewiet, "Explaining Patterns of Candidate Competition in Congressional Elections," *American Journal of Political Science* 33 (November 1989): 997–1015.

38. David Canon, *Actors, Athletes, and Astronauts: Political Amateurism in the United States Congress* (Chicago: University of Chicago Press, 1990).

39. See Kenneth J. Cooper, "Riding High Name Recognition to Hill," *Washington Post*, December 24, 1992, A4.

40. See Thomas E. Mann and Raymond E. Wolfinger, "Candidates and Parties in Congressional Elections," *American Political Science Review* 74 (September 1980): 617–632.

41. See David R. Mayhew, "Congressional Elections: The Case of the Vanishing Marginals," *Polity* 6 (spring 1974): 295–317; Robert S. Erikson, "Malapportionment, Gerrymandering, and Party Fortunes in Congressional Elections," *American Political Science Review* 66 (December 1972): 1234–1245;

Warren Lee Kostroski, "Party and Incumbency in Postwar Senate Elections: Trends, Patterns, and Models," *American Political Science Review* 67 (December 1973): 1213–1234.

42. Edward R. Tufte, "Communication," *American Political Science Review* 68 (March 1974): 211–213. The communication involved a discussion of Tufte's earlier article "The Relationship Between Seats and Votes in Two-Party Systems," *American Political Science Review* 67 (June 1973): 540–554.

43. See John A. Ferejohn, "On the Decline in Competition in Congressional Elections," *American Political Science Review* 71 (March 1977): 166–176; Albert D. Cover, "One Good Term Deserves Another: The Advantage of Incumbency in Congressional Elections," *American Journal of Political Science* 21 (August 1977): 523–541; and Albert D. Cover and David R. Mayhew, "Congressional Dynamics and the Decline of Competition in Congressional Elections," in *Congress Reconsidered*, 2d ed., ed. Lawrence C. Dodd and Bruce I. Oppenheimer (Washington, D.C.: CQ Press, 1981), 62–82.

44. Morris P. Fiorina, *Congress: Keystone of the Washington Establishment*, 2d ed. (New Haven: Yale University Press, 1989), esp. chaps. 4–6.

45. See several conflicting arguments and conclusions in the following articles published in the *American Journal of Political Science* 25 (August 1981): John R. Johannes and John C. McAdams, "The Congressional Incumbency Effect: Is It Casework, Policy Compatibility, or Something Else? An Examination of the 1978 Election" (512–542); Morris P. Fiorina, "Some Problems in Studying the Effects of Resource Allocation in Congressional Elections" (543–567); Diana Evans Yiannakis, "The Grateful Electorate: Casework and Congressional Elections" (568–580); and McAdams and Johannes, "Does Casework Matter? A Reply to Professor Fiorina" (581–604). See also Johannes, *To Serve the People: Congress and Constituency Service* (Lincoln: University of Nebraska Press, 1984), esp. chap. 8; and Albert D. Cover and Bruce S. Brumberg, "Baby Books and Ballots: The Impact of Congressional Mail on Constituent Opinion," *American Political Science Review* 76 (June 1982): 347–359. The evidence in Cover and Brumberg for a positive electoral effect is quite strong, but the result may be applicable only to limited circumstances.

46. Ferejohn, "On the Decline of Competition," 174.

47. Cover, "One Good Term," 535.

48. More recent research shows that the link between party identification and voting has strengthened again. See Larry M. Bartels, "Partisanship and Voting Behavior, 1952–1996," *American Journal of Political Science* 44 (January 2000), 35–50.

49. The data for 1974–1990 were taken from "House Incumbents' Average Vote Percentage," *Congressional Quarterly Weekly Report*, November 10, 1990, 3800. The 1994 figures are from the *New York Times*, November 10, 1994. The data for 1992 and 1996 are from *USA Today*, November 8, 1996, 4A. The data for 1998 and 2000 were computed by the authors.

50. For an excellent analysis of the growth of, and reasons for, anti-Congress sentiment, see John R. Hibbing and Elizabeth Theiss-Morse, *Congress as Public Enemy* (New York: Cambridge University Press, 1995).

51. Fenno, *Home Style,* 163–169.

52. However, we note again that these results ignore races which do not have candidates from both major parties. There was a sharp increase in these races in 1998: ninety-four, compared with only seventeen in 1996 and fifty-two in 1994. The number was almost as large in 2000: eighty-one.

53. The body of literature on this subject has grown to be quite large. Some salient examples, in addition to those cited later, are: Gary C. Jacobson, *Money in Congressional Elections* (New Haven: Yale University Press, 1980); Jacobson, "Parties and PACs in Congressional Elections," in *Congress Reconsidered,* 4th ed., ed. Lawrence C. Dodd and Bruce I. Oppenheimer (Washington, D.C.: CQ Press, 1989), 117–152; Jacobson and Samuel Kernell, *Strategy and Choice in Congressional Elections,* 2d ed. (New Haven: Yale University Press, 1983); John A. Ferejohn and Morris P. Fiorina, "Incumbency and Realignment in Congressional Elections," in *The New Direction in American Politics,* ed. John E. Chubb and Paul E. Peterson (Washington, D.C.: Brookings Institution, 1985), 91–115.

54. See Jacobson, *Electoral Origins of Divided Government,* 63–65.

55. The 1990 data were taken from Phil Duncan, ed., *Politics in America, 1992: The 102nd Congress,* (Washington, D.C.: CQ Press, 1991); the 1992 data are from the *Washington Post,* May 26, 1993, A17. For both elections the data include all incumbents, not just those who had major-party opposition.

56. See Gary C. Jacobson and Samuel Kernell, *Strategy and Choice in Congressional Elections.*

57. The 2000 spending data were obtained from the Web site of the Federal Election Commission (www.fec.gov).

58. These figures from the Federal Election Commission include a substantial number of races with unavailable spending data for challengers. Thus final data may be somewhat different.

59. Thirteen of the 32 targeted representatives (41 percent) lost. HOTLINE November 6, 1997.

60. See Abramson, Aldrich, and Rohde, *Change and Continuity in the 1996 and 1998 Elections,* 218–223, and the earlier work cited there.

61. See Jacobson, *Electoral Origins of Divided Government,* 54–55, and the work cited in note 49.

62. Donald Philip Green and Jonathan S. Krasno, "Salvation for the Spendthrift Incumbent: Reestimating the Effects of Campaign Spending in House Elections," *American Journal of Political Science* 32 (November 1988): 884–907.

63. Gary C. Jacobson, "The Effects of Campaign Spending in House Elections: New Evidence for Old Arguments," *American Journal of Political Science* 34 (May 1990): 334–362. Green and Kranno's response can be found in the same issue on pages 363–372.

64. Alan I. Abramowitz, "Explaining Senate Election Outcomes," *American Political Science Review* 82 (June 1988): 385–403. Alan Gerber, "Estimating the Effect of Campaign Spending on Senate Election Outcomes Using Instrumental Variables," *American Political Science Review* 92 (June 1998): 401–411.

65. Gary C. Jacobson, "Campaign Spending and Voter Awareness of Congressional Candidates" (paper presented at the annual meeting of the Public Choice Society, New Orleans, May 11–13, 1977), 16.

66. Challengers were categorized as having strong experience if they had been elected U.S. representative, to statewide office, to the state legislature, or to countywide or citywide office (for example, mayor, prosecutor, and so on).

67. Paul R. Abramson, John H. Aldrich, and David W. Rohde, *Change and Continuity in the 1980 Elections*, rev. ed. (Washington, D.C.: CQ Press, 1983), 202–203. See also Paul Gronke, *The Electorate, the Campaign, and the Office: A Unified Approach to Senate and House Elections* (Ann Arbor: University of Michigan Press, 2001).

68. Other Democratic Senate winners in 2000 who spent millions of their own money include Maria Cantwell of Washington and Mark Dayton of Minnesota.

69. Quoted in Angela Herrin, "Big Outside Money Backfired in GOP Loss of Senate to Dems," *Washington Post,* November 6, 1986, A46.

70. See David W. Rohde, *Parties and Leaders in the Postreform House* (Chicago: University of Chicago Press, 1991), especially chap. 3; and Rohde, "Electoral Forces, Political Agendas, and Partisanship in the House and Senate," in *The Postreform Congress,* ed. Roger H. Davidson (New York: St. Martin's Press, 1992), 27–47.

71. See Abramson, Aldrich, and Rohde, *Change and Continuity in the 1992 Elections,* rev. ed., 339–342; and John H. Aldrich and David W. Rohde, "The Transition to Republican Rule in the House: Implications for Theories of Congressional Politics," *Political Science Quarterly* 112 (winter, 1997–98): 541–567.

72. *Roll Call,* November 16, 2001, 1.

73. *The Hill,* January 10, 2001, 19.

74. List of the membership of the two groups can be found in Brian Nutting and H. Amy Stern, eds., *CQ's Politics in America 2002* (Washington, D.C.: CQ Press, 2001), 1135.

75. See *The Hill,* November 22, 2000, 3.

76. Ibid., December 6, 2000, 4.

77. *Roll Call,* December 11, 2000, 14.

78. *Washington Post,* January 6, 2001, A1.

79. See *Roll Call,* December 7, 2000, 19.

80. *The Hill,* January 17, 2001, 3.

81. Associated Press, January 25, 2001. (Downloaded from the *New York Times,* Web site: www.nytimes.com).

82. *USA Today,* January 19, 2001, 6A; based on a Gallup poll.

83. *Washington Post,* February 5, 2001, A1.

84. *The Hill,* February 14, 2001, 16.

85. See *Congressional Quarterly Weekly Report,* May 5, 2001, 1009–1011.

86. *Roll Call,* March 8, 2001, 6.

87. *Washington Post,* December 7, 2000, A23.

88. *Roll Call,* April 26, 2001, 1.

89. *The Hill,* May 9, 2001, 1.

90. *Congressional Quarterly Weekly Report,* May 26, 2001, 1246.

91. *Washington Post,* May 25, 2001, A15.

92. *Washington Post,* June 7, 2001, A1.

93. *The Hill,* July 5, 2001, 5.

94. See *Washington Post,* May 26, 2001, A1.

95. Earlier research indicated that for these purposes voters may tend to regard a president whose predecessor either died or resigned from office as a continuation of the first president's administration. Therefore these data are organized by term of administration, rather than term of president. See Abramson, Aldrich, and Rohde, *Change and Continuity in the 1980 Elections,* rev. ed., 252–253.

96. Edward R. Tufte, "Determinants of the Outcomes of Midterm Congressional Elections," *American Political Science Review* 69 (September 1975): 812–826; and Tufte, *Political Control of the Economy* (Princeton: Princeton University Press, 1978); Jacobson and Kernell, *Strategy and Choice in Congressional Elections.*

97. The Jacobson-Kernell hypothesis was challenged by Richard Born in "Strategic Politicians and Unresponsive Voters," *American Political Science Review* 80 (June 1986): 599–612. Born argued that economic and approval data at the time of the election were more closely related to outcomes than were parallel data from earlier in the year. Jacobson, however, offered renewed support for the hypothesis in an analysis of both district-level and aggregate data. See Gary C. Jacobson, "Strategic Politicians and the Dynamics of House Elections, 1946–86," *American Political Science Review* 83 (September 1989): 773–793.

98. Alan I. Abramowitz, Albert D. Cover, and Helmut Norpoth, "The President's Party in Midterm Elections: Going from Bad to Worse," *American Journal of Political Science* 30 (August 1986): 562–576.

99. Bruce I. Oppenheimer, James A. Stimson, and Richard W. Waterman, "Interpreting U.S. Congressional Elections: The Exposure Thesis," *Legislative Studies Quarterly* 11 (May 1986): 228.

100. Robin F. Marra and Charles W. Ostrom Jr., "Explaining Seat Change in the U.S. House of Representatives 1950–86," *American Journal of Political Science* 33 (August 1989): 541–569.

101. In addition, evidence indicates that divided government may also reduce the vulnerability of the president's party in midterms. See Stephen P. Nicholson and Gary M. Segura, "Midterm Elections and Divided Government: An Information Driven Theory of Electoral Volatility," *Political Research Quarterly* 52 (September 1999): 609–629.

102. The gaining states were: Arizona, Florida, Georgia, and Texas (two seats each) and California, Colorado, Nevada, and North Carolina (one each). The

losers were: New York and Pennsylvania (two each) and Connecticut, Illinois, Indiana, Michigan, Mississippi, Ohio, Oklahoma, and Wisconsin (one each).

103. The seven states are: Alaska, Delaware, Montana, North Dakota, South Dakota, Vermont, and Wyoming.

104. See *Congressional Quarterly Weekly Report,* January 13, 2001, 114–119.

105. Much has been written about the political consequences of this process. See, for example, the articles in the special issue (April 1995) of *American Politics Quarterly* on "Legislative Redistricting in the 1980s and 1990s," and the many other studies referenced therein. See also David T. Canon, *Race, Redistricting, and Representation* (Chicago: University of Chicago Press, 1999).

106. See *Congressional Quarterly Weekly Report,* July 1, 1995, 1944–1946.

107. See ibid., April 21, 2001, 882.

108. See *National Journal,* May 5, 2001, 1346.

109. *Roll Call,* March 26, 2001, 15.

110. Ibid., March 15, 2001, 11.

111. Ibid., December 11, 2000, 9.

112. *USA Today,* July 26, 2001, 1A, 8A. For a set of analyses of the role of soft money in the 1998 congressional elections, see David B. Magleby, ed., *Outside Money* (Lanham, Md.: Rowman and Littlefield, 2000).

113. *Washington Post,* July 8, 2001, A5.

114. Ibid.

115. The first case was *Nixon v. Shrink Missouri Government PAC,* 328 U.S. 377, and the second was *Federal Election Commission v. Colorado Republican Federal Campaign Committee,* 150 L.Ed.2d. 461.

10. THE CONGRESSIONAL ELECTORATE IN 2000

1. As we saw in chapter 5, the 2000 NES survey results overreported the Democratic share of the presidential vote. There is also a small pro-Democratic bias in the House vote. According to the 2000 NES survey, the Democrats received 52 percent of the major-party vote; official results show that the actual national vote was almost evenly divided. To simplify the presentation of the data, we have eliminated from consideration votes for minor-party candidates in all the tables in this chapter. Furthermore, to ensure that our study of choice is meaningful, in all tables except 10-1 and 10-2 we include only voters who lived in congressional districts in which both major parties ran candidates.

2. We will confine our attention in this section to voting for the House because this group of voters is more directly comparable to the presidential electorate. We here employ the same definitions for social and demographic categories as used in chapters 4 and 5.

3. See Larry M. Bartels, "Partisanship and Voting Behavior, 1952–1996," *American Journal of Political Science* 44 (January 2000): 35–50.

4. Paul R. Abramson, John H. Aldrich, and David W. Rohde, *Change and Continuity in the 1980 Elections,* rev. ed. (Washington, D.C.: CQ Press, 1983), 213–216.

5. Alan I. Abramowitz, "Choices and Echoes in the 1978 U.S. Senate Elections: A Research Note," *American Journal of Political Science* 25 (February 1981): 112–118; and Abramowitz, "National Issues, Strategic Politicians, and Voting Behavior in the 1980 and 1982 Congressional Elections," *American Journal of Political Science* 28 (November 1984): 710–721.

6. Robert S. Erikson and Gerald C. Wright, "Voters, Candidates, and Issues in Congressional Elections," in *Congress Reconsidered,* 3d ed., ed. Lawrence C. Dodd and Bruce I. Oppenheimer (Washington, D.C.: CQ Press, 1985), 91–116.

7. Robert S. Erikson and Gerald C. Wright, "Voters, Candidates, and Issues in Congressional Elections," in *Congress Reconsidered,* 6th ed., ed. Lawrence C. Dodd and Bruce I. Oppenheimer (Washington, D.C.: CQ Press, 1997), 148–150.

8. Robert S. Erikson and Gerald C. Wright, "Voters, Candidates, and Issues in Congressional Elections," in *Congress Reconsidered,* 7th ed., ed. Lawrence C. Dodd and Bruce I. Oppenheimer (Washington, D.C.: CQ Press, 2001), 84–85. See also Stephen Ansolabehere, James M. Snyder Jr., and Charles Stewart III, "Candidate Positioning in U.S. House Elections," *American Journal of Political Science* 45 (January 2001): 136–159.

9. Albert D. Cover, "One Good Term Deserves Another: The Advantage of Incumbency in Congressional Elections," *American Journal of Political Science* 21 (August 1977): 523–541. Cover includes in his analysis not only strong and weak partisans, but also independents with partisan leanings.

10. It should be noted that the 2000 NES survey may contain biases that inflate the percentage who report voting for House incumbents. For a discussion of this problem in earlier years, see Robert B. Eubank and David John Gow, "The Pro-Incumbent Bias in the 1978 and 1980 Election Studies," *American Journal of Political Science* 27 (February 1983): 122–139; and Gow and Eubank, "The Pro-Incumbent Bias in the 1982 Election Study," *American Journal of Political Science* 28 (February 1984): 224–230.

11. Richard F. Fenno Jr., "If, as Ralph Nader Says, Congress Is 'The Broken Branch,' How Come We Love Our Congressmen So Much?" in *Congress in Change: Evolution and Reform,* ed. Norman J. Ornstein (New York: Praeger, 1975), 277–287. This theme is expanded and analyzed in Richard F. Fenno Jr., *Home Style: House Members in Their Districts* (Boston: Little, Brown, 1978).

12. Abramson, Aldrich, and Rohde, *Change and Continuity in the 1980 Elections,* rev. ed., 220–221.

13. Opinion on this last point is not unanimous, however. See Richard Born, "Reassessing the Decline of Presidential Coattails: U.S. House Elections from 1952–80," *Journal of Politics* 46 (February 1984): 60–79.

14. John A. Ferejohn and Randall L. Calvert, "Presidential Coattails in Historical Perspective," *American Journal of Political Science* 28 (February 1984): 127–146.

15. Randall L. Calvert and John A. Ferejohn, "Coattail Voting in Recent Presidential Elections," *American Political Science Review* 77 (June 1983): 407–419.

16. James E. Campbell and Joe A. Sumners, "Presidential Coattails in Senate Elections," *American Political Science Review* 84 (June 1990): 513–524.

17. See Paul R. Abramson, John H. Aldrich, and David W. Rohde, *Change and Continuity in the 1996 and 1998 Elections* (Washington, D.C.: CQ Press, 1999), 246–248, for the 1996 data. For the locations of data from earlier years, see note 15 on page 337 of that volume.

11. THE 2002 CONGRESSIONAL ELECTIONS

1. The independent was Bernard Sanders of Vermont. As we indicated in chapter 9 (note 1), we treat Sanders as a Democrat in our analyses. In 2002 Virgil H. Goode Jr. of Virginia, who had been a self-declared independent (chapter 9, note 1), became a Republican.

2. Recall that, as with the data in chapter 9, we count as incumbent senators only those who were elected to the office. Thus Sen. Jean Carnahan of Missouri is not counted as an incumbent because she was appointed.

3. Eleven of these twelve cases are districts added by reapportionment. The twelfth district added by reapportionment had an incumbent Republican who switched districts. The remaining open seat in this category was in Pennsylvania's Eighteenth District. It was so radically redesigned that previous party control could not be assigned.

4. These data are drawn from Norman J. Ornstein, Thomas E. Mann, and Michael J. Malbin, eds., *Vital Statistics on Congress 1995–1996* (Washington, D.C.: Congressional Quarterly, 1996), 53; updated with 1998 data.

5. "Cook Election Preview" (a supplement to *National Journal*), April 27, 2002, 12.

6. *Rothenberg Political Report,* May 8, 2002, 10.

7. *Rothenberg Political Report,* May 8, 2002, 1.

8. Kerry Kantin, "GOP Fears Poll Lead Could Hurt," *The Hill,* February 6, 2002, 1, 44.

9. *Roll Call,* February 4, 2002, 1, 24.

10. *Roll Call,* July 18, 2002, 1.

11. *Roll Call,* September 23, 2002, 1.

12. See Chris Cillizza, "No Wave In Sight," *Roll Call,* September 23, 2002, 1.

13. *Washington Post,* November 3, 2002, B1.

14. *New York Times*/CBS News poll taken October 27–31, 2002. Data are from www.newyorktimes.com, November 26, 2002.

15. Ibid.

16. *USA Today,* January 16, 2002, 4A.

17. James Carney and John F. Dickerson, "W. and the 'Boy Genius'," *Time,* November 18, 2002, 43–44.

18. *USA Today,* July 2, 2002, 4A.

19. *New York Times*/CBS News poll, op. cit. fn. 13.

20. Howard Fineman, "How Bush Did It," *Newsweek,* November 18, 2002, 35.

21. *Washington Post,* January 19, 2002, A2.

22. See Allison Stevens, "Dems Abandon Gun Issue in 2002 Races," *The Hill,* May 22, 2002, 1; and Lauren W. Whittington, "Vets Tout Service," *Roll Call,* September 30, 2002, 13.

23. *Washington Post,* November 5, 2002, A6.

24. *New York Times*/CBS News poll, op. cit. fn. 13.

25. Recent research has raised questions about whether voter turnout among the U.S. citizen population has declined. See Michael P. McDonald and Samuel L. Popkin, "The Myth of the Vanishing Voter," *American Political Science Review* 95 (December 2001), 963–974. For an important critique of the McDonald and Popkin thesis, see Thomas E. Patterson, *The Vanishing Voter: Public Involvement in an Age of Uncertainty* (New York: Knopf, 2002), 8–11.

26. See Paul R. Abramson, John H. Aldrich, and David W. Rohde, *Change and Continuity in the 1996 and 1998 Elections* (Washington, D.C.: CQ Press, 1999), 257–260.

27. *Washington Post,* October 31, 2002, A21.

28. *Washington Post,* September 30, 2002, A5.

29. *Roll Call,* September 26, 2002, 13.

30. *Washington Post,* November 10, 2002, A7. "Soft money" is donations to parties and political groups that can be used for TV ads, mass mailings, get-out-the-vote activities, and so on, as long as these do not advocate the election of a particular candidate. Through the election of 2002, these donations were not limited by law, but they are affected by the new campaign finance law.

31. *Roll Call,* October 21, 2002, 1, 17.

32. *Washington Post,* November 8, 2002, A10.

33. Ibid.

34. The 1998 figures are from the *New York Times,* November 6, 1998, A22; the 2002 data are from *USA Today,* November 7, 2002, 4A.

35. *The Rothenberg Political Report,* December 18, 2002, 9.

36. *Roll Call,* January 7, 2002, 9.

37. *Roll Call,* April 4, 2002, 7.

38. *Washington Post,* October 4, 2001, A8; *Washington Post,* October 12, 2001, A3; *Roll Call,* October 15, 2001, 1.

39. *Washington Post,* January 23, 2002, A2; *CQ Weekly,* June 22, 2002, 1661.

40. See chapter 9, fn. 102 for the list of states gaining and losing seats.

41. See Bob Benenson, Gregory L. Giroux, and Jonathan Allen, "Safe House: Incumbents Face Worry-Free Election," *CQ Weekly,* May 18, 2002, 1274–1286.

42. For a discussion of the increased role of national party organizations in congressional elections over the past two decades, see Paul S. Herrnson, *Congressional Elections,* 2d. ed. (Washington, D.C.: CQ Press, 1998), ch. 4.

43. For a discussion of the 1994 congressional elections, see Paul R. Abramson, John H. Aldrich, and David W. Rohde, *Change and Continuity in the 1992 Elections,* rev. ed. (Washington, D.C.: CQ Press, 1995), 317–336.

44. Ibid., 257–282.

45. The Pew Research Center, http://people-press.org/results/, downloaded October 11, 2002.

46. These figures on the 2002 vote, and those used later in this chapter, are taken from the *New York Times,* November 7, 2002, B10–B11. Data on races that were not complete by that time were taken from the online version of the *Washington Post,* www.washingtonpost.com.

47. The data on candidate experience were taken from the online versions of the *New York Times* (www.newyorktimes.com) and the *Washington Post* (www.washingtonpost.com).

48. These numbers, and those cited below, are derived from Paul R. Abramson, John H. Aldrich, and David W. Rohde, *Change and Continuity in the 1988 Elections,* rev. ed. (Washington, D.C.: CQ Press, 1991), 240, 322; Abramson, Aldrich, and Rohde, *Change and Continuity in the 1992 Elections,* rev. ed., 274, 334; and Abramson, Aldrich, and Rohde, *Change and Continuity in the 1996 and 1998 Elections,* 214, 261.

49. Herrnson, *Congressional Elections,* 40.

50. Carney and Dickerson, "W. and the 'Boy Genius' ," op. cit., 42–43.

51. Fineman, "How Bush Did It," op. cit., 32.

52. *Roll Call,* February 25, 2002, 16.

53. *Roll Call,* March 31, 2002, 14.

54. *Roll Call,* December 17, 2002, 1.

55. Federal Elections Commission, www.fec.gov, downloaded January 10, 2003.

56. *USA Today,* October 17, 2002, 1A.

57. Political Money Line, www.tray.com, downloaded December 20, 2002.

58. *Roll Call,* October 21, 2002, 4.

59. Thomas B. Edsall, "GOP Wins Race for Cash, Too," *Washington Post,* November 7, 2002, A37.

60. Ibid.

61. *Washington Post,* November 7, 2002, A27.

62. Ibid., A27, A33.

63. *Washington Post,* November 24, 2002, A4.

64. See *CQ Weekly,* November 23, 2002, 3072–3073.

65. *Washington Post,* November 20, 2002, A5.

66. *Washington Post,* November 15, 2002, A4.

67. *Washington Post,* November 11, 2002, A4.

68. *Washington Post,* November 25, 2002, A1.

69. Katharine Q. Seelye, "Industry Seeking Rewards from GOP-Led Congress," *New York Times,* December 3, 2002. Downloaded from www.nytimes.com.

70. *Roll Call,* November 18, 2002, 1, 18.

71. See John H. Aldrich and David W. Rohde, "The Republican Revolution and the House Appropriations Committee," *Journal of Politics* 62 (February 2000), 1–33.

72. *Roll Call,* November 18, 2002, 7.

73. *The Hill,* November 27, 2002, 1.

74. *The Hill,* June 26, 2002, 1.

75. *CQ Weekly,* November 16, 2002, 3012.

76. *Washington Post,* December 7, 2002, A6.

77. *USA Today,* December 12, 2002, 18A.

78. *CQ Weekly,* December 14, 2002, 3248; *USA Today,* December 12, 2002, 18A.

79. *USA Today,* December 13, 2002, 4A.

80. These quotations and other details in this paragraph are taken from Elisabeth Bulmer, "Bush Orchestrates an Ouster," *New York Times,* December 21, 2002. Downloaded from www.nytimes.com.

81. David Firestone, "Leadership in Recapturing the Senate Pushed Frist into the Spotlight," *New York Times,* December 21, 2002. Downloaded from www.nytimes.com.

82. Adam Nagourney and Janet Elder, "Positive Ratings for the GOP, If Not Its Policy," *New York Times,* November 26, 2002. Downloaded from www.nytimes.com.

83. *National Journal,* December 14, 2002, 3682.

84. *CQ Weekly,* December 7, 2002, 3171.

85. *National Journal,* September 7, 2002, 2543.

86. *New York Times,* November 2, 2002, A1.

87. *Washington Post,* November 27, 2002, A1, A4.

88. *Roll Call,* December 2, 2002, 1, 10; *USA Today,* December 4, 2002, 2A.

89. *Roll Call,* November 18, 2002, 9.

90. *Roll Call,* November 14, 2002, 11.

91. *Roll Call,* December 5, 2002, 11.

92. *Roll Call,* December 12, 2002, 7.

93. For Dorgan the strongest opponent would probably be former GOP governor Ed Schaeffer, whereas for Feingold it would be Health and Human Services secretary and former governor Tommy Thompson.

94. *Roll Call,* December 19, 2002, 9.

95. *Washington Post,* November 7, 2002, A39.

96. *USA Today,* November 11, 2002, 11A.

INTRODUCTION TO PART 4

1. Nicolò Machiavelli, *The Prince,* 2d ed., trans. Harvey Mansfield Jr. (Chicago: University of Chicago Press, 1998), 98.

2. Jefferson was accused of fathering a son by his slave, Sally Hemmings. Jackson was accused of marrying his wife, Rachel Donaldson Robards, while she was still married to her first husband; these charges were technically true.

And Cleveland was accused of fathering an out-of-wedlock son before he became president.

3. Recent tests, however, suggest the charges against Jefferson were probably true.

4. Arend Lijphart, *Democracies: Patterns of Majoritarian and Consensus Government in Twenty-One Countries* (New Haven: Yale University Press, 1984). Finland and France could also be considered to have presidential systems, but in Finland the president and prime minister have roughly equal powers. Since Lijphart's book was written, experience has shown that France is not as much of a presidential system as Lijphart thought. He wrote, "The French president is not only the head of state but also the real head of government; the prime minister is the president's principal advisor and assistant" (93). This appeared to be true in 1984, but after the 1986 legislative election it became clear that the president's power is diminished substantially if he does not have support in the National Assembly.

5. In France a new election is held to select a new president for a full presidential term. This has occurred twice: once in 1969, after Charles de Gaulle resigned, and once in 1974, after Georges Pompidou died in office.

12. THE 2000 AND 2002 ELECTIONS AND THE FUTURE OF AMERICAN POLITICS

1. Maurice Duverger, *Political Parties: Their Organization and Activity in the Modern World*, trans. Barbara North and Robert North (New York: Wiley, 1963), 308–309. In this book we have used the term *majority* to mean winning more than half the vote. It is clear that Duverger used the term *majorité* to mean what we would call a plurality of the vote—that is, more votes than any other party received.

2. Other democracies that might also be classified as having, or as having had, a dominant party, include Chile, Columbia, Denmark, Iceland, India, Norway, and Venezuela. The four countries discussed here are those examined extensively in a book edited by T. J. Pempel, *Uncommon Democracies: The One-Party Dominant Regimes* (Ithaca, N.Y.: Cornell University Press, 1990). See also Asher Arian and Samuel H. Barnes, "The Dominant Party System: A Neglected Model of Democratic Stability," *Journal of Politics* 36 (August 1974), 592–614, which compares Italy and Israel. *Mapai* is the Hebrew acronym for the Israel Workers' Party. In 1968 Mapai merged with two smaller parties and became the Alignment. That coalition fell apart in 1984. In 1999 the Labor Party ran in a joint list with two smaller parties under the name "One Israel," but it is now generally referred to as the Labor Party. See also Gøsta Epsing-Andersen, "Single-Party Democracies in Sweden: The Saga of Social Democracy," in *Uncommon Democracies*, 33–57, and Scott C. Flanagan et al., *The Japanese Voter* (New Haven: Yale University Press, 1991).

3. Duverger, *Political Parties*, 312.

4. Admittedly, Duverger was vague about the reasons why dominant parties tend to fall. He suggests that they become too bureaucratized to govern effectively. Although dominant parties lost their dominance in Israel, Italy, Sweden, and Japan, a variety of factors led to their decline.

5. Asher Arian, *The Second Republic: Politics in Israel* (Chatham, N.J.: Chatham House, 1998), 111.

6. There was no Knesset election in 2001. The Knesset abandoned the direct election of the prime minister in 2001.

7. For an analysis of the gradual decline of the Christian Democrats, see Sidney Tarrow, "Maintaining Hegemony in Italy: 'The Softer They Rise, the Slower They Fall!' " in *Uncommon Democracies*, 306–332.

8. Maurice Duverger, *Les Partis Politique*, 3d ed. (Paris: Armand Colin, 1958), 352. The English-language translation we use appeared in 1963 (see note 1).

9. See, for example, Michael Nelson, "Constitutional Aspects of the Elections," in *The Elections of 1988*, ed. Michael Nelson (Washington, D.C.: CQ Press, 1989), 161–209. See also Byron E. Shafer, "The Election of 1988 and the Structure of American Politics: Notes on Explaining a New Political Order," *Electoral Studies* 8 (April 1989), 5–21,

10. The other exception was in 1934 during Franklin D. Roosevelt's first term.

11. James W. Ceaser and Andrew W. Busch, *Losing to Win: The 1996 Elections and American Politics* (Lanham, Md.: Rowman and Littlefield, 1997), 170, 171.

12. James W. Ceaser and Andrew W. Busch, *The Perfect Tie: The True Story of the 2000 Presidential Election* (Lanham, Md.: Rowman and Littlefield, 2001), 17–47.

13. In both years the percentage was the same when independents who felt closer to the two major parties were included in the analysis. We are grateful to Tom Rice of the National Opinion Research Center for providing us with the results of the 2002 General Social Survey.

14. John B. Judis and Ruy Teixeira, *The Emerging Democratic Majority* (New York: Scribner, 2002).

15. Ibid., 116. For a brief critique of the Judis-Teixeira thesis, see David Kusnet, "Wait Till Next Year," *New York Times Book Review*, November 24, 2002, 35.

16. For more information on primaries and caucuses, see Eric M. Appleman, "More Primaries," http://www.gwu.edu/~action/2004/chrnothp.html, accessed January 22, 2003.

17. The last Republican convention to take more than a single ballot to choose its presidential nominee was the convention of 1948, when it took three ballots to nominate Thomas E. Dewey.

18. Wilson Carey McWilliams, "The Meaning of the Election," in *The Election of 2000: Reports and Interpretations*, ed. Gerald M. Pomper et al. (New York: Chatham House, 2001), 182.

19. Ibid., 191.

20. Richard L. Berke, "Bush Appears to Have Straddled the G.O.P. Divide," *New York Times,* August 11, 2001, A9.

21. Donald Green and Eric Schickler, "Winning a Battle, Not a War," *New York Times,* November 12, 2002, A31. For a discussion of the importance of party identification by these authors, see Donald Green, Bradley Palmquist, and Eric Schickler, *Partisan Hearts and Minds: Political Parties and the Social Identities of Voters* (New Haven: Yale University Press, 2002).

22. Arend Lijphart, *Electoral Systems and Party Systems: A Study of Twenty-Seven Democracies, 1945–1990* (New York: Oxford University Press, 1994), 160–162.

23. "The Mouse that Roared," *The Economist,* September 30, 1995, 32.

24. Under proportional representation, an environmentalist party may be successful with a relatively small share of the vote. For example, in the 1988 German Bundestag election, the Green Party won only 6.7 percent of the second-ballot votes, but it won 7 percent of the seats and became part of the governing coalition. In the 2002 election the Greens won 8.6 percent of the second-ballot votes and captured 9 percent of the seats, again becoming part of the governing coalition formed after the election.

25. Joseph A. Schlesinger, *Political Parties and the Winning of Political Office* (Ann Arbor: University of Michigan Press, 1991).

26. For a discussion of the distinction between selective and collective goods, see Mancur Olson Jr., *The Logic of Collective Action: Public Goods and the Theory of Groups* (Cambridge: Harvard University Press, 1965). For an application of this difference to the study of political parties, see John H. Aldrich, *Why Parties?: The Origin and Transformation of Political Parties in America* (Chicago: University of Chicago Press, 1995).

27. We are grateful to Joseph A. Schlesinger for reminding us of this point.

28. Philip E. Converse, *The Dynamics of Party Support: Cohort-Analyzing Party Identification* (Beverly Hills, Calif.: Sage, 1976).

29. As we saw in chapter 4, in the 2000 General Social Survey, 20 percent of the respondents were independents who leaned toward neither the Republican nor the Democratic Party. In 2002, 20 percent of the respondents were once again classified as independents who leaned toward neither party.

30. The "hidden partisan" thesis is advanced most forcefully by Bruce E. Keith et al., *The Myth of the Independent Voter* (Berkeley: University of California Press, 1992). For the strongest evidence supporting the position that independence indicates a lack of commitment to a political party, see Martin P. Wattenberg, *The Decline of American Political Parties, 1952–1996* (Cambridge: Harvard University Press, 1998), 31–46. See also Wattenberg, *The Rise of Candidate-Centered Politics: Presidential Elections of the 1980s* (Cambridge: Harvard University Press, 1991), 31–46.

Suggested Readings

(Readings preceded by an asterisk include materials on the 2000 elections.)

Chapter 1: The Nomination Struggle

Abramson, Paul R., John H. Aldrich, Phil Paolino, and David W. Rohde. "'Sophisticated' Voting in 1988 Presidential Primaries." *American Political Science Review* 86 (March 1992): 55–69.

Abramson, Paul R., John H. Aldrich, and David W. Rohde. "Progressive Ambition among United States Senators: 1972–1988." *Journal of Politics* 49 (February 1987): 3–35.

Aldrich, John H. *Before the Convention: Strategies and Choices in Presidential Nomination Campaigns.* Chicago: University of Chicago Press, 1980.

Bartels, Larry M. *Presidential Primaries and the Dynamics of Public Choice.* Princeton: Princeton University Press, 1988.

Brams, Steven J. *The Presidential Election Game.* New Haven: Yale University Press, 1978, 1–79.

*Ceaser, James W., and Andrew E. Busch. *The Perfect Tie: The True Story of the 2000 Presidential Election.* Lanham, Md.: Rowman and Littlefield, 2001, 49–131.

*Crotty, William. "The Presidential Primaries: Triumph of the Frontrunners." In *America's Choice 2000,* edited by William Crotty. Boulder, Colo.: Westview, 2001, 95–114.

*Mayer, William G. "The Presidential Nominations." In *The Election of 2000: Reports and Interpretations,* by Gerald M. Pomper with colleagues. New York: Chatham House, 2001, 12–45.

*Morton, Rebecca, and Kenneth C. Williams. *Learning by Voting: Sequential Choices in Presidential Primaries and Other Elections.* Ann Arbor: University of Michigan Press, 2001.

Norrander, Barbara. "The End Game in Post-Reform Presidential Nominations." *Journal of Politics* 62 (November 2000): 999–1013.

Polsby, Nelson W., and Aaron Wildavsky. *Presidential Elections: Strategies and Structures of American Politics,* 10th ed. New York: Chatham House, 2000, 97–150.

*Stanley, Harold W. "The Nominations: The Return of the Party Leaders." In *The Elections of 2000,* edited by Michael Nelson. Washington, D.C.: CQ Press, 2001, 27–53.

Chapter 2: The General Election Campaign

Brams, Steven J. *The Presidential Election Game.* New Haven: Yale University Press, 1978, 80–133.

*Campbell, James E. "The Curious and Close Presidential Campaign of 2000." In *America's Choice 2000,* edited by William Crotty. Boulder, Colo.: Westview, 2001, 115–137.

*Ceaser, James W., and Andrew E. Busch. *The Perfect Tie: The True Story of the 2000 Presidential Election.* Lanham, Md.: Rowman and Littlefield, 2001, 133–170.

*Crotty, William. "The Election of 2000: Close, Chaotic, and Unforgettable." In *America's Choice 2000,* edited by William Crotty. Boulder, Colo. Westview, 2001, 1–35.

*Hershey, Marjorie Randon. "The Campaign and the Media." In *The Election of 2000: Reports and Interpretations,* by Gerald M. Pomper with colleagues. New York: Chatham House, 2001, 46–72.

———. "The Constructed Explanation: Interpreting Election Results in the 1984 Presidential Race." *Journal of Politics* 54 (November 1992): 943–976.

*Kerbel, Matthew Robert. "The Media: Old Frames in a Time of Transition." In *The Elections of 2000,* edited by Michael Nelson. Washington, D.C.: CQ Press, 2001, 109–132.

Kessel, John H. *Presidential Campaign Politics: Coalition Strategies and Citizen Response,* 4th ed. Pacific Groves, Calif.: Brooks/Cole, 1992.

Polsby, Nelson W., and Aaron Wildavsky. *Presidential Elections: Strategies and Structures of American Politics,* 10th ed. New York: Chatham House, 2000, 150–259.

Shaw, Daron R. "The Methods Behind the Madness: Presidential Electoral College Strategies, 1988–1996." *Journal of Politics* 61 (November 1999): 893–913.

Thomas, Dan B., and Larry R. Bass. "The Postelection Campaign: Competing Constructions of the Clinton Victory in 1992." *Journal of Politics* 58 (May 1996): 309–331.

Chapter 3: The Election Results

Abramson, Paul R., John H. Aldrich, Phil Paolino, and David W. Rohde. "Third-Party and Independent Candidates in American Politics: Wallace, Anderson, and Perot." *Political Science Quarterly* 110 (fall 1995): 349–367.

Black, Earl, and Merle Black. *The Vital South: How Presidential Elections Are Won.* Cambridge: Harvard University Press, 1992.

Burnham, Walter Dean. *Critical Elections and the Mainsprings of American Politics.* New York: Norton, 1970.

Chubb, Jerome M., William H. Flanigan, and Nancy H. Zingale. *Partisan Realignment: Voters, Parties, and Government in American History.* Beverly Hills., Calif.: Sage, 1980.

Kelley, Stanley, Jr. *Interpreting Elections.* Princeton: Princeton University Press, 1983.

Lamis, Alexander P. *The Two-Party South,* 2d exp. ed. New York: Oxford University Press, 1990.

Nardulli, Peter F. "The Concept of a Critical Realignment, Electoral Behavior, and Political Change." *American Political Science Review* 89 (March 1995): 10–22.

*Scammon, Richard M., Alice V. McGillivray, and Rhodes Cook, eds. *America Votes 24: A Handbook of Contemporary American Election Statistics.* Washington, D.C.: CQ Press, 2001.

Schlesinger, Joseph A. *Political Parties and the Winning of Office.* Ann Arbor: University of Michigan Press, 1991.

Sundquist, James L. *Dynamics of the Party System: Alignment and Realignment of Political Parties in the United States,* rev. ed. Washington, D.C.: Brookings Institution, 1983.

Chapter 4: Who Voted?

Aldrich, John H. "Rational Choice and Turnout." *American Journal of Political Science* 37 (February 1993): 246–278.

Ansolabehere, Stephen, and Shanto Iyengar. *Going Negative: How Attack Ads Shrink and Polarize the Electorate.* New York: Free Press, 1996.

Burnham, Walter Dean. "The Turnout Problem." In *Elections American Style,* edited by James A. Reichley. Washington, D.C.: Brookings Institution, 1987, 97–133.

*Conway, M. Margaret. "Political Participation in American Elections: Who Decides What?" In *America's Choice 2000,* edited by William Crotty. Boulder, Colo.: Westview, 2001, 79–94.

Hill, Kim Quaile, and Jan E. Leighley. "Political Parties and Class Mobilization in Contemporary United States Elections." *American Journal of Political Science* 40 (August 1996): 787–804.

*McDonald, Michael P., and Samuel L. Popkin. "The Myth of the Vanishing Voter." *American Political Science Review* 95 (December 2001): 963–974.

Miller, Warren E., and J. Merrill Shanks. *The New American Voter.* Cambridge: Harvard University Press, 1996, 95–114.

Putnam, Robert D. *Bowling Alone: The Collapse and Revival of American Community.* New York: Simon and Schuster, 2000.

Rosenstone, Steven J., and John Mark Hansen. *Mobilization, Participation, and Democracy in America.* New York: Macmillan, 1993.

Teixeira, Ruy A. *The Disappearing American Voter.* Washington, D.C.: The Brookings Institution, 1992.

Wolfinger, Raymond E., and Steven J. Rosenstone. *Who Votes?* New Haven: Yale University Press, 1980.

Chapter 5: Social Forces and the Vote

Alford, Robert R. *Party and Society: The Anglo-American Democracies.* Chicago: Rand McNally, 1963.

Axelrod, Robert. "Where the Votes Come From: An Analysis of Electoral Coalitions, 1952–1968." *American Political Science Review* 66 (March 1972): 11–20.

Dawson, Michael C. *Behind the Mule: Race and Class in American Politics.* Princeton: Princeton University Press, 1994.

Hamilton, Richard F. *Class and Politics in the United States.* New York: Wiley, 1972.

Huckfeldt, Robert, and Carol Weitzel Kohfeld. *Race and the Decline of Class in American Politics.* Urbana: University of Illinois Press, 1989.

Lipset, Seymour Martin. *Political Man: The Social Bases of Politics,* exp. ed. Baltimore: Johns Hopkins University Press, 1981.

Manza, Jeff, and Clem Brooks. *Social Cleavages and Political Change: Voter Alignments and U.S. Party Coalitions.* Oxford: Oxford University Press, 1999.

Miller, Warren E., and J. Merrill Shanks. *The New American Voter.* Cambridge: Harvard University Press, 1996, 212–282.

Norrander, Barbara. "The Evolution of the Gender Gap." *Public Opinion Quarterly* 63 (winter 1999): 566–576.

Stanley, Harold W., and Richard G. Niemi. "Party Coalitions in Transition: Partisanship and Group Support, 1952–96." In *Reelection 1996: How Americans Voted,* edited by Herbert F. Weisberg and Janet M. Box-Steffensmeier. New York: Chatham House, 1999, 162–180.

Tate, Katherine. *From Protest to Politics: The New Black Voters in American Elections,* enl. ed. Cambridge: Harvard University Press, 1994.

Chapter 6: Candidates, Issues, and the Vote

Campbell, Angus, Philip E. Converse, Warren E. Miller, and Donald E. Stokes. *The American Voter.* New York: Wiley, 1960, 168–265.

Carmines, Edward G., and James A. Stimson. *Issue Evolution: Race and the Transformation of American Politics.* Princeton: Princeton University Press, 1989.

Gerber, Elisabeth R., and John E. Jackson. "Endogenous Preferences and the Study of Institutions." *American Political Science Review* 87 (September 1993): 639–656.

Popkin, Samuel L. *The Reasoning Voter: Communication and Persuasion in Presidential Campaigns.* Chicago: University of Chicago Press, 1991.

Shafer, Byron E., and William J. M. Claggett. *The Two Majorities: The Issue Context of Modern American Politics.* Baltimore: Johns Hopkins University Press, 1995.

Stimson, James A., Michael B. MacKuen, and Robert S. Erikson. "Dynamic Representation." *American Political Science Review* 89 (September 1995): 543–565.

Chapter 7: Presidential Performance and Candidate Choice

Downs, Anthony. *An Economic Theory of Democracy.* New York: Harper and Row, 1957.

Fiorina, Morris P. *Retrospective Voting in American National Elections.* New Haven: Yale University Press, 1981.

*Frankovic, Kathleen A., and Monika L. McDermott. "Public Opinion in the 2000 Election: The Ambivalent Electorate." In *The Election of 2000: Reports and Interpretations,* by Gerald M. Pomper with colleagues. New York: Chatham House, 2001, 73–91.

Key, V. O., Jr. *The Responsible Electorate: Rationality in Presidential Voting, 1936–1960.* Cambridge: Harvard University Press, 1966.

Kiewiet, D. Roderick. *Macroeconomics and Micropolitics: The Electoral Effects of Economic Issues.* Chicago: University of Chicago Press, 1983.

Lewis-Beck, Michael S. *Economics and Elections: The Major Western Democracies.* Ann Arbor: University of Michigan Press, 1988.

MacKuen, Michael B., Robert S. Erikson, and James A. Stimson. "Peasants or Bankers? The American Electorate and the U.S. Economy." *American Political Science Review* 86 (September 1992): 597–611.

Riker, William H. *Liberalism Against Populism: A Confrontation Between the Theory of Democracy and the Theory of Social Choice.* San Francisco: W. H. Freeman, 1982.

Tufte, Edward R. *Political Control of the Economy*. Princeton: Princeton University Press, 1978.

Chapter 8: Party Loyalties, Policy Preferences, and the Vote

Abramowitz, Alan I., and Kyle Saunders. "Ideological Realignment in the U.S. Electorate." *Journal of Politics* 60 (August 1998): 634–652.

Abramson, Paul R. *Political Attitudes in America: Formation and Change*. San Francisco: W. H. Freeman, 1983.

Aldrich, John H. *Why Parties? The Origin and Transformation of Political Parties in America*. Chicago: University of Chicago Press, 1995.

Bartels, Larry M. "Partisanship and Voting Behavior, 1952–1996." *American Journal of Political Science* 44 (January 2000): 35–50.

Campbell, Angus, Philip E. Converse, Warren E. Miller, and Donald E. Stokes. *The American Voter*. New York: Wiley, 1960, 120–167.

Keith, Bruce E., David B. Magleby, Candice J. Nelson, Elizabeth Orr, Mark C. Westlye, and Raymond E. Wolfinger. *The Myth of the Independent Voter*. Berkeley: University of California Press, 1992.

Miller, Warren E., and J. Merrill Shanks. *The New American Voter*. Cambridge: Harvard University Press, 1996, 117–185.

Niemi, Richard G., and Herbert F. Weisberg. "How Much Does Politics Affect Party Identification?" In *Controversies in Voting Behavior*, 4th ed., edited by Richard G. Niemi and Herbert F. Weisberg. Washington, D.C.: CQ Press, 2001, 322–337.

Rapoport, Ronald B. "Partisanship Change in a Candidate-Centered Era." *Journal of Politics* 59 (February 1997): 185–199.

Wattenberg, Martin P. *The Decline of American Political Parties, 1952–1996*. Cambridge: Harvard University Press, 1998.

Chapter 9: Candidates and Outcomes in 2000

Brunell, Thomas L., and Bernard Grofman. "Explaining Divided U.S. Senate Delegations, 1788–1996: A Realignment Approach." *American Political Science Review* 92 (June 1998): 391–399.

*Ceaser, James W., and Andrew E. Busch. *The Perfect Tie: The True Story of the 2000 Presidential Election.* Lanham, Md.: Rowman and Littlefield, 2001, 213–239.

Fenno, Richard E., Jr. *Home Style: House Members in Their Districts.* Boston: Little, Brown, 1978.

Fiorina, Morris P. *Congress: Keystone of the Washington Establishment,* 2d ed. New Haven: Yale University Press, 1989.

*Herrnson, Paul S. "The Congressional Elections." In *The 2000 Election: Reports and Interpretations,* by Gerald M. Pomper with colleagues. New York: Chatham House, 2001, 155–176.

*Jackson, John S., III. "The Congressional Races: Continuing Battleground for the Parties." In *America's Choice 2000.* Boulder, Colo.: Westview, 2001, 138–162.

*Jacobson, Gary C. "Congress: Elections and Stalemate." In *The Elections of 2000,* edited by Michael Nelson. Washington, D.C. CQ Press, 2001, 185–209.

———. *The Politics of Congressional Elections,* 5th ed. New York: Longman, 2001, 1–100, 141–270.

Rohde, David W. *Parties and Leaders in the Postreform House.* Chicago: University of Chicago Press, 1991.

Schlesinger, Joseph A. *Ambition and Politics: Political Careers in the United States.* Chicago: Rand McNally, 1966.

Chapter 10: The Congressional Electorate in 2000

Abramowitz, Alan I., and Jeffrey A. Segal. *Senate Elections.* Ann Arbor: University of Michigan Press, 1992.

Beck, Paul Allen, Lawrence Baum, Aage R. Clausen, and Charles E. Smith Jr. "Patterns and Sources of Ticket Splitting in Subpresidential Voting." *American Political Science Review* 86 (December 1992): 916–928.

Dalager, Jon K. "Voters, Issues, and Elections: Are the Candidates' Messages Getting Through?" *Journal of Politics* 58 (May 1996): 486–515.

Fenno, Richard F., Jr. "If, as Ralph Nader Says, Congress Is 'The Broken Branch,' Why Do We Love Our Congressmen So Much?" In *Congress in Change: Elections and Reform,* edited by Norman J. Ornstein. New York: Praeger, 1975, 277–287.

Jacobson, Gary C. *The Electoral Origins of Divided Government: Competition in U.S. House Elections, 1946–1988.* Boulder, Colo.: Westview, 1990.

*————. "A House and Senate Divided: The Clinton Legacy and the Congressional Elections of 2000." *Political Science Quarterly* 116 (spring 2001): 5–27.

————. *The Politics of Congressional Elections,* 5th ed. New York: Longman, 2001, 101–139.

Sigelman, Lee, Paul Wahlbeck, and Emmett H. Buell Jr. "Vote Choice and the Preference for Divided Government: Lessons of 1992." *American Journal of Political Science* 41 (July 1997): 879–894.

Chapter 11: The 2002 Congressional Elections

*Ceaser, James W., and Andrew E. Busch. *The Perfect Tie: The True Story of the 2000 Presidential Election.* Lanham, Md.: Rowman and Littlefield, 2001, 1–47, 241–263.

*Erikson, Robert S. "The 2000 Presidential Election in Historical Perspective." *Political Science Quarterly* 116 (spring 2001): 29–52.

*McWilliams, Wilson Carey. "The Meaning of the Election." In *The Election of 2000: Reports and Interpretations,* by Gerald M. Pomper with colleagues. New York: Chatham House, 2001, 177–201.

*Nelson, Michael. "The Election: Ordinary Politics, Extraordinary Outcome." In *The Elections of 2000,* edited by Michael Nelson. Washington, D.C.: CQ Press, 2001, 55–91.

*Pomper, Gerald M. "The Presidential Election." In *The Election of 2000: Reports and Interpretations,* by Gerald M. Pomper with colleagues. New York: Chatham House, 2001, 125–154.

*White, John Kenneth. "The Election in Perspective: Two Nations, Four Parties." In *America's Choice 2000,* edited by William Crotty. Boulder, Colo.: Westview, 2001, 180–206.

The following readings on the 2000 elections appeared after Change and Continuity in the 2000 Elections *was published in March 2002.*

Abramowitz, Alan I. "Gubernatorial Influence in Presidential Elections: Fact or Myth?" *PS: Political Science and Politics* 35 (December 2002): 701–703.

Black, Earl, and Merle Black. *The Rise of Southern Republicans.* Cambridge: Harvard University Press, 2002.

CQ Press. *Presidential Elections, 1789–2000.* Washington, D.C.: 2002.

Erikson, Robert S., and Kent L. Tedin. *American Public Opinion: Its Origins, Content, and Impact,* 6th ed., updated. New York: Longman, 2003.

Fiorina, Morris P. "Parties, Participation, and Representation in America: Old Theories Face New Realities." In *Political Science: The State of the Discipline,* edited by Ira Katznelson and Helen V. Milner. New York: Norton, 2002, 511–541.

Green, Donald, Bradley Palmquist, and Eric Schickler. *Partisan Hearts and Minds: Political Parties and the Social Identities of Voters.* New Haven: Yale University Press, 2002.

Jamieson, Kathleen Hall, and Paul Waldman. *The Press Effect: Politicians, Journalists, and the Stories that Shape the Political World.* New York: Oxford University Press, 2003.

Judis, John B., and Ruy Teixeira. *The Emerging Democratic Majority.* New York: Scribner, 2002.

Layman, Geoffrey C., and Thomas M. Carsey. "Party Polarization and 'Conflict Extension' in the American Electorate." *American Journal of Political Science* 46 (October 2002): 786–802.

Mayhew, David R. *Electoral Realignments: A Critique of the American Genre.* New Haven: Yale University Press, 2002.

Patterson, Thomas E. *The Vanishing Voter: Public Involvement in an Age of Uncertainty.* New York: Knopf, 2002.

Uggen, Christopher, and Jeff Manza. "Democratic Contraction? Political Consequences of Felon Disenfranchisement in the United States." *American Sociological Review* 67 (December 2002): 777–803.

U.S. Bureau of the Census. *Voting and Registration in the Election of November 2000: Population Characteristics.* (P20-542). February 2002.

Wlezien, Christopher, and Robert S. Erikson. "The Timeline of Presidential Election Campaigns." *Journal of Politics* 64 (November 2002): 969–993.

Index